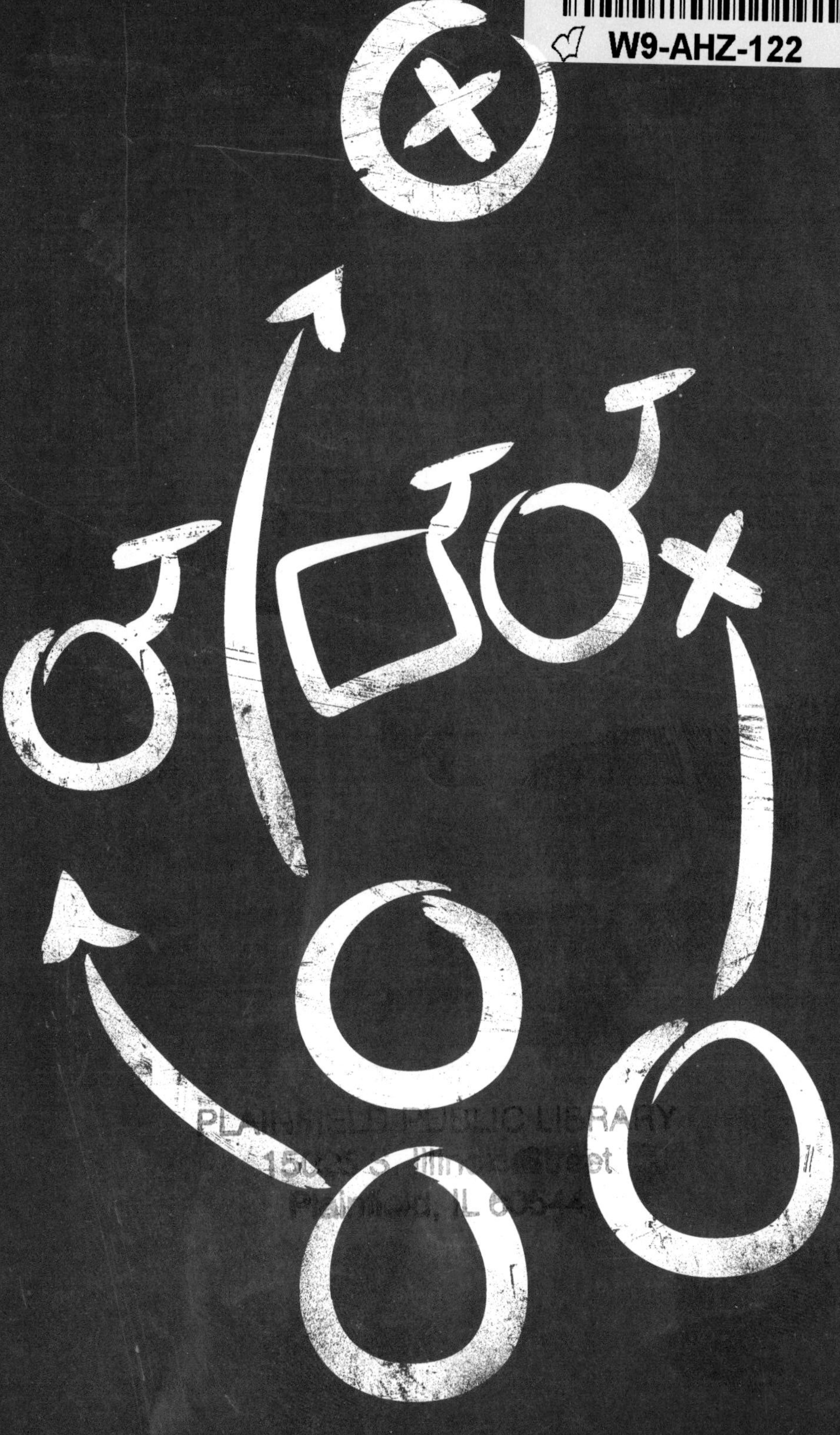

DOWN. SET. FIGHT!

WRITTEN BY
CHAD BOWERS & CHRIS SIMS

ILLUSTRATED & COLORED BY
SCOTT KOWALCHUK

LETTERED BY
JOSH KRACH

COLOR FLATS BY
JASON FISCHER

DESIGNED BY
JASON STOREY

EDITED BY
CHARLIE CHU

AN ONI PRESS PUBLICATION

ONI PRESS, INC.

PUBLISHER, JOE NOZEMACK
EDITOR IN CHIEF, JAMES LUCAS JONES
ART DIRECTOR, KEITH WOOD
DIRECTOR OF PUBLICITY, JOHN SCHORK
DIRECTOR OF SALES, CHEYENNE ALLOTT
EDITOR, JILL BEATON
EDITOR, CHARLIE CHU
GRAPHIC DESIGNER, JASON STOREY
DIGITAL PREPRESS LEAD, TROY LOOK
ADMINISTRATIVE ASSISTANT, ROBIN HERRERA

MONSTERPLUSCOMIC.COM / @CHADBOWERS
SCOTTKOWALCHUK.COM / @SCOTTKOWALCHUK
THE-ISB.COM / @THEISB

DOWN SET FIGHT!, February 2014. Published by Oni Press, Inc. 1305 SE Martin Luther King Jr. Blvd., Suite A, Portland, OR 97214. DOWN SET FIGHT! is ™ & © 2014 Chad Bowers, Scott Kowalchuk, and Chris Sims. All rights reserved. Oni Press logo and icon ™ & © 2014 Oni Press, Inc. All rights reserved. Oni Press logo and icon artwork created by Keith A. Wood. The events, institutions, and characters presented in this book are fictional. Any resemblance to actual persons, living or dead, is purely coincidental. No portion of this publication may be reproduced, by any means, without the express written permission of the copyright holders.

1305 SE Martin Luther King Jr. Blvd.
Suite A
Portland, OR 97214

ONIPRESS.COM
FACEBOOK.COM/ONIPRESS · TWITTER.COM/ONIPRESS · ONIPRESS.TUMBLR.COM

FIRST EDITION: FEBRUARY 2014

ISBN 978-1-62010-116-2 · EISBN 978-1-62010-125-4

1 3 5 7 9 10 8 6 4 2

LIBRARY OF CONGRESS CONTROL NUMBER: 2013949084

PRINTED IN CHINA.

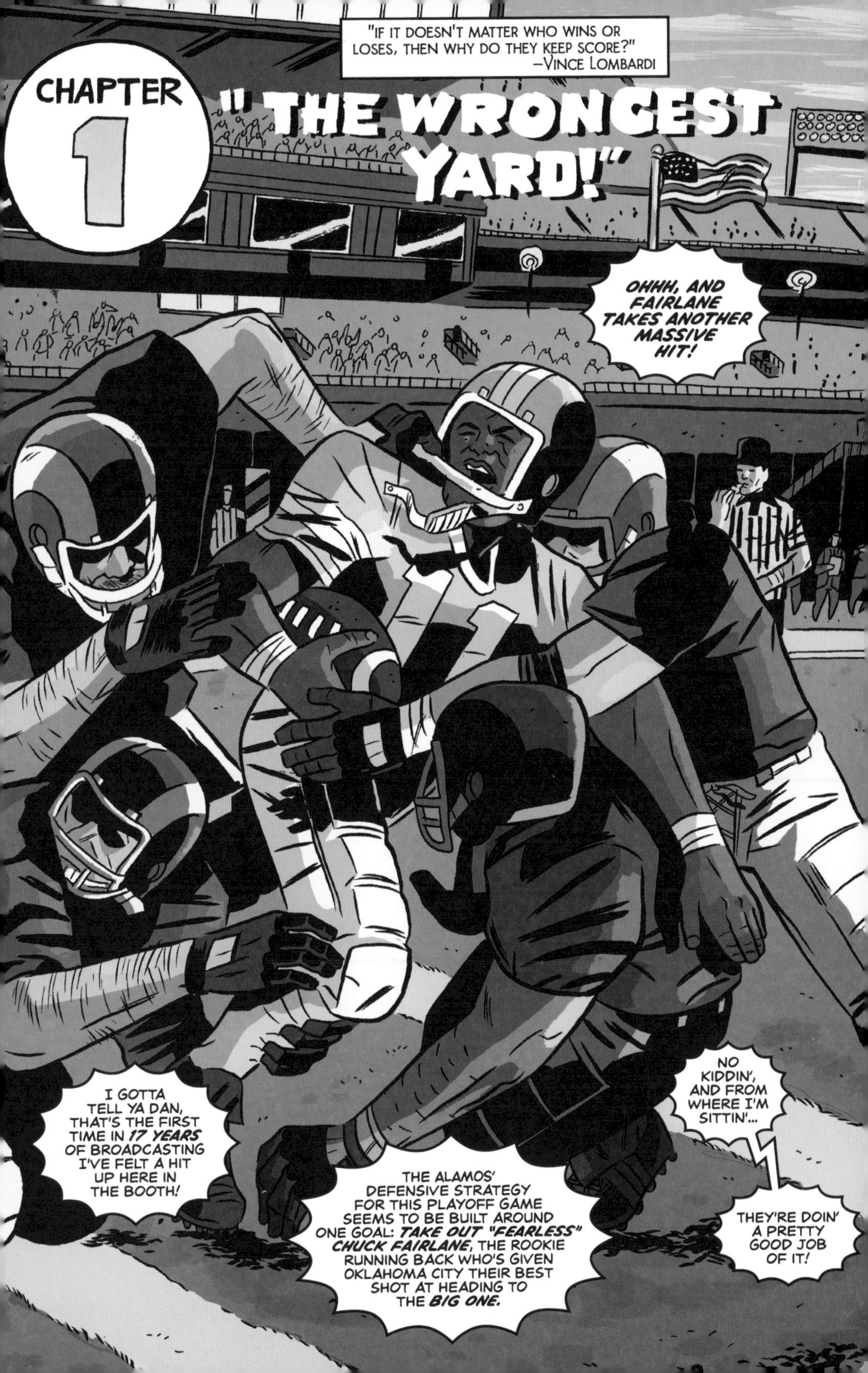

"IF IT DOESN'T MATTER WHO WINS OR LOSES, THEN WHY DO THEY KEEP SCORE?" –VINCE LOMBARDI
CHAPTER 1
"THE WRONGEST YARD!"
OHHH, AND FAIRLANE TAKES ANOTHER MASSIVE HIT!
I GOTTA TELL YA DAN, THAT'S THE FIRST TIME IN 17 YEARS OF BROADCASTING I'VE FELT A HIT UP HERE IN THE BOOTH!
NO KIDDIN', AND FROM WHERE I'M SITTIN'...
THEY'RE DOIN' A PRETTY GOOD JOB OF IT!
THE ALAMOS' DEFENSIVE STRATEGY FOR THIS PLAYOFF GAME SEEMS TO BE BUILT AROUND ONE GOAL: TAKE OUT "FEARLESS" CHUCK FAIRLANE, THE ROOKIE RUNNING BACK WHO'S GIVEN OKLAHOMA CITY THEIR BEST SHOT AT HEADING TO THE BIG ONE.

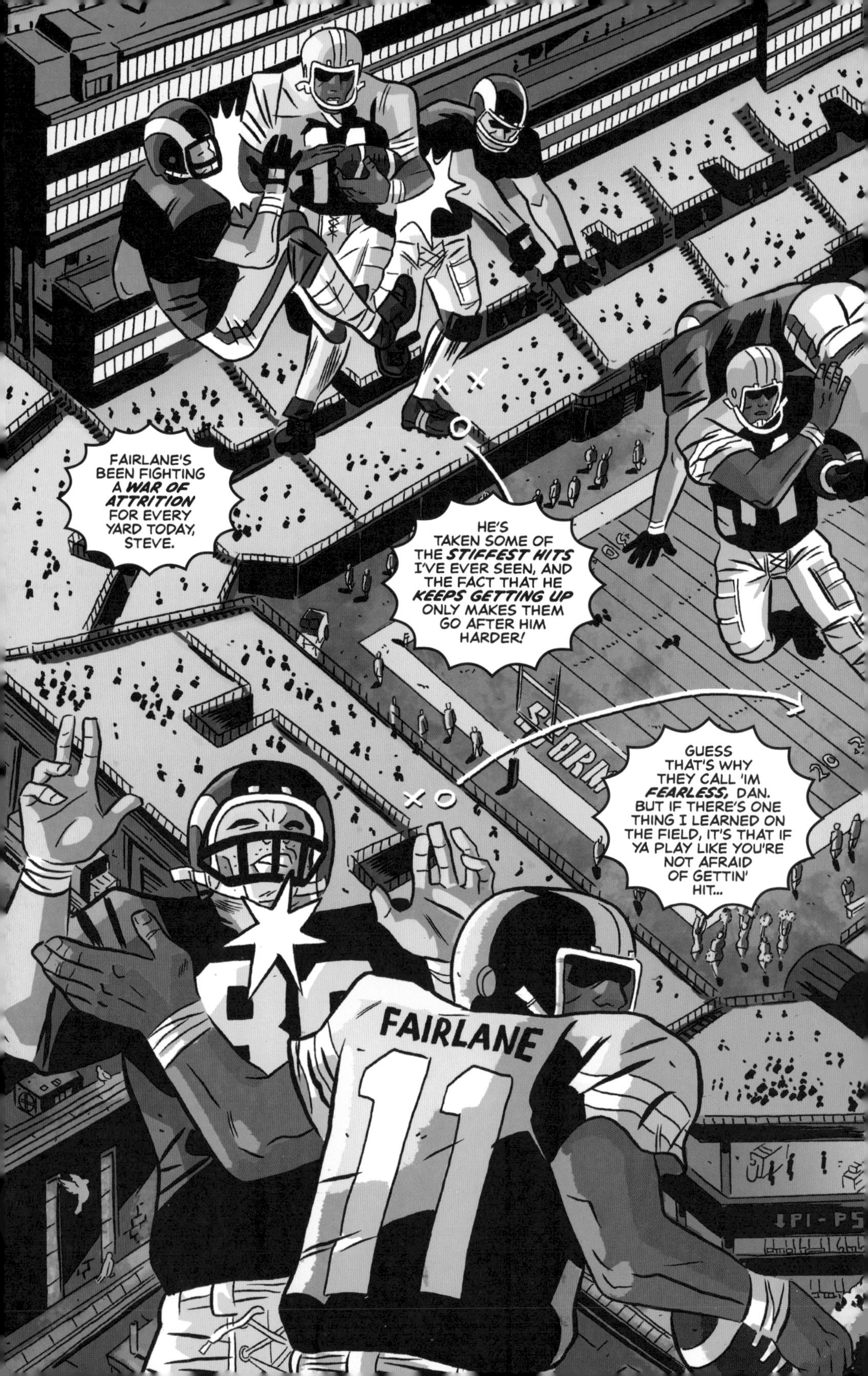

FAIRLANE'S BEEN FIGHTING A **WAR OF ATTRITION** FOR EVERY YARD TODAY, STEVE.
HE'S TAKEN SOME OF THE **STIFFEST HITS** I'VE EVER SEEN, AND THE FACT THAT HE **KEEPS GETTING UP** ONLY MAKES THEM GO AFTER HIM HARDER!
GUESS THAT'S WHY THEY CALL 'IM **FEARLESS,** DAN. BUT IF THERE'S ONE THING I LEARNED ON THE FIELD, IT'S THAT IF YA PLAY LIKE YOU'RE NOT AFRAID OF GETTIN' HIT...
FAIRLANE
11

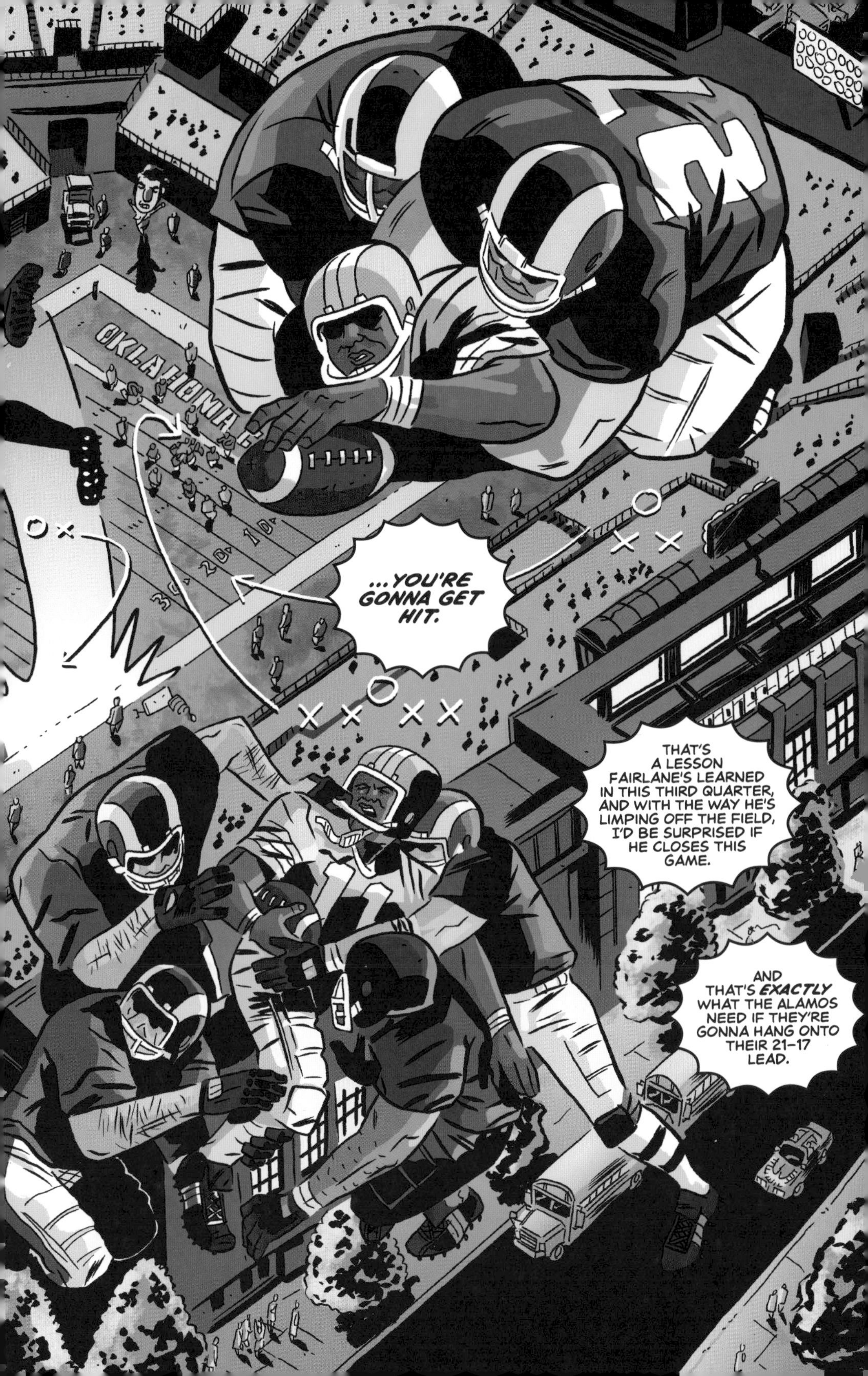
OKLAHOMA
...YOU'RE GONNA GET HIT.
THAT'S A LESSON FAIRLANE'S LEARNED IN THIS THIRD QUARTER, AND WITH THE WAY HE'S LIMPING OFF THE FIELD, I'D BE SURPRISED IF HE CLOSES THIS GAME.
AND THAT'S *EXACTLY* WHAT THE ALAMOS NEED IF THEY'RE GONNA HANG ONTO THEIR 21–17 LEAD.

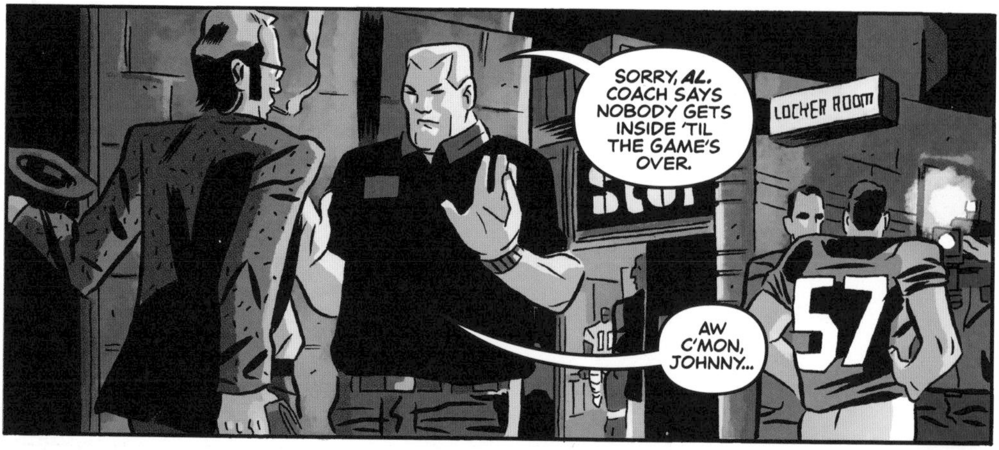
SORRY, AL. COACH SAYS NOBODY GETS INSIDE 'TIL THE GAME'S OVER.
LOCKER ROOM
57
AW C'MON, JOHNNY...

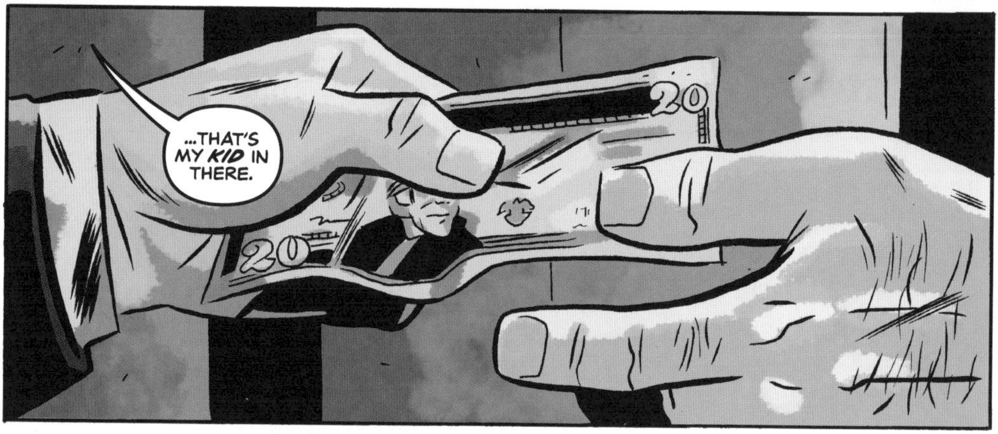
...THAT'S MY KID IN THERE.
20
20

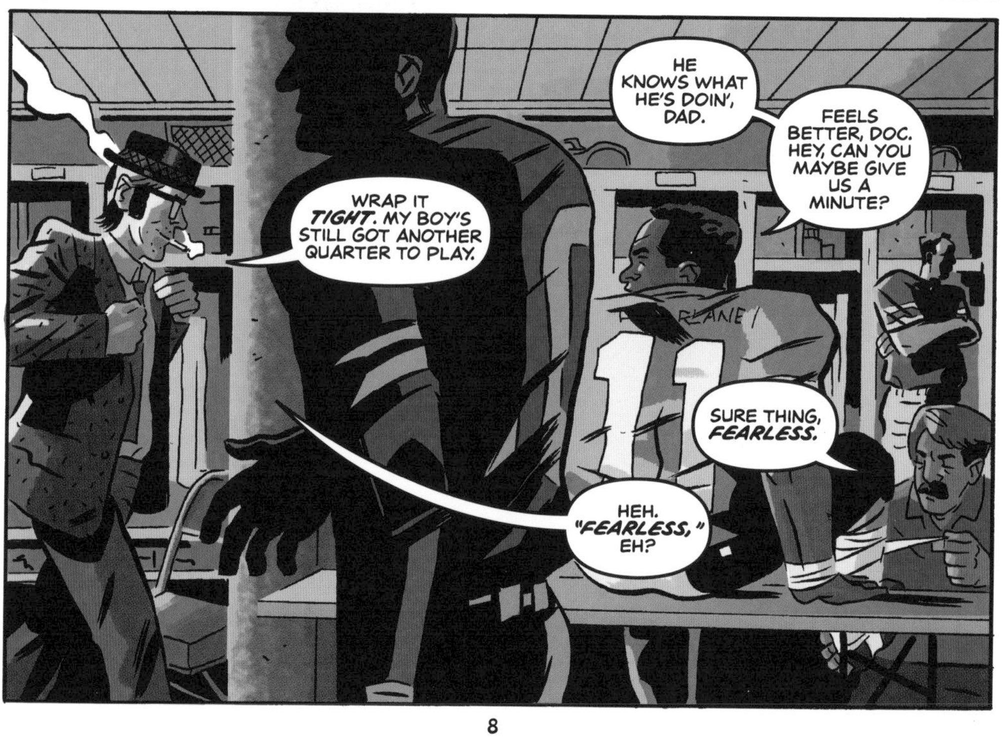
WRAP IT TIGHT. MY BOY'S STILL GOT ANOTHER QUARTER TO PLAY.
HE KNOWS WHAT HE'S DOIN', DAD.
FEELS BETTER, DOC. HEY, CAN YOU MAYBE GIVE US A MINUTE?
SURE THING, FEARLESS.
HEH. "FEARLESS," EH?
11

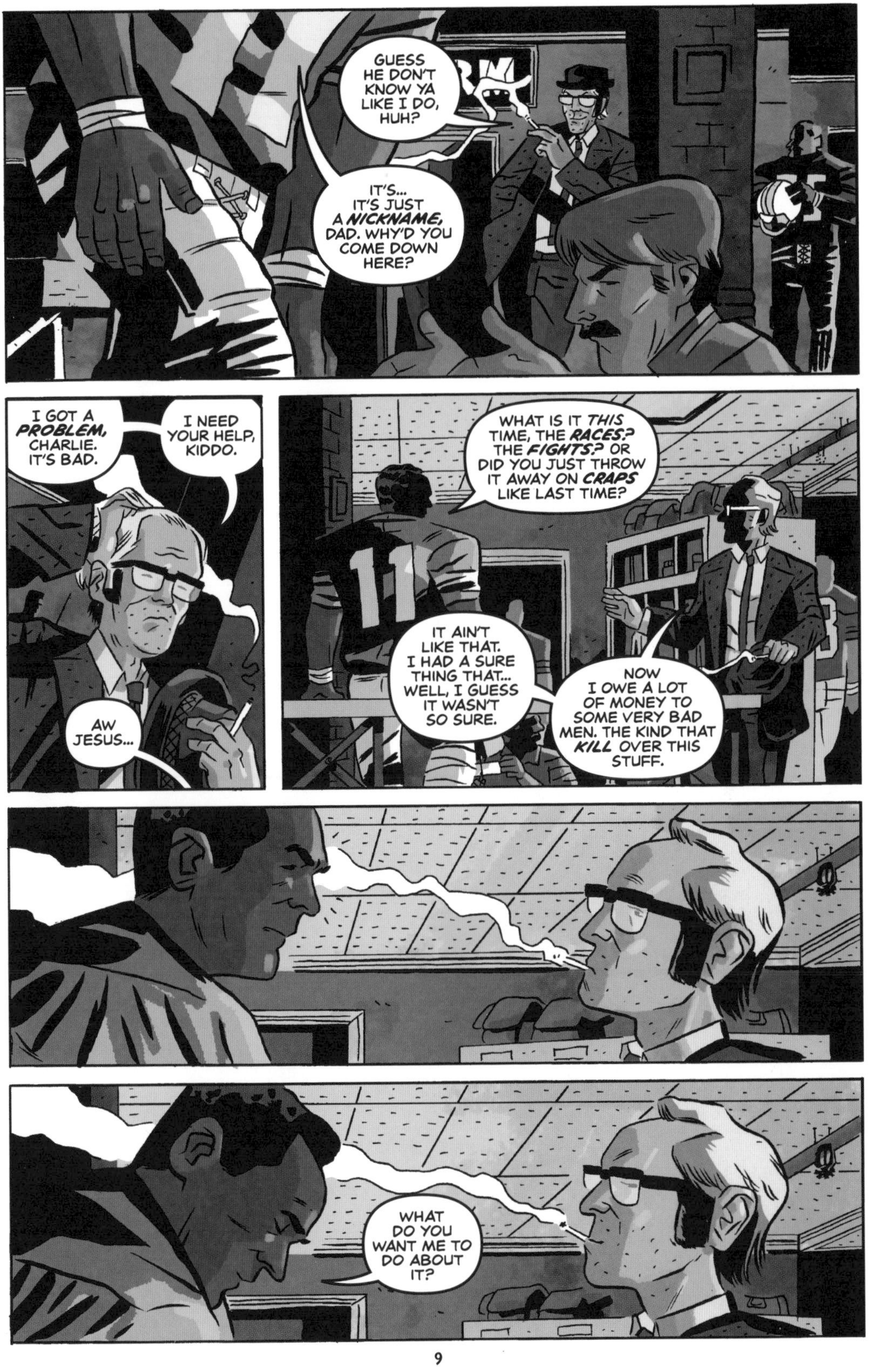
GUESS HE DON'T KNOW YA LIKE I DO, HUH?
IT'S... IT'S JUST A NICKNAME, DAD. WHY'D YOU COME DOWN HERE?
I GOT A PROBLEM, CHARLIE. IT'S BAD.
I NEED YOUR HELP, KIDDO.
AW JESUS...
WHAT IS IT THIS TIME, THE RACES? THE FIGHTS? OR DID YOU JUST THROW IT AWAY ON CRAPS LIKE LAST TIME?
IT AIN'T LIKE THAT. I HAD A SURE THING THAT... WELL, I GUESS IT WASN'T SO SURE.
NOW I OWE A LOT OF MONEY TO SOME VERY BAD MEN. THE KIND THAT KILL OVER THIS STUFF.
WHAT DO YOU WANT ME TO DO ABOUT IT?

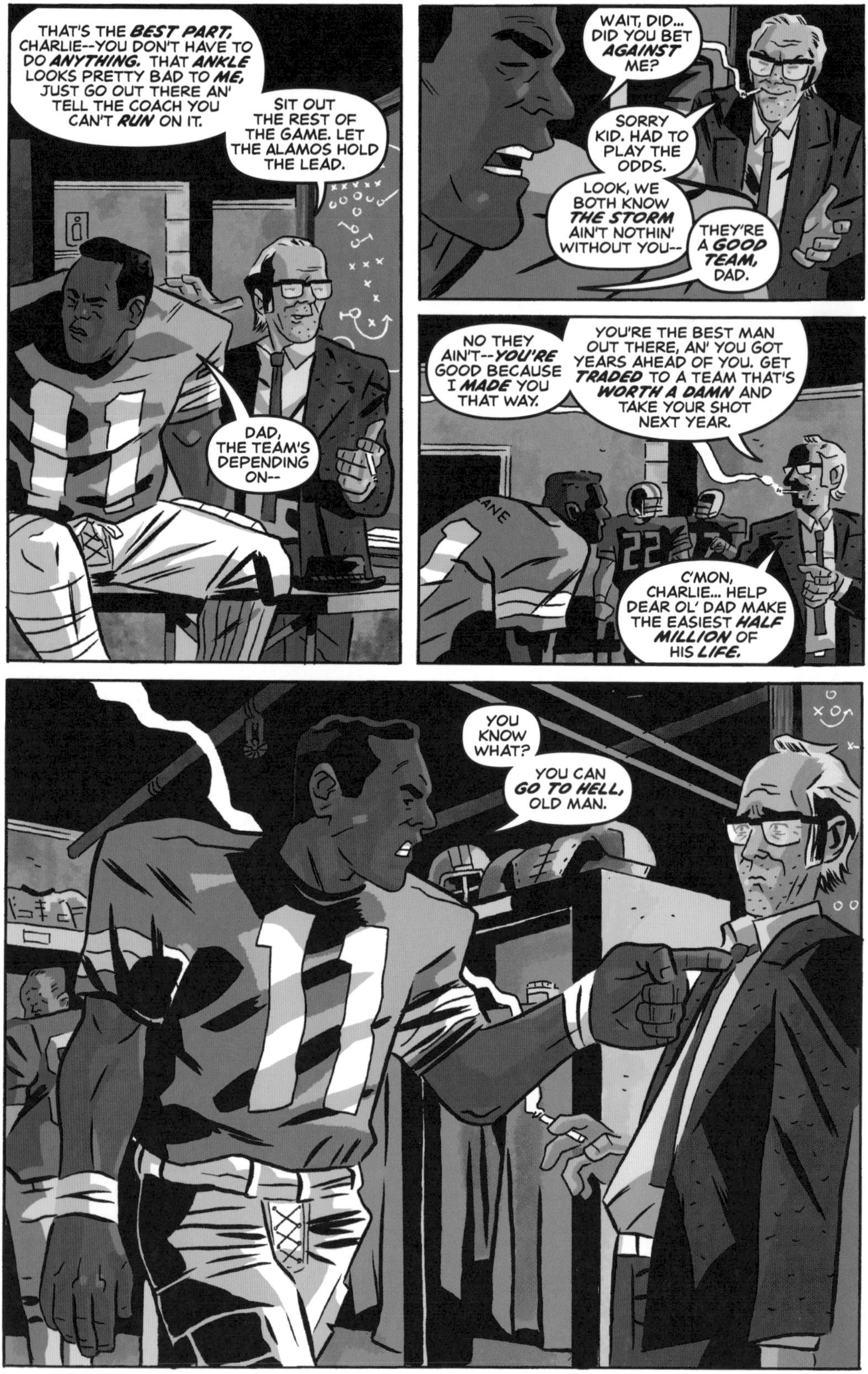
THAT'S THE ***BEST PART,*** CHARLIE--YOU DON'T HAVE TO DO ***ANYTHING.*** THAT ***ANKLE*** LOOKS PRETTY BAD TO ***ME,*** JUST GO OUT THERE AN' TELL THE COACH YOU CAN'T ***RUN*** ON IT.
SIT OUT THE REST OF THE GAME. LET THE ALAMOS HOLD THE LEAD.
DAD, THE TEAM'S DEPENDING ON--
WAIT, DID... DID YOU BET ***AGAINST*** ME?
SORRY KID. HAD TO PLAY THE ODDS.
LOOK, WE BOTH KNOW ***THE STORM*** AIN'T NOTHIN' WITHOUT YOU--
THEY'RE A ***GOOD TEAM,*** DAD.
NO THEY AIN'T--***YOU'RE*** GOOD BECAUSE I ***MADE*** YOU THAT WAY.
YOU'RE THE BEST MAN OUT THERE, AN' YOU GOT YEARS AHEAD OF YOU. GET ***TRADED*** TO A TEAM THAT'S ***WORTH A DAMN*** AND TAKE YOUR SHOT NEXT YEAR.
C'MON, CHARLIE... HELP DEAR OL' DAD MAKE THE EASIEST ***HALF MILLION*** OF HIS ***LIFE.***
YOU KNOW WHAT?
YOU CAN ***GO TO HELL,*** OLD MAN.

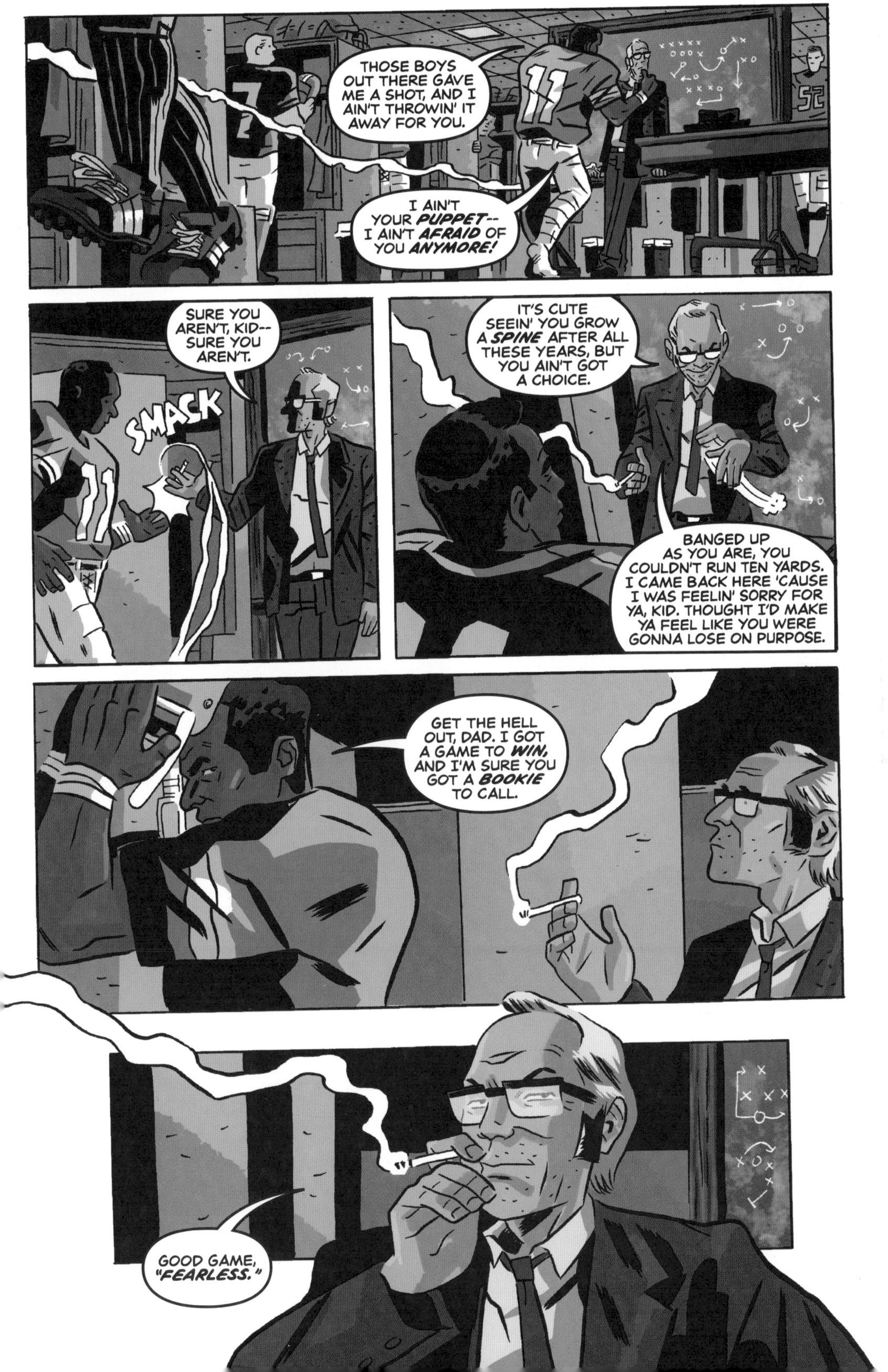
THOSE BOYS OUT THERE GAVE ME A SHOT, AND I AIN'T THROWIN' IT AWAY FOR YOU.
I AIN'T YOUR ***PUPPET***-- I AIN'T ***AFRAID*** OF YOU ***ANYMORE!***
SURE YOU AREN'T, KID-- SURE YOU AREN'T.
SMACK
IT'S CUTE SEEIN' YOU GROW A ***SPINE*** AFTER ALL THESE YEARS, BUT YOU AIN'T GOT A CHOICE.
BANGED UP AS YOU ARE, YOU COULDN'T RUN TEN YARDS. I CAME BACK HERE 'CAUSE I WAS FEELIN' SORRY FOR YA, KID. THOUGHT I'D MAKE YA FEEL LIKE YOU WERE GONNA LOSE ON PURPOSE.
GET THE HELL OUT, DAD. I GOT A GAME TO ***WIN,*** AND I'M SURE YOU GOT A ***BOOKIE*** TO CALL.
GOOD GAME, ***"FEARLESS."***

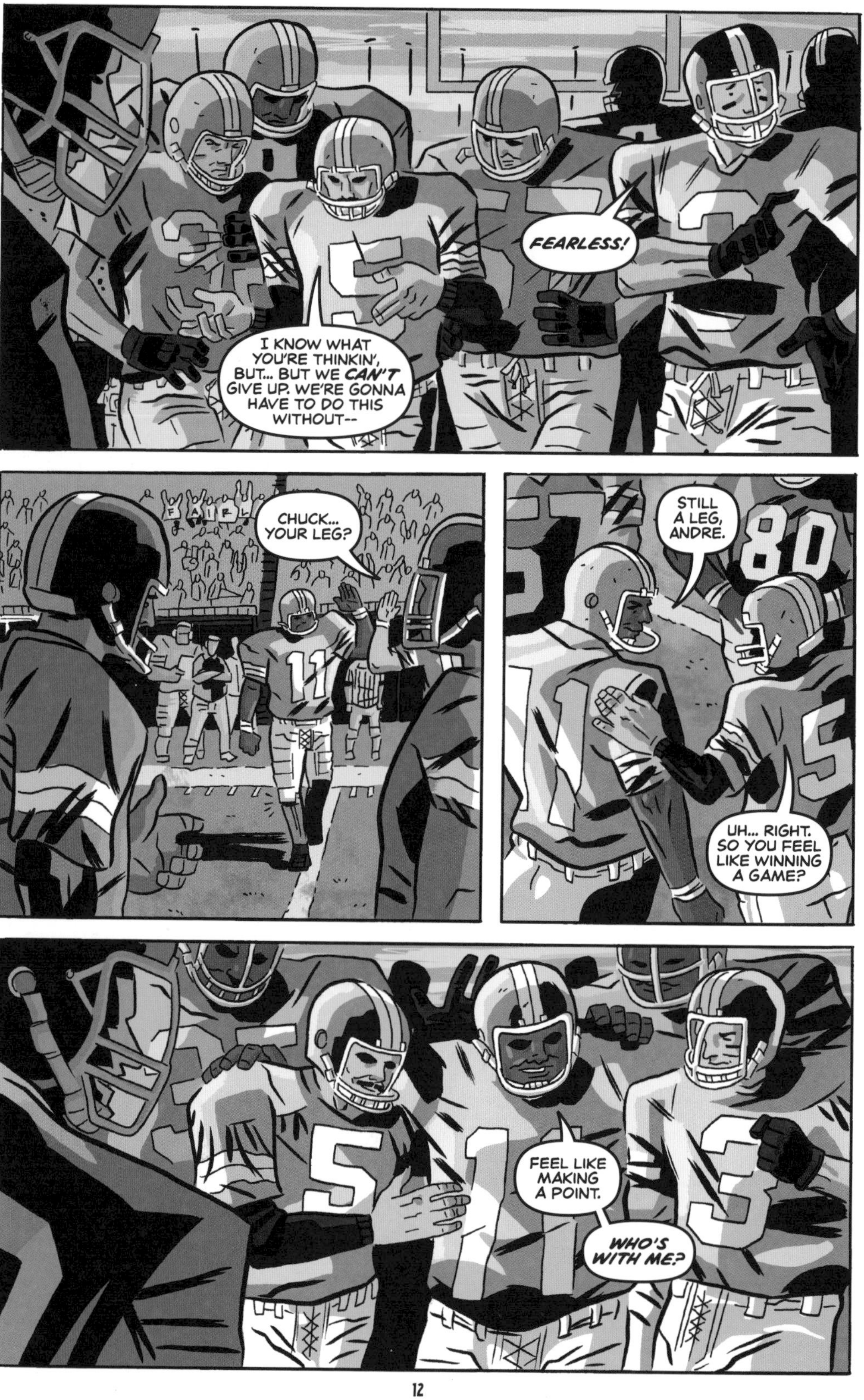
FEARLESS!
I KNOW WHAT YOU'RE THINKIN', BUT... BUT WE CAN'T GIVE UP. WE'RE GONNA HAVE TO DO THIS WITHOUT--
CHUCK... YOUR LEG?
STILL A LEG, ANDRE.
UH... RIGHT. SO YOU FEEL LIKE WINNING A GAME?
FEEL LIKE MAKING A POINT.
WHO'S WITH ME?

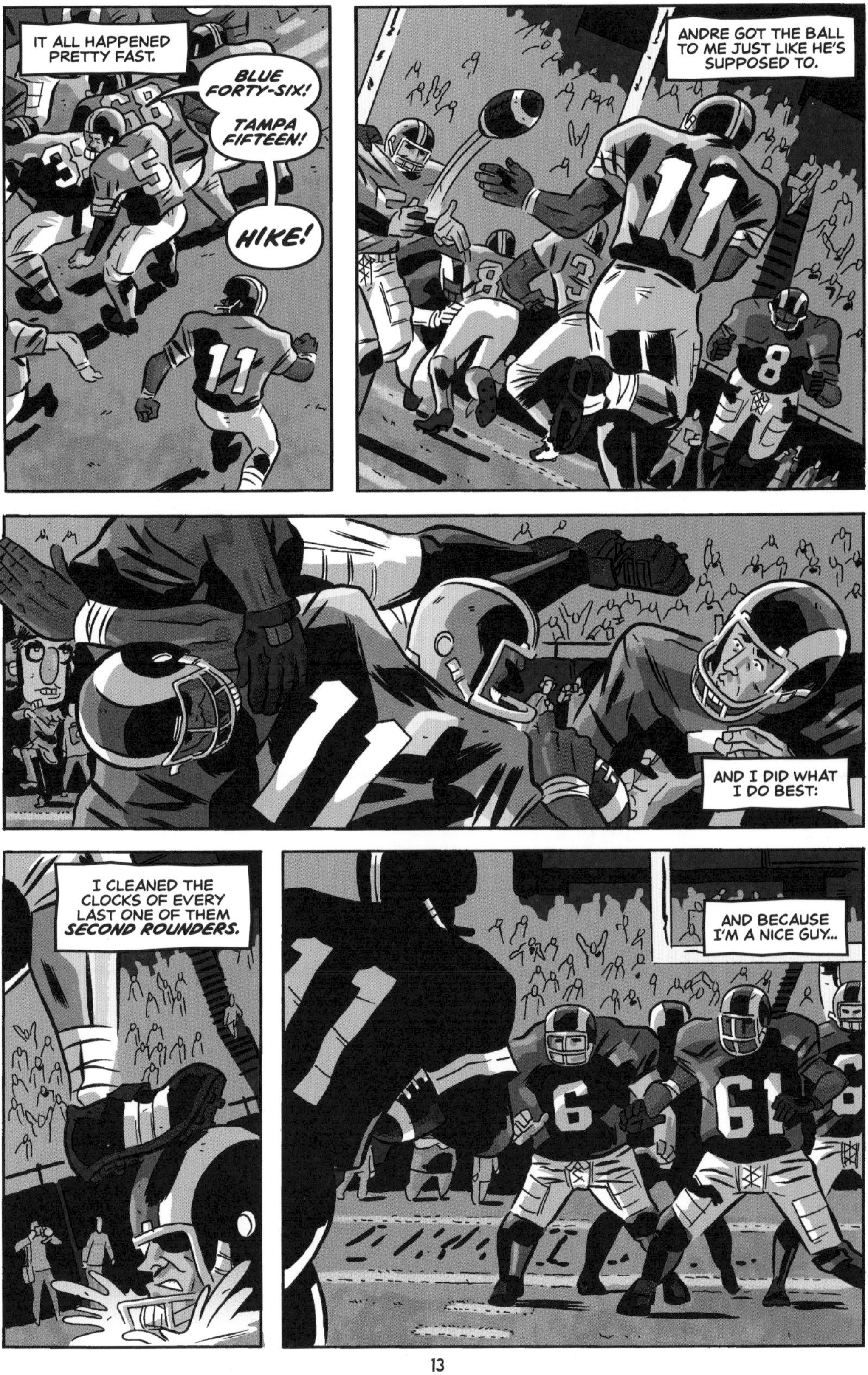
IT ALL HAPPENED PRETTY FAST.
BLUE FORTY-SIX!
TAMPA FIFTEEN!
HIKE!
ANDRE GOT THE BALL TO ME JUST LIKE HE'S SUPPOSED TO.
AND I DID WHAT I DO BEST:
I CLEANED THE CLOCKS OF EVERY LAST ONE OF THEM SECOND ROUNDERS.
AND BECAUSE I'M A NICE GUY...

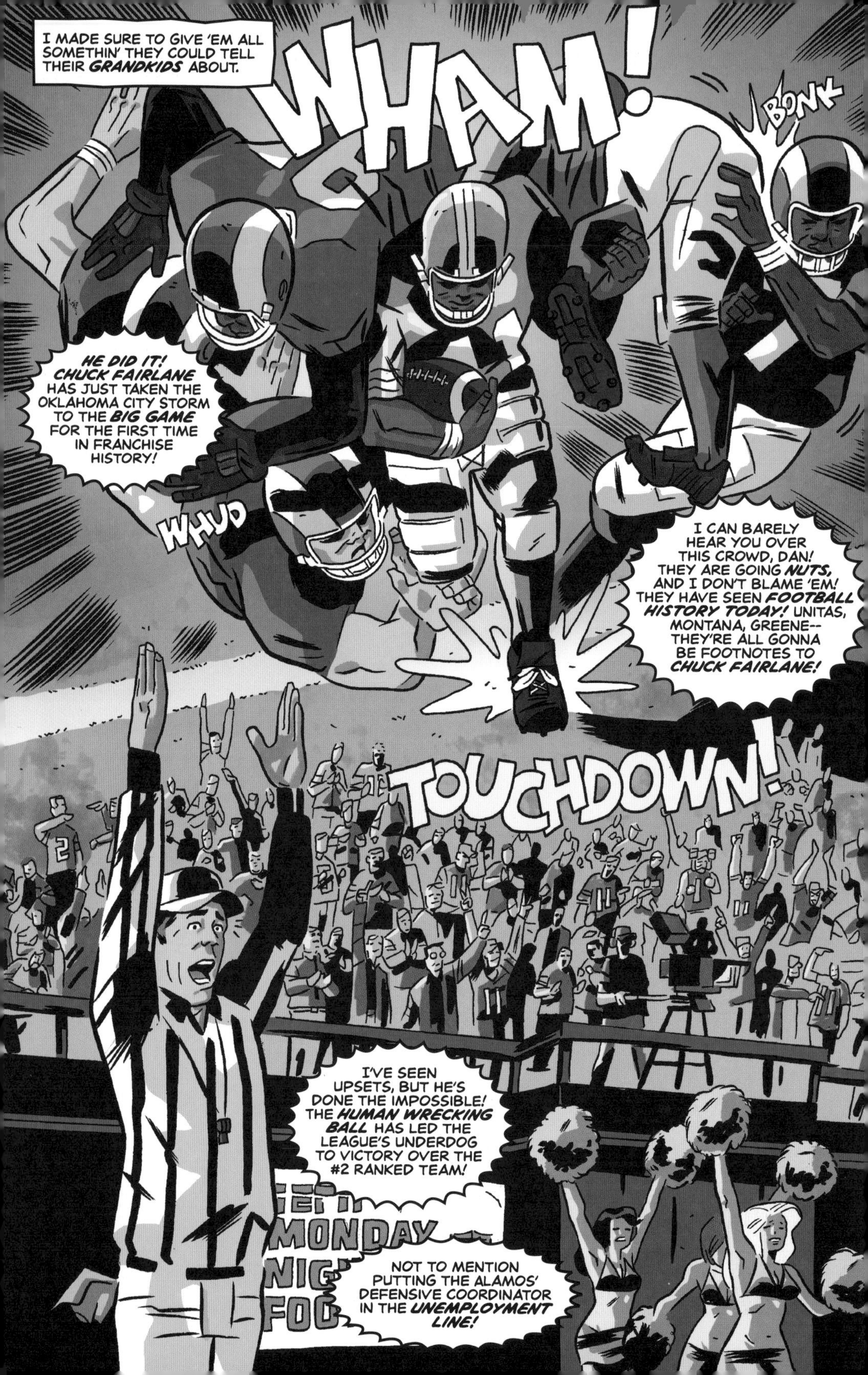
I MADE SURE TO GIVE 'EM ALL SOMETHIN' THEY COULD TELL THEIR GRANDKIDS ABOUT.
WHAM!
BONK
HE DID IT! CHUCK FAIRLANE HAS JUST TAKEN THE OKLAHOMA CITY STORM TO THE BIG GAME FOR THE FIRST TIME IN FRANCHISE HISTORY!
WHUD
I CAN BARELY HEAR YOU OVER THIS CROWD, DAN! THEY ARE GOING NUTS, AND I DON'T BLAME 'EM! THEY HAVE SEEN FOOTBALL HISTORY TODAY! UNITAS, MONTANA, GREENE-- THEY'RE ALL GONNA BE FOOTNOTES TO CHUCK FAIRLANE!
TOUCHDOWN!
I'VE SEEN UPSETS, BUT HE'S DONE THE IMPOSSIBLE! THE HUMAN WRECKING BALL HAS LED THE LEAGUE'S UNDERDOG TO VICTORY OVER THE #2 RANKED TEAM!
MONDAY
NOT TO MENTION PUTTING THE ALAMOS' DEFENSIVE COORDINATOR IN THE UNEMPLOYMENT LINE!

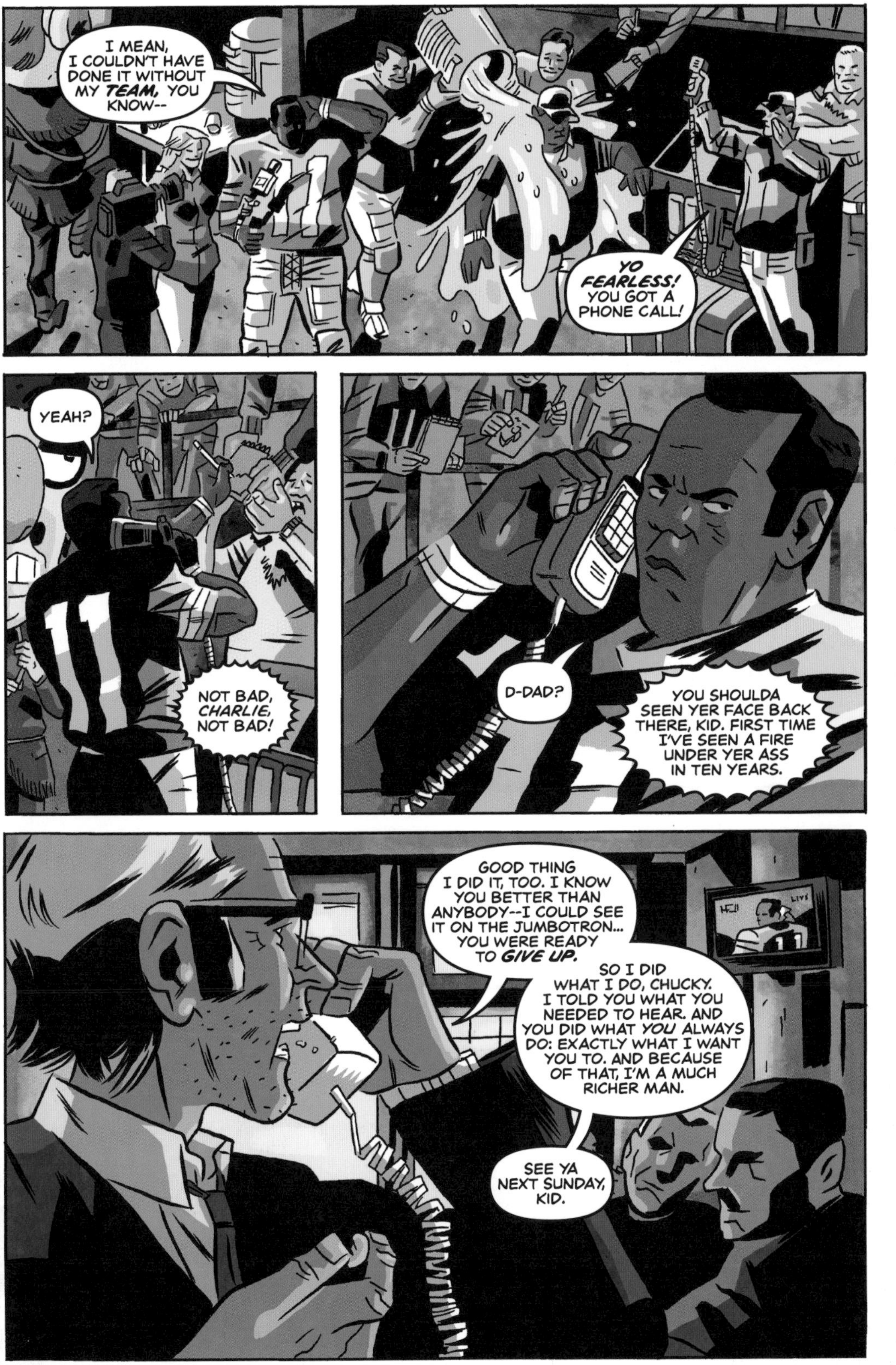

I MEAN, I COULDN'T HAVE DONE IT WITHOUT MY *TEAM,* YOU KNOW--
YO FEARLESS! YOU GOT A PHONE CALL!
YEAH?
NOT BAD, *CHARLIE,* NOT BAD!
D-DAD?
YOU SHOULDA SEEN YER FACE BACK THERE, KID. FIRST TIME I'VE SEEN A FIRE UNDER YER ASS IN TEN YEARS.
GOOD THING I DID IT, TOO. I KNOW YOU BETTER THAN ANYBODY--I COULD SEE IT ON THE JUMBOTRON... YOU WERE READY TO *GIVE UP.*
SO I DID WHAT I DO, CHUCKY. I TOLD YOU WHAT YOU NEEDED TO HEAR. AND YOU DID WHAT *YOU* ALWAYS DO: EXACTLY WHAT I WANT YOU TO. AND BECAUSE OF THAT, I'M A MUCH RICHER MAN.
SEE YA NEXT SUNDAY, KID.

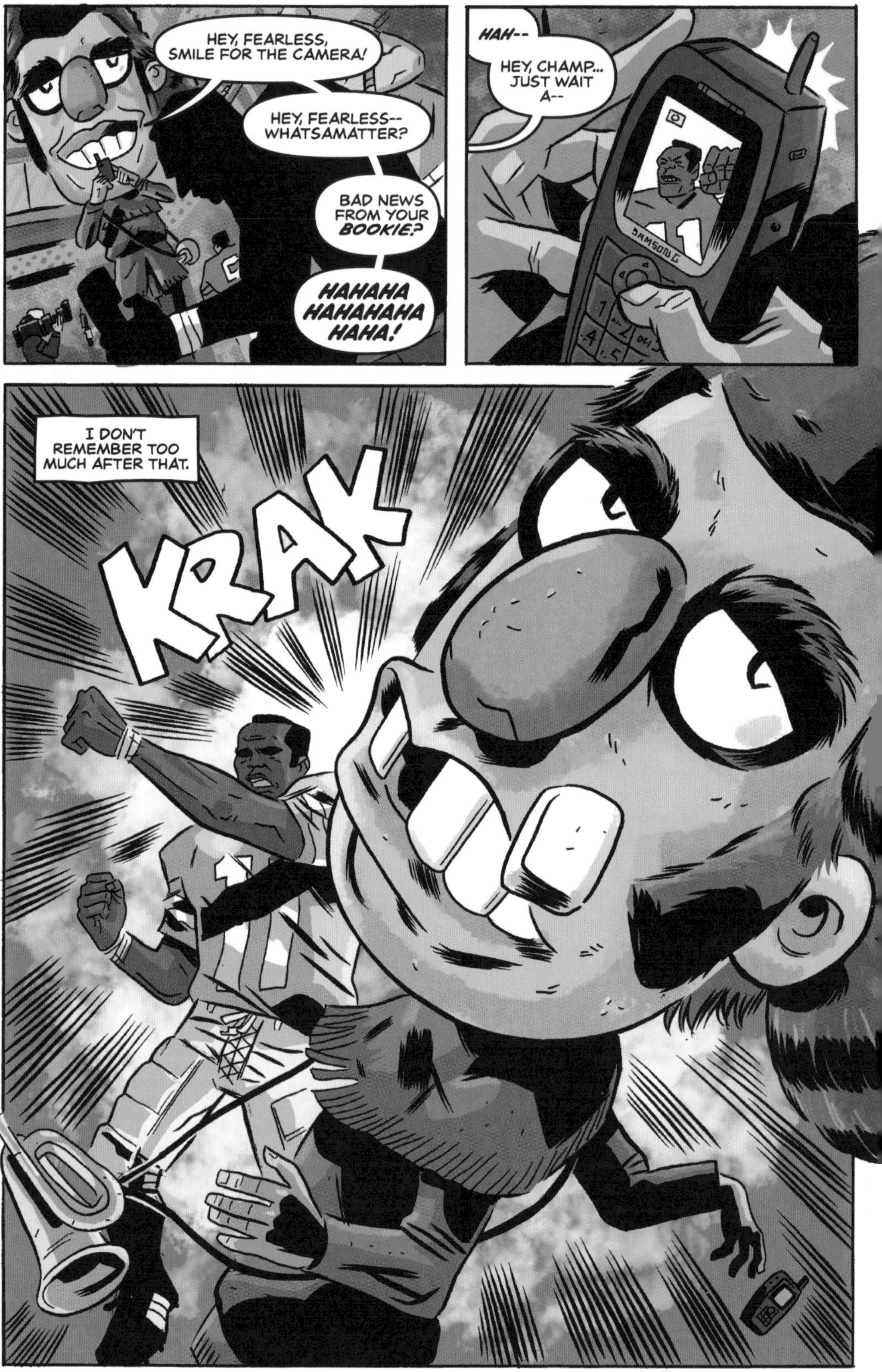
HEY, FEARLESS, SMILE FOR THE CAMERA!
HEY, FEARLESS-- WHATSAMATTER?
BAD NEWS FROM YOUR *BOOKIE?*
HAHAHA HAHAHAHA HAHA!
HAH--
HEY, CHAMP... JUST WAIT A--
SAMSUNG
I DON'T REMEMBER TOO MUCH AFTER THAT.
KRAK

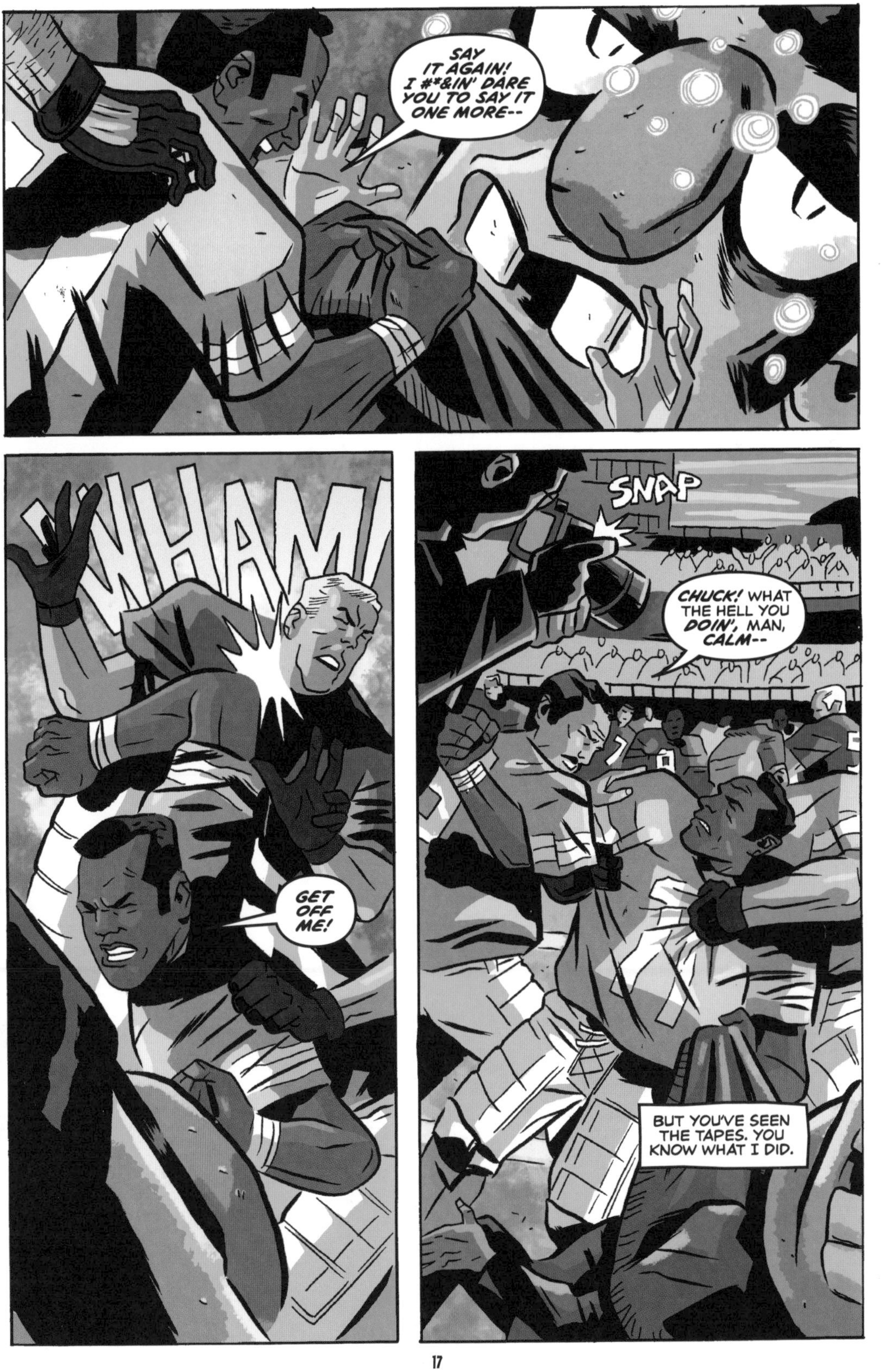
SAY IT AGAIN! I #*&IN' DARE YOU TO SAY IT ONE MORE--
WHAM!
GET OFF ME!
SNAP
CHUCK! WHAT THE HELL YOU DOIN', MAN, CALM--
BUT YOU'VE SEEN THE TAPES. YOU KNOW WHAT I DID.

I FOUGHT THE *ALAMOS*...
I FOUGHT THE *STORM*...

I FOUGHT THE *COACHES* ON BOTH SIDES...

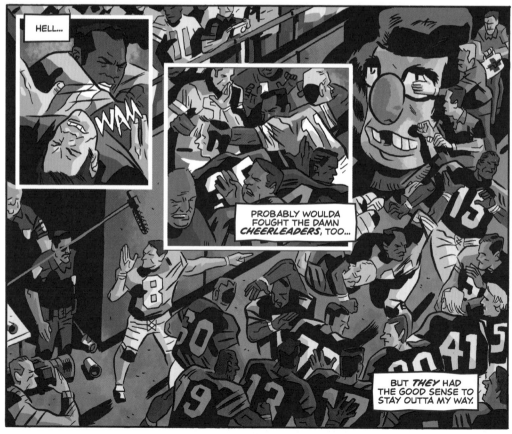

HELL...

PROBABLY WOULDA FOUGHT THE DAMN *CHEERLEADERS*, TOO...

BUT *THEY* HAD THE GOOD SENSE TO STAY OUTTA MY WAY.

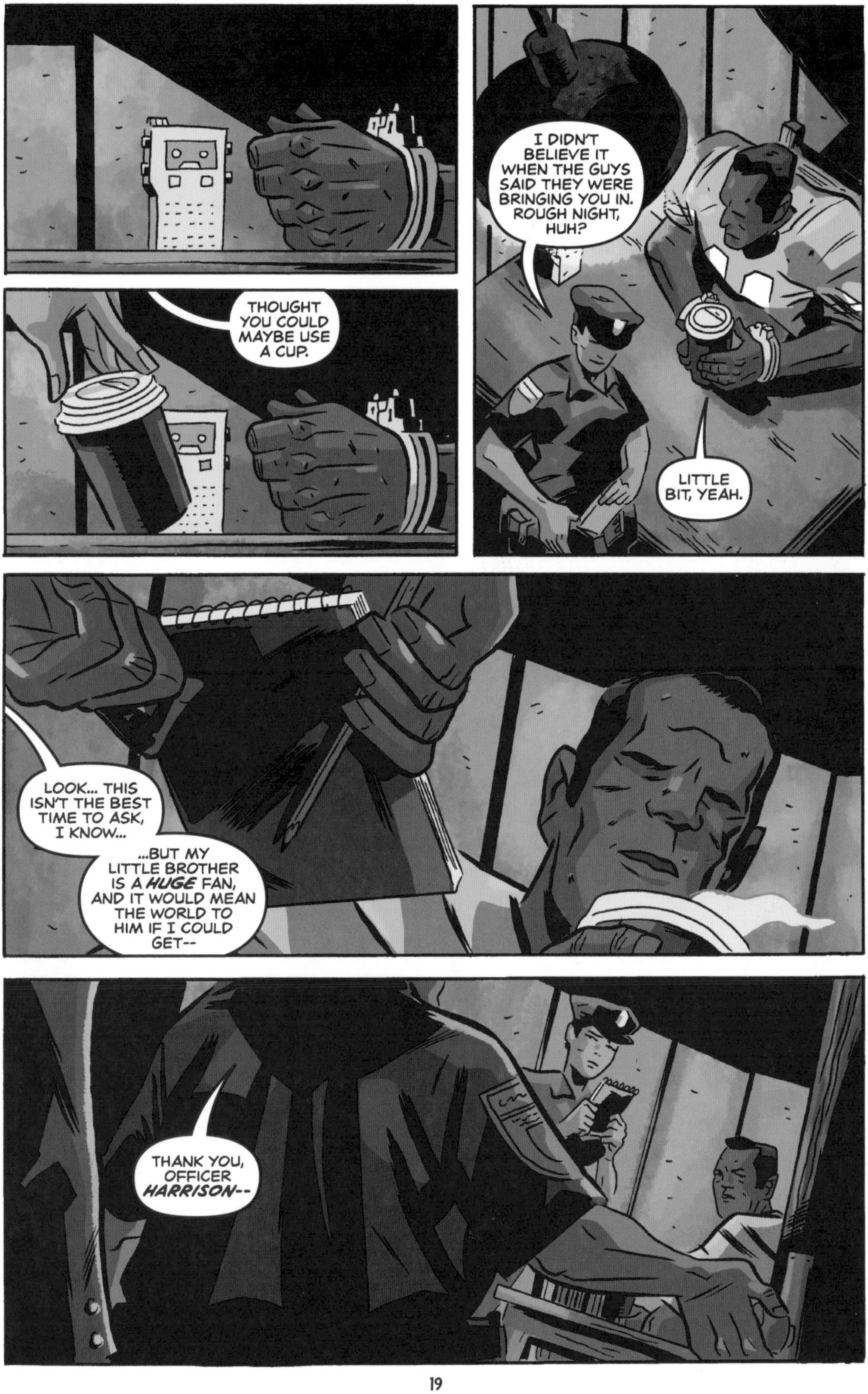
THOUGHT YOU COULD MAYBE USE A CUP.
I DIDN'T BELIEVE IT WHEN THE GUYS SAID THEY WERE BRINGING YOU IN. ROUGH NIGHT, HUH?
LITTLE BIT, YEAH.
LOOK... THIS ISN'T THE BEST TIME TO ASK, I KNOW...
...BUT MY LITTLE BROTHER IS A *HUGE* FAN, AND IT WOULD MEAN THE WORLD TO HIM IF I COULD GET--
THANK YOU, OFFICER *HARRISON*--

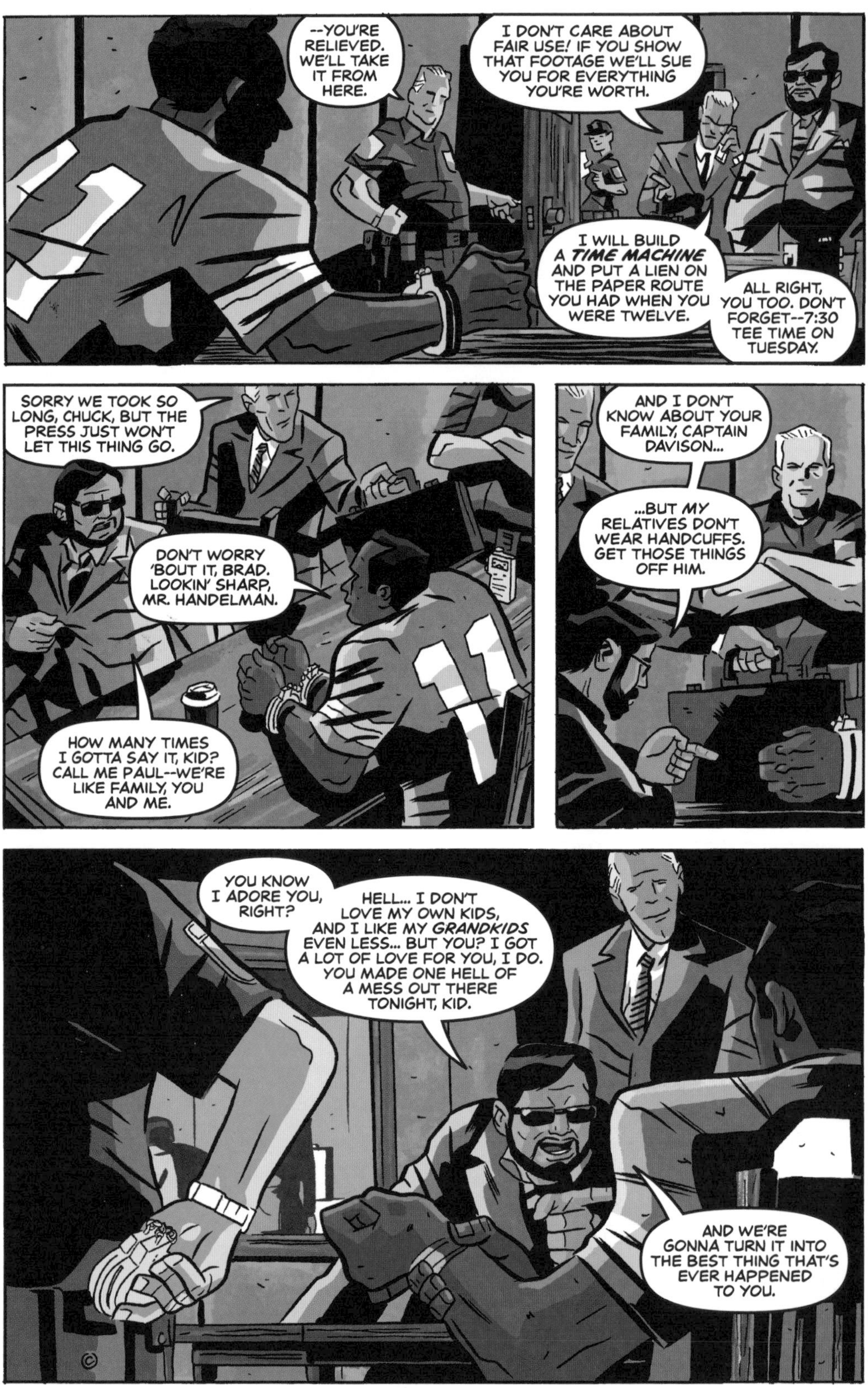
--YOU'RE RELIEVED. WE'LL TAKE IT FROM HERE.
I DON'T CARE ABOUT FAIR USE! IF YOU SHOW THAT FOOTAGE WE'LL SUE YOU FOR EVERYTHING YOU'RE WORTH.
I WILL BUILD A *TIME MACHINE* AND PUT A LIEN ON THE PAPER ROUTE YOU HAD WHEN YOU WERE TWELVE.
ALL RIGHT, YOU TOO. DON'T FORGET--7:30 TEE TIME ON TUESDAY.
SORRY WE TOOK SO LONG, CHUCK, BUT THE PRESS JUST WON'T LET THIS THING GO.
DON'T WORRY 'BOUT IT, BRAD. LOOKIN' SHARP, MR. HANDELMAN.
HOW MANY TIMES I GOTTA SAY IT, KID? CALL ME PAUL--WE'RE LIKE FAMILY, YOU AND ME.
AND I DON'T KNOW ABOUT YOUR FAMILY, CAPTAIN DAVISON...
...BUT *MY* RELATIVES DON'T WEAR HANDCUFFS. GET THOSE THINGS OFF HIM.
YOU KNOW I ADORE YOU, RIGHT?
HELL... I DON'T LOVE MY OWN KIDS, AND I LIKE MY *GRANDKIDS* EVEN LESS... BUT YOU? I GOT A LOT OF LOVE FOR YOU, I DO. YOU MADE ONE HELL OF A MESS OUT THERE TONIGHT, KID.
AND WE'RE GONNA TURN IT INTO THE BEST THING THAT'S EVER HAPPENED TO YOU.
©

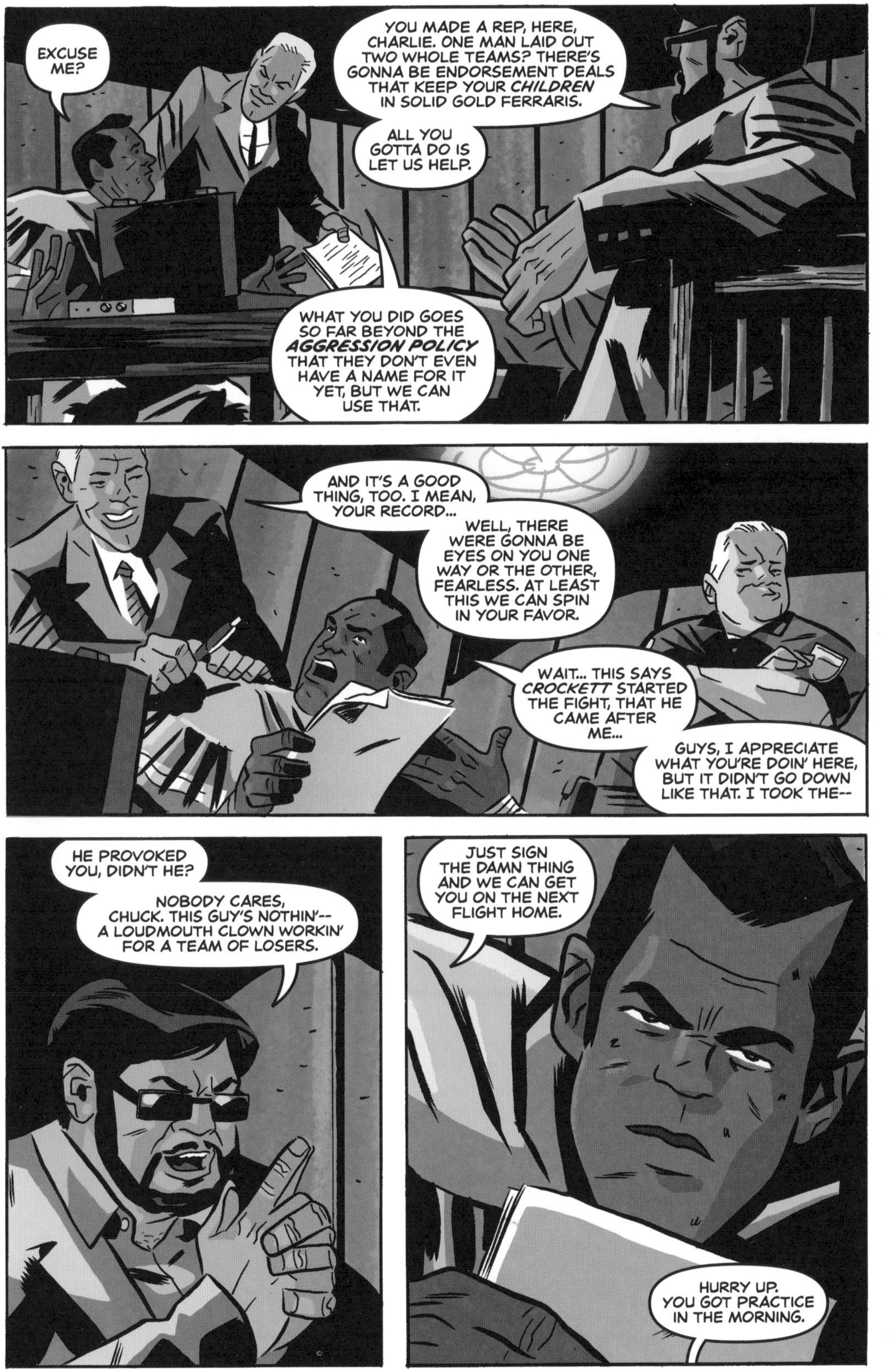
EXCUSE ME?
YOU MADE A REP, HERE, CHARLIE. ONE MAN LAID OUT TWO WHOLE TEAMS? THERE'S GONNA BE ENDORSEMENT DEALS THAT KEEP YOUR *CHILDREN* IN SOLID GOLD FERRARIS.
ALL YOU GOTTA DO IS LET US HELP.
WHAT YOU DID GOES SO FAR BEYOND THE ***AGGRESSION POLICY*** THAT THEY DON'T EVEN HAVE A NAME FOR IT YET, BUT WE CAN USE THAT.
AND IT'S A GOOD THING, TOO. I MEAN, YOUR RECORD...
WELL, THERE WERE GONNA BE EYES ON YOU ONE WAY OR THE OTHER, FEARLESS. AT LEAST THIS WE CAN SPIN IN YOUR FAVOR.
WAIT... THIS SAYS *CROCKETT* STARTED THE FIGHT, THAT HE CAME AFTER ME...
GUYS, I APPRECIATE WHAT YOU'RE DOIN' HERE, BUT IT DIDN'T GO DOWN LIKE THAT. I TOOK THE--
HE PROVOKED YOU, DIDN'T HE?
NOBODY CARES, CHUCK. THIS GUY'S NOTHIN'-- A LOUDMOUTH CLOWN WORKIN' FOR A TEAM OF LOSERS.
JUST SIGN THE DAMN THING AND WE CAN GET YOU ON THE NEXT FLIGHT HOME.
HURRY UP. YOU GOT PRACTICE IN THE MORNING.

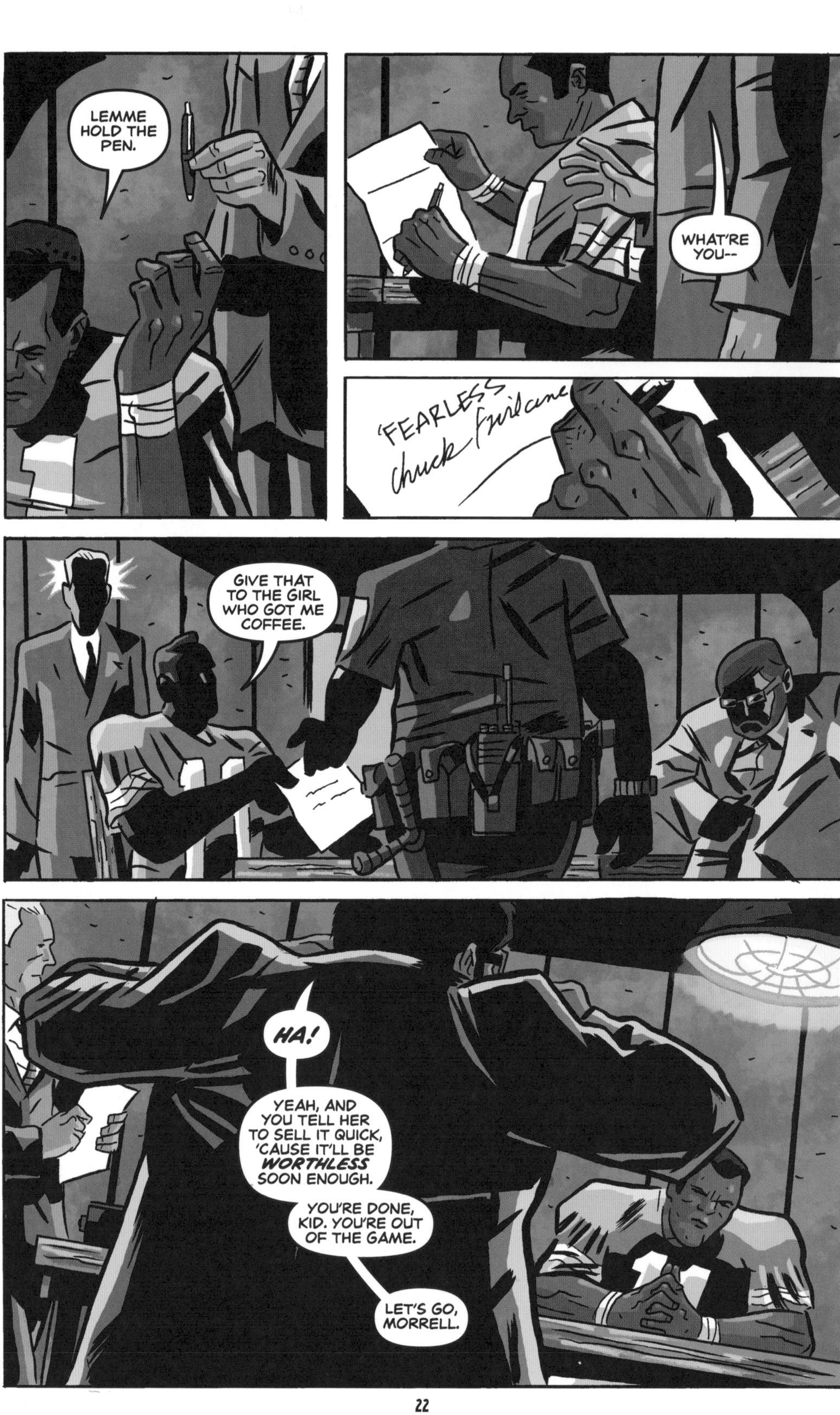
LEMME HOLD THE PEN.
WHAT'RE YOU--
'FEARLESS' Chuck Frilcane
GIVE THAT TO THE GIRL WHO GOT ME COFFEE.
HA!
YEAH, AND YOU TELL HER TO SELL IT QUICK, 'CAUSE IT'LL BE WORTHLESS SOON ENOUGH.
YOU'RE DONE, KID. YOU'RE OUT OF THE GAME.
LET'S GO, MORRELL.

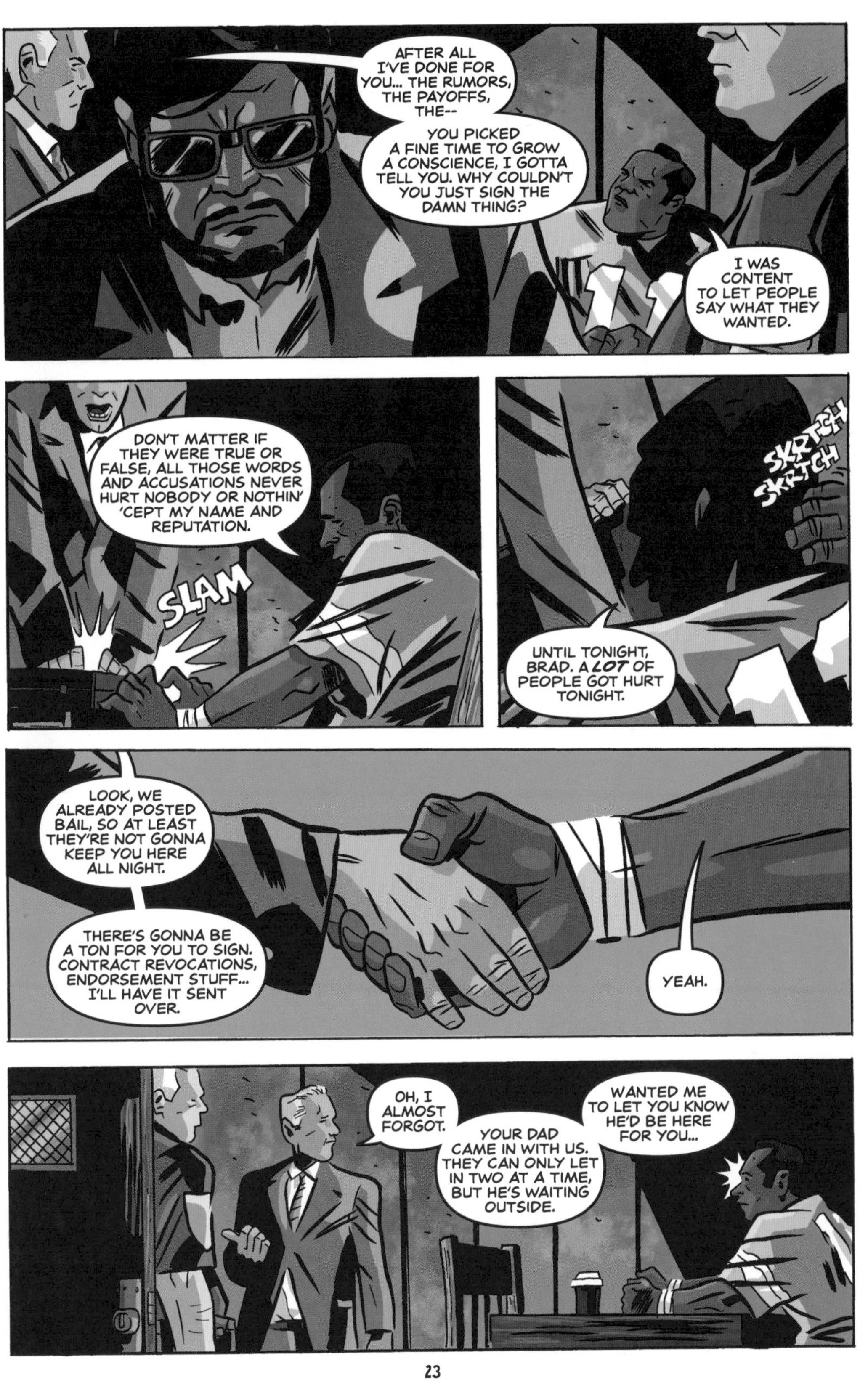
AFTER ALL I'VE DONE FOR YOU... THE RUMORS, THE PAYOFFS, THE--
YOU PICKED A FINE TIME TO GROW A CONSCIENCE, I GOTTA TELL YOU. WHY COULDN'T YOU JUST SIGN THE DAMN THING?
I WAS CONTENT TO LET PEOPLE SAY WHAT THEY WANTED.
DON'T MATTER IF THEY WERE TRUE OR FALSE, ALL THOSE WORDS AND ACCUSATIONS NEVER HURT NOBODY OR NOTHIN' 'CEPT MY NAME AND REPUTATION.
SLAM
SKRTCH SKRTCH
UNTIL TONIGHT, BRAD. A LOT OF PEOPLE GOT HURT TONIGHT.
LOOK, WE ALREADY POSTED BAIL, SO AT LEAST THEY'RE NOT GONNA KEEP YOU HERE ALL NIGHT.
THERE'S GONNA BE A TON FOR YOU TO SIGN. CONTRACT REVOCATIONS, ENDORSEMENT STUFF... I'LL HAVE IT SENT OVER.
YEAH.
OH, I ALMOST FORGOT.
YOUR DAD CAME IN WITH US. THEY CAN ONLY LET IN TWO AT A TIME, BUT HE'S WAITING OUTSIDE.
WANTED ME TO LET YOU KNOW HE'D BE HERE FOR YOU...

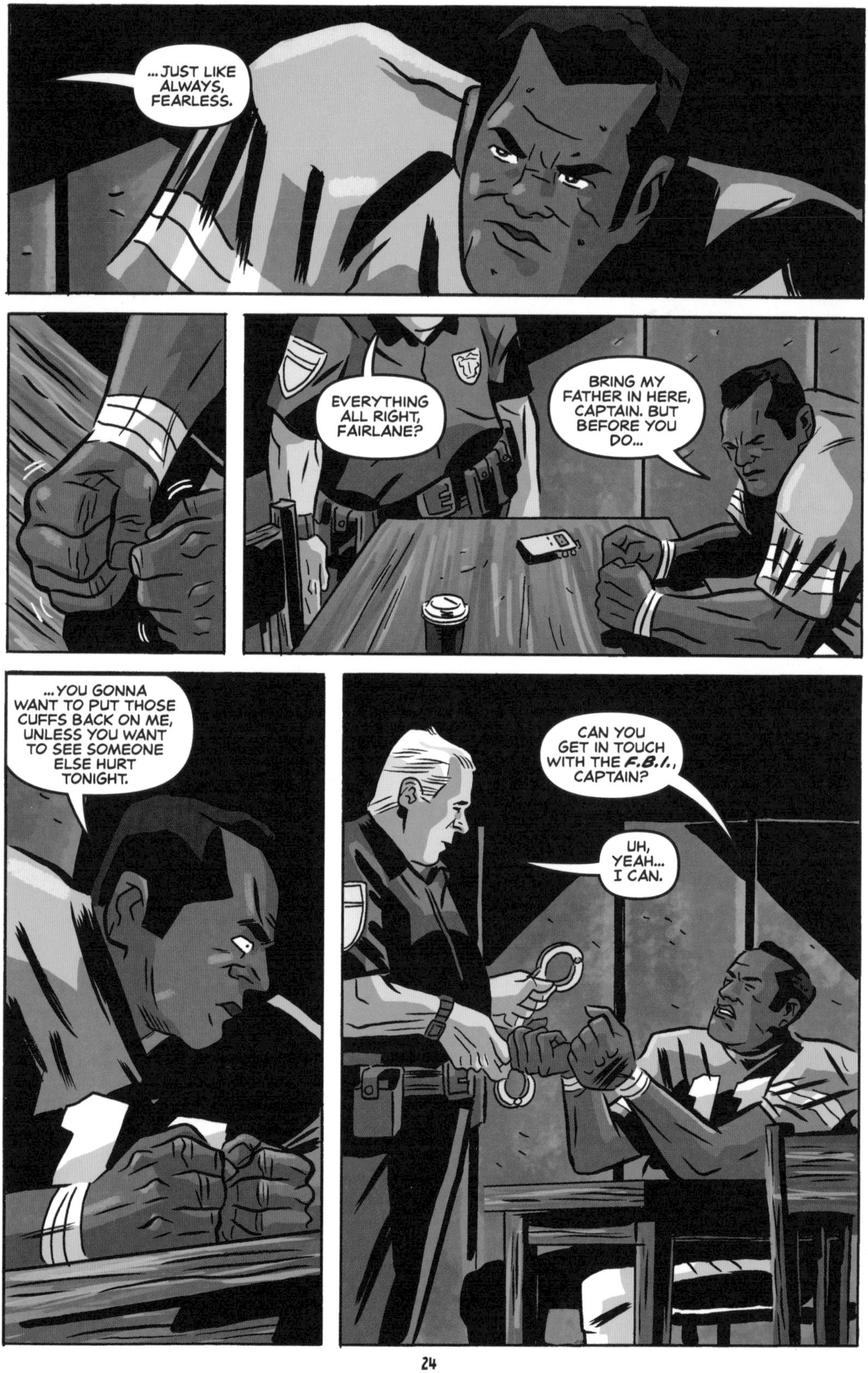
...JUST LIKE ALWAYS, FEARLESS.
EVERYTHING ALL RIGHT, FAIRLANE?
BRING MY FATHER IN HERE, CAPTAIN. BUT BEFORE YOU DO...
...YOU GONNA WANT TO PUT THOSE CUFFS BACK ON ME, UNLESS YOU WANT TO SEE SOMEONE ELSE HURT TONIGHT.
CAN YOU GET IN TOUCH WITH THE *F.B.I.*, CAPTAIN?
UH, YEAH... I CAN.

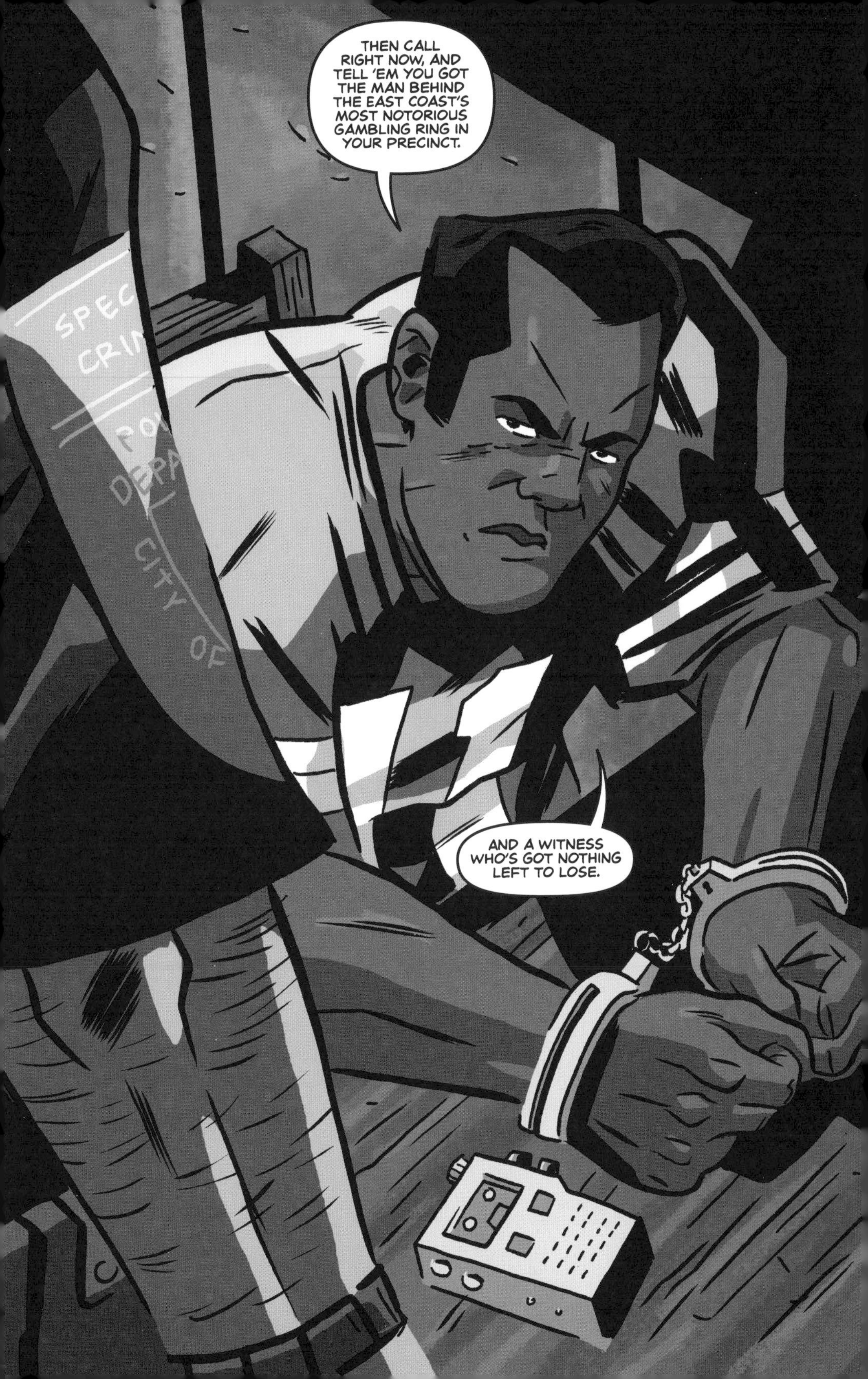
THEN CALL RIGHT NOW, AND TELL 'EM YOU GOT THE MAN BEHIND THE EAST COAST'S MOST NOTORIOUS GAMBLING RING IN YOUR PRECINCT.
AND A WITNESS WHO'S GOT NOTHING LEFT TO LOSE.

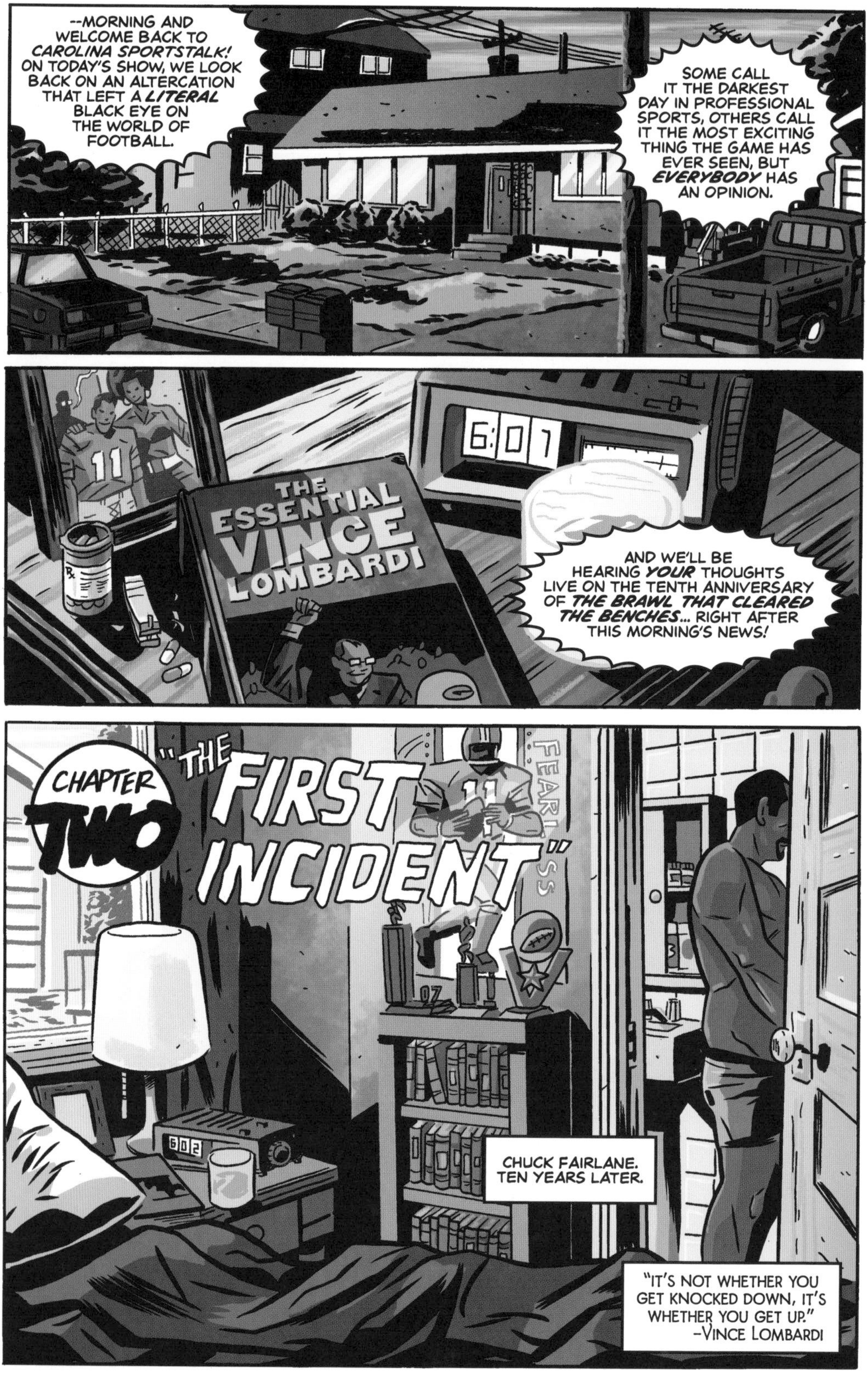
--MORNING AND WELCOME BACK TO *CAROLINA SPORTSTALK!* ON TODAY'S SHOW, WE LOOK BACK ON AN ALTERCATION THAT LEFT A *LITERAL* BLACK EYE ON THE WORLD OF FOOTBALL.
SOME CALL IT THE DARKEST DAY IN PROFESSIONAL SPORTS, OTHERS CALL IT THE MOST EXCITING THING THE GAME HAS EVER SEEN, BUT ***EVERYBODY*** HAS AN OPINION.
6:01
THE ESSENTIAL VINCE LOMBARDI
AND WE'LL BE HEARING ***YOUR*** THOUGHTS LIVE ON THE TENTH ANNIVERSARY OF ***THE BRAWL THAT CLEARED THE BENCHES***... RIGHT AFTER THIS MORNING'S NEWS!
CHAPTER TWO "THE FIRST INCIDENT"
CHUCK FAIRLANE. TEN YEARS LATER.
"IT'S NOT WHETHER YOU GET KNOCKED DOWN, IT'S WHETHER YOU GET UP." –VINCE LOMBARDI

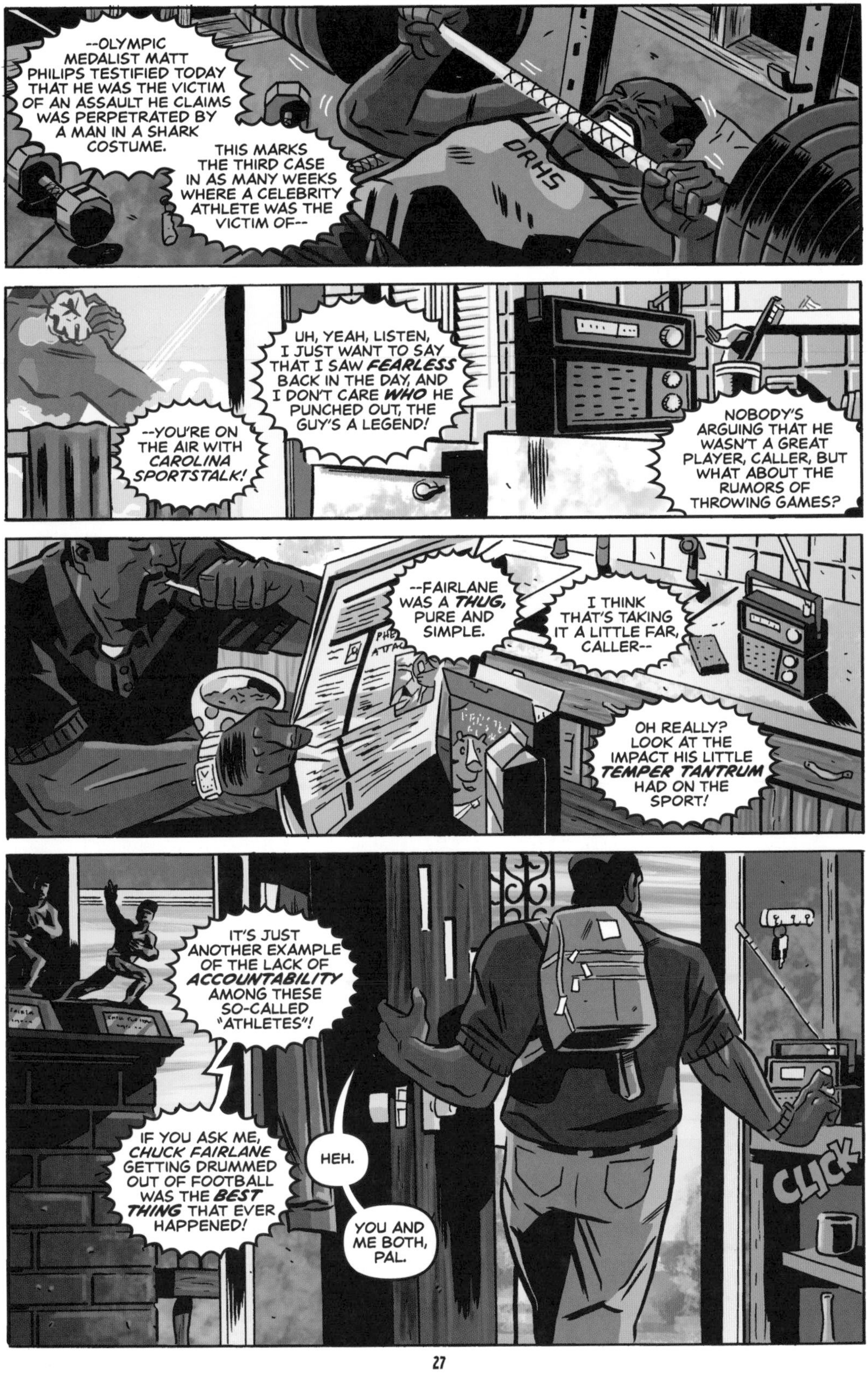
--OLYMPIC MEDALIST MATT PHILIPS TESTIFIED TODAY THAT HE WAS THE VICTIM OF AN ASSAULT HE CLAIMS WAS PERPETRATED BY A MAN IN A SHARK COSTUME.
THIS MARKS THE THIRD CASE IN AS MANY WEEKS WHERE A CELEBRITY ATHLETE WAS THE VICTIM OF--
DRHS
--YOU'RE ON THE AIR WITH CAROLINA SPORTSTALK!
UH, YEAH, LISTEN, I JUST WANT TO SAY THAT I SAW FEARLESS BACK IN THE DAY, AND I DON'T CARE WHO HE PUNCHED OUT, THE GUY'S A LEGEND!
NOBODY'S ARGUING THAT HE WASN'T A GREAT PLAYER, CALLER, BUT WHAT ABOUT THE RUMORS OF THROWING GAMES?
--FAIRLANE WAS A THUG, PURE AND SIMPLE.
I THINK THAT'S TAKING IT A LITTLE FAR, CALLER--
OH REALLY? LOOK AT THE IMPACT HIS LITTLE TEMPER TANTRUM HAD ON THE SPORT!
IT'S JUST ANOTHER EXAMPLE OF THE LACK OF ACCOUNTABILITY AMONG THESE SO-CALLED "ATHLETES"!
IF YOU ASK ME, CHUCK FAIRLANE GETTING DRUMMED OUT OF FOOTBALL WAS THE BEST THING THAT EVER HAPPENED!
HEH.
YOU AND ME BOTH, PAL.
CLICK

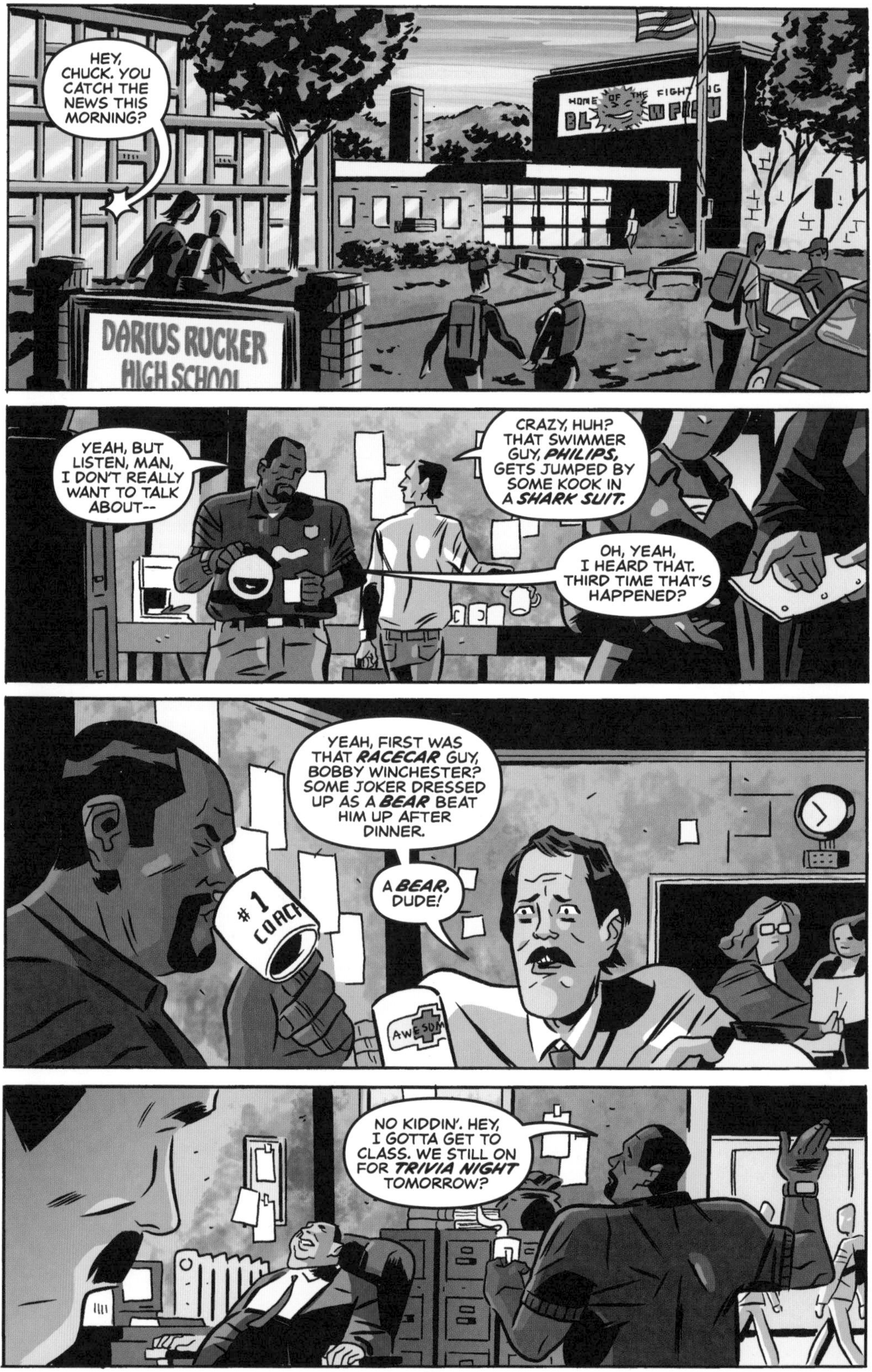
HEY, CHUCK. YOU CATCH THE NEWS THIS MORNING?
DARIUS RUCKER HIGH SCHOOL
YEAH, BUT LISTEN, MAN, I DON'T REALLY WANT TO TALK ABOUT--
CRAZY, HUH? THAT SWIMMER GUY, PHILIPS, GETS JUMPED BY SOME KOOK IN A SHARK SUIT.
OH, YEAH, I HEARD THAT. THIRD TIME THAT'S HAPPENED?
YEAH, FIRST WAS THAT RACECAR GUY, BOBBY WINCHESTER? SOME JOKER DRESSED UP AS A BEAR BEAT HIM UP AFTER DINNER.
A BEAR, DUDE!
NO KIDDIN'. HEY, I GOTTA GET TO CLASS. WE STILL ON FOR TRIVIA NIGHT TOMORROW?

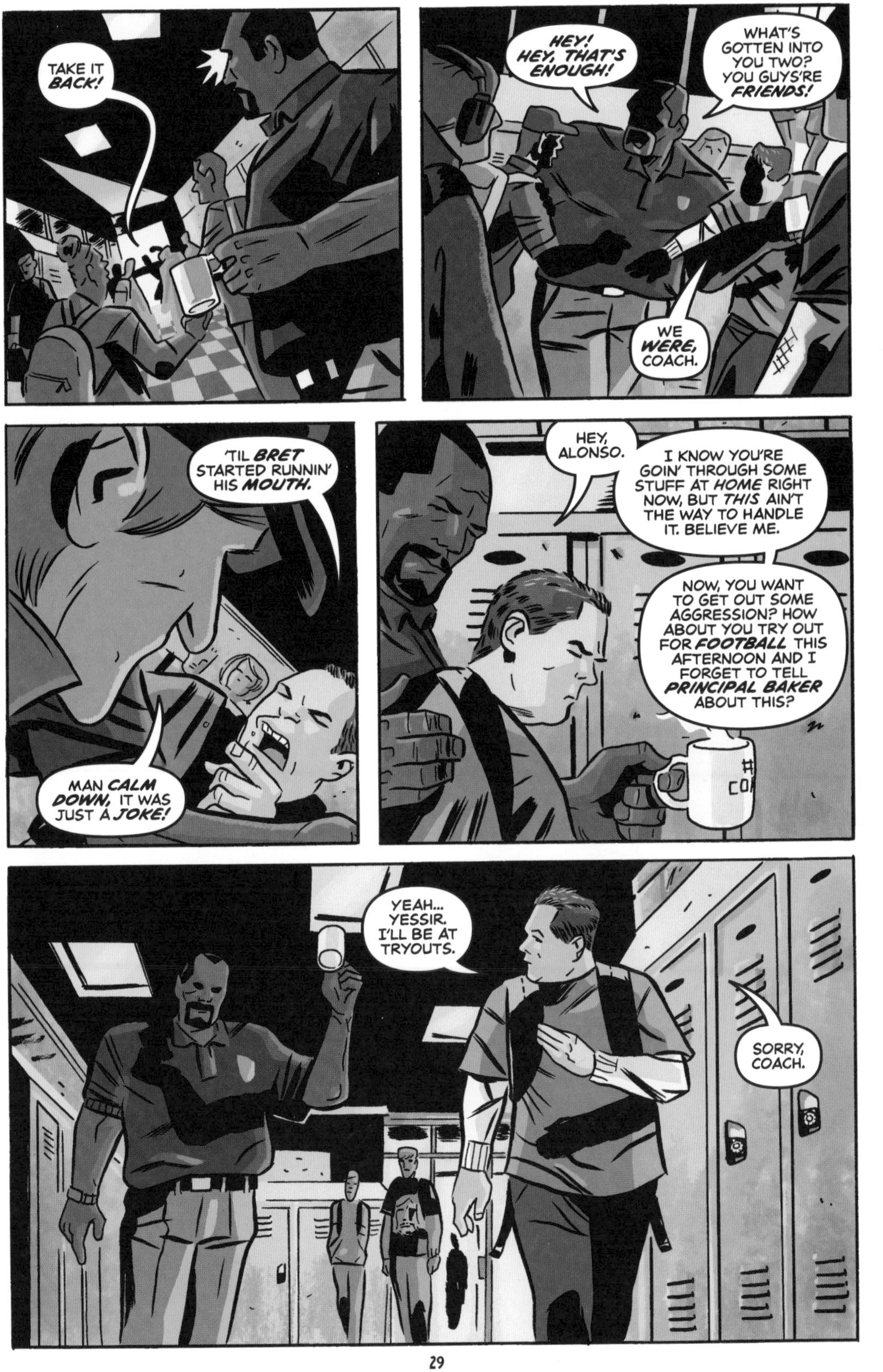
TAKE IT BACK!
HEY! HEY, THAT'S ENOUGH!
WHAT'S GOTTEN INTO YOU TWO? YOU GUYS'RE FRIENDS!
WE WERE, COACH.
'TIL BRET STARTED RUNNIN' HIS MOUTH.
MAN CALM DOWN, IT WAS JUST A JOKE!
HEY, ALONSO.
I KNOW YOU'RE GOIN' THROUGH SOME STUFF AT HOME RIGHT NOW, BUT THIS AIN'T THE WAY TO HANDLE IT. BELIEVE ME.
NOW, YOU WANT TO GET OUT SOME AGGRESSION? HOW ABOUT YOU TRY OUT FOR FOOTBALL THIS AFTERNOON AND I FORGET TO TELL PRINCIPAL BAKER ABOUT THIS?
YEAH... YESSIR. I'LL BE AT TRYOUTS.
SORRY, COACH.

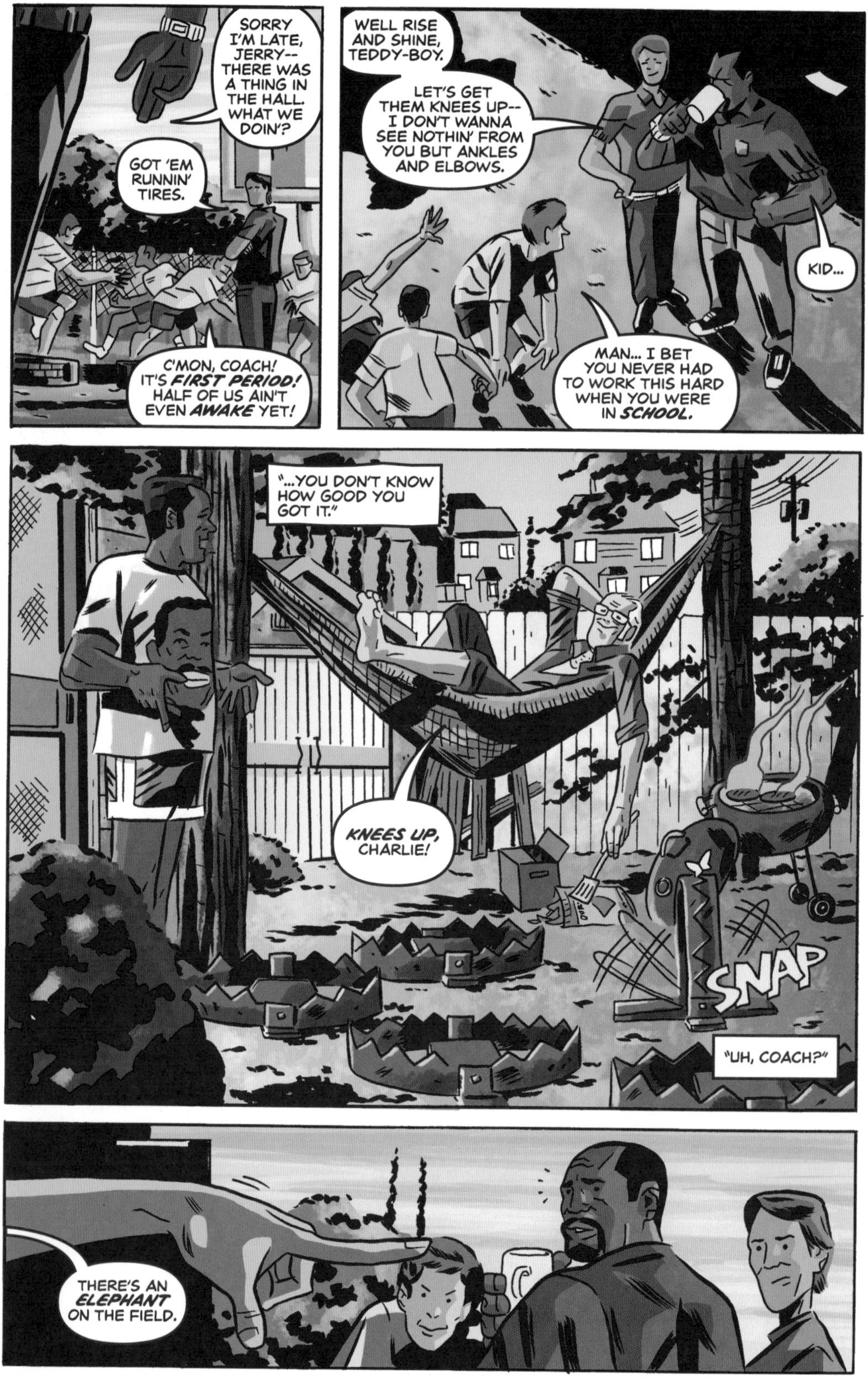
SORRY I'M LATE, JERRY-- THERE WAS A THING IN THE HALL. WHAT WE DOIN'?
GOT 'EM RUNNIN' TIRES.
C'MON, COACH! IT'S FIRST PERIOD! HALF OF US AIN'T EVEN AWAKE YET!
WELL RISE AND SHINE, TEDDY-BOY.
LET'S GET THEM KNEES UP-- I DON'T WANNA SEE NOTHIN' FROM YOU BUT ANKLES AND ELBOWS.
KID...
MAN... I BET YOU NEVER HAD TO WORK THIS HARD WHEN YOU WERE IN SCHOOL.
"...YOU DON'T KNOW HOW GOOD YOU GOT IT."
KNEES UP, CHARLIE!
SNAP
"UH, COACH?"
THERE'S AN ELEPHANT ON THE FIELD.

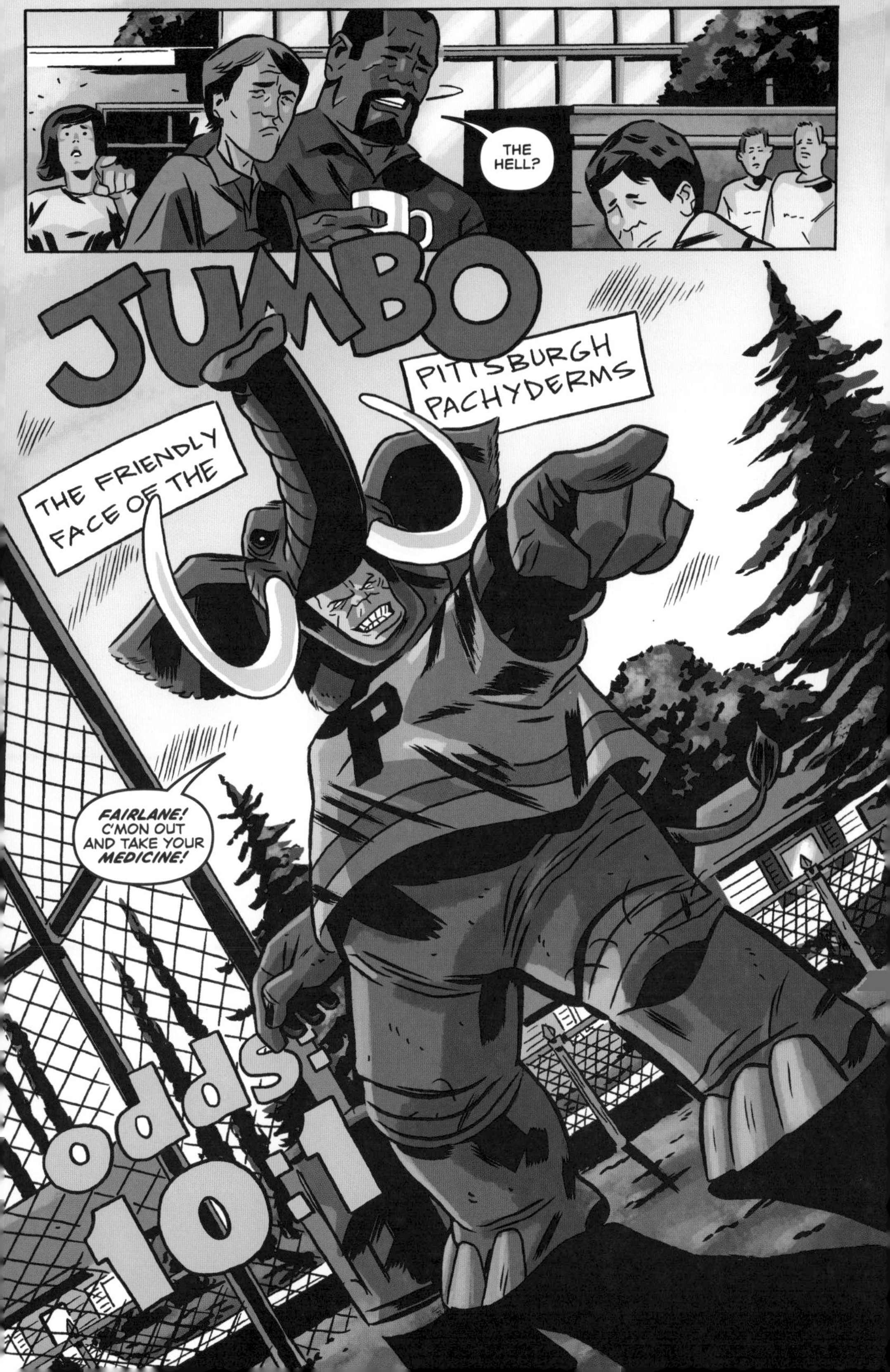
THE HELL?
JUMBO
PITTSBURGH PACHYDERMS
THE FRIENDLY FACE OF THE
FAIRLANE! C'MON OUT AND TAKE YOUR MEDICINE!
POP!

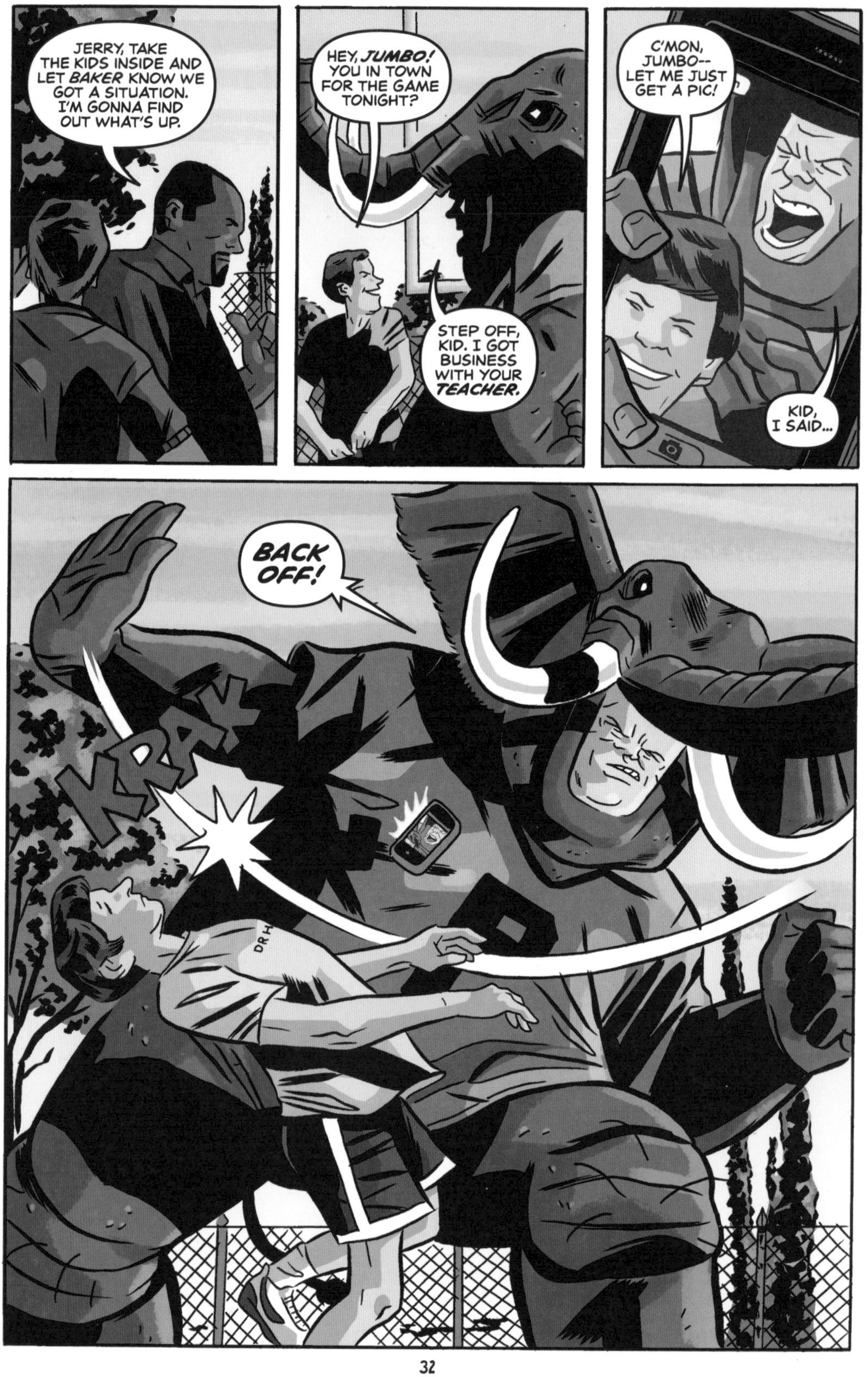
JERRY, TAKE THE KIDS INSIDE AND LET BAKER KNOW WE GOT A SITUATION. I'M GONNA FIND OUT WHAT'S UP.
HEY, JUMBO! YOU IN TOWN FOR THE GAME TONIGHT?
STEP OFF, KID. I GOT BUSINESS WITH YOUR TEACHER.
C'MON, JUMBO-- LET ME JUST GET A PIC!
KID, I SAID...
BACK OFF!
KRAK

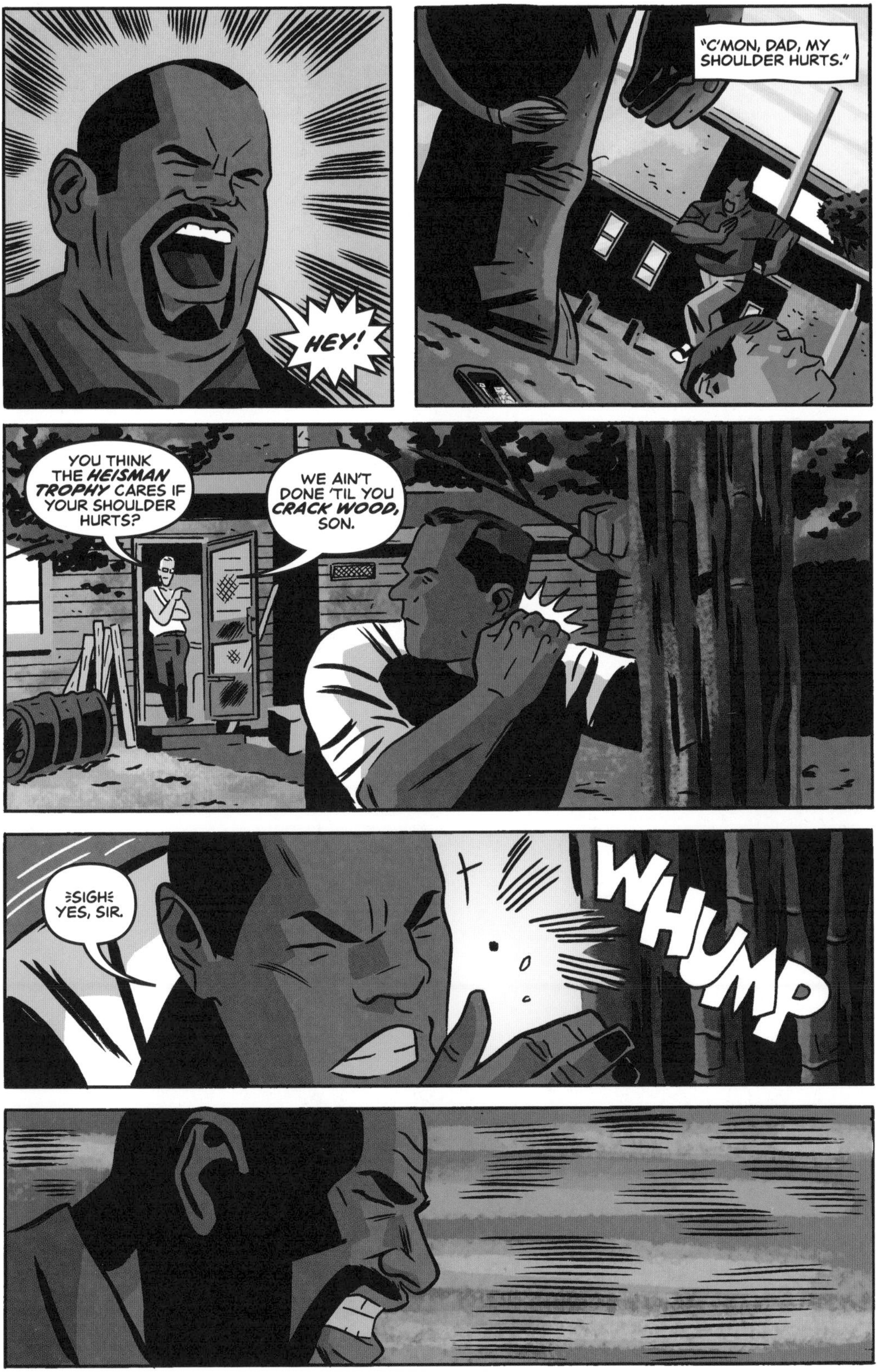
HEY!
"C'MON, DAD, MY SHOULDER HURTS."
YOU THINK THE HEISMAN TROPHY CARES IF YOUR SHOULDER HURTS?
WE AIN'T DONE 'TIL YOU CRACK WOOD, SON.
SIGH YES, SIR.
WHUMP

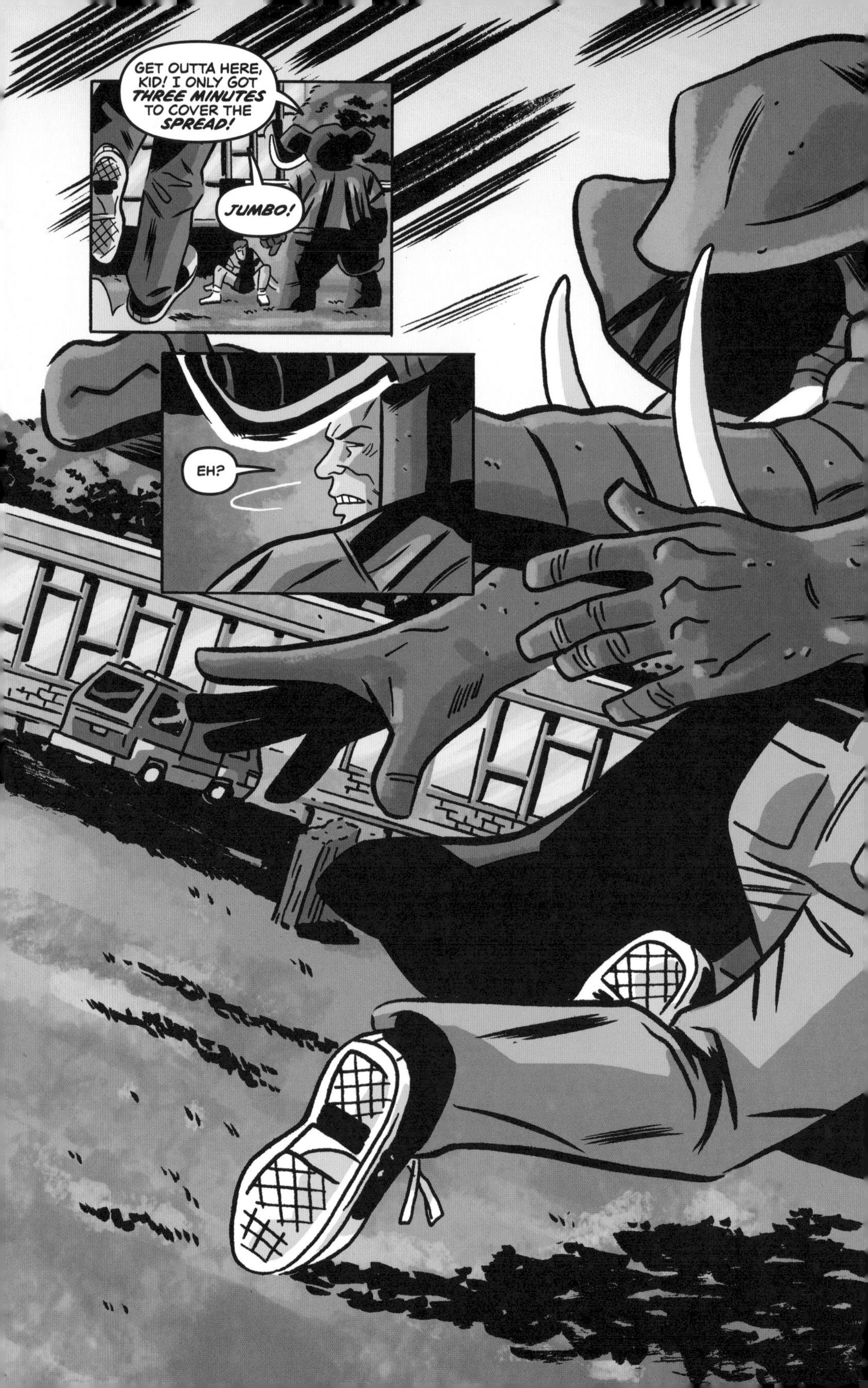
GET OUTTA HERE, KID! I ONLY GOT THREE MINUTES TO COVER THE SPREAD!
JUMBO!
EH?

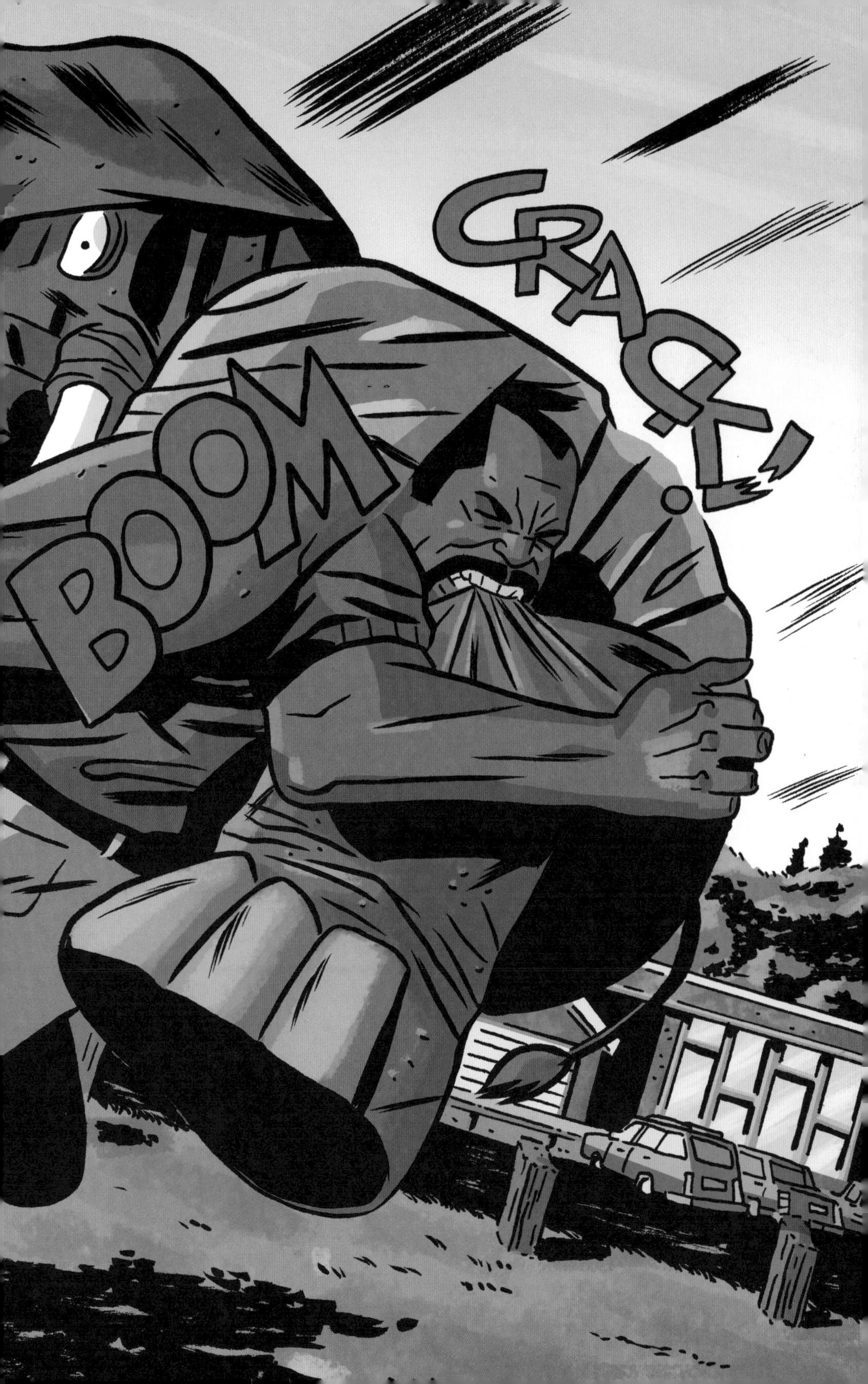
CRACK!
BOOM

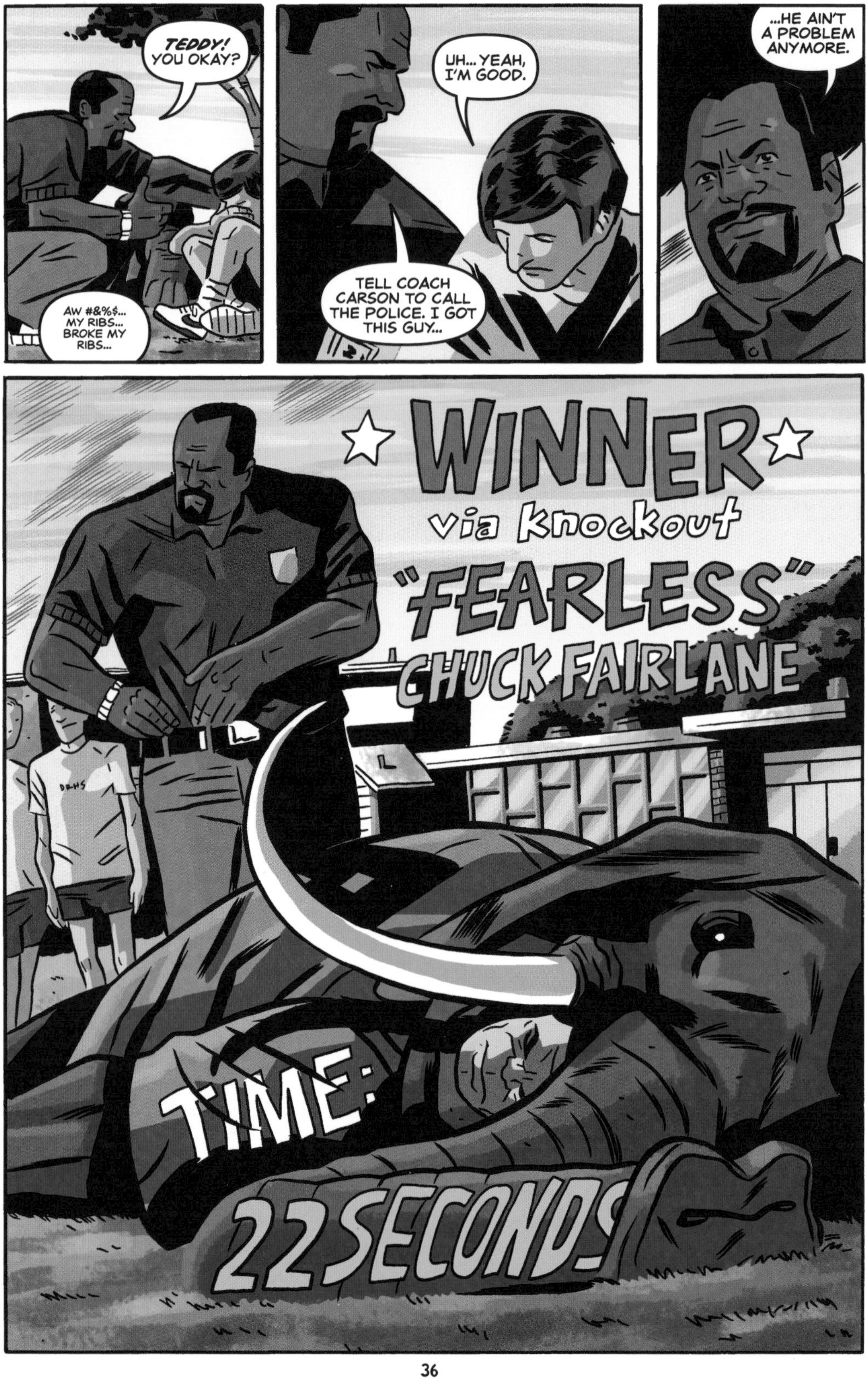
TEDDY! YOU OKAY?
AW #&%$... MY RIBS... BROKE MY RIBS...
UH... YEAH, I'M GOOD.
TELL COACH CARSON TO CALL THE POLICE. I GOT THIS GUY...
...HE AIN'T A PROBLEM ANYMORE.
WINNER
via knockout
"FEARLESS"
CHUCK FAIRLANE
TIME:
22 SECONDS

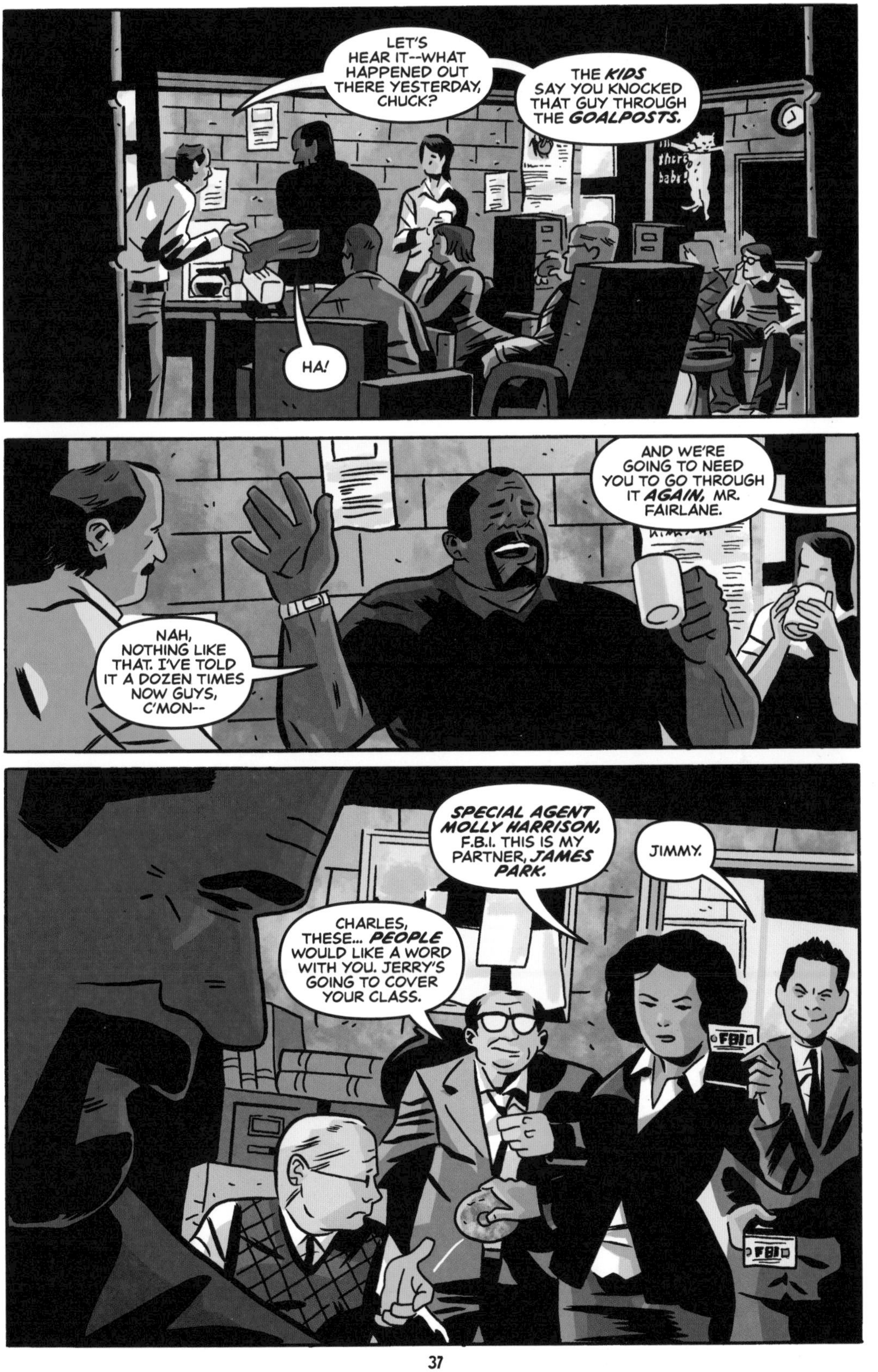
LET'S HEAR IT--WHAT HAPPENED OUT THERE YESTERDAY, CHUCK?
THE *KIDS* SAY YOU KNOCKED THAT GUY THROUGH THE *GOALPOSTS.*
HA!
AND WE'RE GOING TO NEED YOU TO GO THROUGH IT *AGAIN,* MR. FAIRLANE.
NAH, NOTHING LIKE THAT. I'VE TOLD IT A DOZEN TIMES NOW GUYS, C'MON--
CHARLES, THESE... *PEOPLE* WOULD LIKE A WORD WITH YOU. JERRY'S GOING TO COVER YOUR CLASS.
SPECIAL AGENT MOLLY HARRISON, F.B.I. THIS IS MY PARTNER, *JAMES PARK.*
JIMMY.
FBI
FBI

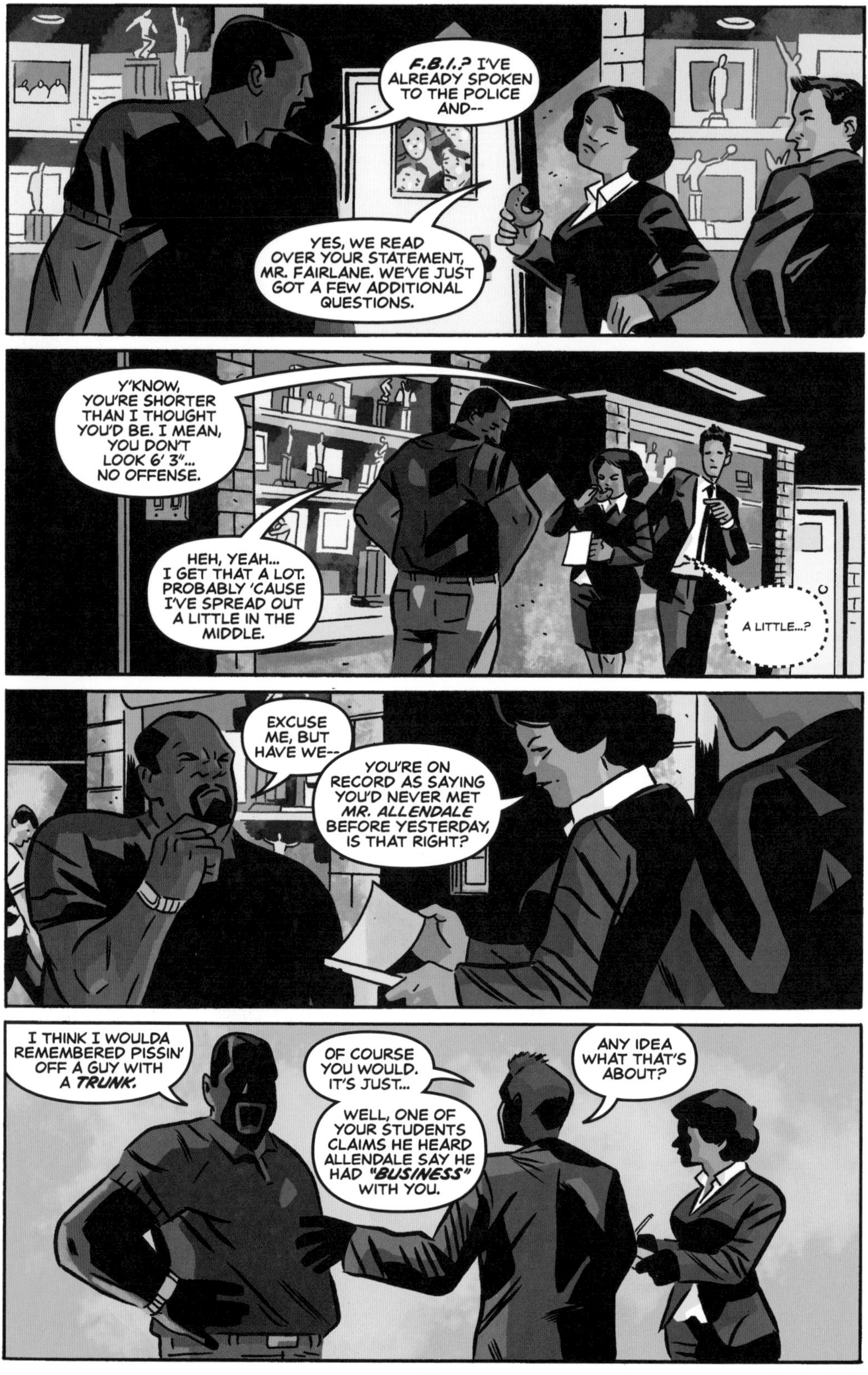
F.B.I.? I'VE ALREADY SPOKEN TO THE POLICE AND--
YES, WE READ OVER YOUR STATEMENT, MR. FAIRLANE. WE'VE JUST GOT A FEW ADDITIONAL QUESTIONS.
Y'KNOW, YOU'RE SHORTER THAN I THOUGHT YOU'D BE. I MEAN, YOU DON'T LOOK 6' 3"... NO OFFENSE.
HEH, YEAH... I GET THAT A LOT. PROBABLY 'CAUSE I'VE SPREAD OUT A LITTLE IN THE MIDDLE.
A LITTLE...?
EXCUSE ME, BUT HAVE WE--
YOU'RE ON RECORD AS SAYING YOU'D NEVER MET MR. ALLENDALE BEFORE YESTERDAY, IS THAT RIGHT?
I THINK I WOULDA REMEMBERED PISSIN' OFF A GUY WITH A TRUNK.
OF COURSE YOU WOULD. IT'S JUST...
WELL, ONE OF YOUR STUDENTS CLAIMS HE HEARD ALLENDALE SAY HE HAD "BUSINESS" WITH YOU.
ANY IDEA WHAT THAT'S ABOUT?

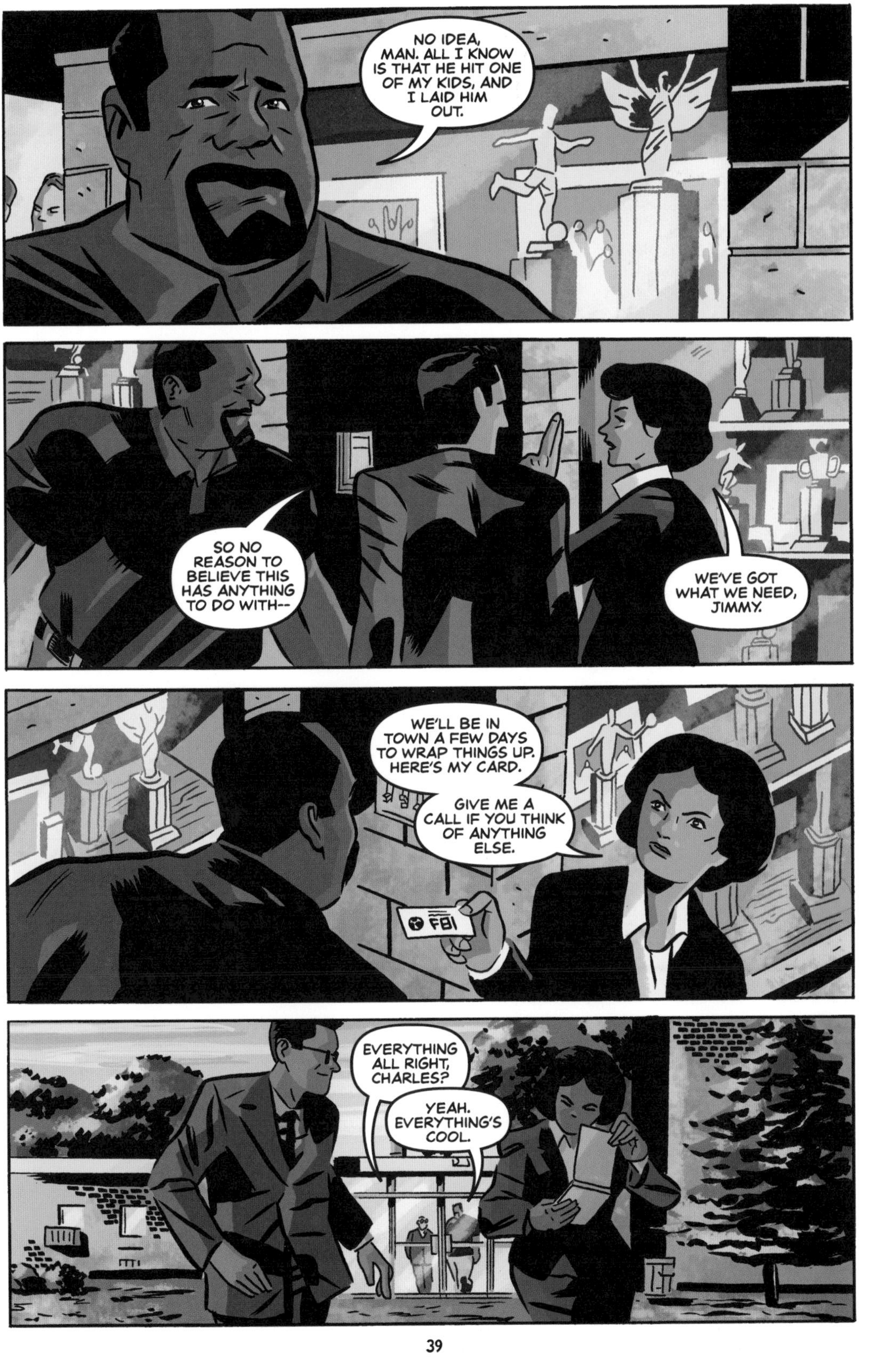
NO IDEA, MAN. ALL I KNOW IS THAT HE HIT ONE OF MY KIDS, AND I LAID HIM OUT.
SO NO REASON TO BELIEVE THIS HAS ANYTHING TO DO WITH--
WE'VE GOT WHAT WE NEED, JIMMY.
WE'LL BE IN TOWN A FEW DAYS TO WRAP THINGS UP. HERE'S MY CARD.
GIVE ME A CALL IF YOU THINK OF ANYTHING ELSE.
FBI
EVERYTHING ALL RIGHT, CHARLES?
YEAH. EVERYTHING'S COOL.

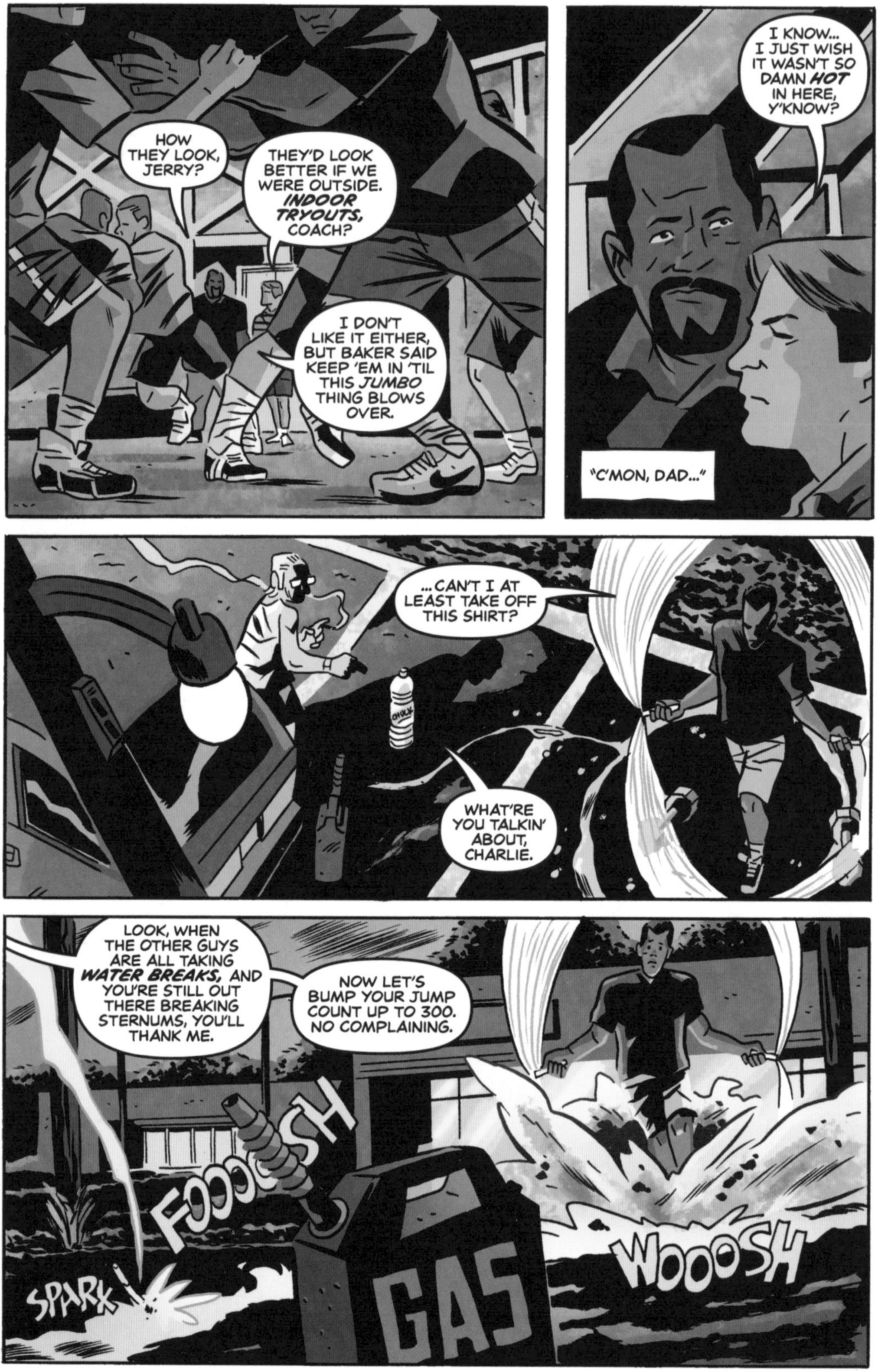
HOW THEY LOOK, JERRY?
THEY'D LOOK BETTER IF WE WERE OUTSIDE. INDOOR TRYOUTS, COACH?
I DON'T LIKE IT EITHER, BUT BAKER SAID KEEP 'EM IN 'TIL THIS JUMBO THING BLOWS OVER.
I KNOW... I JUST WISH IT WASN'T SO DAMN HOT IN HERE, Y'KNOW?
"C'MON, DAD..."
...CAN'T I AT LEAST TAKE OFF THIS SHIRT?
WHAT'RE YOU TALKIN' ABOUT, CHARLIE.
LOOK, WHEN THE OTHER GUYS ARE ALL TAKING WATER BREAKS, AND YOU'RE STILL OUT THERE BREAKING STERNUMS, YOU'LL THANK ME.
NOW LET'S BUMP YOUR JUMP COUNT UP TO 300. NO COMPLAINING.
FOOOOSH
SPARK
GAS
WOOOSH

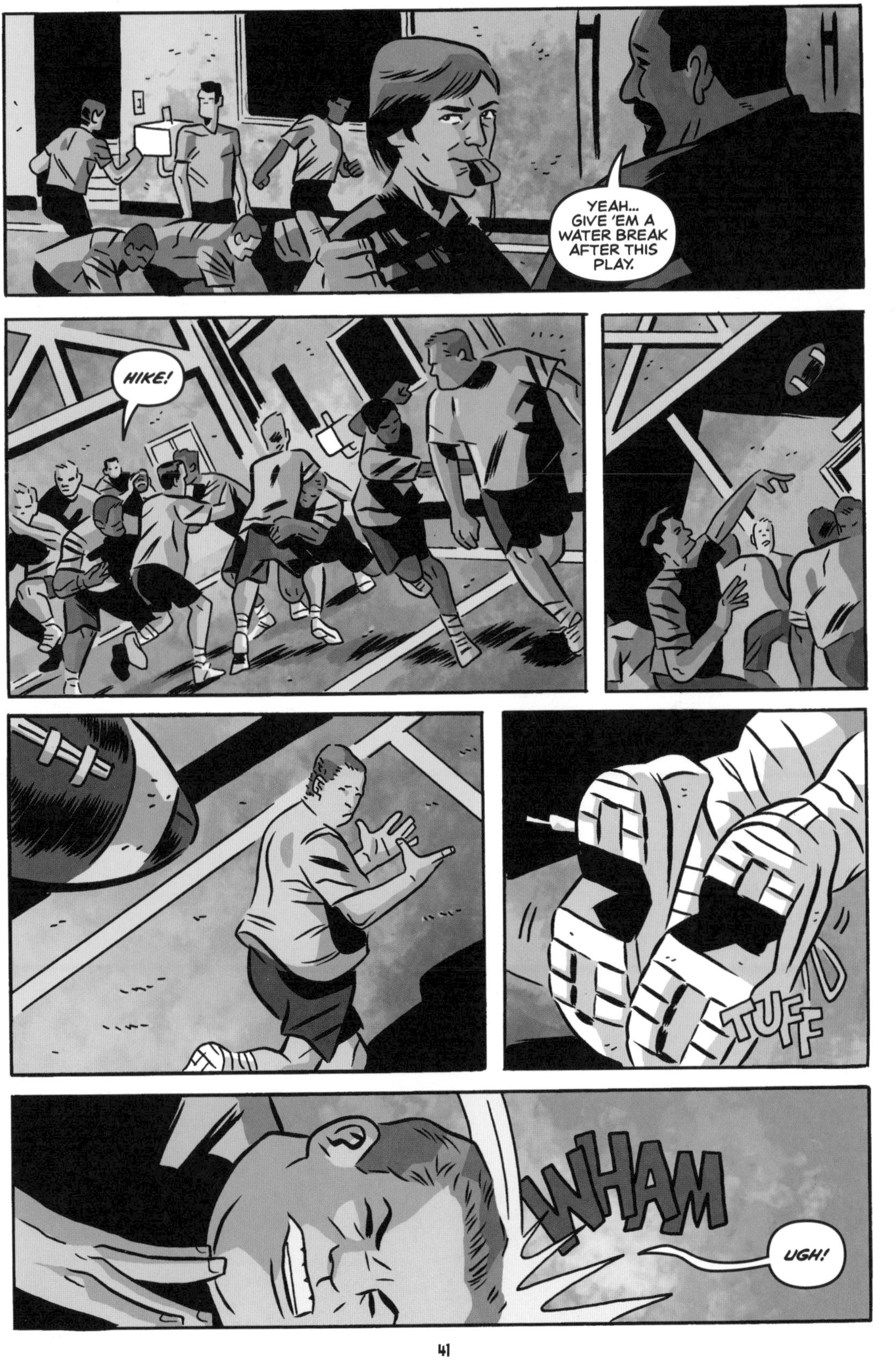
YEAH... GIVE 'EM A WATER BREAK AFTER THIS PLAY.
HIKE!
TUFF
WHAM
UGH!

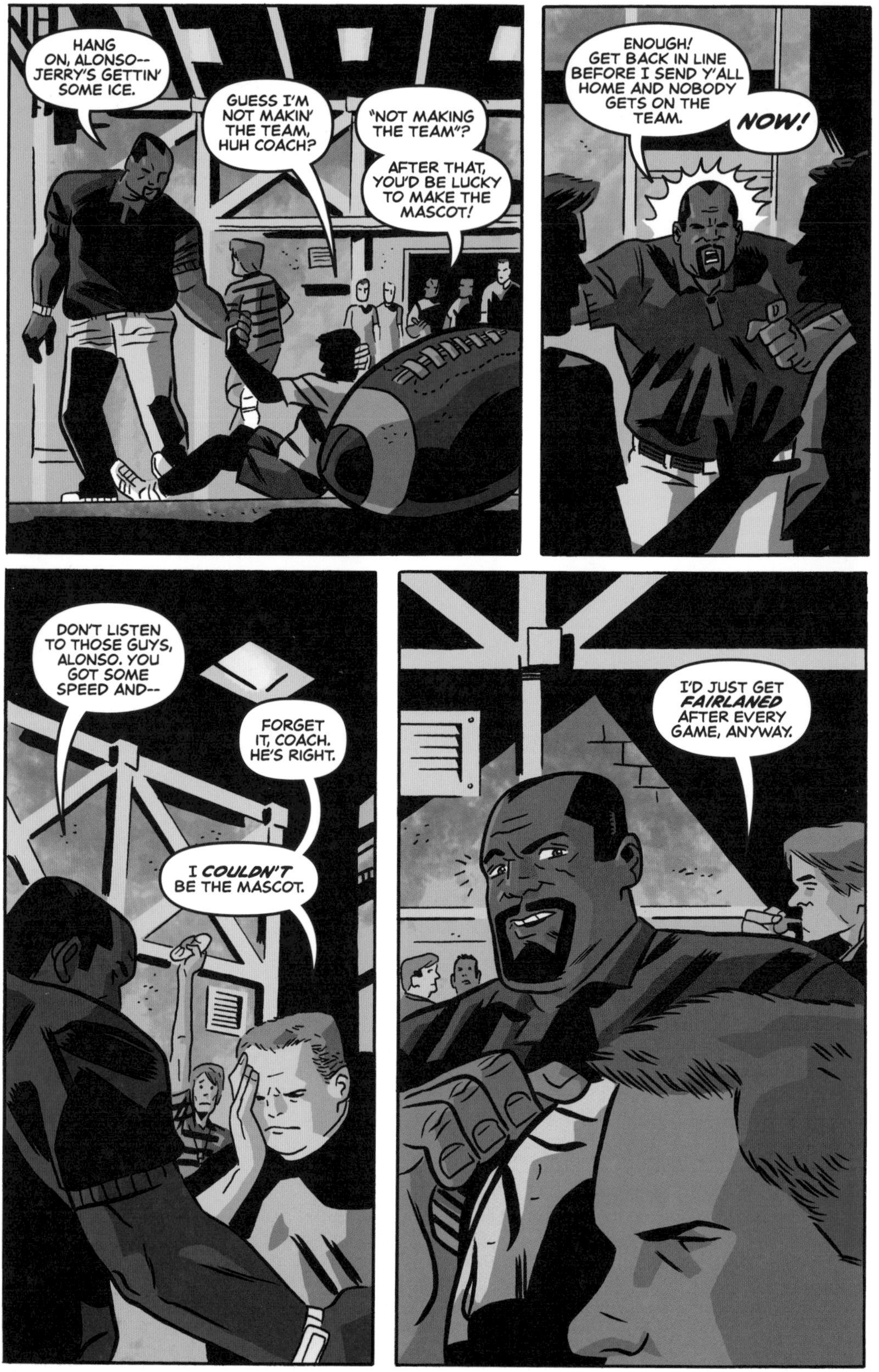
HANG ON, ALONSO-- JERRY'S GETTIN' SOME ICE.
GUESS I'M NOT MAKIN' THE TEAM, HUH COACH?
"NOT MAKING THE TEAM"?
AFTER THAT, YOU'D BE LUCKY TO MAKE THE MASCOT!
ENOUGH! GET BACK IN LINE BEFORE I SEND Y'ALL HOME AND NOBODY GETS ON THE TEAM.
NOW!
DON'T LISTEN TO THOSE GUYS, ALONSO. YOU GOT SOME SPEED AND--
FORGET IT, COACH. HE'S RIGHT.
I COULDN'T BE THE MASCOT.
I'D JUST GET FAIRLANED AFTER EVERY GAME, ANYWAY.

ALL RIGHT, COACH, I'M HEADIN' OUT. YOU NEED ANYTHING 'FORE I GO?

NAH, JERRY, I'M SOLID. HAVE, A GOOD EVE--

HEY, YEAH-- LEMME ASK...

YEAH, COACH?

WHAT DO YOU KNOW ABOUT GETTING "FAIRLANED"?

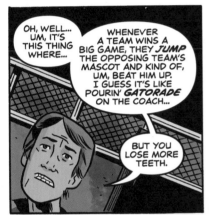

OH, WELL... UM, IT'S THIS THING WHERE...

WHENEVER A TEAM WINS A BIG GAME, THEY JUMP THE OPPOSING TEAM'S MASCOT AND KIND OF, UM, BEAT HIM UP. I GUESS IT'S LIKE POURIN' GATORADE ON THE COACH...

BUT YOU LOSE MORE TEETH.

HAHAHAHAHA... UH, YEAH, I KNOW WHAT IT IS, JER. BUT YOU DON'T THINK... MAYBE, THIS JUMBO... IS RELATED?

THOUGHT ABOUT IT? YEAH, IT'S PROBABLY NOTHING.

WHAT, LIKE THE MASCOTS ARE FIGHTING BACK OR SOMETHING? I DON'T KNOW, I NEVER REALLY--

JUST THINKING OUT LOUD AFTER A LONG PRACTICE.

SORRY TO HOLD YOU UP. GO ON HOME. I'LL SEE YOU TOMORROW.

UH, OKAY, COACH. YOU HAVE A GOOD NIGHT.

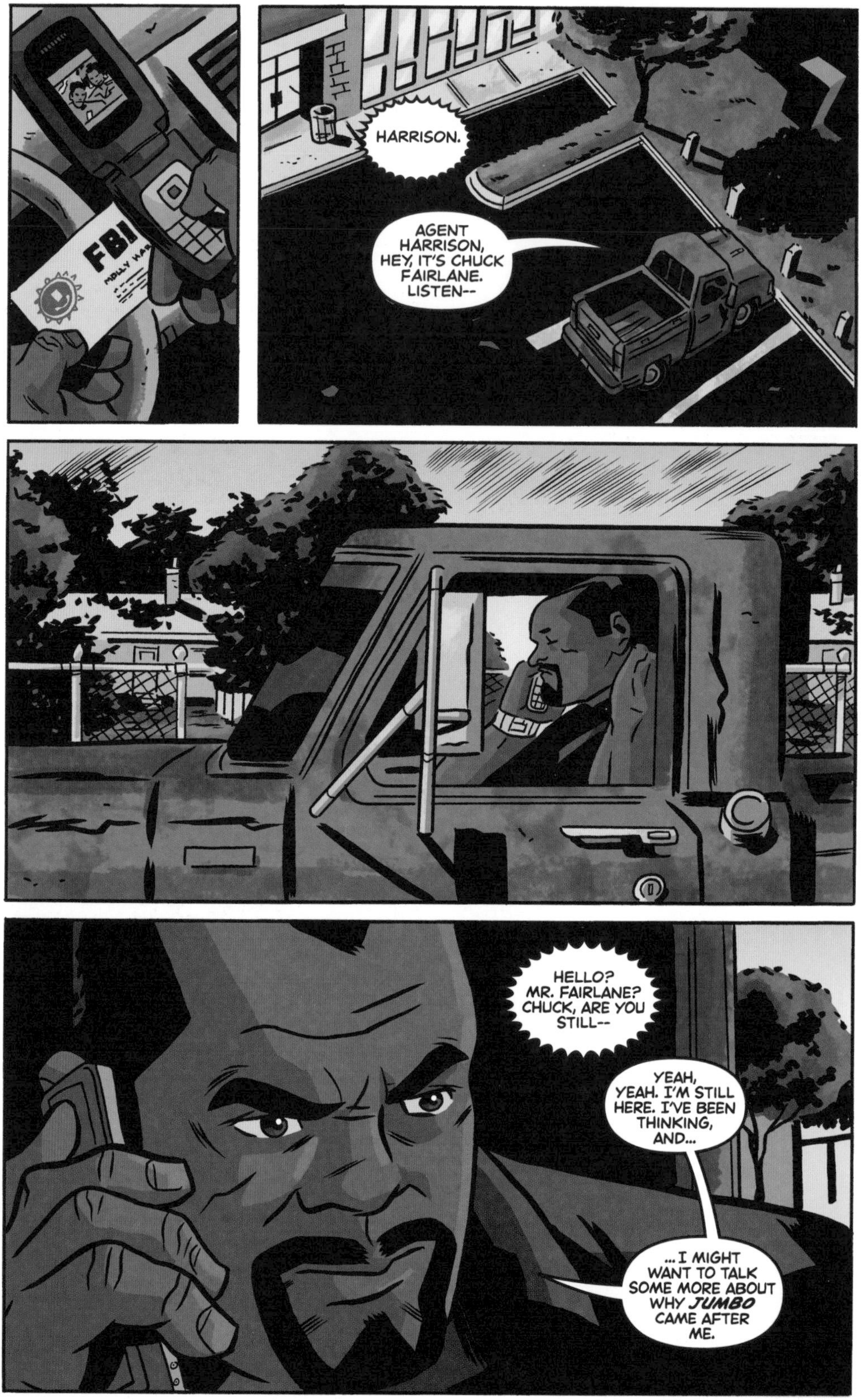
FBI
HARRISON.
AGENT HARRISON, HEY, IT'S CHUCK FAIRLANE. LISTEN--
HELLO? MR. FAIRLANE? CHUCK, ARE YOU STILL--
YEAH, YEAH. I'M STILL HERE. I'VE BEEN THINKING, AND...
...I MIGHT WANT TO TALK SOME MORE ABOUT WHY *JUMBO* CAME AFTER ME.

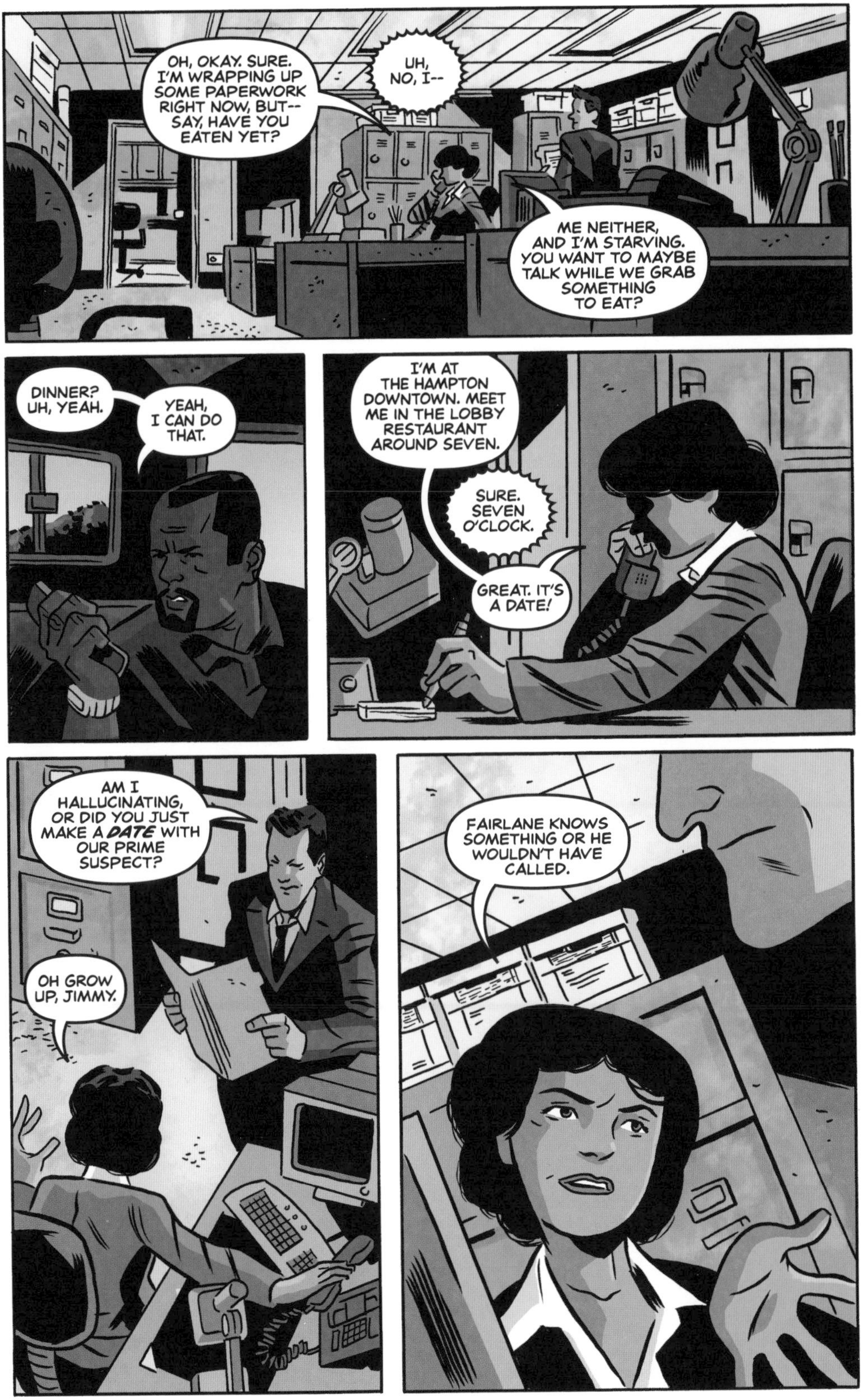
OH, OKAY. SURE. I'M WRAPPING UP SOME PAPERWORK RIGHT NOW, BUT-- SAY, HAVE YOU EATEN YET?
UH, NO, I--
ME NEITHER, AND I'M STARVING. YOU WANT TO MAYBE TALK WHILE WE GRAB SOMETHING TO EAT?
DINNER? UH, YEAH.
YEAH, I CAN DO THAT.
I'M AT THE HAMPTON DOWNTOWN. MEET ME IN THE LOBBY RESTAURANT AROUND SEVEN.
SURE. SEVEN O'CLOCK.
GREAT. IT'S A DATE!
AM I HALLUCINATING, OR DID YOU JUST MAKE A *DATE* WITH OUR PRIME SUSPECT?
OH GROW UP, JIMMY.
FAIRLANE KNOWS SOMETHING OR HE WOULDN'T HAVE CALLED.

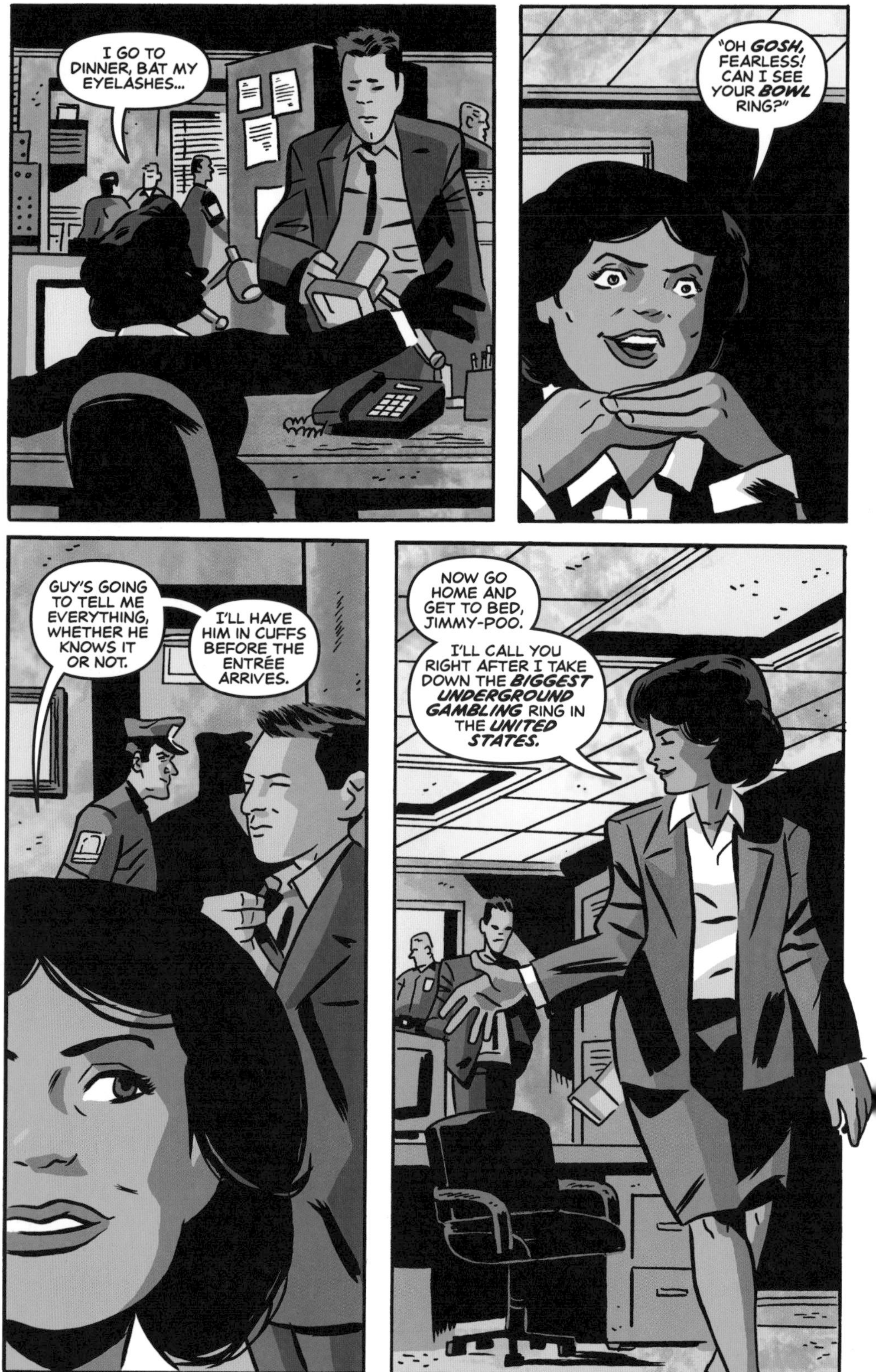
I GO TO DINNER, BAT MY EYELASHES...
"OH *GOSH,* FEARLESS! CAN I SEE YOUR *BOWL* RING?"
GUY'S GOING TO TELL ME EVERYTHING, WHETHER HE KNOWS IT OR NOT.
I'LL HAVE HIM IN CUFFS BEFORE THE ENTRÉE ARRIVES.
NOW GO HOME AND GET TO BED, JIMMY-POO.
I'LL CALL YOU RIGHT AFTER I TAKE DOWN THE *BIGGEST UNDERGROUND GAMBLING* RING IN THE *UNITED STATES.*

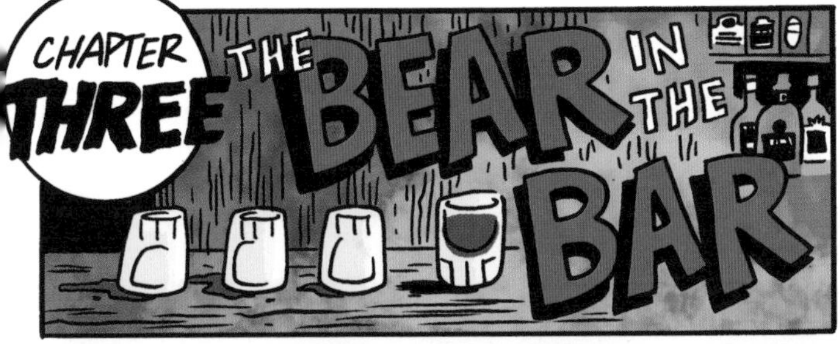
CHAPTER THREE
THE BEAR IN THE BAR

"IF YOU DON'T THINK YOU'RE A WINNER, YOU DON'T BELONG HERE."
–VINCE LOMBARDI

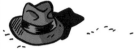

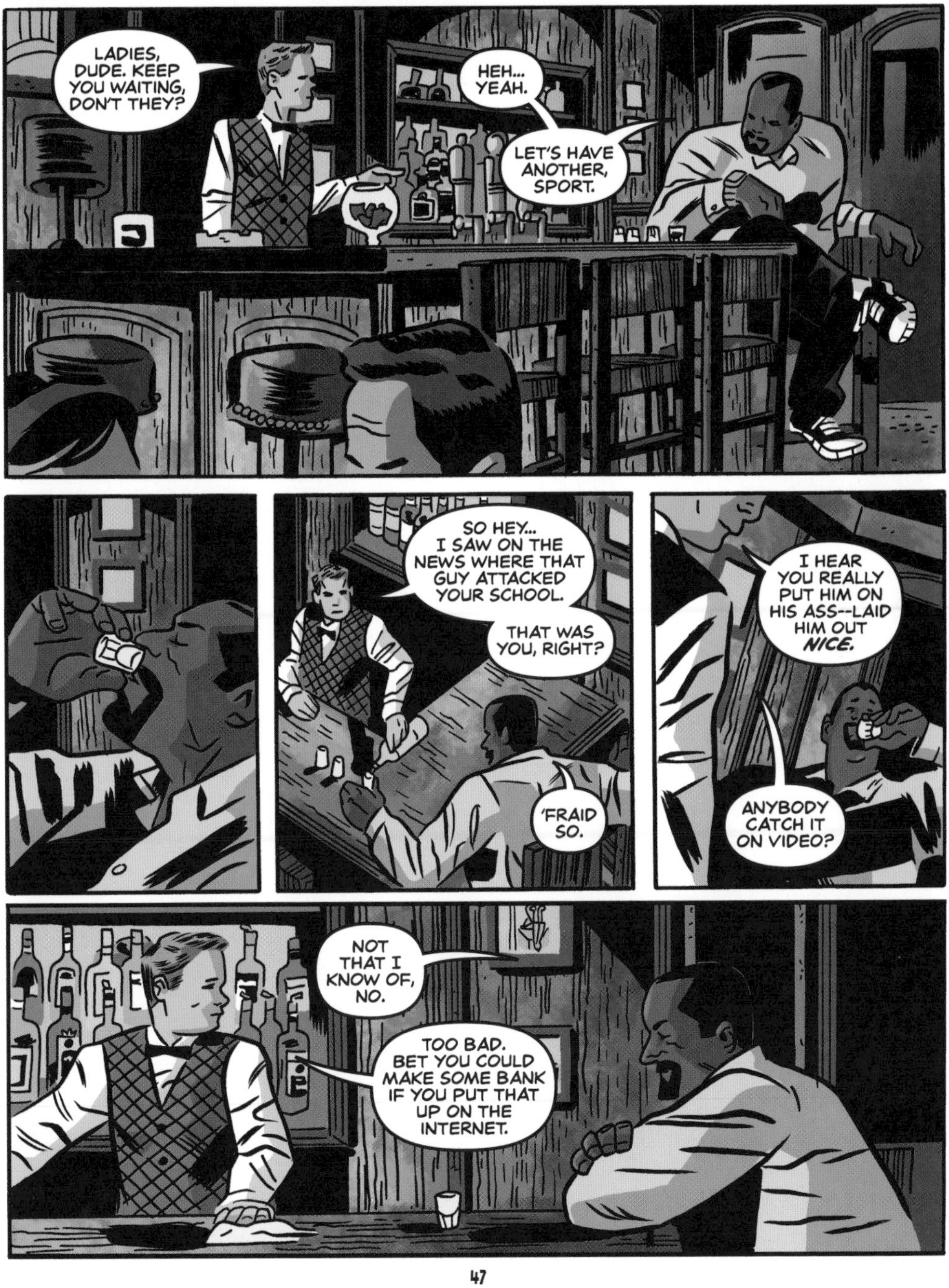
LADIES, DUDE. KEEP YOU WAITING, DON'T THEY?
HEH... YEAH.
LET'S HAVE ANOTHER, SPORT.
SO HEY... I SAW ON THE NEWS WHERE THAT GUY ATTACKED YOUR SCHOOL.
THAT WAS YOU, RIGHT?
'FRAID SO.
I HEAR YOU REALLY PUT HIM ON HIS ASS--LAID HIM OUT NICE.
ANYBODY CATCH IT ON VIDEO?
NOT THAT I KNOW OF, NO.
TOO BAD. BET YOU COULD MAKE SOME BANK IF YOU PUT THAT UP ON THE INTERNET.

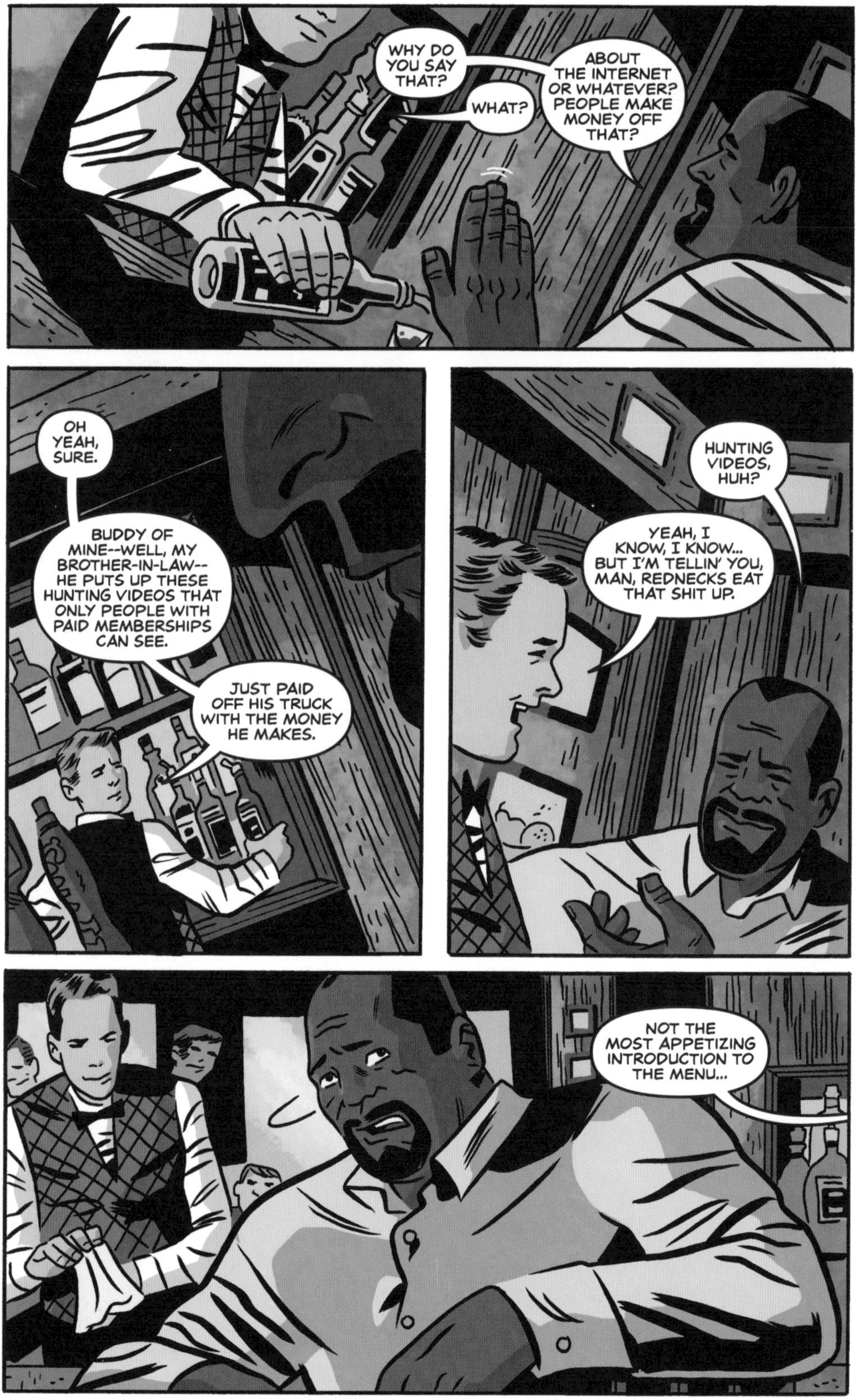
WHY DO YOU SAY THAT?
WHAT?
ABOUT THE INTERNET OR WHATEVER? PEOPLE MAKE MONEY OFF THAT?
OH YEAH, SURE.
BUDDY OF MINE--WELL, MY BROTHER-IN-LAW--HE PUTS UP THESE HUNTING VIDEOS THAT ONLY PEOPLE WITH PAID MEMBERSHIPS CAN SEE.
JUST PAID OFF HIS TRUCK WITH THE MONEY HE MAKES.
HUNTING VIDEOS, HUH?
YEAH, I KNOW, I KNOW... BUT I'M TELLIN' YOU, MAN, REDNECKS EAT THAT SHIT UP.
NOT THE MOST APPETIZING INTRODUCTION TO THE MENU...

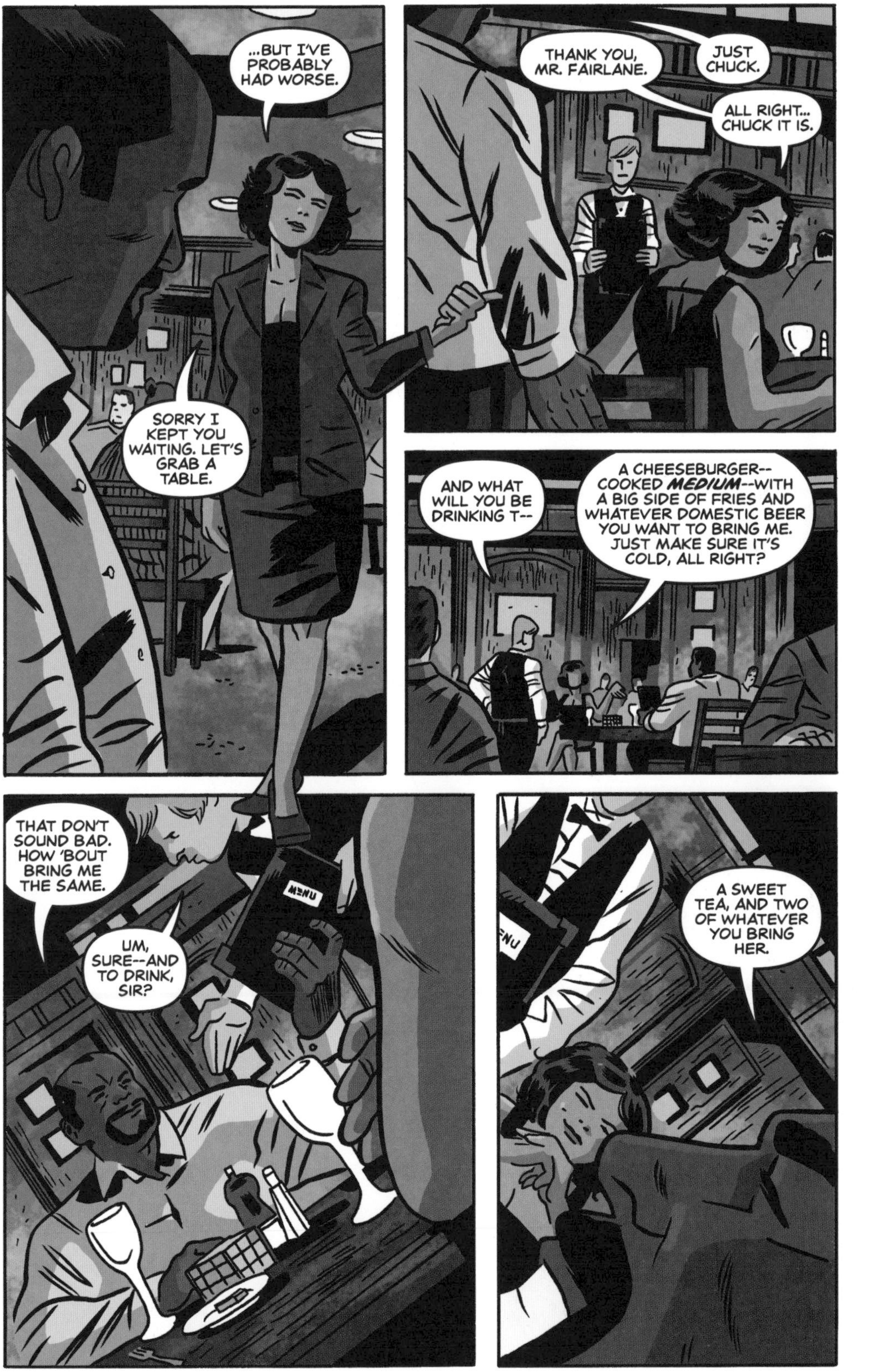
...BUT I'VE PROBABLY HAD WORSE.
SORRY I KEPT YOU WAITING. LET'S GRAB A TABLE.
THANK YOU, MR. FAIRLANE.
JUST CHUCK.
ALL RIGHT... CHUCK IT IS.
AND WHAT WILL YOU BE DRINKING T--
A CHEESEBURGER-- COOKED MEDIUM--WITH A BIG SIDE OF FRIES AND WHATEVER DOMESTIC BEER YOU WANT TO BRING ME. JUST MAKE SURE IT'S COLD, ALL RIGHT?
THAT DON'T SOUND BAD. HOW 'BOUT BRING ME THE SAME.
MENU
UM, SURE--AND TO DRINK, SIR?
A SWEET TEA, AND TWO OF WHATEVER YOU BRING HER.

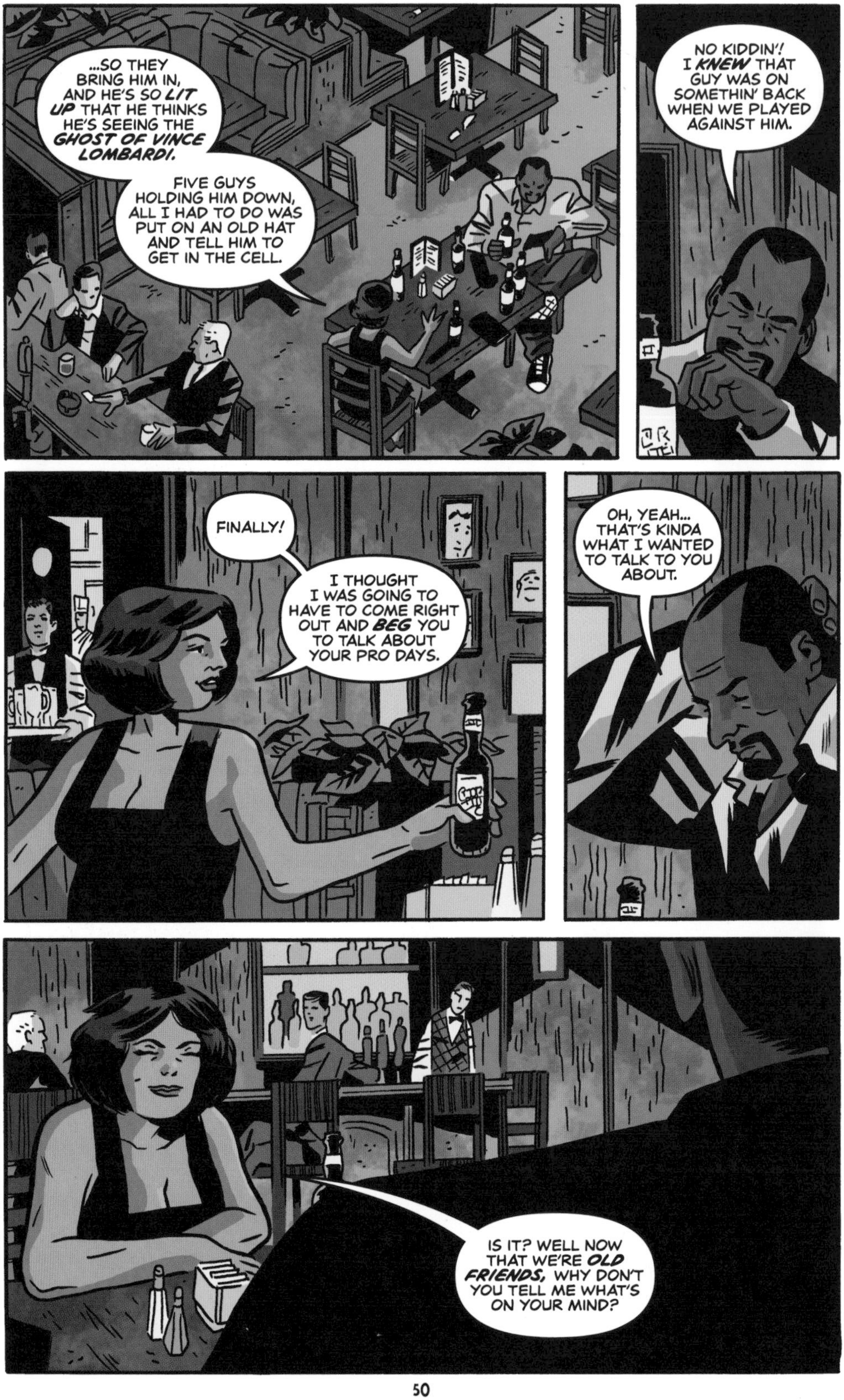
...SO THEY BRING HIM IN, AND HE'S SO *LIT UP* THAT HE THINKS HE'S SEEING THE *GHOST OF VINCE LOMBARDI.*
FIVE GUYS HOLDING HIM DOWN, ALL I HAD TO DO WAS PUT ON AN OLD HAT AND TELL HIM TO GET IN THE CELL.
NO KIDDIN'! I *KNEW* THAT GUY WAS ON SOMETHIN' BACK WHEN WE PLAYED AGAINST HIM.
FINALLY!
I THOUGHT I WAS GOING TO HAVE TO COME RIGHT OUT AND *BEG* YOU TO TALK ABOUT YOUR PRO DAYS.
OH, YEAH... THAT'S KINDA WHAT I WANTED TO TALK TO YOU ABOUT.
IS IT? WELL NOW THAT WE'RE *OLD FRIENDS,* WHY DON'T YOU TELL ME WHAT'S ON YOUR MIND?

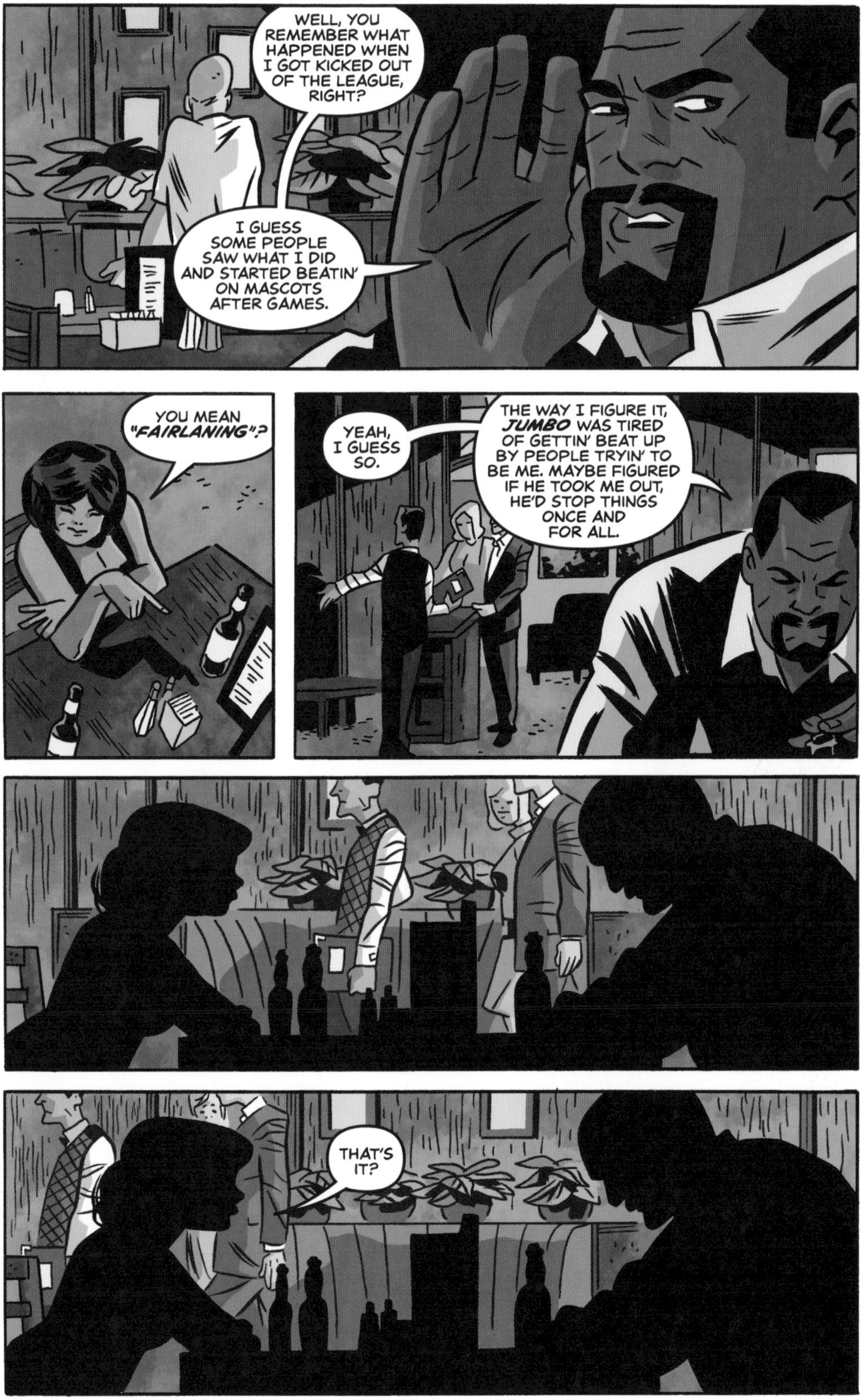
WELL, YOU REMEMBER WHAT HAPPENED WHEN I GOT KICKED OUT OF THE LEAGUE, RIGHT?
I GUESS SOME PEOPLE SAW WHAT I DID AND STARTED BEATIN' ON MASCOTS AFTER GAMES.
YOU MEAN "FAIRLANING"?
YEAH, I GUESS SO.
THE WAY I FIGURE IT, JUMBO WAS TIRED OF GETTIN' BEAT UP BY PEOPLE TRYIN' TO BE ME. MAYBE FIGURED IF HE TOOK ME OUT, HE'D STOP THINGS ONCE AND FOR ALL.
THAT'S IT?

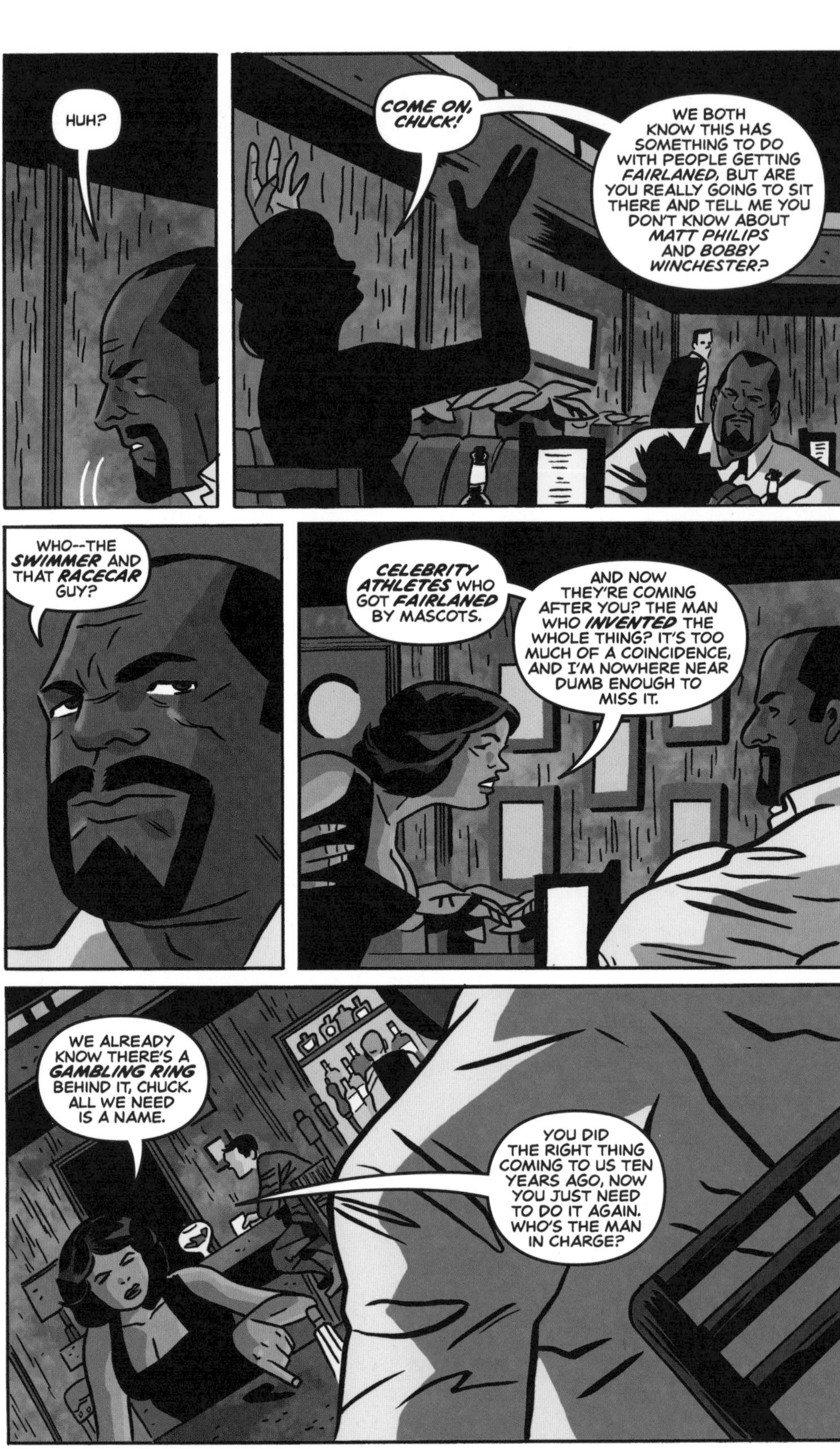
HUH?
COME ON, CHUCK!
WE BOTH KNOW THIS HAS SOMETHING TO DO WITH PEOPLE GETTING FAIRLANED, BUT ARE YOU REALLY GOING TO SIT THERE AND TELL ME YOU DON'T KNOW ABOUT MATT PHILIPS AND BOBBY WINCHESTER?
WHO--THE SWIMMER AND THAT RACECAR GUY?
CELEBRITY ATHLETES WHO GOT FAIRLANED BY MASCOTS.
AND NOW THEY'RE COMING AFTER YOU? THE MAN WHO INVENTED THE WHOLE THING? IT'S TOO MUCH OF A COINCIDENCE, AND I'M NOWHERE NEAR DUMB ENOUGH TO MISS IT.
WE ALREADY KNOW THERE'S A GAMBLING RING BEHIND IT, CHUCK. ALL WE NEED IS A NAME.
YOU DID THE RIGHT THING COMING TO US TEN YEARS AGO, NOW YOU JUST NEED TO DO IT AGAIN. WHO'S THE MAN IN CHARGE?

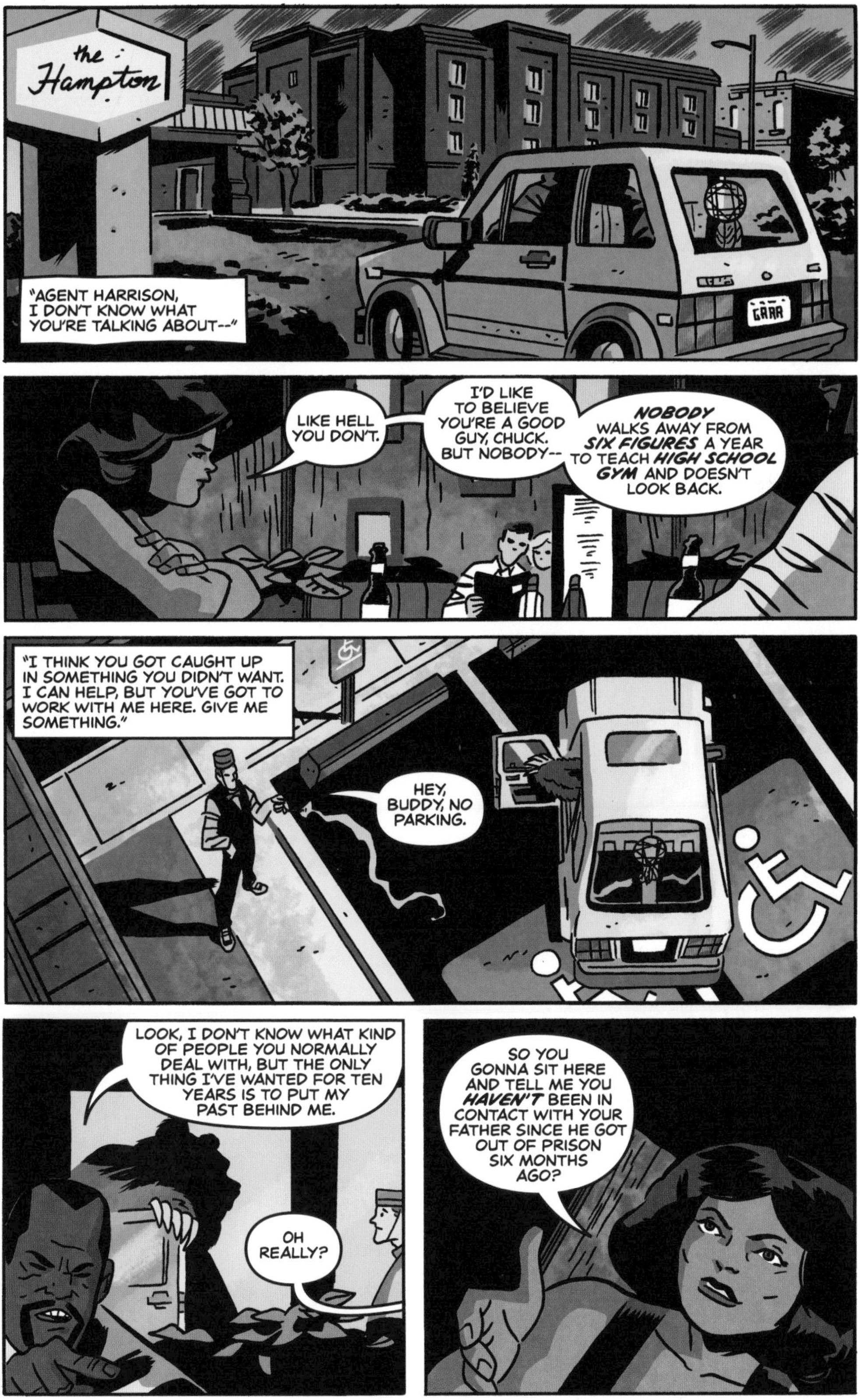
the Hampton
"AGENT HARRISON, I DON'T KNOW WHAT YOU'RE TALKING ABOUT--"
LIKE HELL YOU DON'T.
I'D LIKE TO BELIEVE YOU'RE A GOOD GUY, CHUCK. BUT NOBODY--
NOBODY WALKS AWAY FROM SIX FIGURES A YEAR TO TEACH HIGH SCHOOL GYM AND DOESN'T LOOK BACK.
"I THINK YOU GOT CAUGHT UP IN SOMETHING YOU DIDN'T WANT. I CAN HELP, BUT YOU'VE GOT TO WORK WITH ME HERE. GIVE ME SOMETHING."
HEY, BUDDY, NO PARKING.
LOOK, I DON'T KNOW WHAT KIND OF PEOPLE YOU NORMALLY DEAL WITH, BUT THE ONLY THING I'VE WANTED FOR TEN YEARS IS TO PUT MY PAST BEHIND ME.
OH REALLY?
SO YOU GONNA SIT HERE AND TELL ME YOU HAVEN'T BEEN IN CONTACT WITH YOUR FATHER SINCE HE GOT OUT OF PRISON SIX MONTHS AGO?

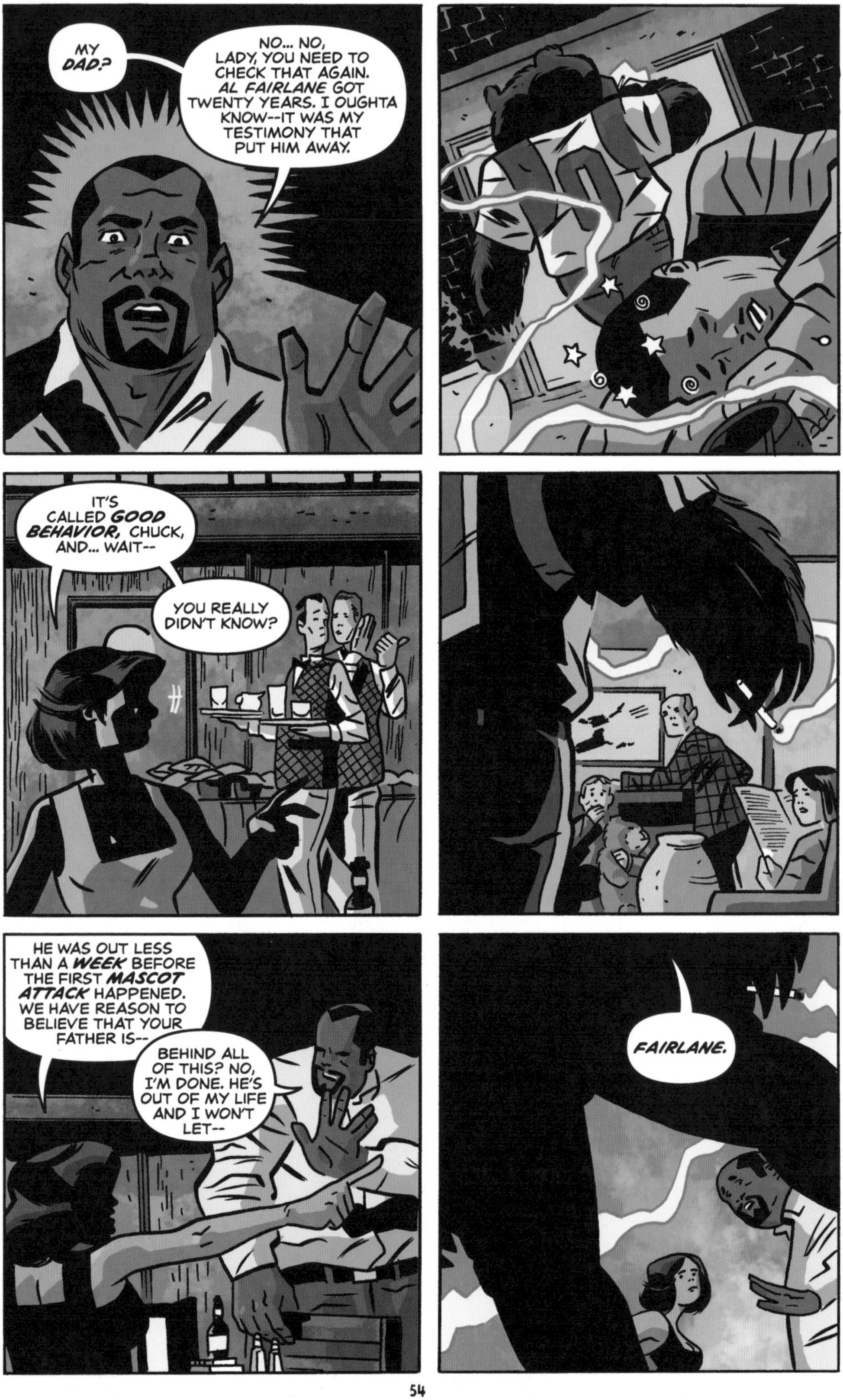
MY DAD?
NO... NO, LADY, YOU NEED TO CHECK THAT AGAIN. AL FAIRLANE GOT TWENTY YEARS. I OUGHTA KNOW--IT WAS MY TESTIMONY THAT PUT HIM AWAY.
IT'S CALLED GOOD BEHAVIOR, CHUCK, AND... WAIT--
YOU REALLY DIDN'T KNOW?
HE WAS OUT LESS THAN A WEEK BEFORE THE FIRST MASCOT ATTACK HAPPENED. WE HAVE REASON TO BELIEVE THAT YOUR FATHER IS--
BEHIND ALL OF THIS? NO, I'M DONE. HE'S OUT OF MY LIFE AND I WON'T LET--
FAIRLANE.

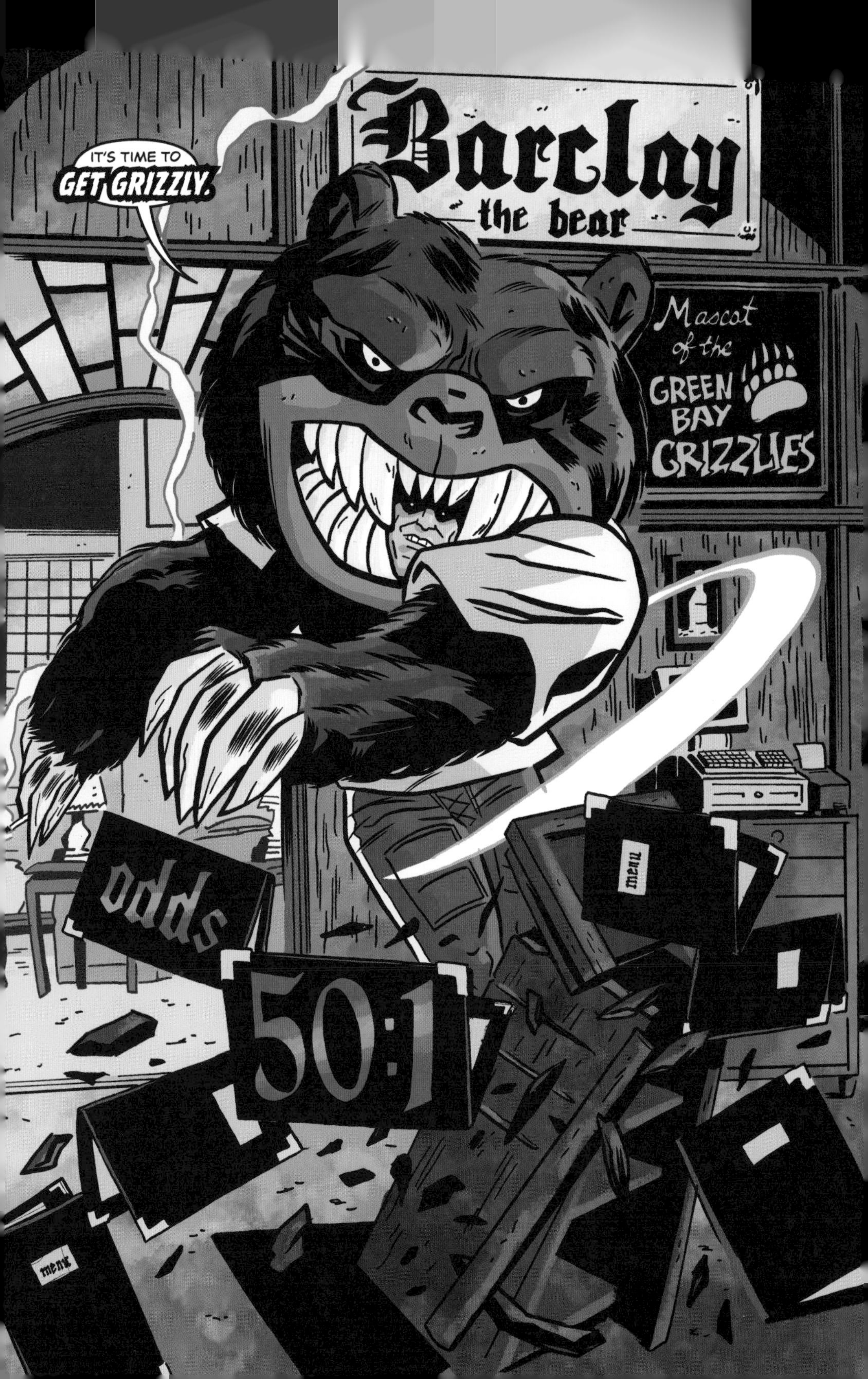

IT'S TIME TO GET GRIZZLY.
Barclay
the bear
Mascot of the GREEN BAY GRIZZLIES
odds
50:1
menu
menu

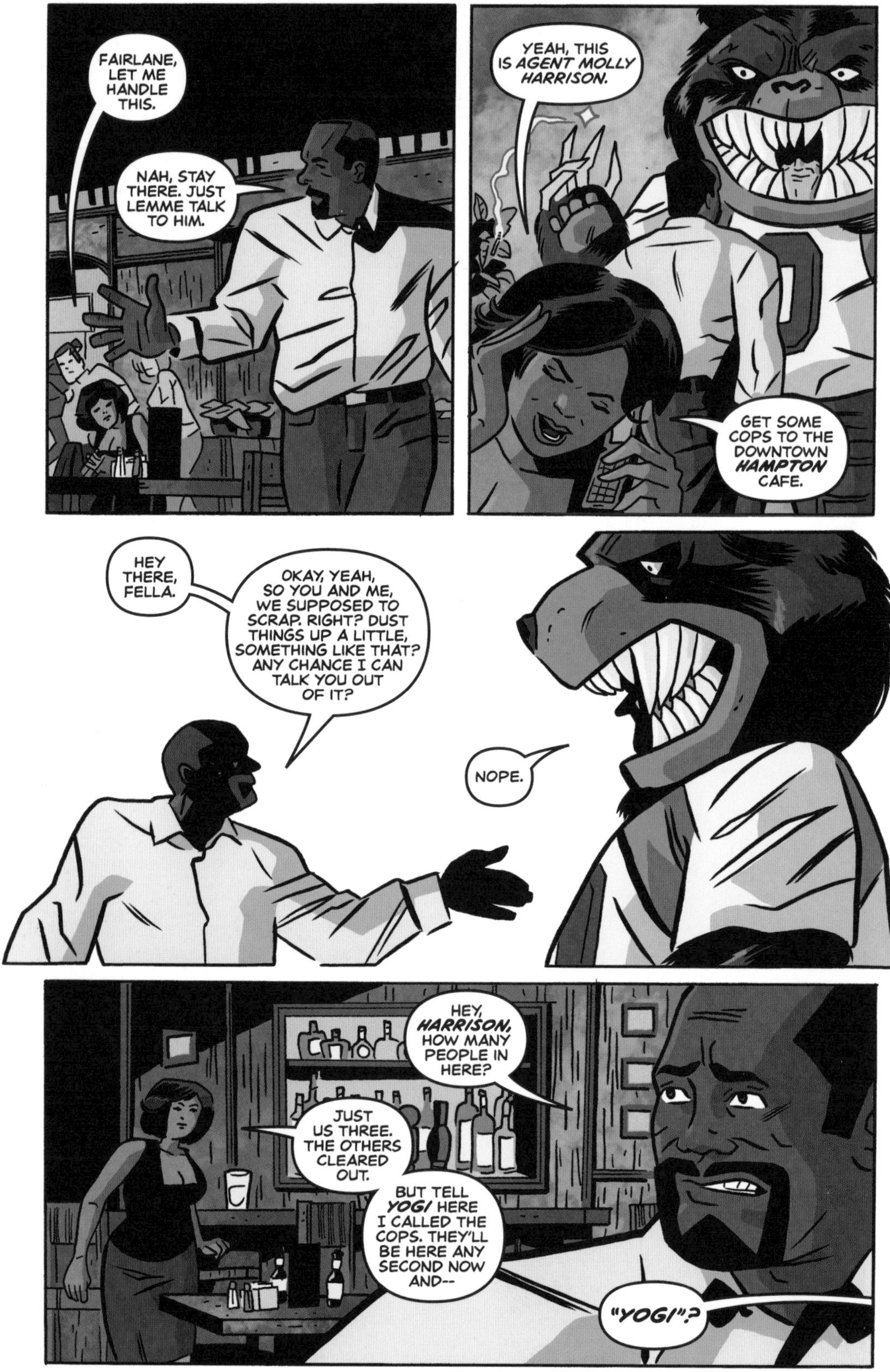
FAIRLANE, LET ME HANDLE THIS.
NAH, STAY THERE. JUST LEMME TALK TO HIM.
YEAH, THIS IS AGENT MOLLY HARRISON.
GET SOME COPS TO THE DOWNTOWN HAMPTON CAFE.
HEY THERE, FELLA.
OKAY, YEAH, SO YOU AND ME, WE SUPPOSED TO SCRAP. RIGHT? DUST THINGS UP A LITTLE, SOMETHING LIKE THAT? ANY CHANCE I CAN TALK YOU OUT OF IT?
NOPE.
HEY, HARRISON, HOW MANY PEOPLE IN HERE?
JUST US THREE. THE OTHERS CLEARED OUT.
BUT TELL YOGI HERE I CALLED THE COPS. THEY'LL BE HERE ANY SECOND NOW AND--
"YOGI"?

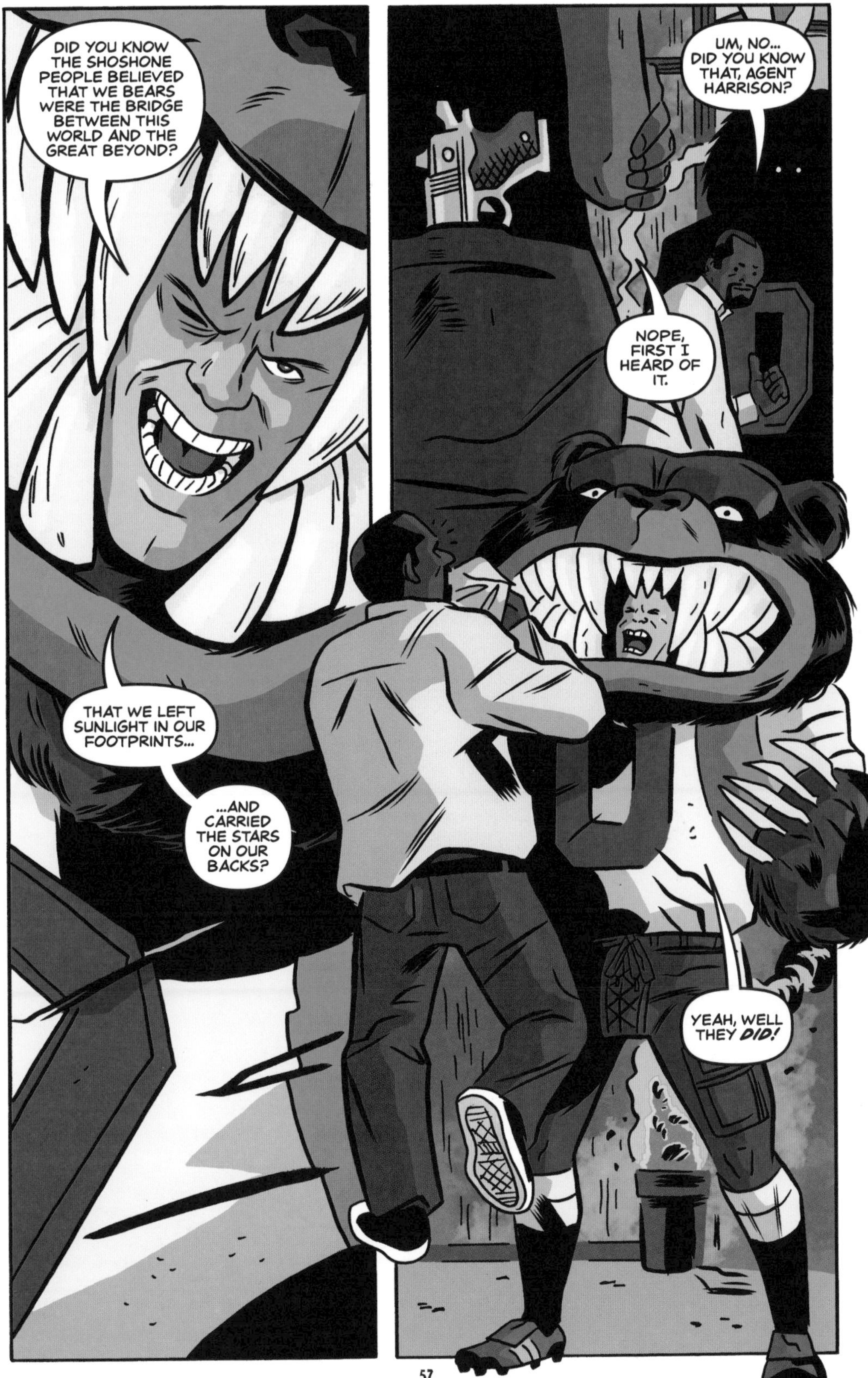
DID YOU KNOW THE SHOSHONE PEOPLE BELIEVED THAT WE BEARS WERE THE BRIDGE BETWEEN THIS WORLD AND THE GREAT BEYOND?
THAT WE LEFT SUNLIGHT IN OUR FOOTPRINTS...
...AND CARRIED THE STARS ON OUR BACKS?
UM, NO... DID YOU KNOW THAT, AGENT HARRISON?
NOPE, FIRST I HEARD OF IT.
YEAH, WELL THEY *DID!*

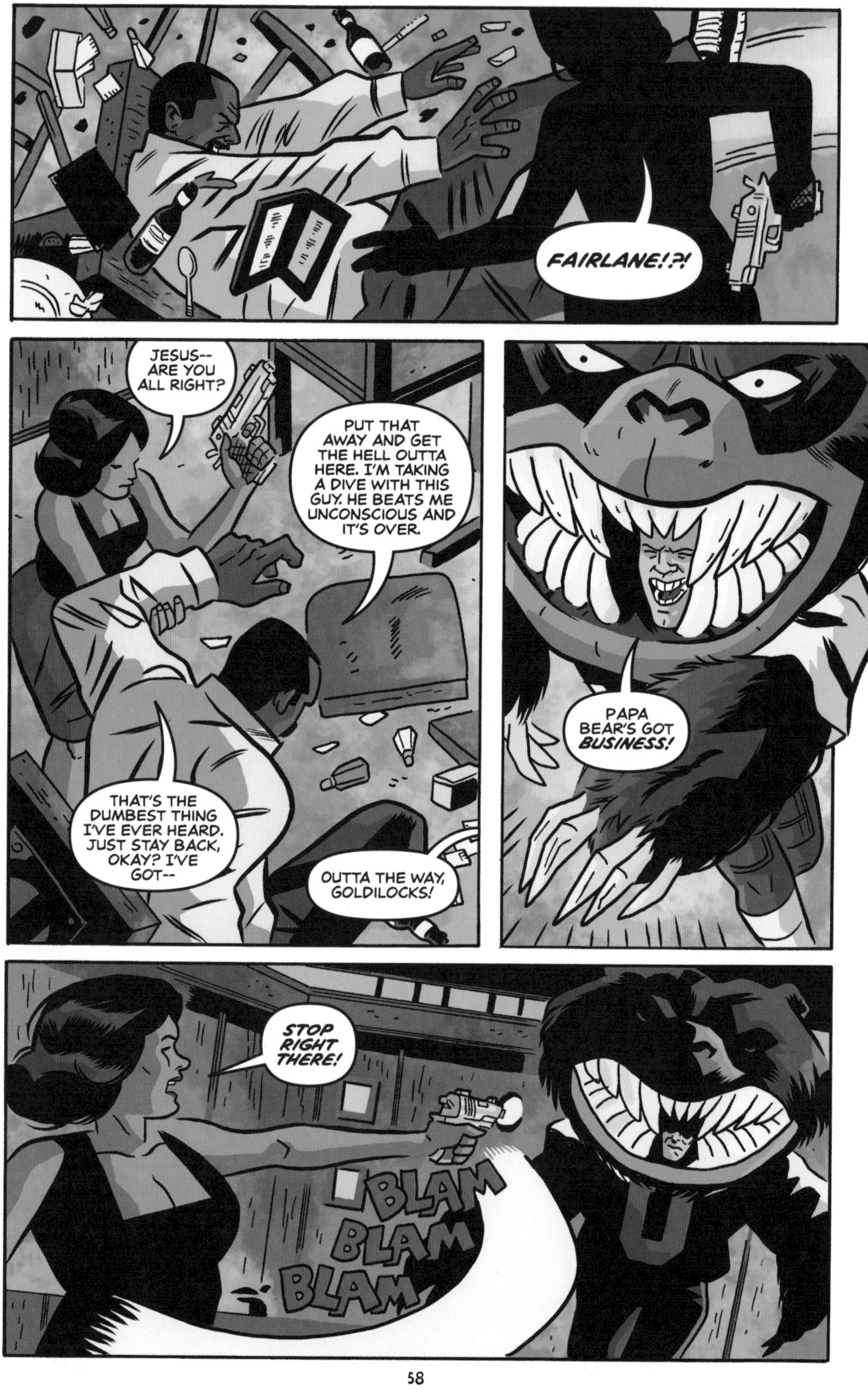
FAIRLANE!?!
JESUS-- ARE YOU ALL RIGHT?
PUT THAT AWAY AND GET THE HELL OUTTA HERE. I'M TAKING A DIVE WITH THIS GUY. HE BEATS ME UNCONSCIOUS AND IT'S OVER.
THAT'S THE DUMBEST THING I'VE EVER HEARD. JUST STAY BACK, OKAY? I'VE GOT--
OUTTA THE WAY, GOLDILOCKS!
PAPA BEAR'S GOT BUSINESS!
STOP RIGHT THERE!
BLAM
BLAM
BLAM

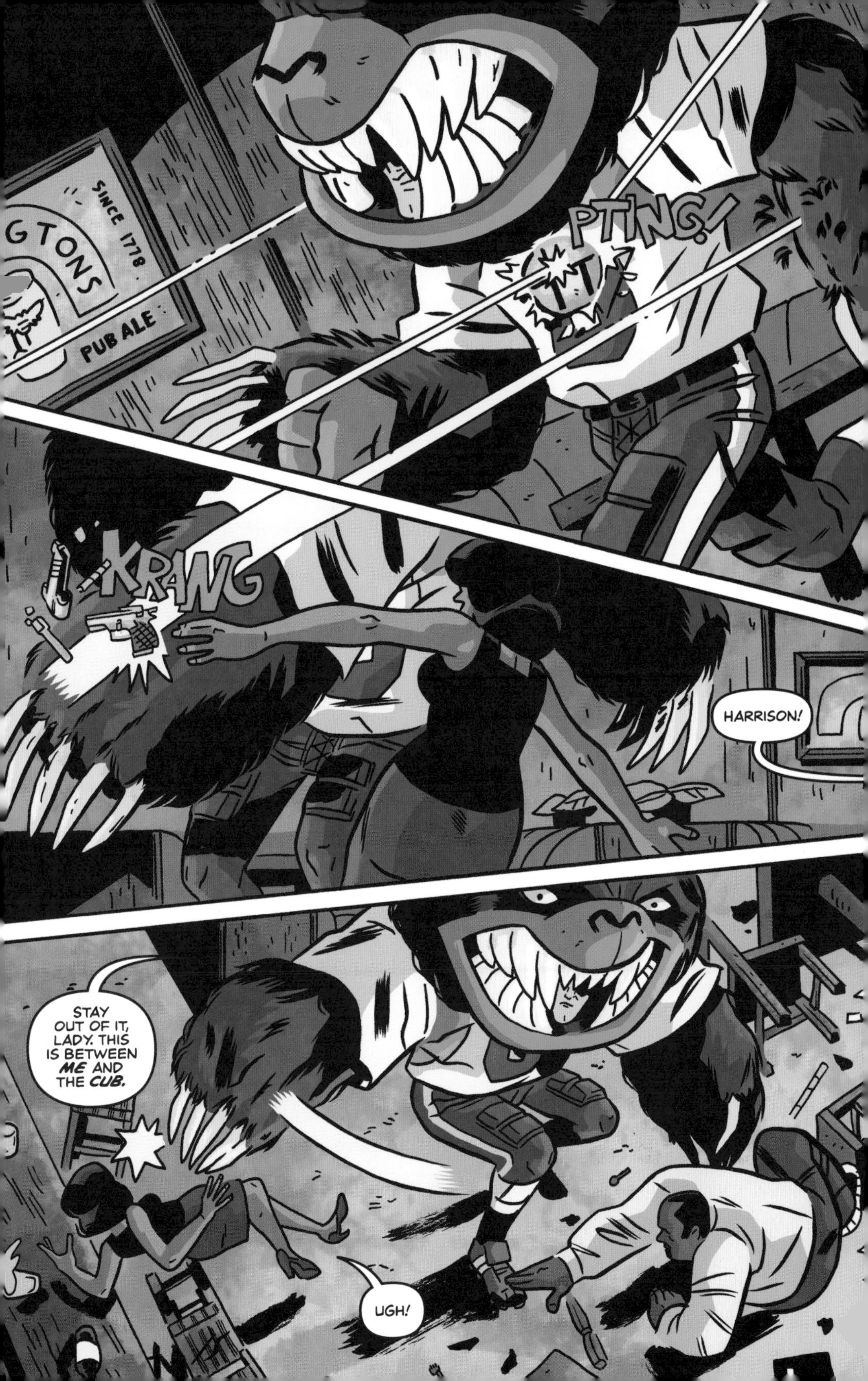
GTONS
SINCE 1778
PUB ALE
PTING!
KRANG
HARRISON!
STAY OUT OF IT, LADY. THIS IS BETWEEN *ME* AND THE *CUB.*
UGH!

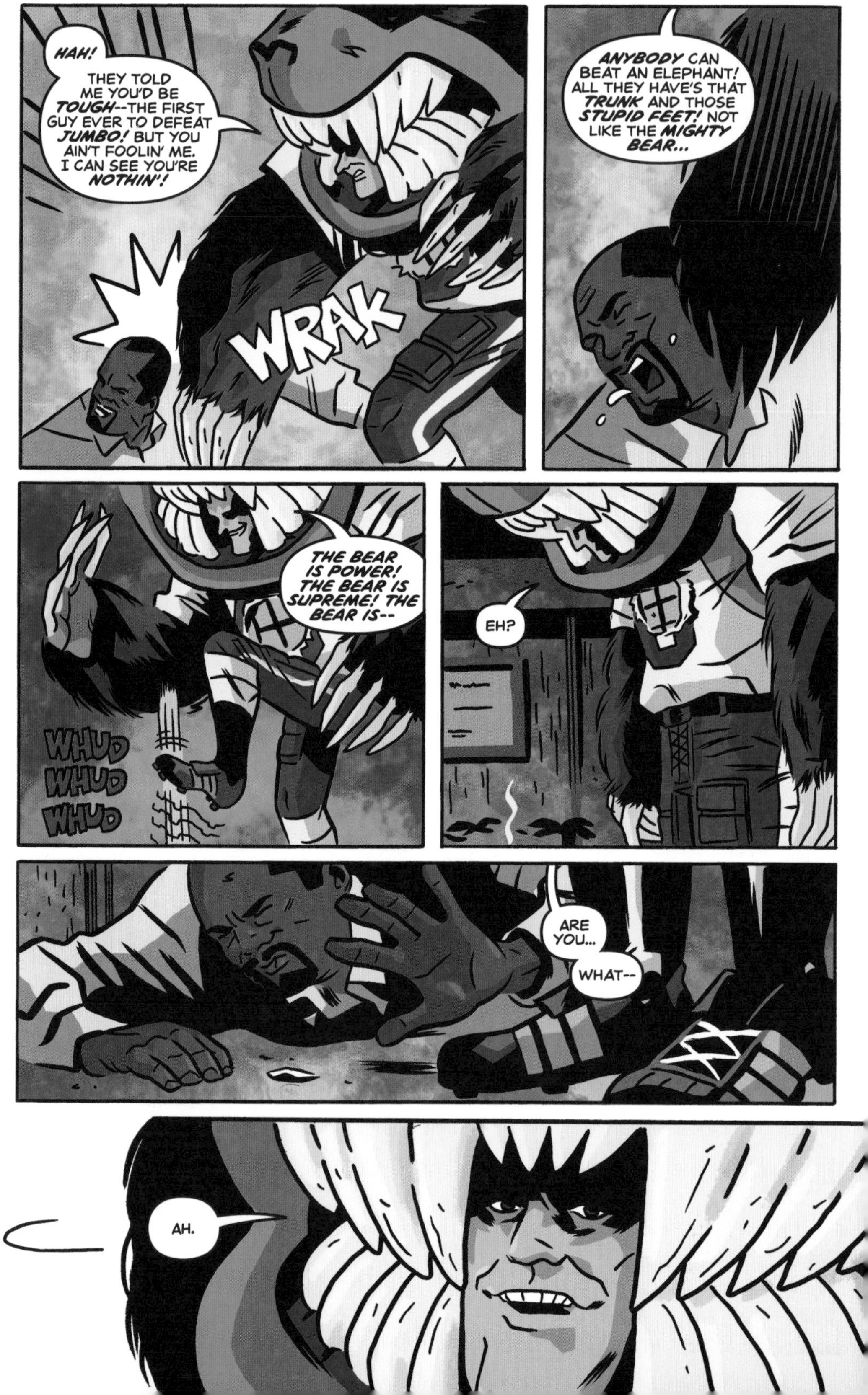
HAH!
THEY TOLD ME YOU'D BE TOUGH--THE FIRST GUY EVER TO DEFEAT JUMBO! BUT YOU AIN'T FOOLIN' ME. I CAN SEE YOU'RE NOTHIN'!
WRAK
ANYBODY CAN BEAT AN ELEPHANT! ALL THEY HAVE'S THAT TRUNK AND THOSE STUPID FEET! NOT LIKE THE MIGHTY BEAR...
THE BEAR IS POWER! THE BEAR IS SUPREME! THE BEAR IS--
WHUD
WHUD
WHUD
EH?
ARE YOU...
WHAT--
AH.

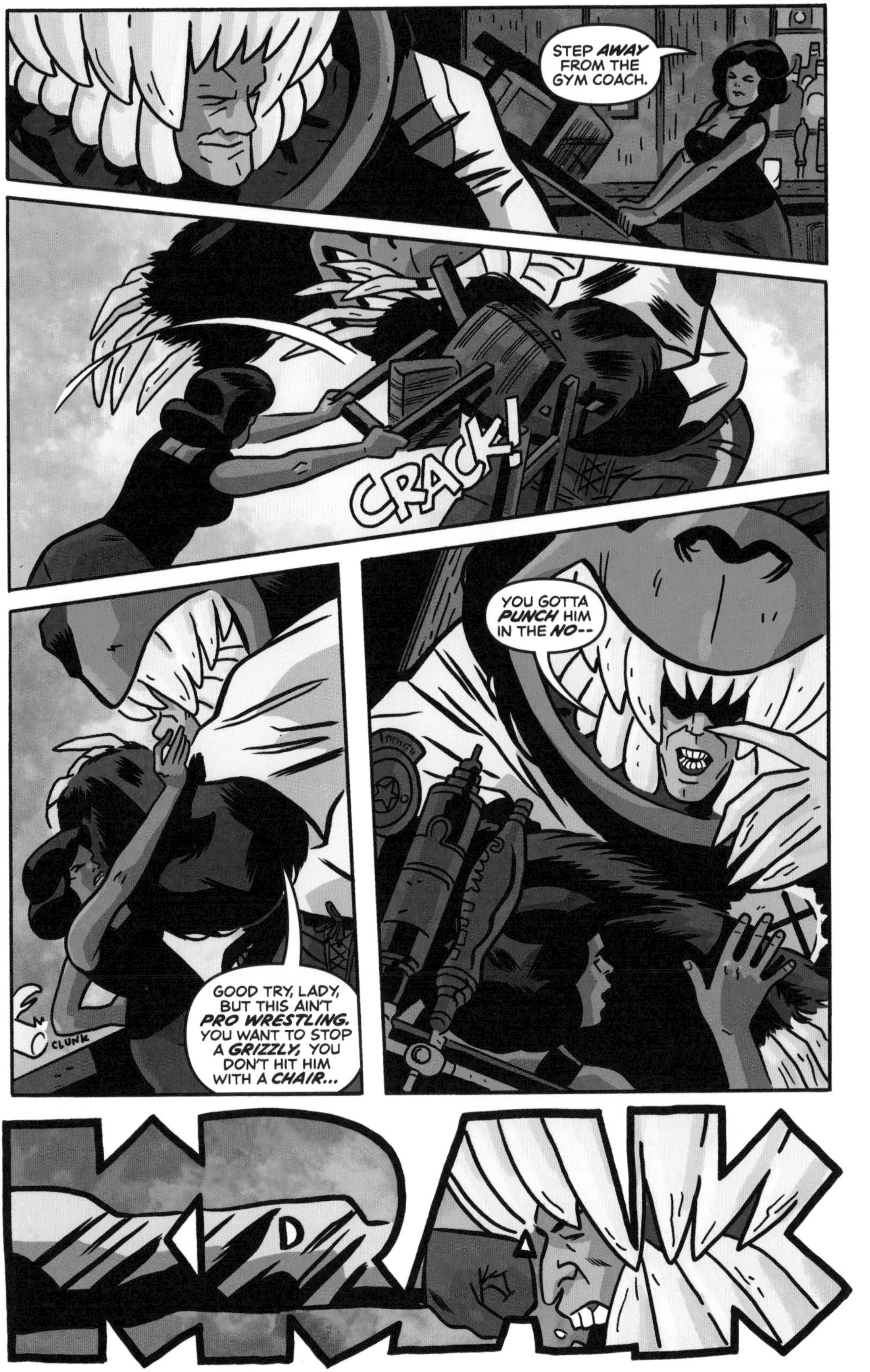
STEP AWAY FROM THE GYM COACH.
CRACK!
GOOD TRY, LADY, BUT THIS AIN'T PRO WRESTLING. YOU WANT TO STOP A GRIZZLY, YOU DON'T HIT HIM WITH A CHAIR...
CLUNK
YOU GOTTA PUNCH HIM IN THE NO--
KRAK

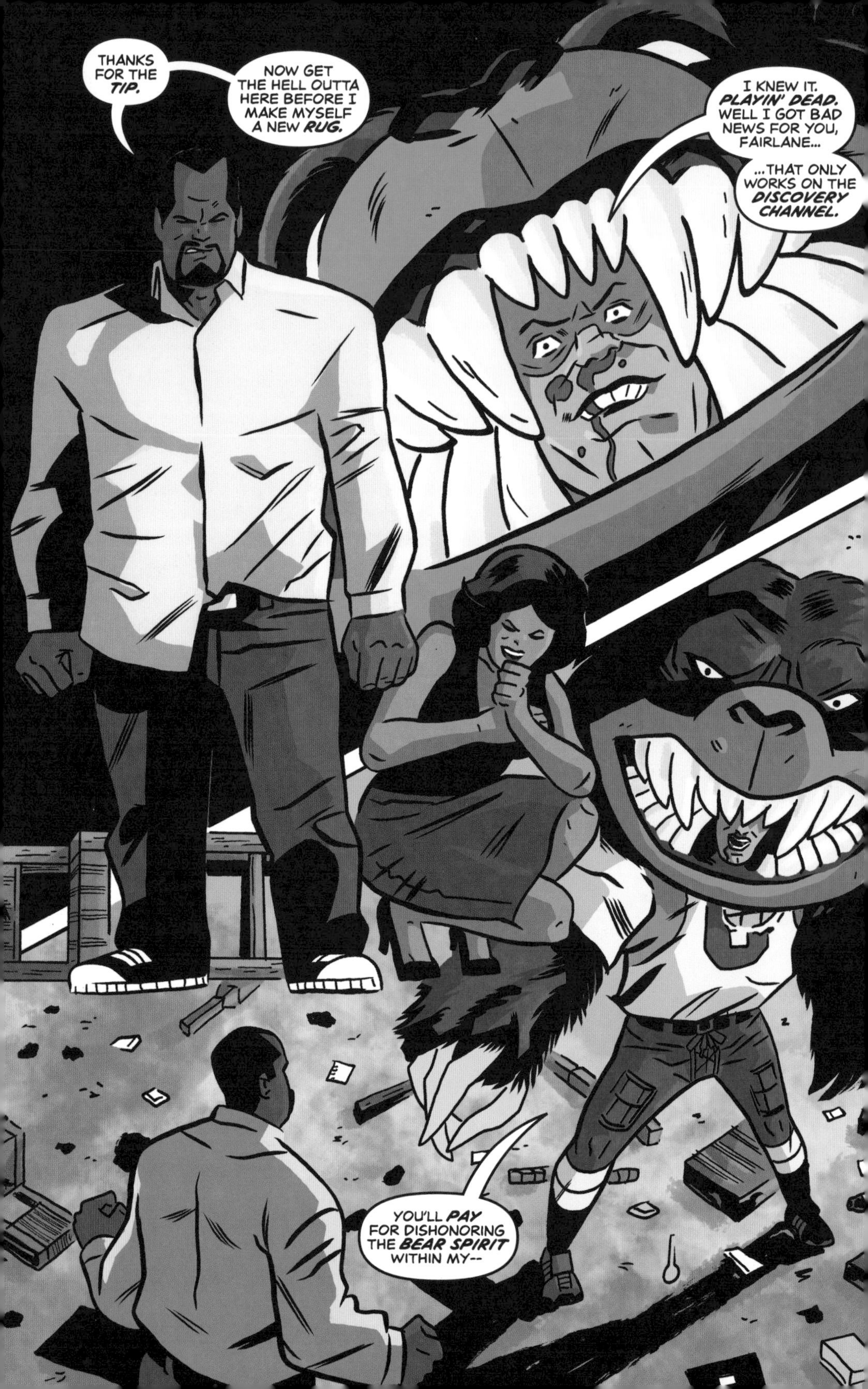
THANKS FOR THE TIP.
NOW GET THE HELL OUTTA HERE BEFORE I MAKE MYSELF A NEW RUG.
I KNEW IT. PLAYIN' DEAD. WELL I GOT BAD NEWS FOR YOU, FAIRLANE...
...THAT ONLY WORKS ON THE DISCOVERY CHANNEL.
YOU'LL PAY FOR DISHONORING THE BEAR SPIRIT WITHIN MY--

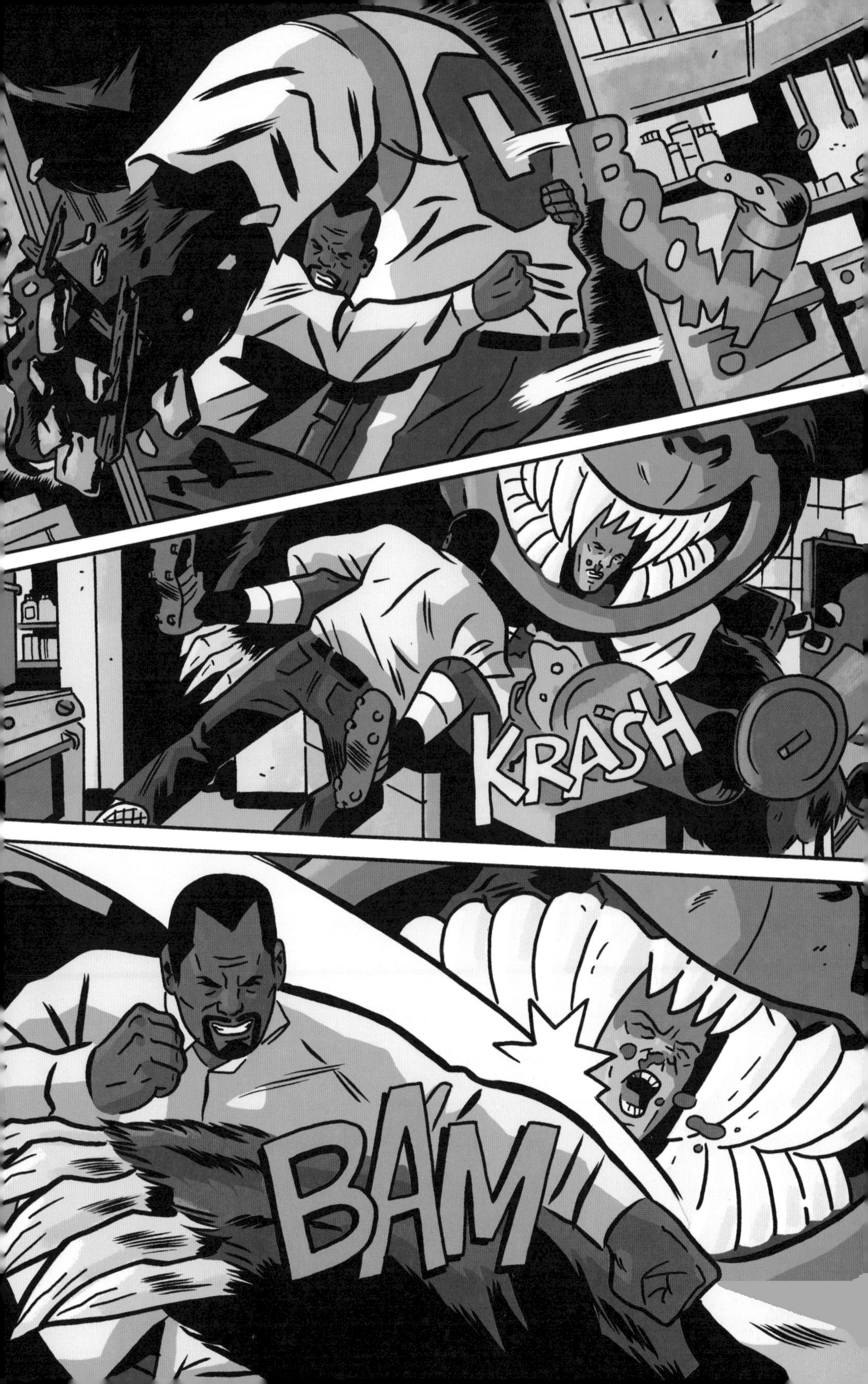
BOOM
KRASH
BAM

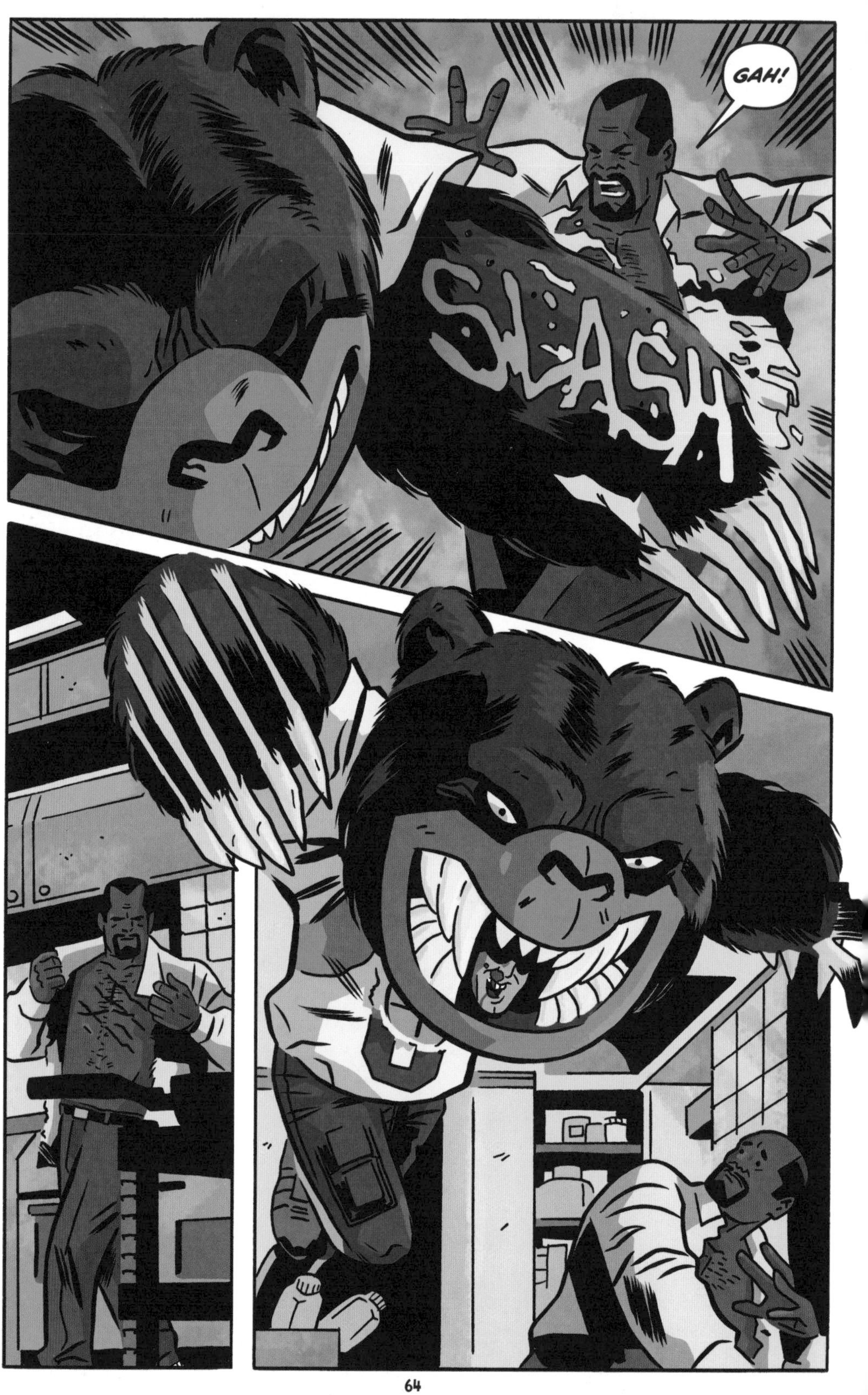
GAH!
SLASH

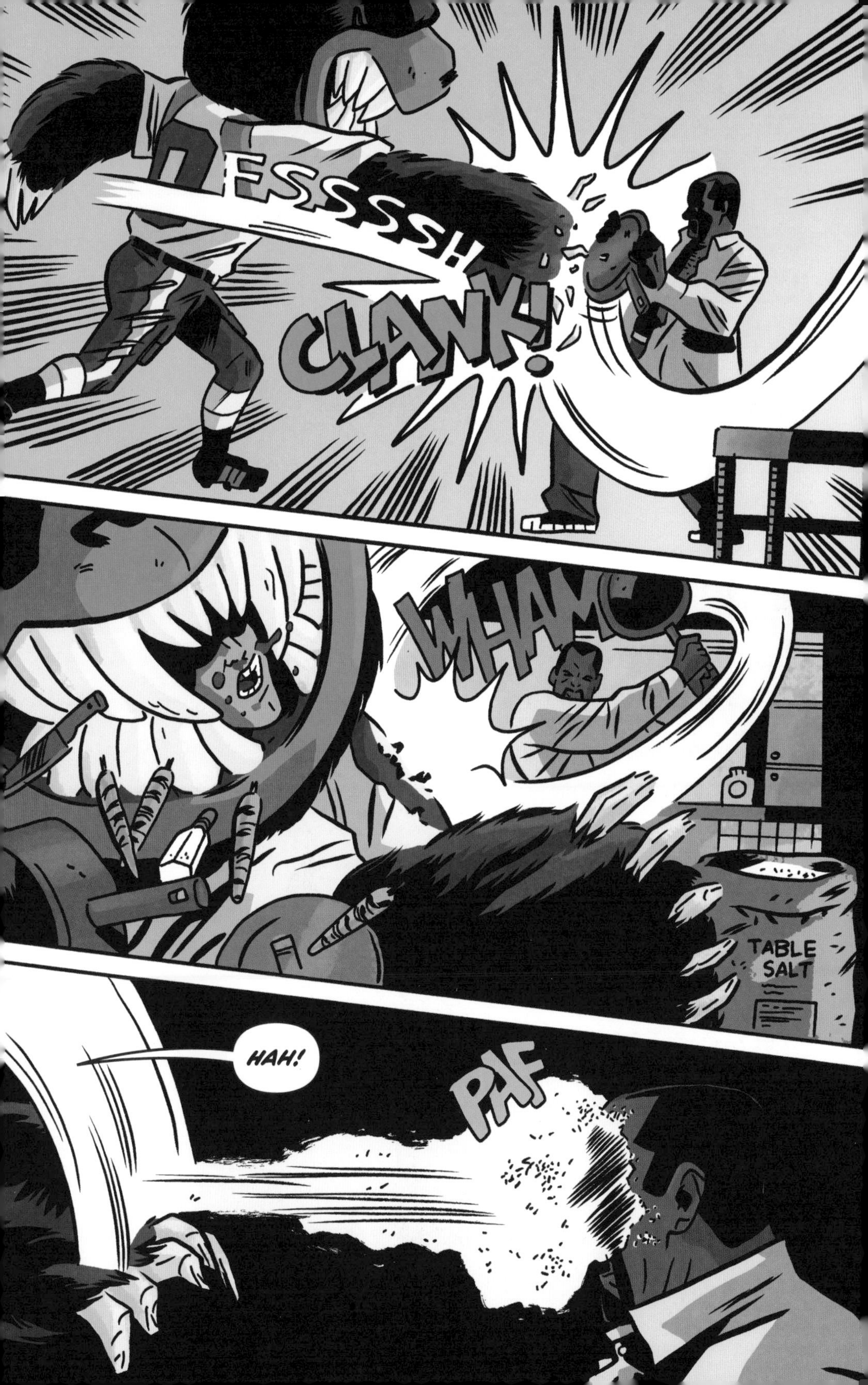
FSSSSSH!
CLANK!
WHAM
TABLE SALT
HAH!
PAF

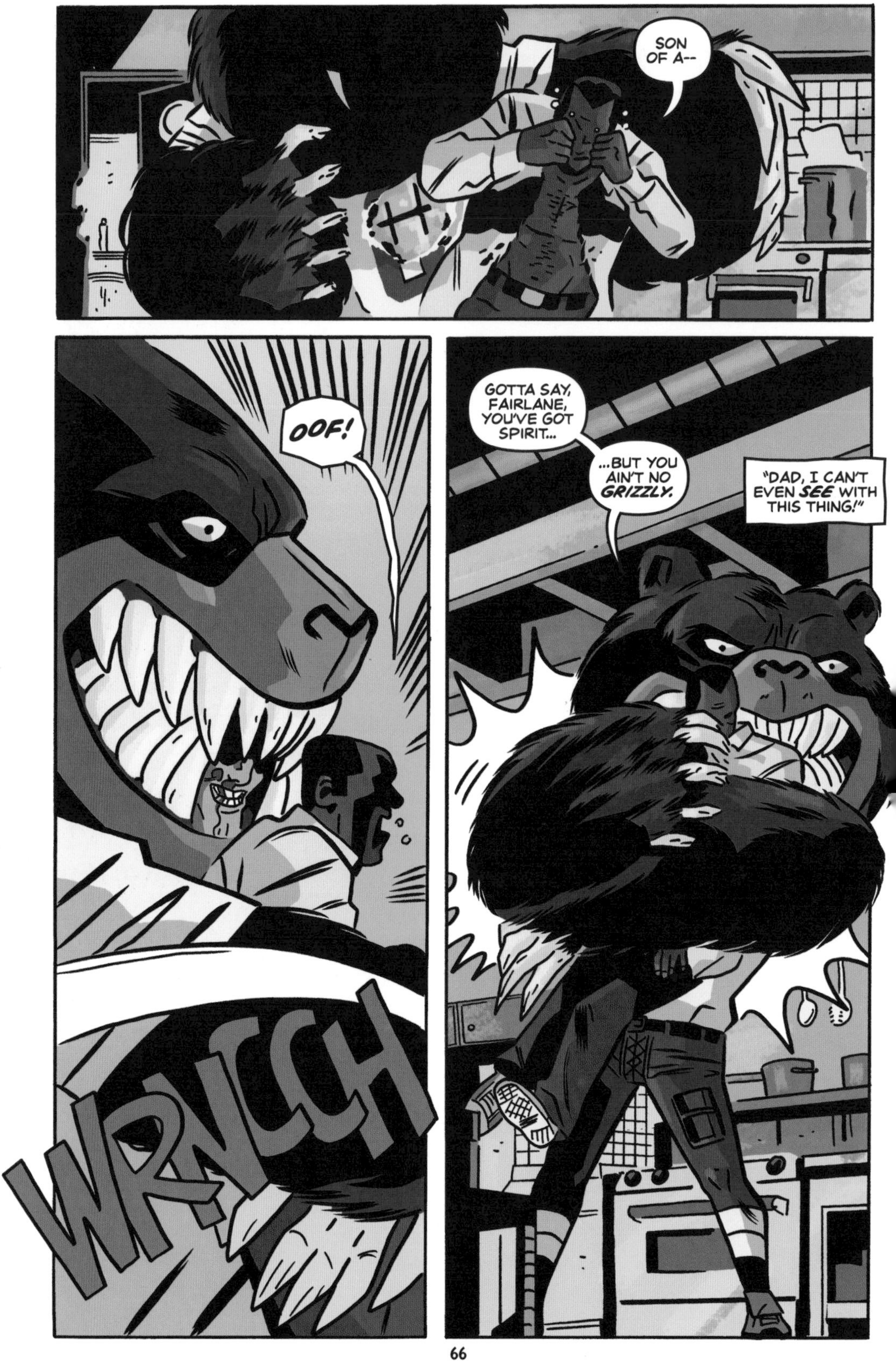
SON OF A--
OOF!
WRNCCH
GOTTA SAY, FAIRLANE, YOU'VE GOT SPIRIT...
...BUT YOU AIN'T NO *GRIZZLY.*
"DAD, I CAN'T EVEN *SEE* WITH THIS THING!"

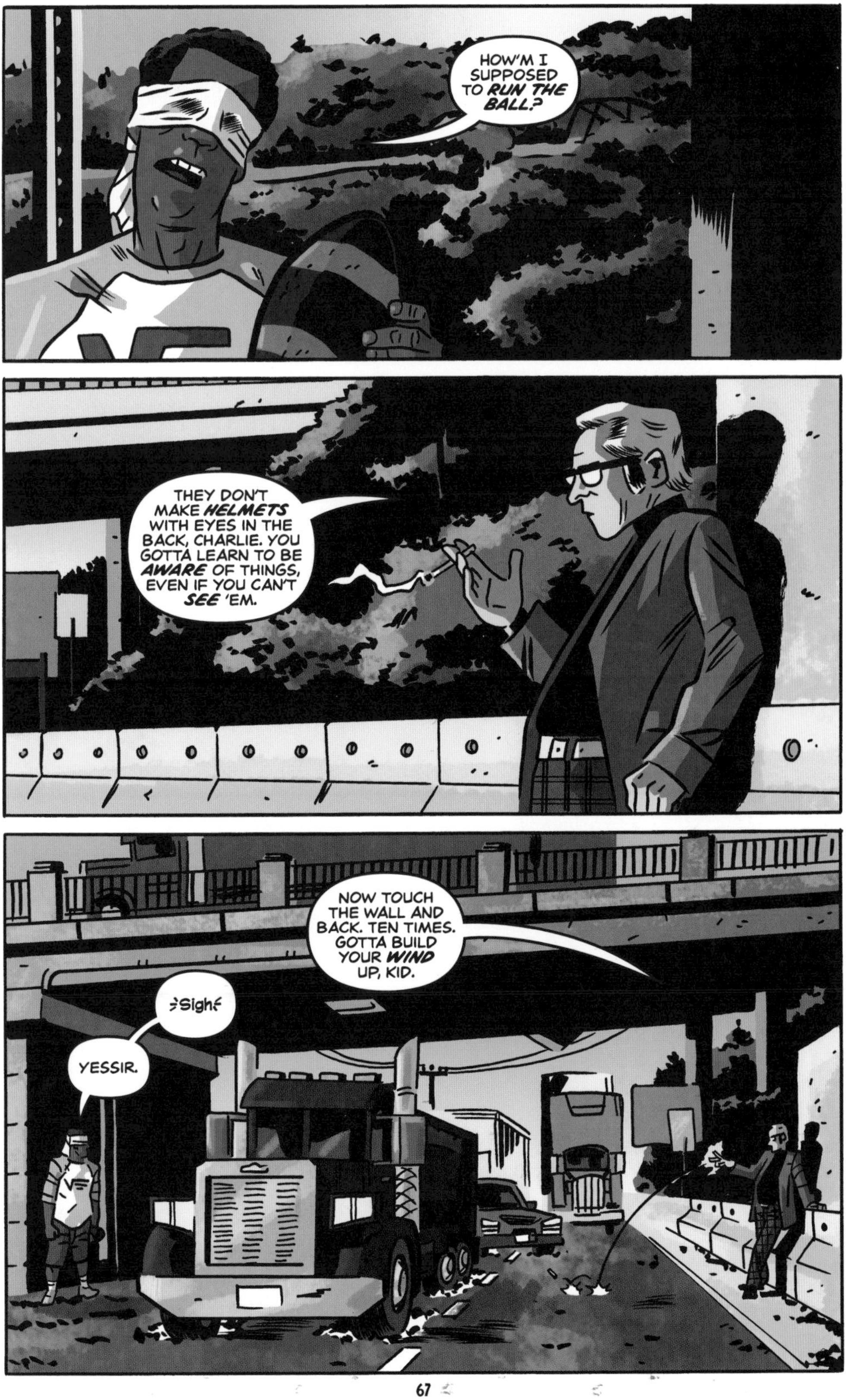
HOW'M I SUPPOSED TO RUN THE BALL?
THEY DON'T MAKE HELMETS WITH EYES IN THE BACK, CHARLIE. YOU GOTTA LEARN TO BE AWARE OF THINGS, EVEN IF YOU CAN'T SEE 'EM.
NOW TOUCH THE WALL AND BACK. TEN TIMES. GOTTA BUILD YOUR WIND UP, KID.
Sigh
YESSIR.

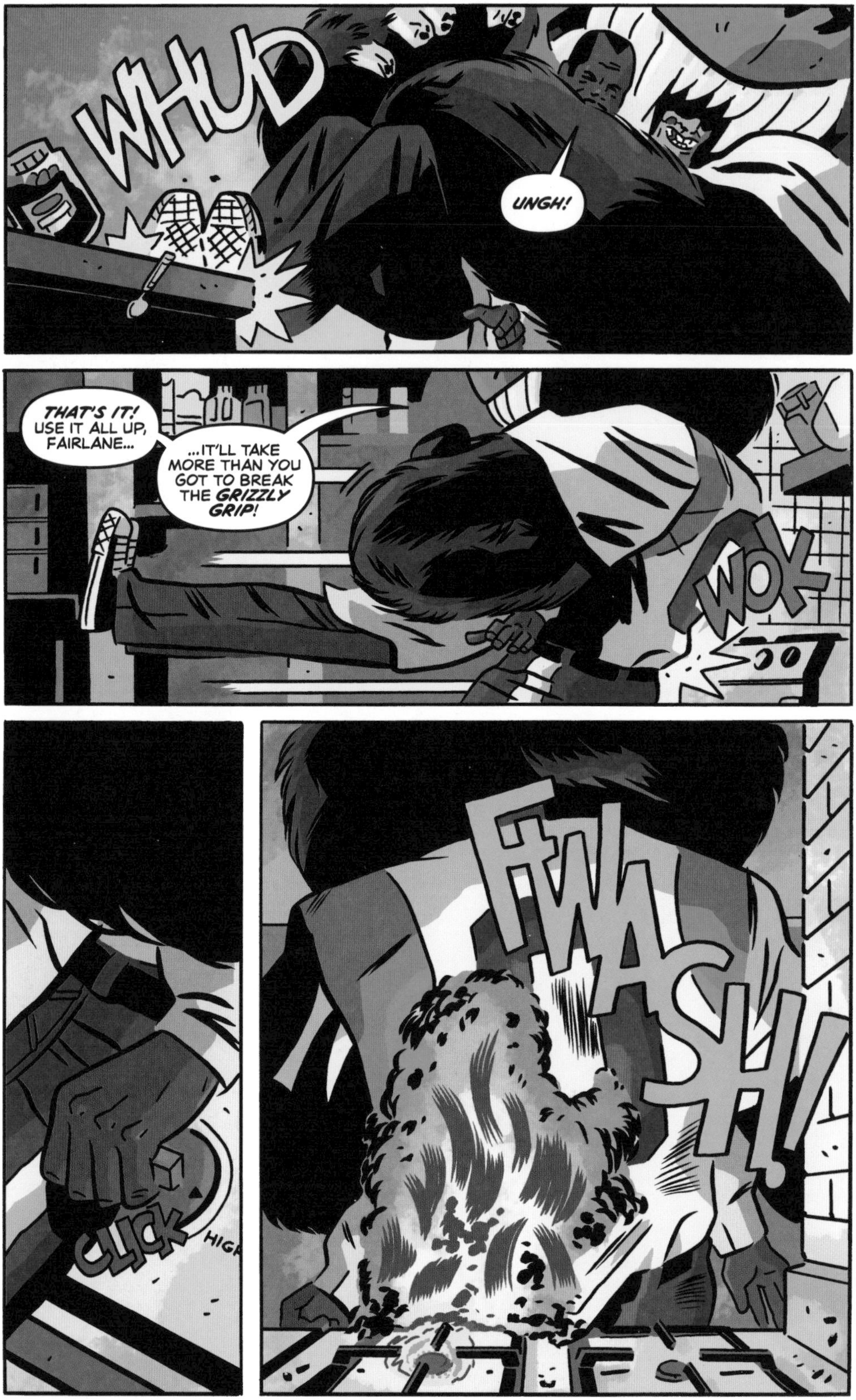
WHUD
UNGH!
THAT'S IT! USE IT ALL UP, FAIRLANE...
...IT'LL TAKE MORE THAN YOU GOT TO BREAK THE GRIZZLY GRIP!
WOK
CLICK
FWASH!!

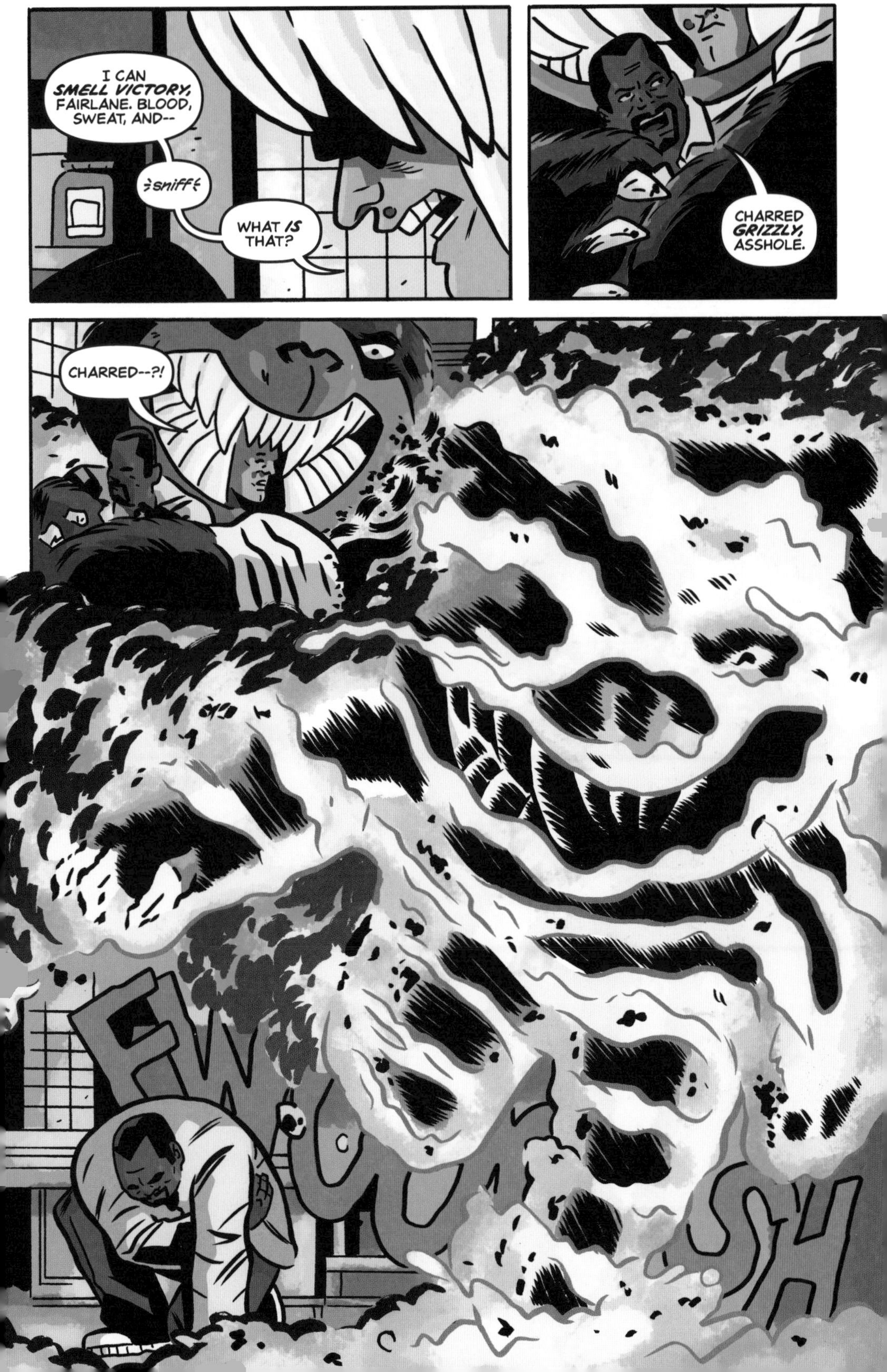
I CAN SMELL VICTORY, FAIRLANE. BLOOD, SWEAT, AND--
sniff
WHAT IS THAT?
CHARRED GRIZZLY, ASSHOLE.
CHARRED--?!
FWOOSH

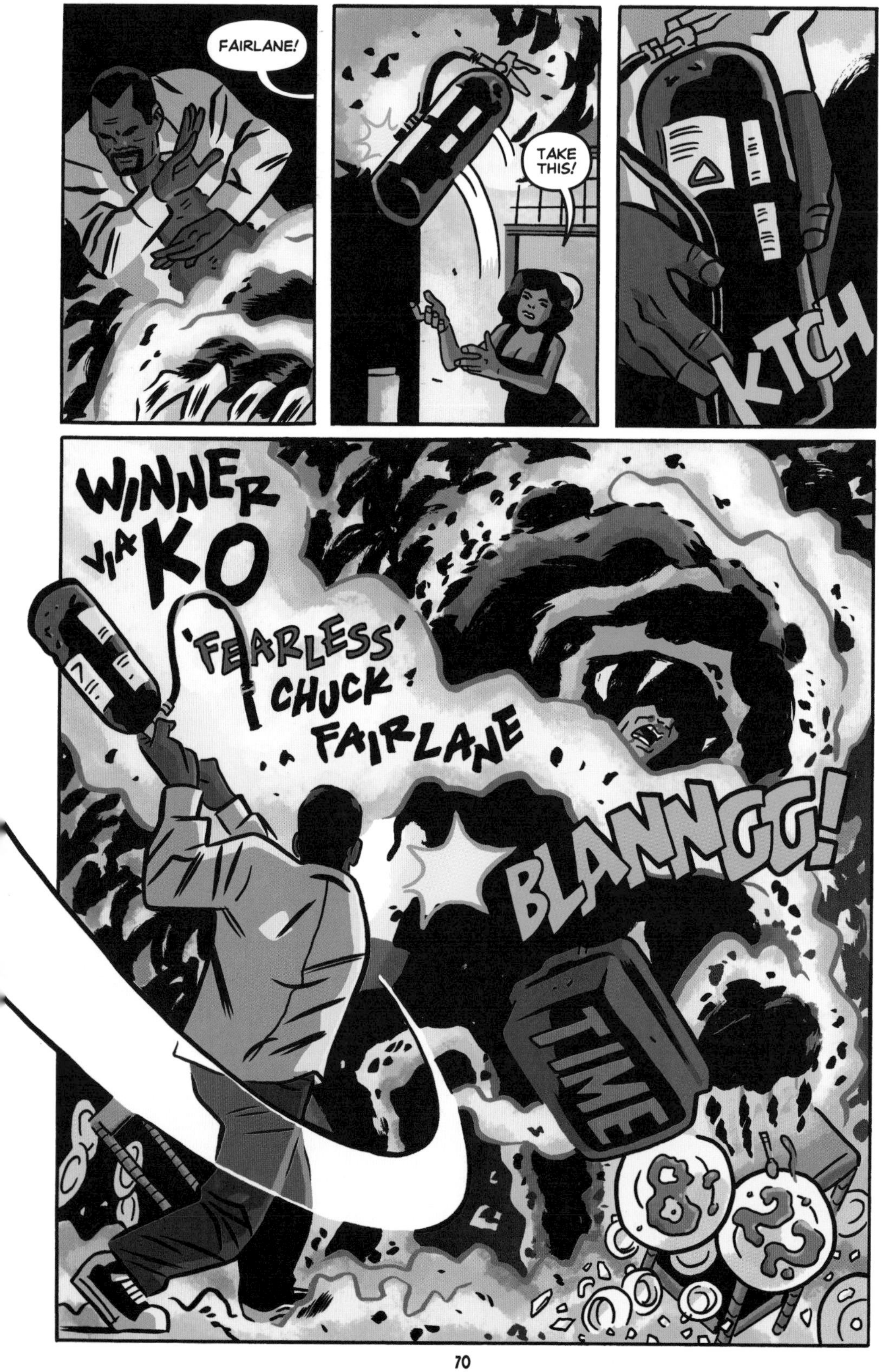
FAIRLANE!
TAKE THIS!
KTCH
WINNER VIA KO
'FEARLESS' CHUCK FAIRLANE
BLANNGG!
TIME

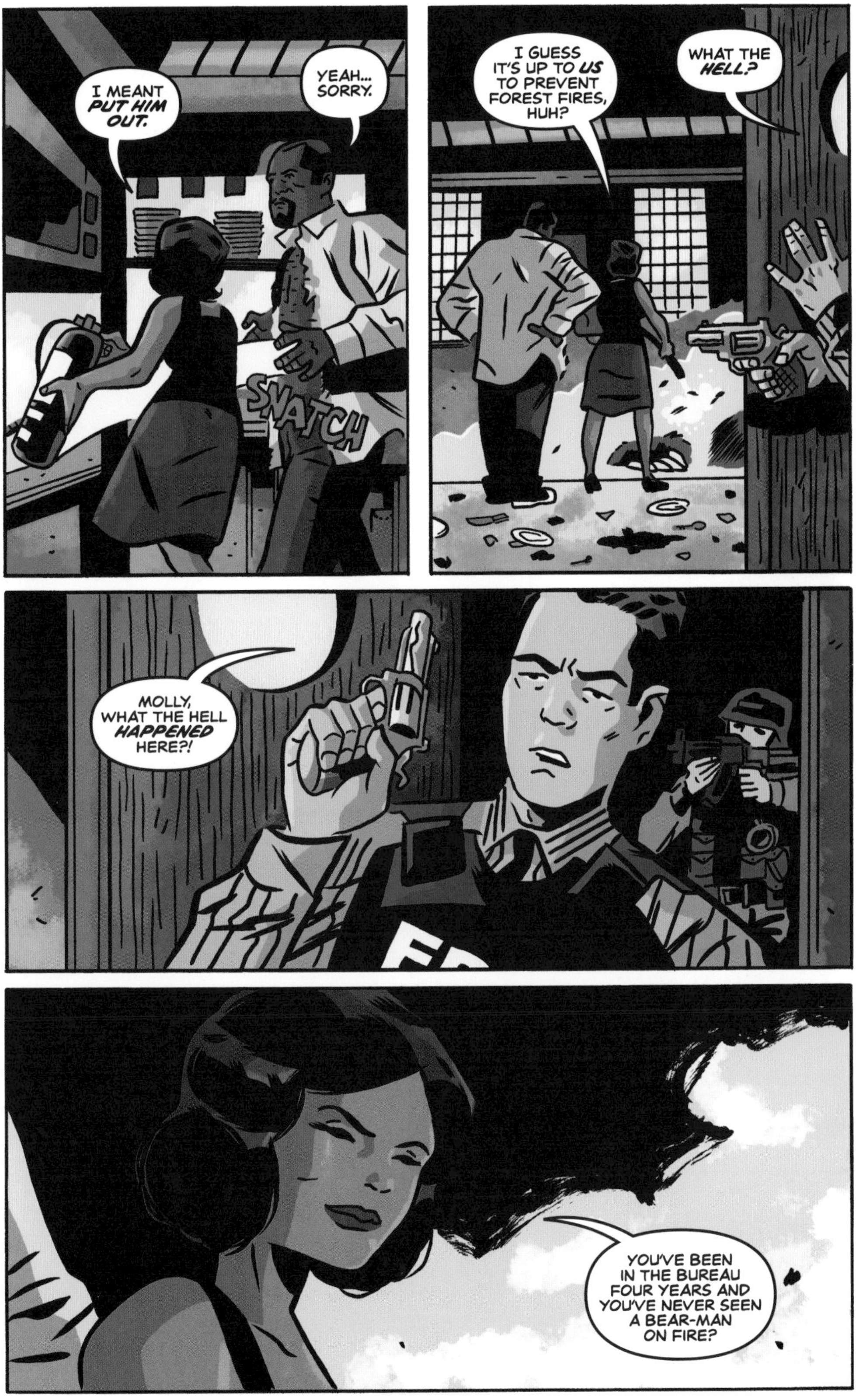
I MEANT *PUT HIM OUT.*
YEAH... SORRY.
SNATCH
I GUESS IT'S UP TO *US* TO PREVENT FOREST FIRES, HUH?
WHAT THE *HELL?*
MOLLY, WHAT THE HELL *HAPPENED* HERE?!
YOU'VE BEEN IN THE BUREAU FOUR YEARS AND YOU'VE NEVER SEEN A BEAR-MAN ON FIRE?

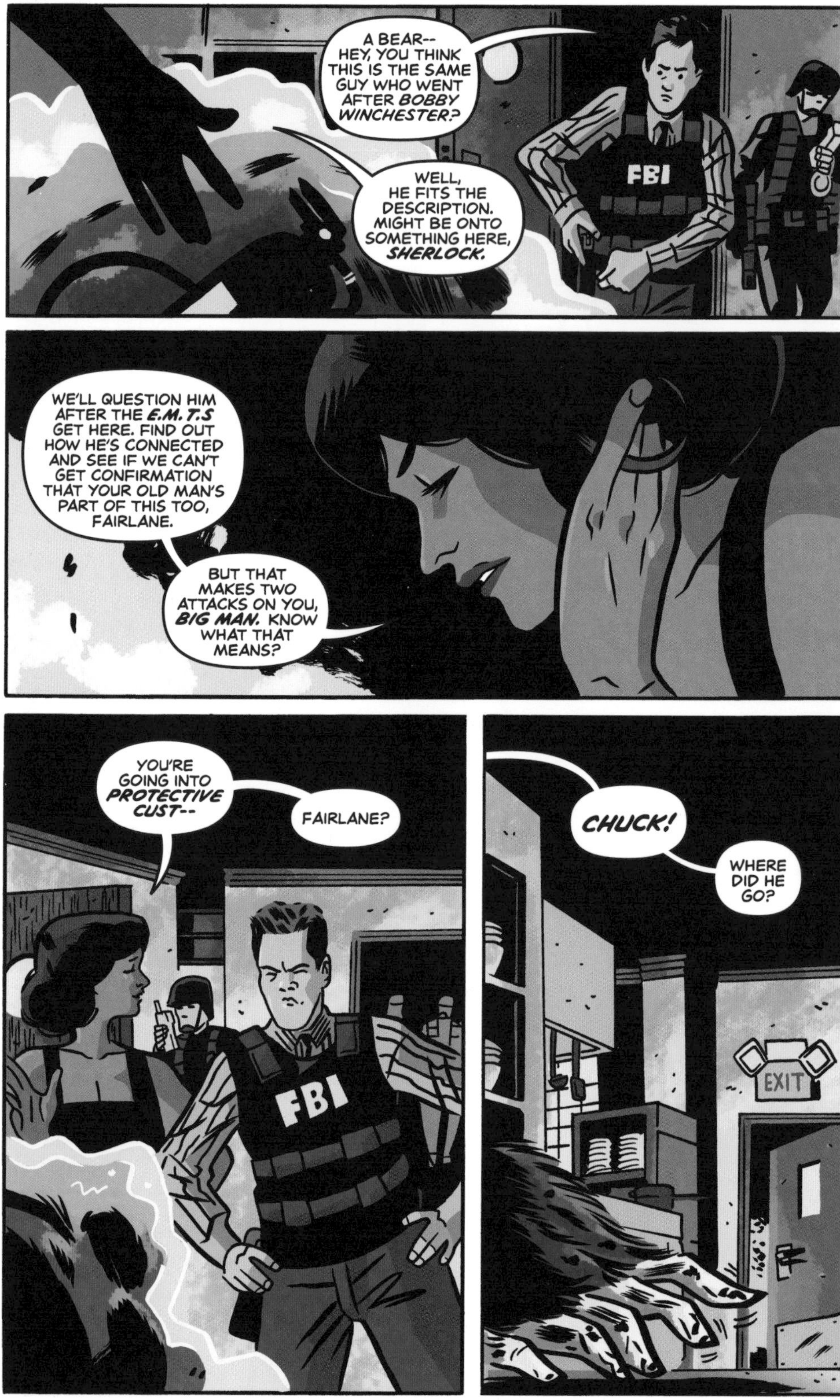
A BEAR-- HEY, YOU THINK THIS IS THE SAME GUY WHO WENT AFTER *BOBBY WINCHESTER?*
WELL, HE FITS THE DESCRIPTION. MIGHT BE ONTO SOMETHING HERE, ***SHERLOCK.***
WE'LL QUESTION HIM AFTER THE ***E.M.T.S*** GET HERE. FIND OUT HOW HE'S CONNECTED AND SEE IF WE CAN'T GET CONFIRMATION THAT YOUR OLD MAN'S PART OF THIS TOO, FAIRLANE.
BUT THAT MAKES TWO ATTACKS ON YOU, ***BIG MAN.*** KNOW WHAT THAT MEANS?
YOU'RE GOING INTO ***PROTECTIVE CUST--***
FAIRLANE?
EXIT
CHUCK!
WHERE DID HE GO?

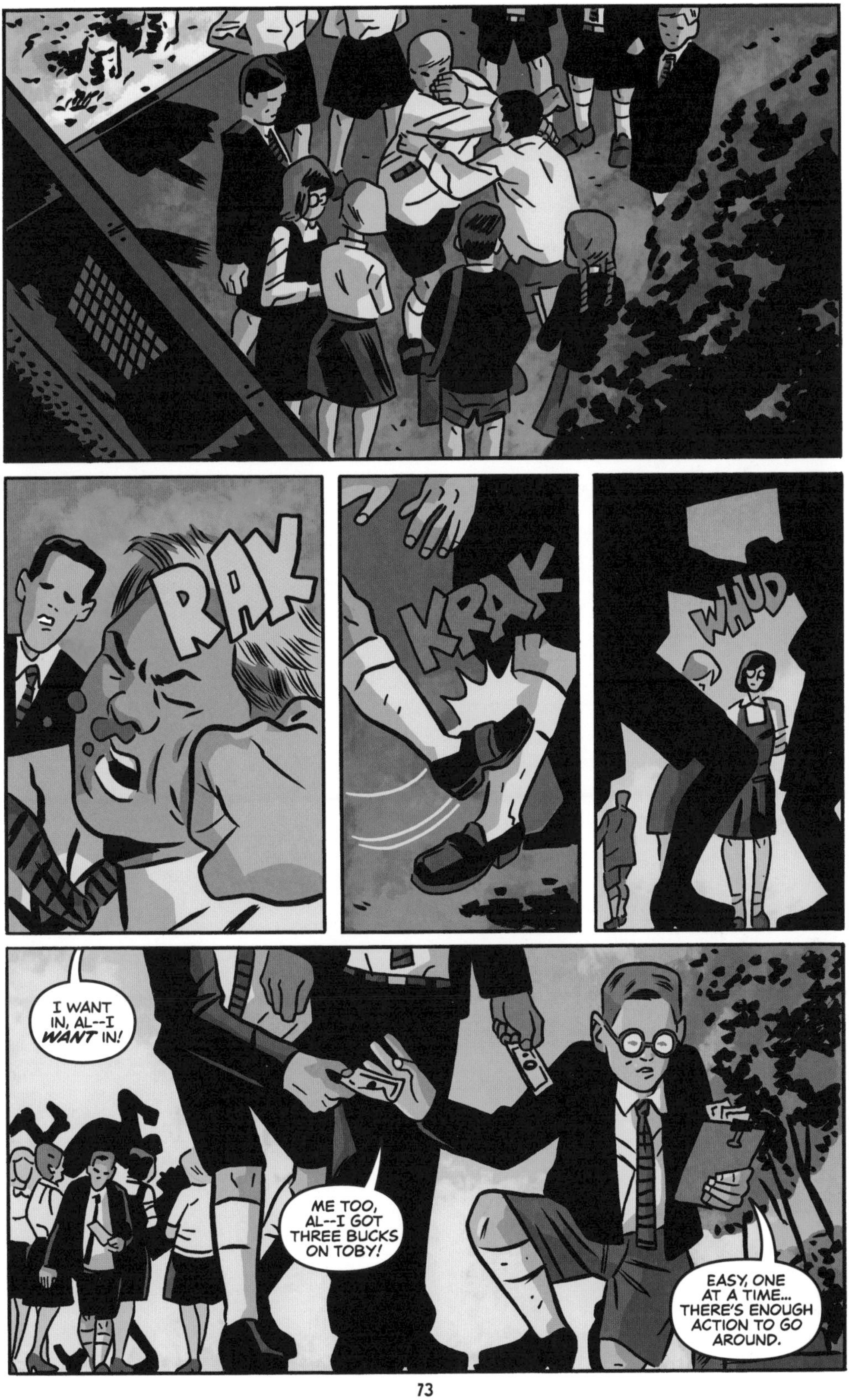
RAK
KRAK
WHUD
I WANT IN, AL--I *WANT* IN!
ME TOO, AL--I GOT THREE BUCKS ON TOBY!
EASY, ONE AT A TIME... THERE'S ENOUGH ACTION TO GO AROUND.

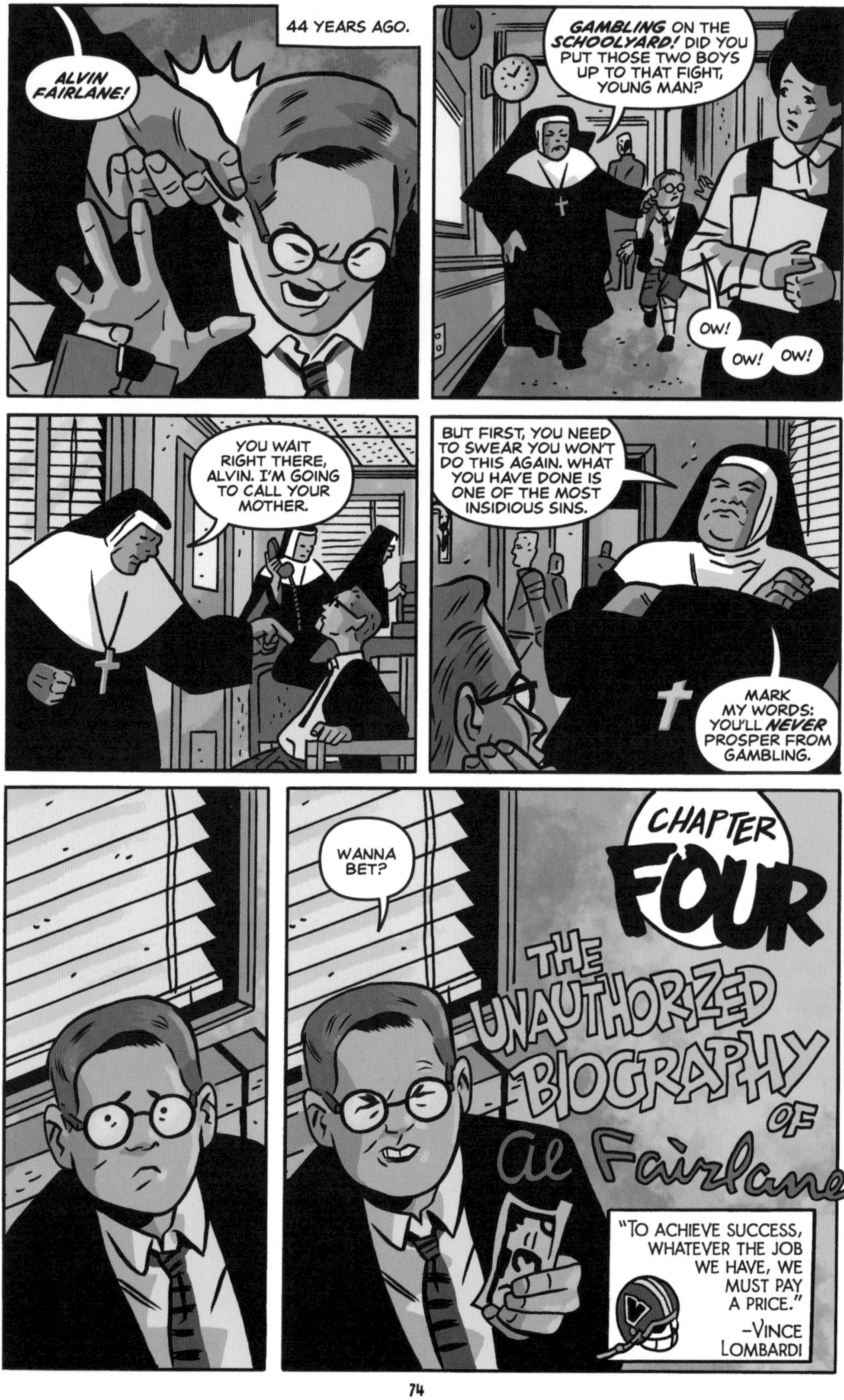
44 YEARS AGO.
ALVIN FAIRLANE!
GAMBLING ON THE SCHOOLYARD! DID YOU PUT THOSE TWO BOYS UP TO THAT FIGHT, YOUNG MAN?
OW!
OW!
OW!
YOU WAIT RIGHT THERE, ALVIN. I'M GOING TO CALL YOUR MOTHER.
BUT FIRST, YOU NEED TO SWEAR YOU WON'T DO THIS AGAIN. WHAT YOU HAVE DONE IS ONE OF THE MOST INSIDIOUS SINS.
MARK MY WORDS: YOU'LL NEVER PROSPER FROM GAMBLING.
WANNA BET?
CHAPTER FOUR
THE UNAUTHORIZED BIOGRAPHY OF Al Fairlane
"TO ACHIEVE SUCCESS, WHATEVER THE JOB WE HAVE, WE MUST PAY A PRICE."
–VINCE LOMBARDI

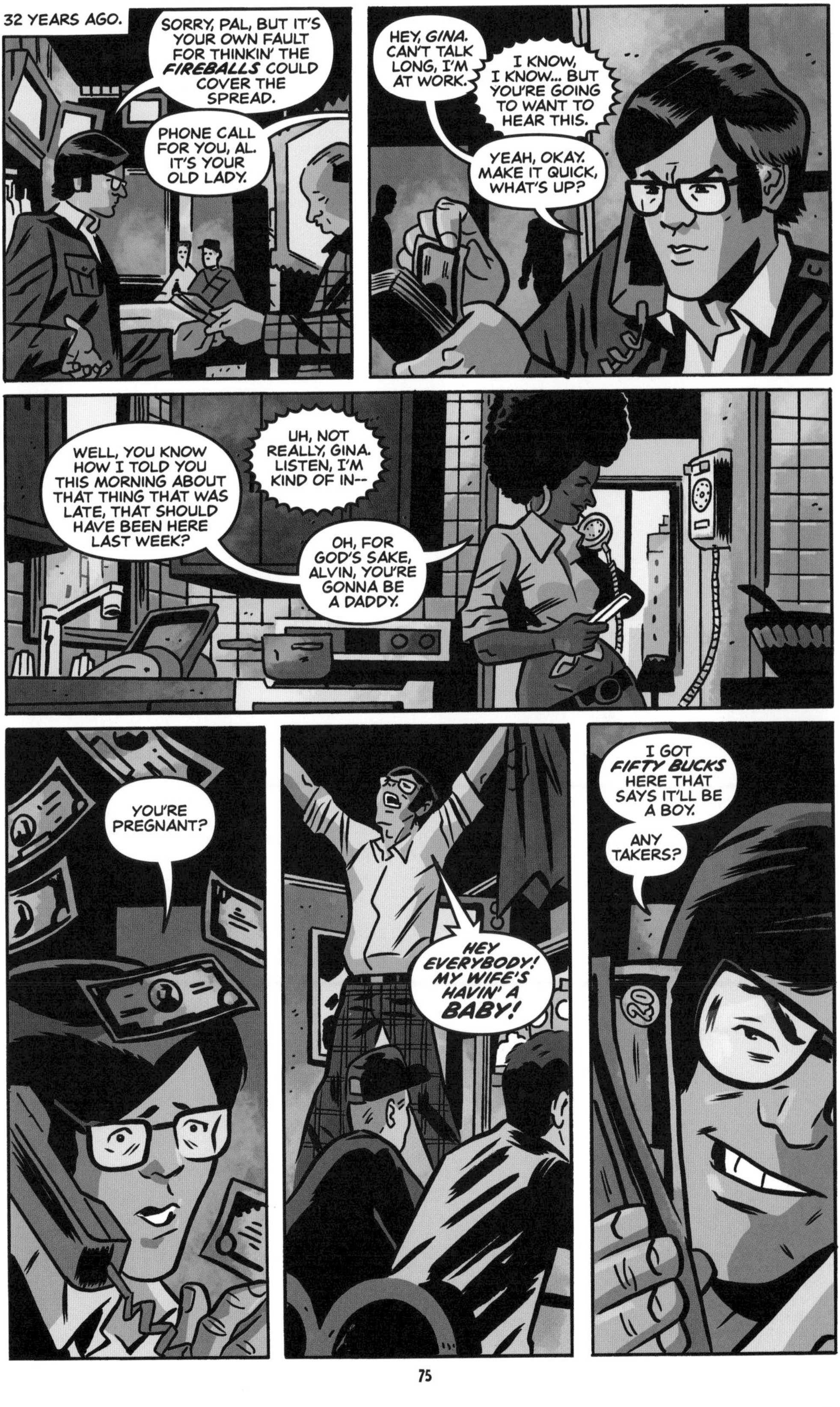
32 YEARS AGO.
SORRY, PAL, BUT IT'S YOUR OWN FAULT FOR THINKIN' THE FIREBALLS COULD COVER THE SPREAD.
PHONE CALL FOR YOU, AL. IT'S YOUR OLD LADY.
HEY, GINA. CAN'T TALK LONG, I'M AT WORK.
I KNOW, I KNOW... BUT YOU'RE GOING TO WANT TO HEAR THIS.
YEAH, OKAY. MAKE IT QUICK, WHAT'S UP?
WELL, YOU KNOW HOW I TOLD YOU THIS MORNING ABOUT THAT THING THAT WAS LATE, THAT SHOULD HAVE BEEN HERE LAST WEEK?
UH, NOT REALLY, GINA. LISTEN, I'M KIND OF IN--
OH, FOR GOD'S SAKE, ALVIN, YOU'RE GONNA BE A DADDY.
YOU'RE PREGNANT?
HEY EVERYBODY! MY WIFE'S HAVIN' A BABY!
I GOT FIFTY BUCKS HERE THAT SAYS IT'LL BE A BOY.
ANY TAKERS?

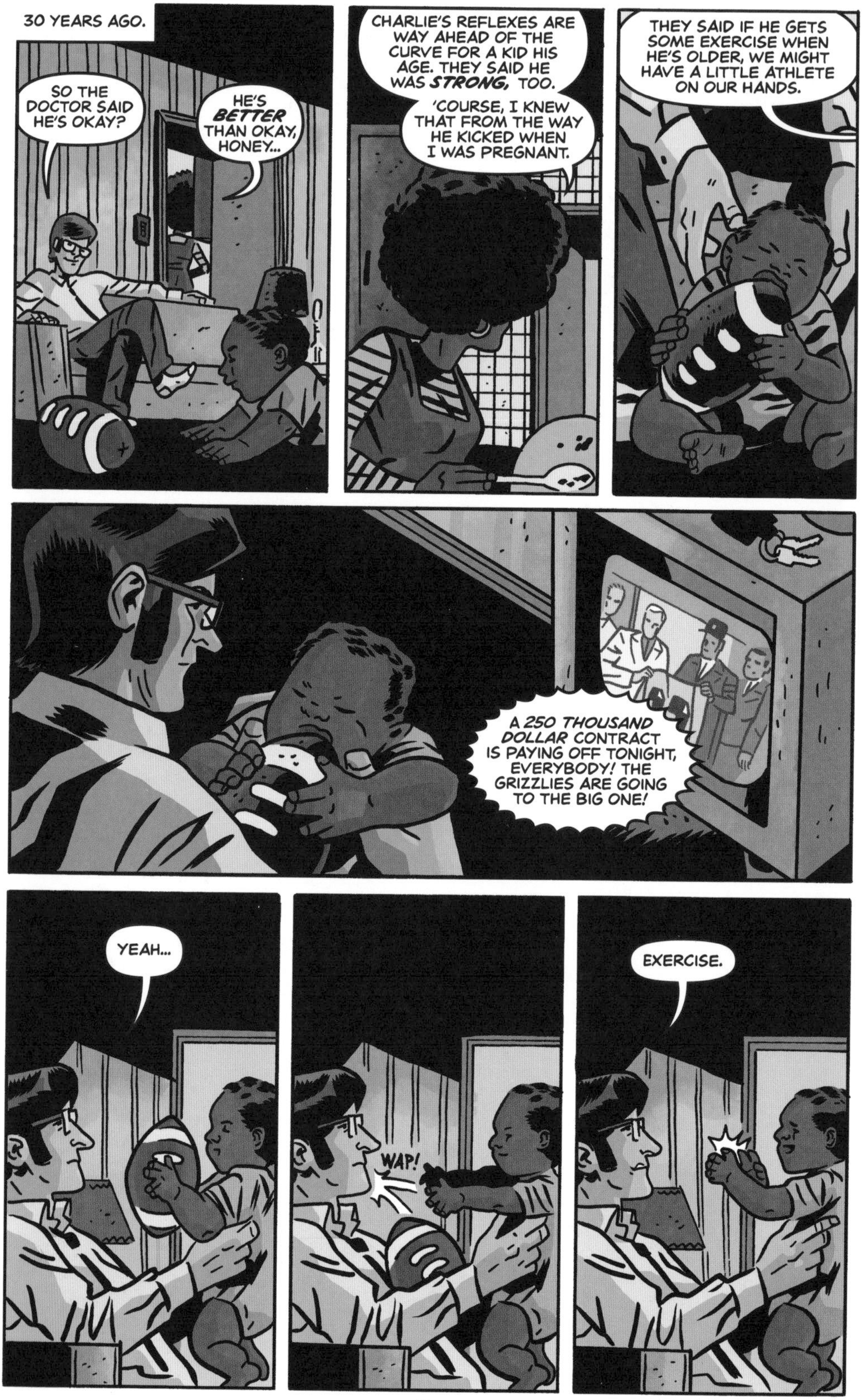
30 YEARS AGO.
SO THE DOCTOR SAID HE'S OKAY?
HE'S *BETTER* THAN OKAY, HONEY...
CHARLIE'S REFLEXES ARE WAY AHEAD OF THE CURVE FOR A KID HIS AGE. THEY SAID HE WAS *STRONG,* TOO.
'COURSE, I KNEW THAT FROM THE WAY HE KICKED WHEN I WAS PREGNANT.
THEY SAID IF HE GETS SOME EXERCISE WHEN HE'S OLDER, WE MIGHT HAVE A LITTLE ATHLETE ON OUR HANDS.
A *250 THOUSAND DOLLAR* CONTRACT IS PAYING OFF TONIGHT, EVERYBODY! THE GRIZZLIES ARE GOING TO THE BIG ONE!
YEAH...
WAP!
EXERCISE.

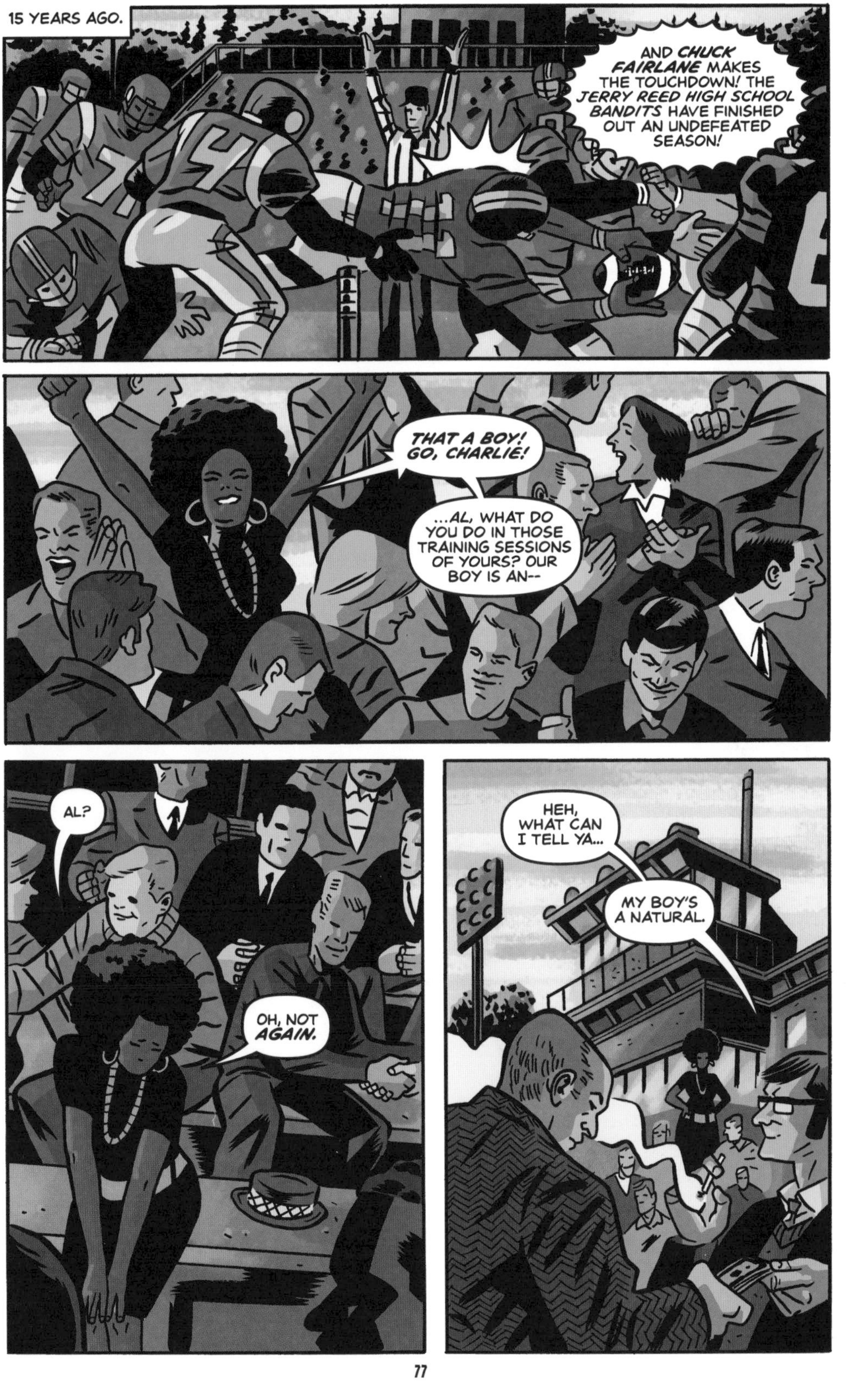
15 YEARS AGO.
AND *CHUCK FAIRLANE* MAKES THE TOUCHDOWN! THE *JERRY REED HIGH SCHOOL BANDITS* HAVE FINISHED OUT AN UNDEFEATED SEASON!
THAT A BOY! GO, CHARLIE!
...*AL*, WHAT DO YOU DO IN THOSE TRAINING SESSIONS OF YOURS? OUR BOY IS AN--
AL?
OH, NOT *AGAIN.*
HEH, WHAT CAN I TELL YA...
MY BOY'S A NATURAL.

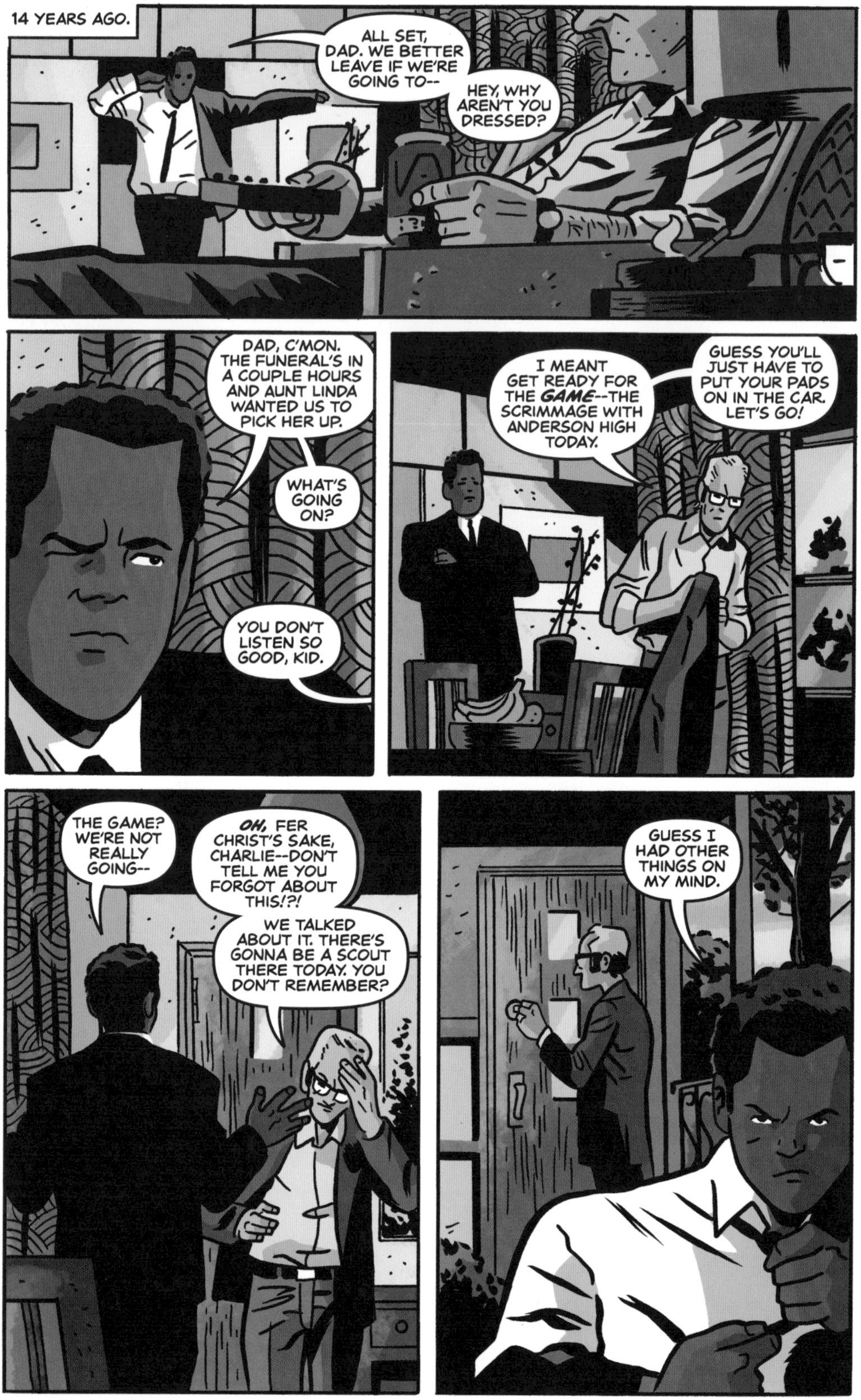
14 YEARS AGO.
ALL SET, DAD. WE BETTER LEAVE IF WE'RE GOING TO--
HEY, WHY AREN'T YOU DRESSED?
DAD, C'MON. THE FUNERAL'S IN A COUPLE HOURS AND AUNT LINDA WANTED US TO PICK HER UP.
WHAT'S GOING ON?
YOU DON'T LISTEN SO GOOD, KID.
I MEANT GET READY FOR THE *GAME*--THE SCRIMMAGE WITH ANDERSON HIGH TODAY.
GUESS YOU'LL JUST HAVE TO PUT YOUR PADS ON IN THE CAR. LET'S GO!
THE GAME? WE'RE NOT REALLY GOING--
OH, FER CHRIST'S SAKE, CHARLIE--DON'T TELL ME YOU FORGOT ABOUT THIS!?!
WE TALKED ABOUT IT. THERE'S GONNA BE A SCOUT THERE TODAY. YOU DON'T REMEMBER?
GUESS I HAD OTHER THINGS ON MY MIND.

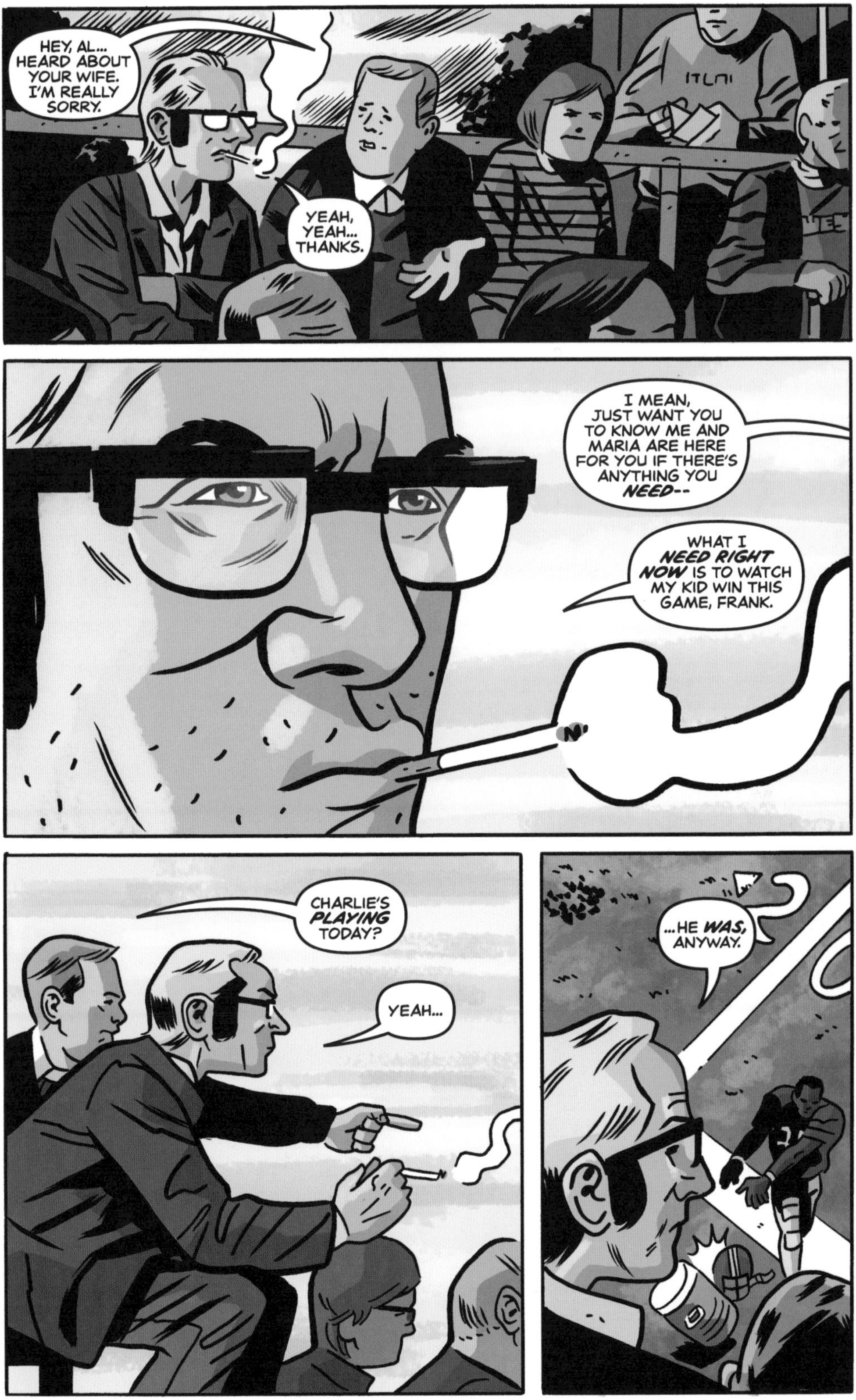
HEY, AL... HEARD ABOUT YOUR WIFE. I'M REALLY SORRY.
YEAH, YEAH... THANKS.
I MEAN, JUST WANT YOU TO KNOW ME AND MARIA ARE HERE FOR YOU IF THERE'S ANYTHING YOU NEED--
WHAT I NEED RIGHT NOW IS TO WATCH MY KID WIN THIS GAME, FRANK.
CHARLIE'S PLAYING TODAY?
YEAH...
...HE WAS, ANYWAY.

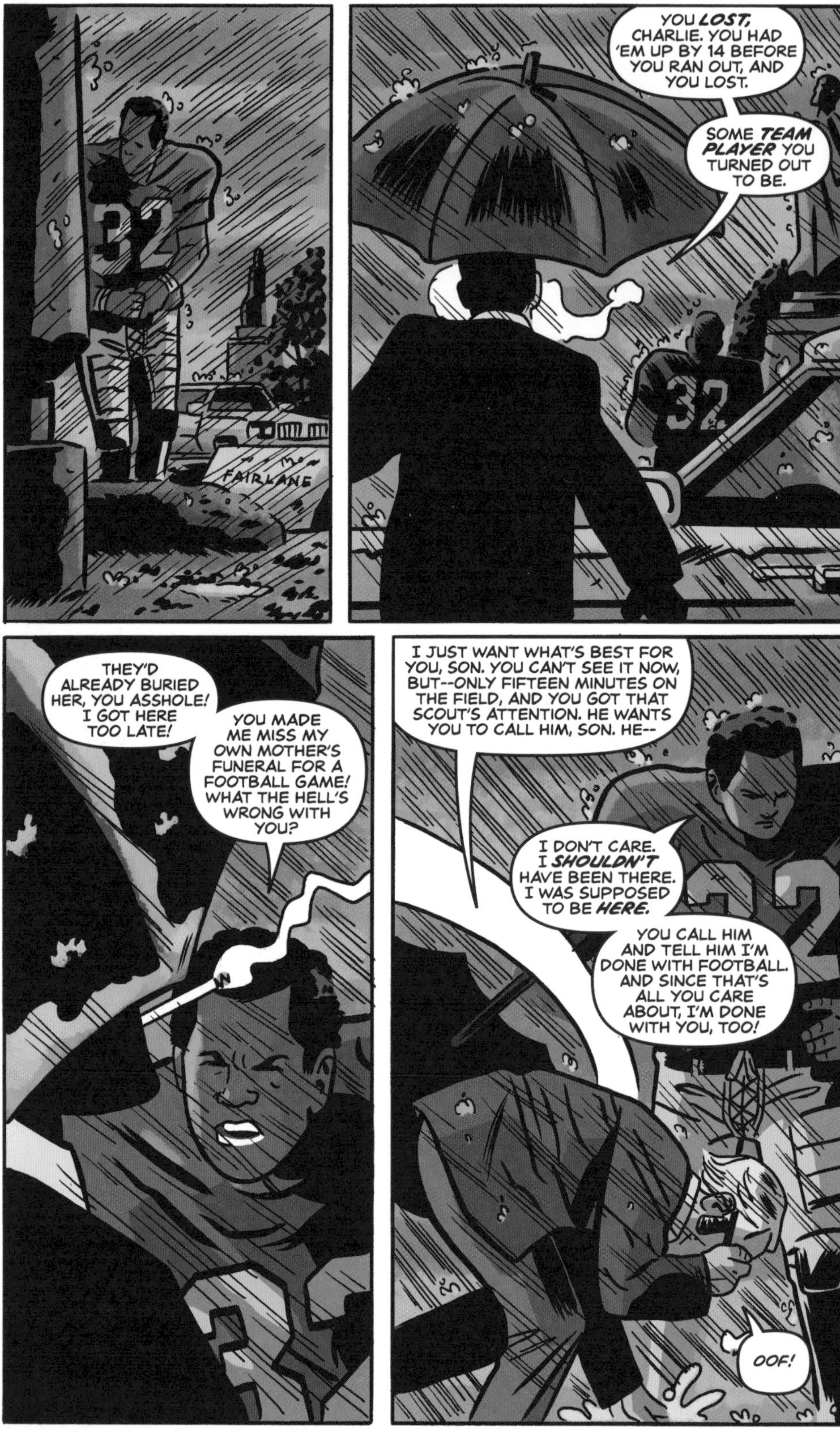
FAIRLANE
YOU LOST, CHARLIE. YOU HAD 'EM UP BY 14 BEFORE YOU RAN OUT, AND YOU LOST.
SOME TEAM PLAYER YOU TURNED OUT TO BE.
THEY'D ALREADY BURIED HER, YOU ASSHOLE! I GOT HERE TOO LATE!
YOU MADE ME MISS MY OWN MOTHER'S FUNERAL FOR A FOOTBALL GAME! WHAT THE HELL'S WRONG WITH YOU?
I JUST WANT WHAT'S BEST FOR YOU, SON. YOU CAN'T SEE IT NOW, BUT--ONLY FIFTEEN MINUTES ON THE FIELD, AND YOU GOT THAT SCOUT'S ATTENTION. HE WANTS YOU TO CALL HIM, SON. HE--
I DON'T CARE. I SHOULDN'T HAVE BEEN THERE. I WAS SUPPOSED TO BE HERE.
YOU CALL HIM AND TELL HIM I'M DONE WITH FOOTBALL. AND SINCE THAT'S ALL YOU CARE ABOUT, I'M DONE WITH YOU, TOO!
OOF!

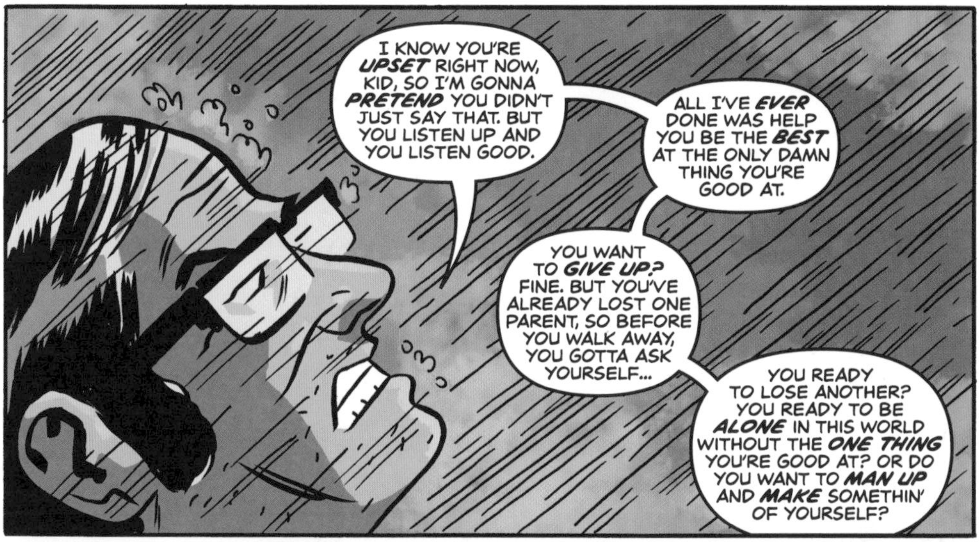
I KNOW YOU'RE *UPSET* RIGHT NOW, KID, SO I'M GONNA *PRETEND* YOU DIDN'T JUST SAY THAT. BUT YOU LISTEN UP AND YOU LISTEN GOOD.
ALL I'VE *EVER* DONE WAS HELP YOU BE THE *BEST* AT THE ONLY DAMN THING YOU'RE GOOD AT.
YOU WANT TO *GIVE UP?* FINE. BUT YOU'VE ALREADY LOST ONE PARENT, SO BEFORE YOU WALK AWAY, YOU GOTTA ASK YOURSELF...
YOU READY TO LOSE ANOTHER? YOU READY TO BE *ALONE* IN THIS WORLD WITHOUT THE *ONE THING* YOU'RE GOOD AT? OR DO YOU WANT TO *MAN UP* AND *MAKE* SOMETHIN' OF YOURSELF?

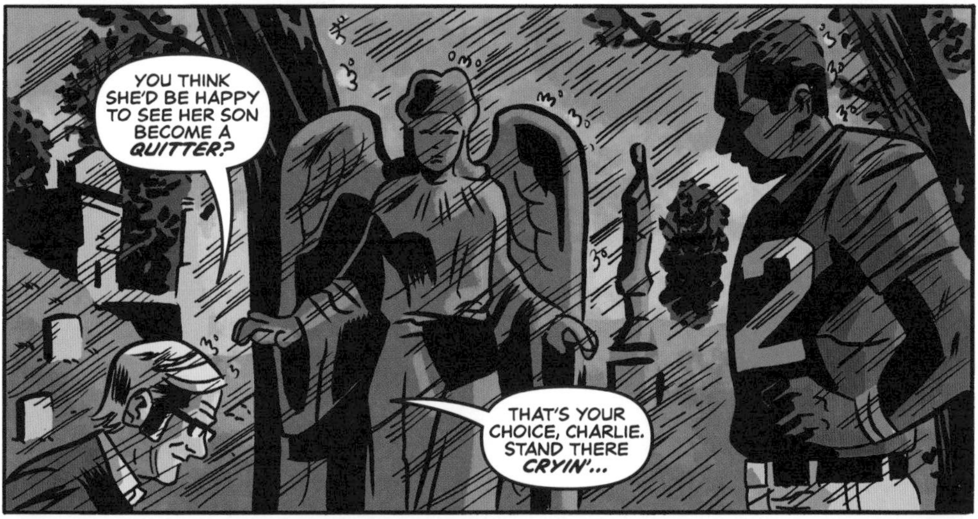
YOU THINK SHE'D BE HAPPY TO SEE HER SON BECOME A *QUITTER?*
THAT'S YOUR CHOICE, CHARLIE. STAND THERE *CRYIN'*...

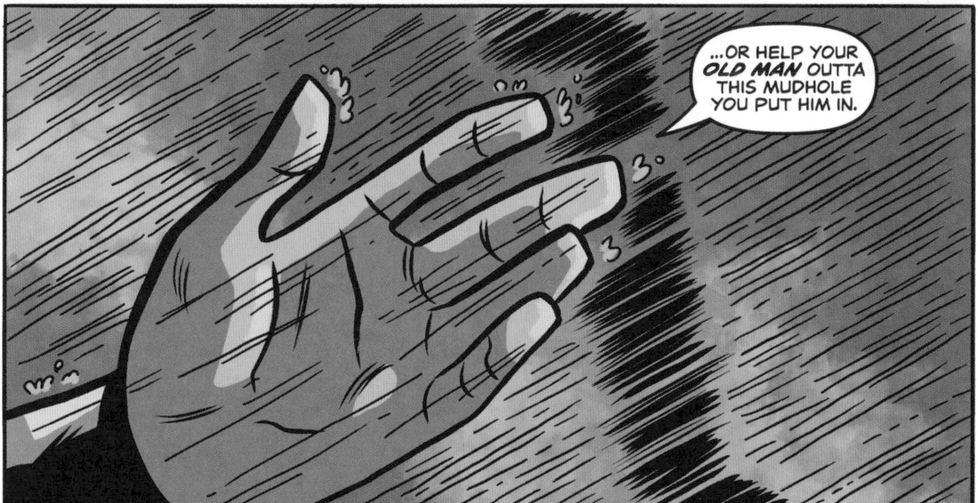
...OR HELP YOUR *OLD MAN* OUTTA THIS MUDHOLE YOU PUT HIM IN.

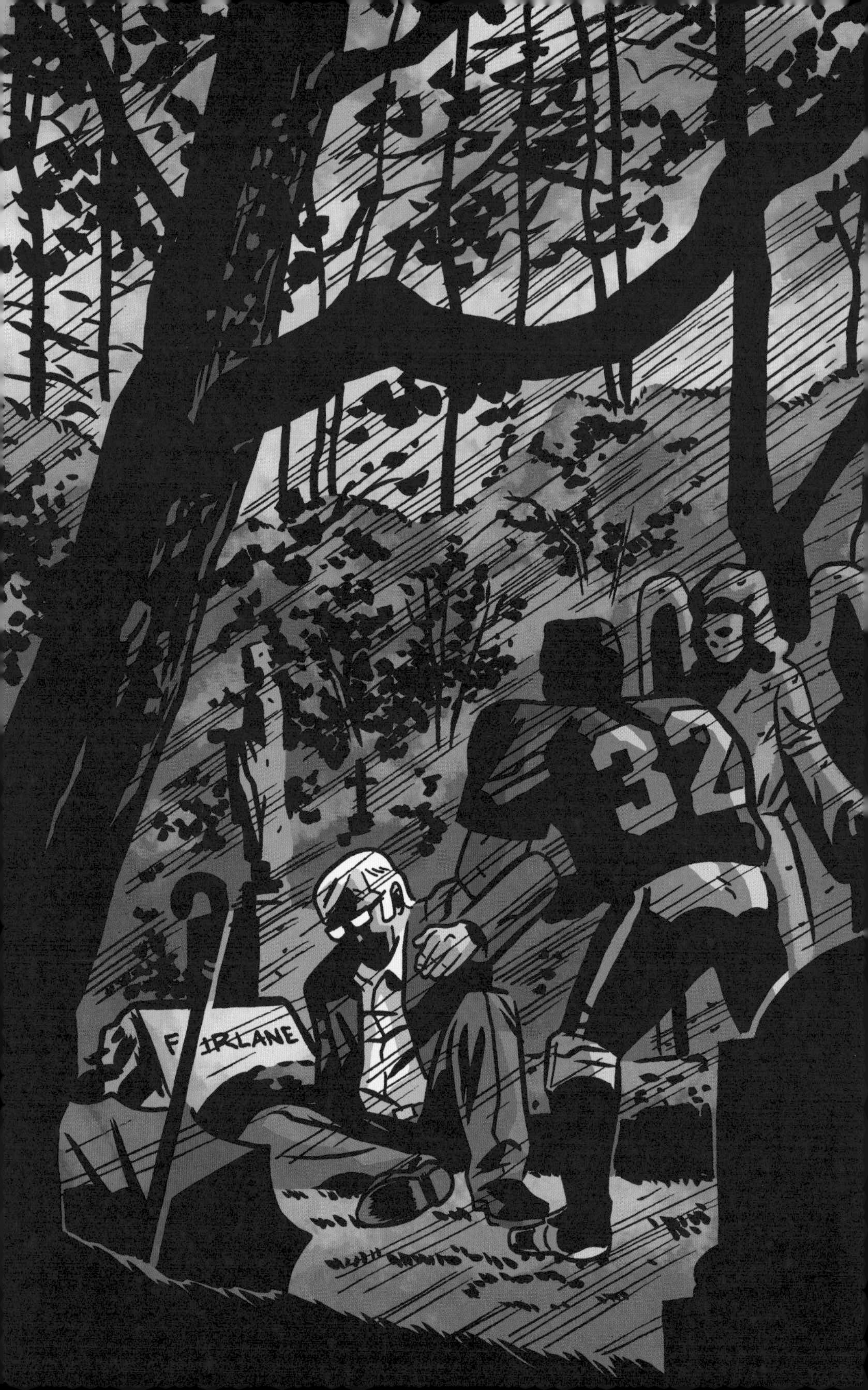
32
F IRLANE

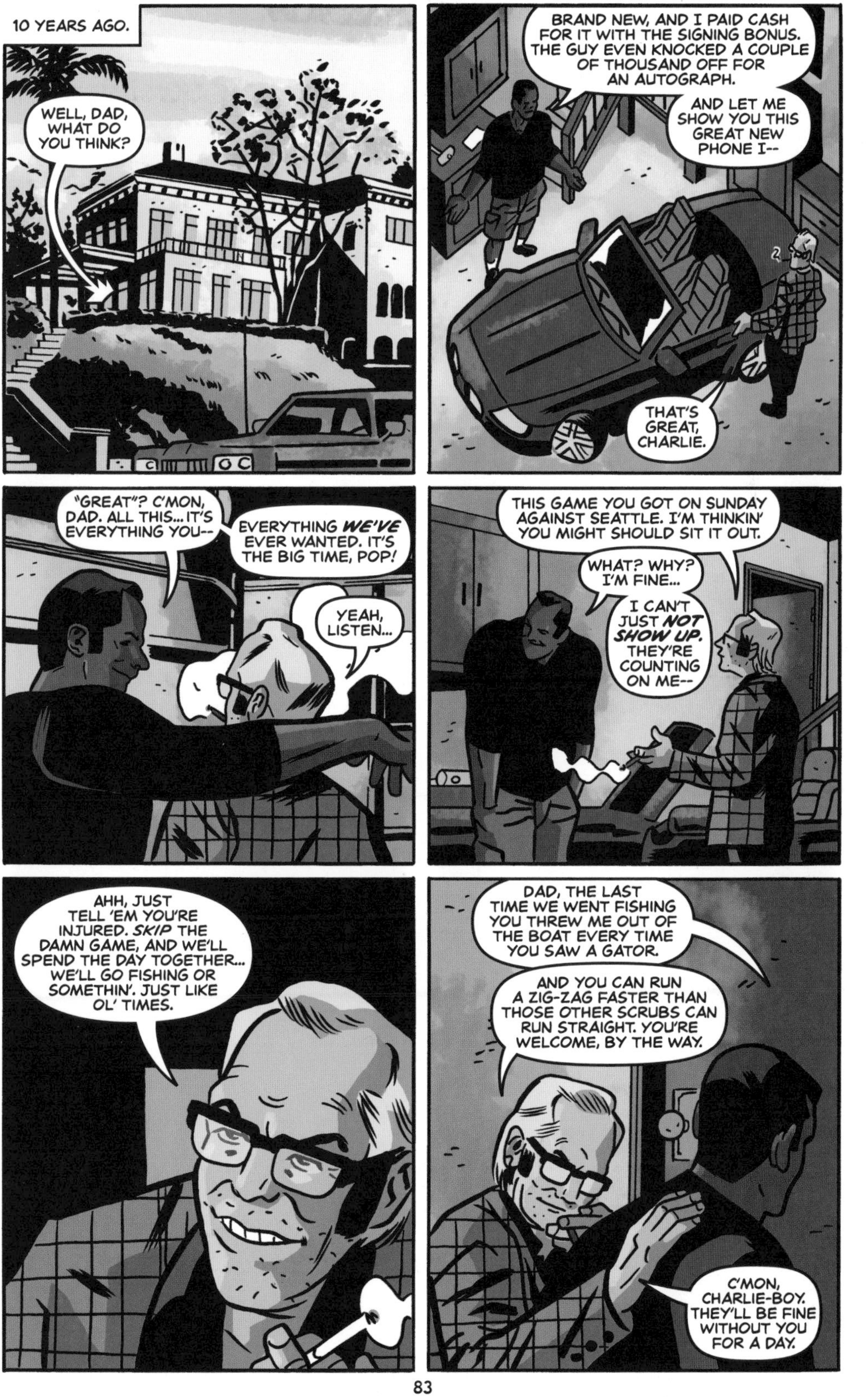
10 YEARS AGO.
WELL, DAD, WHAT DO YOU THINK?
BRAND NEW, AND I PAID CASH FOR IT WITH THE SIGNING BONUS. THE GUY EVEN KNOCKED A COUPLE OF THOUSAND OFF FOR AN AUTOGRAPH.
AND LET ME SHOW YOU THIS GREAT NEW PHONE I--
THAT'S GREAT, CHARLIE.
"GREAT"? C'MON, DAD. ALL THIS... IT'S EVERYTHING YOU--
EVERYTHING *WE'VE* EVER WANTED. IT'S THE BIG TIME, POP!
YEAH, LISTEN...
THIS GAME YOU GOT ON SUNDAY AGAINST SEATTLE. I'M THINKIN' YOU MIGHT SHOULD SIT IT OUT.
WHAT? WHY? I'M FINE...
I CAN'T JUST *NOT SHOW UP.* THEY'RE COUNTING ON ME--
AHH, JUST TELL 'EM YOU'RE INJURED. *SKIP* THE DAMN GAME, AND WE'LL SPEND THE DAY TOGETHER... WE'LL GO FISHING OR SOMETHIN'. JUST LIKE OL' TIMES.
DAD, THE LAST TIME WE WENT FISHING YOU THREW ME OUT OF THE BOAT EVERY TIME YOU SAW A GATOR.
AND YOU CAN RUN A ZIG-ZAG FASTER THAN THOSE OTHER SCRUBS CAN RUN STRAIGHT. YOU'RE WELCOME, BY THE WAY.
C'MON, CHARLIE-BOY. THEY'LL BE FINE WITHOUT YOU FOR A DAY.

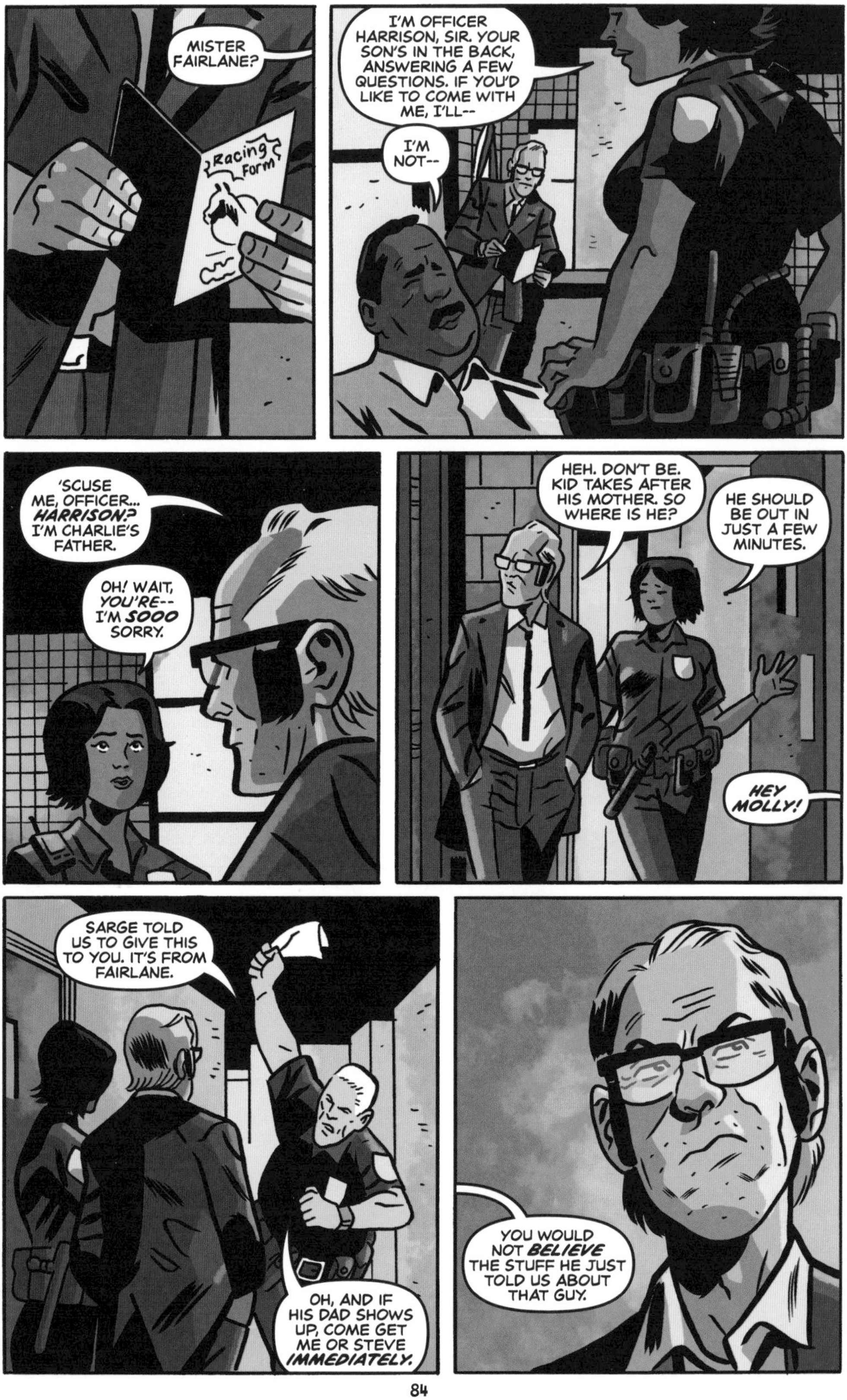
MISTER FAIRLANE?
Racing Form
I'M OFFICER HARRISON, SIR. YOUR SON'S IN THE BACK, ANSWERING A FEW QUESTIONS. IF YOU'D LIKE TO COME WITH ME, I'LL--
I'M NOT--
'SCUSE ME, OFFICER... *HARRISON?* I'M CHARLIE'S FATHER.
OH! WAIT, *YOU'RE*-- I'M *SOOO* SORRY.
HEH. DON'T BE. KID TAKES AFTER HIS MOTHER. SO WHERE IS HE?
HE SHOULD BE OUT IN JUST A FEW MINUTES.
HEY MOLLY!
SARGE TOLD US TO GIVE THIS TO YOU. IT'S FROM FAIRLANE.
OH, AND IF HIS DAD SHOWS UP, COME GET ME OR STEVE *IMMEDIATELY.*
YOU WOULD NOT *BELIEVE* THE STUFF HE JUST TOLD US ABOUT THAT GUY.

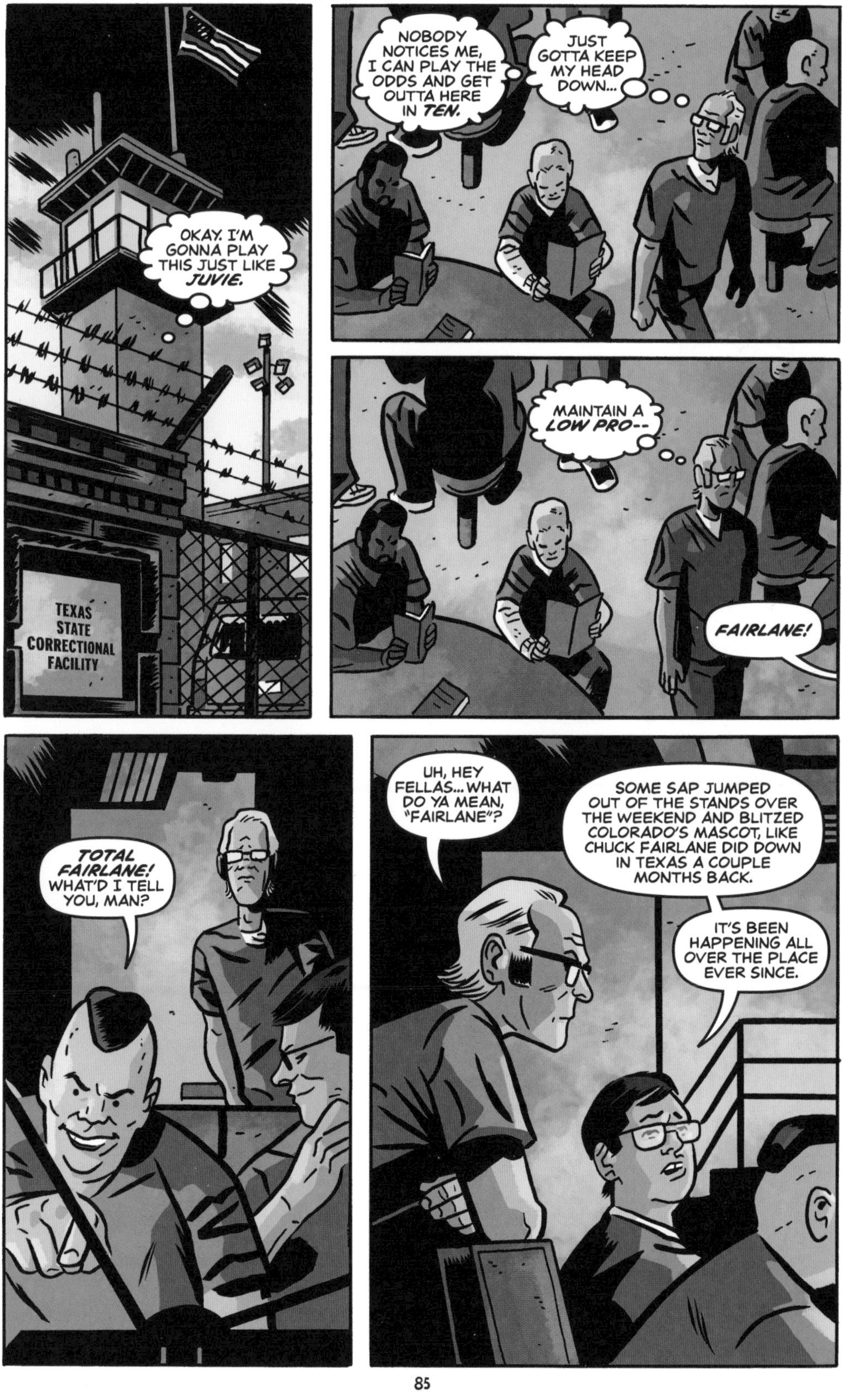
OKAY. I'M GONNA PLAY THIS JUST LIKE JUVIE.
TEXAS STATE CORRECTIONAL FACILITY
NOBODY NOTICES ME, I CAN PLAY THE ODDS AND GET OUTTA HERE IN TEN.
JUST GOTTA KEEP MY HEAD DOWN...
MAINTAIN A LOW PRO--
FAIRLANE!
TOTAL FAIRLANE! WHAT'D I TELL YOU, MAN?
UH, HEY FELLAS... WHAT DO YA MEAN, "FAIRLANE"?
SOME SAP JUMPED OUT OF THE STANDS OVER THE WEEKEND AND BLITZED COLORADO'S MASCOT, LIKE CHUCK FAIRLANE DID DOWN IN TEXAS A COUPLE MONTHS BACK.
IT'S BEEN HAPPENING ALL OVER THE PLACE EVER SINCE.

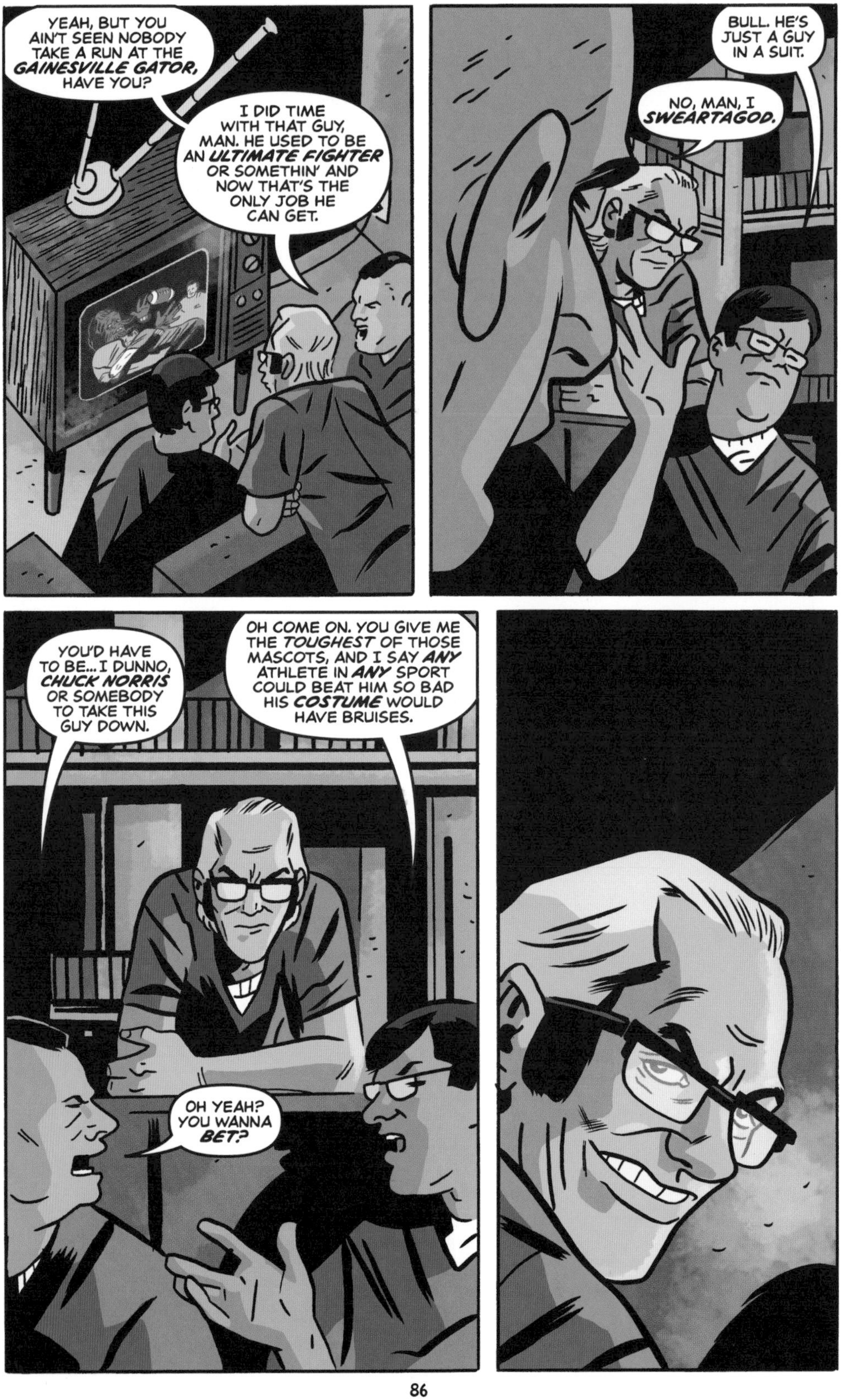
YEAH, BUT YOU AIN'T SEEN NOBODY TAKE A RUN AT THE GAINESVILLE GATOR, HAVE YOU?
I DID TIME WITH THAT GUY, MAN. HE USED TO BE AN ULTIMATE FIGHTER OR SOMETHIN' AND NOW THAT'S THE ONLY JOB HE CAN GET.
BULL. HE'S JUST A GUY IN A SUIT.
NO, MAN, I SWEARTAGOD.
YOU'D HAVE TO BE... I DUNNO, CHUCK NORRIS OR SOMEBODY TO TAKE THIS GUY DOWN.
OH COME ON. YOU GIVE ME THE TOUGHEST OF THOSE MASCOTS, AND I SAY ANY ATHLETE IN ANY SPORT COULD BEAT HIM SO BAD HIS COSTUME WOULD HAVE BRUISES.
OH YEAH? YOU WANNA BET?

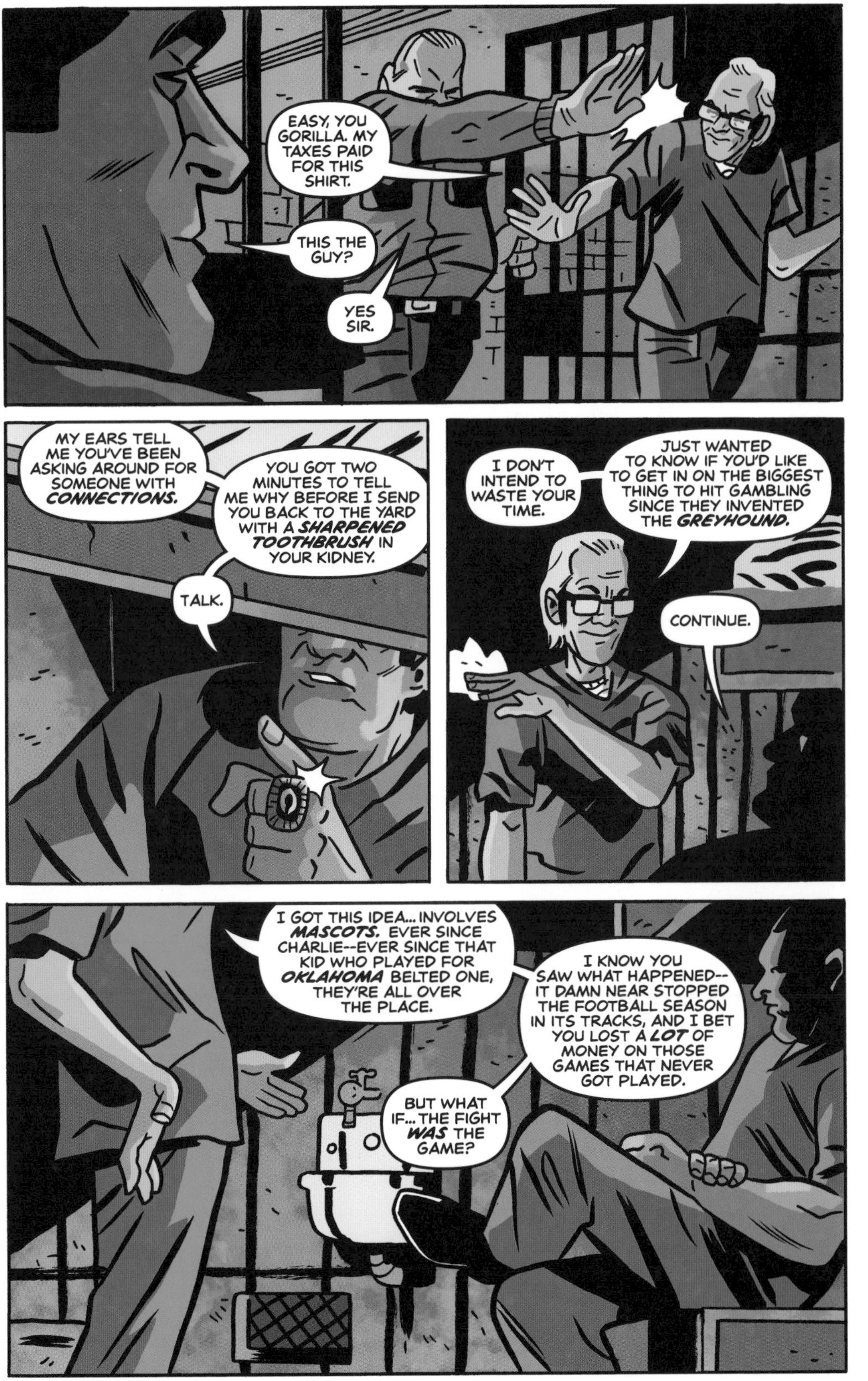

EASY, YOU GORILLA. MY TAXES PAID FOR THIS SHIRT.
THIS THE GUY?
YES SIR.
MY EARS TELL ME YOU'VE BEEN ASKING AROUND FOR SOMEONE WITH CONNECTIONS.
YOU GOT TWO MINUTES TO TELL ME WHY BEFORE I SEND YOU BACK TO THE YARD WITH A SHARPENED TOOTHBRUSH IN YOUR KIDNEY.
TALK.
I DON'T INTEND TO WASTE YOUR TIME.
JUST WANTED TO KNOW IF YOU'D LIKE TO GET IN ON THE BIGGEST THING TO HIT GAMBLING SINCE THEY INVENTED THE GREYHOUND.
CONTINUE.
I GOT THIS IDEA... INVOLVES MASCOTS. EVER SINCE CHARLIE--EVER SINCE THAT KID WHO PLAYED FOR OKLAHOMA BELTED ONE, THEY'RE ALL OVER THE PLACE.
I KNOW YOU SAW WHAT HAPPENED--IT DAMN NEAR STOPPED THE FOOTBALL SEASON IN ITS TRACKS, AND I BET YOU LOST A LOT OF MONEY ON THOSE GAMES THAT NEVER GOT PLAYED.
BUT WHAT IF... THE FIGHT WAS THE GAME?

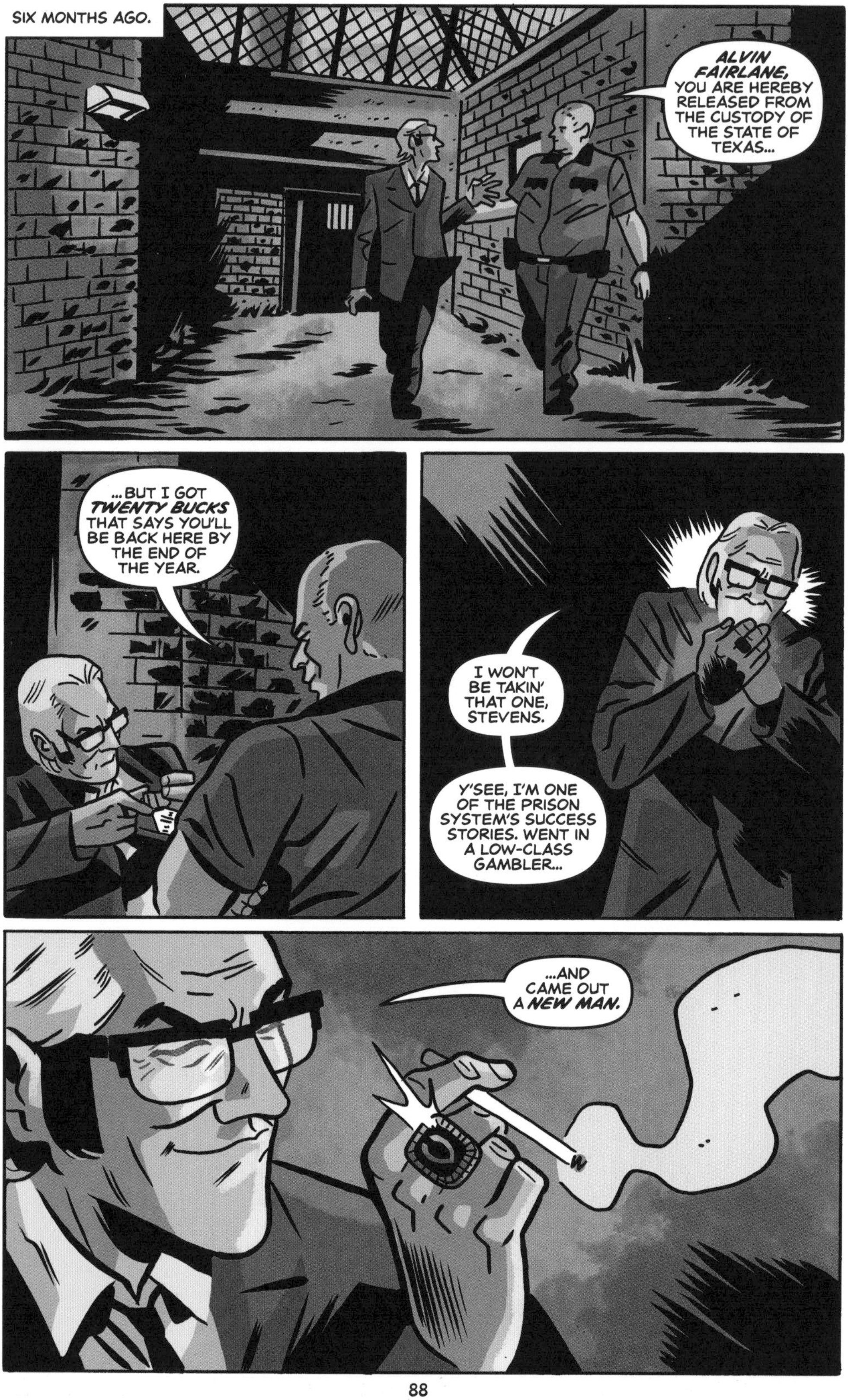
SIX MONTHS AGO.
ALVIN FAIRLANE, YOU ARE HEREBY RELEASED FROM THE CUSTODY OF THE STATE OF TEXAS...
...BUT I GOT TWENTY BUCKS THAT SAYS YOU'LL BE BACK HERE BY THE END OF THE YEAR.
I WON'T BE TAKIN' THAT ONE, STEVENS.
Y'SEE, I'M ONE OF THE PRISON SYSTEM'S SUCCESS STORIES. WENT IN A LOW-CLASS GAMBLER...
...AND CAME OUT A NEW MAN.

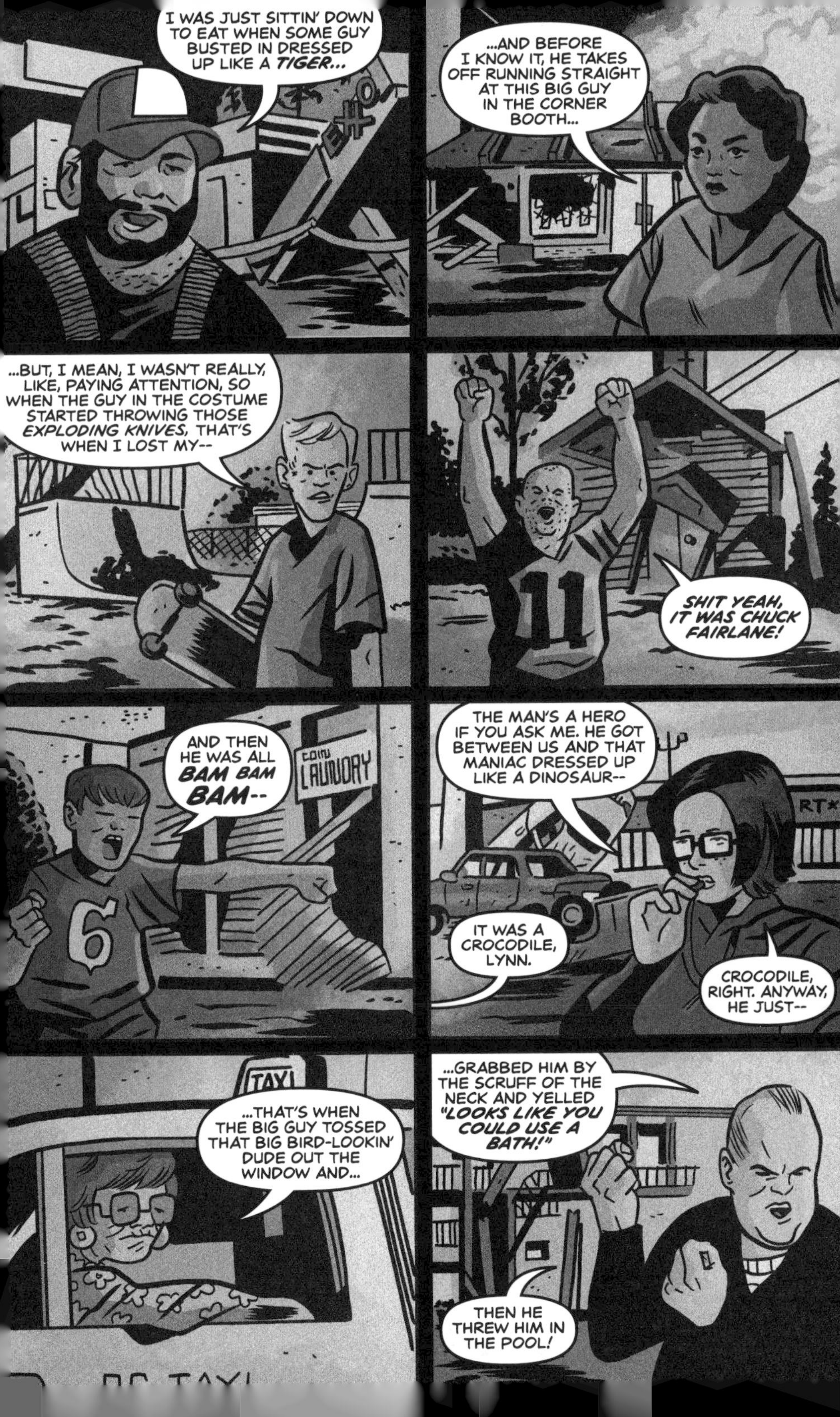

I WAS JUST SITTIN' DOWN TO EAT WHEN SOME GUY BUSTED IN DRESSED UP LIKE A *TIGER*...
...AND BEFORE I KNOW IT, HE TAKES OFF RUNNING STRAIGHT AT THIS BIG GUY IN THE CORNER BOOTH...
...BUT, I MEAN, I WASN'T REALLY, LIKE, PAYING ATTENTION, SO WHEN THE GUY IN THE COSTUME STARTED THROWING THOSE *EXPLODING KNIVES,* THAT'S WHEN I LOST MY--
SHIT YEAH, IT WAS CHUCK FAIRLANE!
AND THEN HE WAS ALL **BAM BAM BAM**--
COIN LAUNDRY
THE MAN'S A HERO IF YOU ASK ME. HE GOT BETWEEN US AND THAT MANIAC DRESSED UP LIKE A DINOSAUR--
IT WAS A CROCODILE, LYNN.
CROCODILE, RIGHT. ANYWAY, HE JUST--
TAXI
...THAT'S WHEN THE BIG GUY TOSSED THAT BIG BIRD-LOOKIN' DUDE OUT THE WINDOW AND...
...GRABBED HIM BY THE SCRUFF OF THE NECK AND YELLED ***"LOOKS LIKE YOU COULD USE A BATH!"***
THEN HE THREW HIM IN THE POOL!

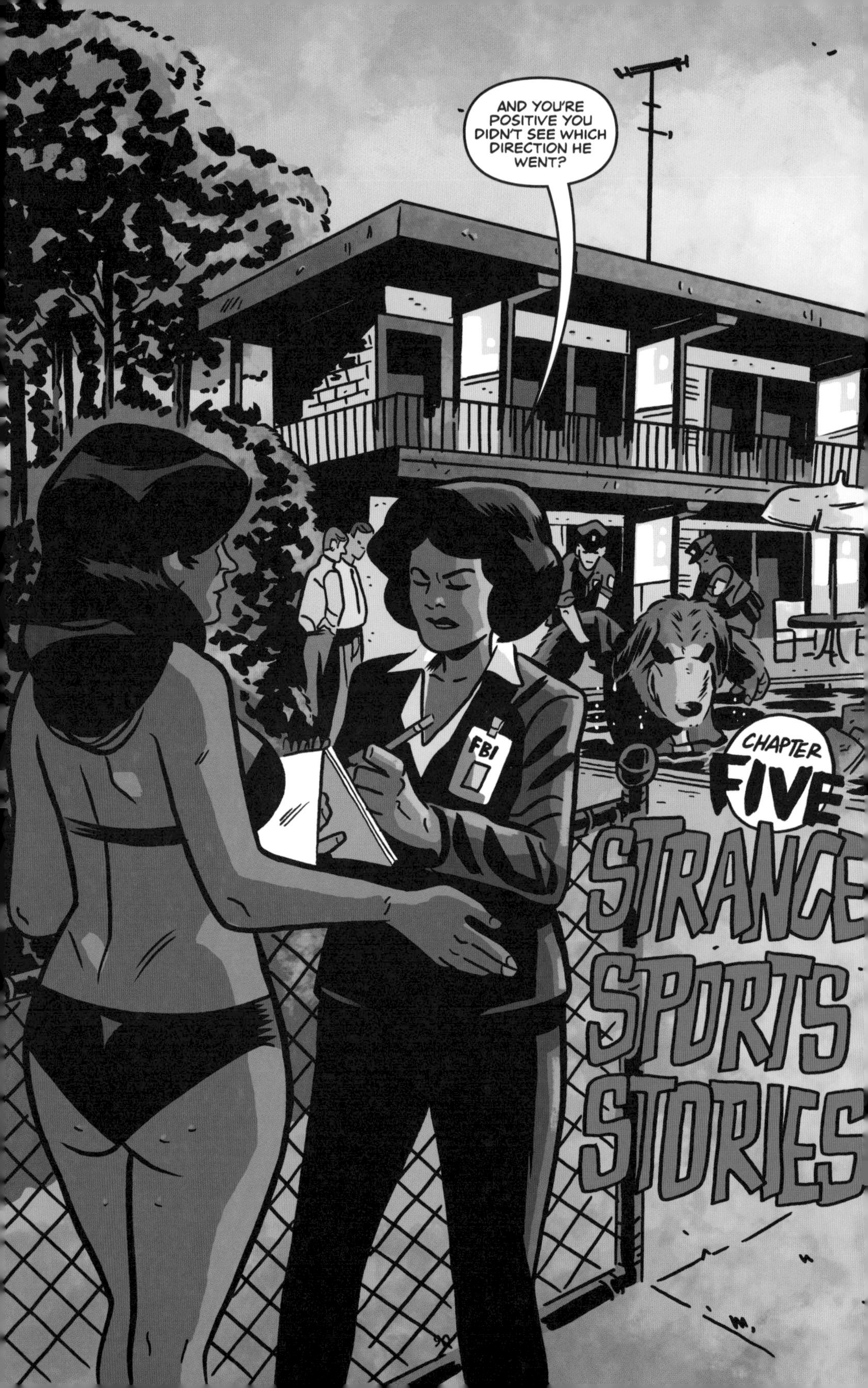
AND YOU'RE POSITIVE YOU DIDN'T SEE WHICH DIRECTION HE WENT?
FBI
CHAPTER FIVE
STRANGE SPORTS STORIES

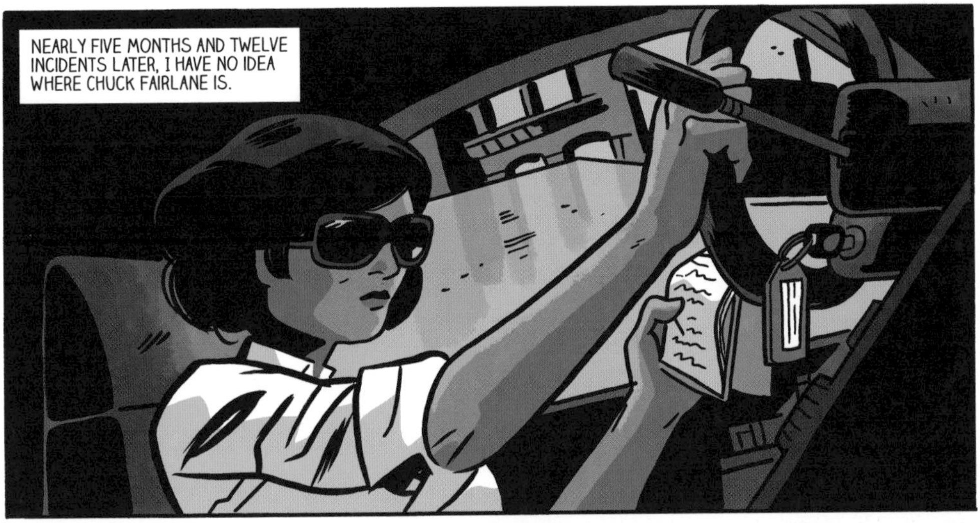
NEARLY FIVE MONTHS AND TWELVE INCIDENTS LATER, I HAVE NO IDEA WHERE CHUCK FAIRLANE IS.

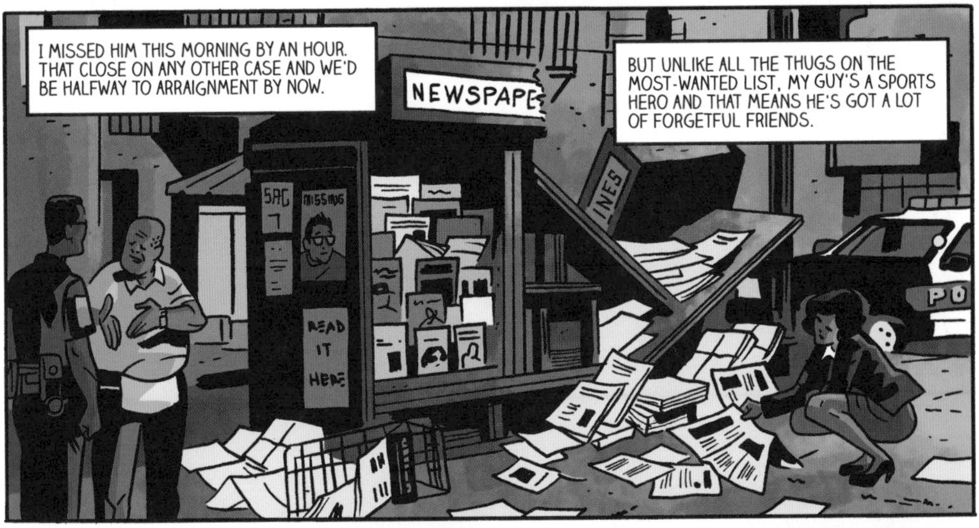
I MISSED HIM THIS MORNING BY AN HOUR. THAT CLOSE ON ANY OTHER CASE AND WE'D BE HALFWAY TO ARRAIGNMENT BY NOW.
NEWSPAPE
BUT UNLIKE ALL THE THUGS ON THE MOST-WANTED LIST, MY GUY'S A SPORTS HERO AND THAT MEANS HE'S GOT A LOT OF FORGETFUL FRIENDS.
MISSING
READ IT HERE

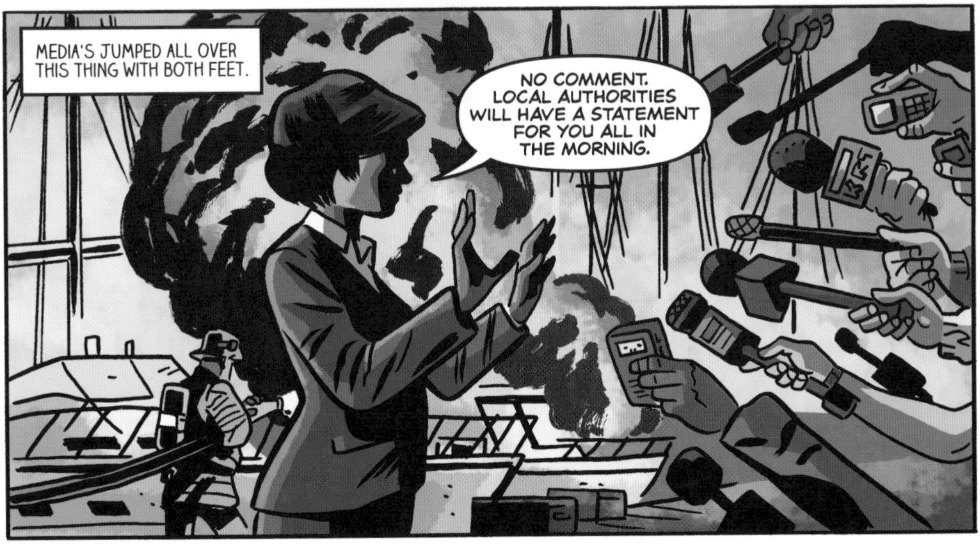
MEDIA'S JUMPED ALL OVER THIS THING WITH BOTH FEET.
NO COMMENT. LOCAL AUTHORITIES WILL HAVE A STATEMENT FOR YOU ALL IN THE MORNING.

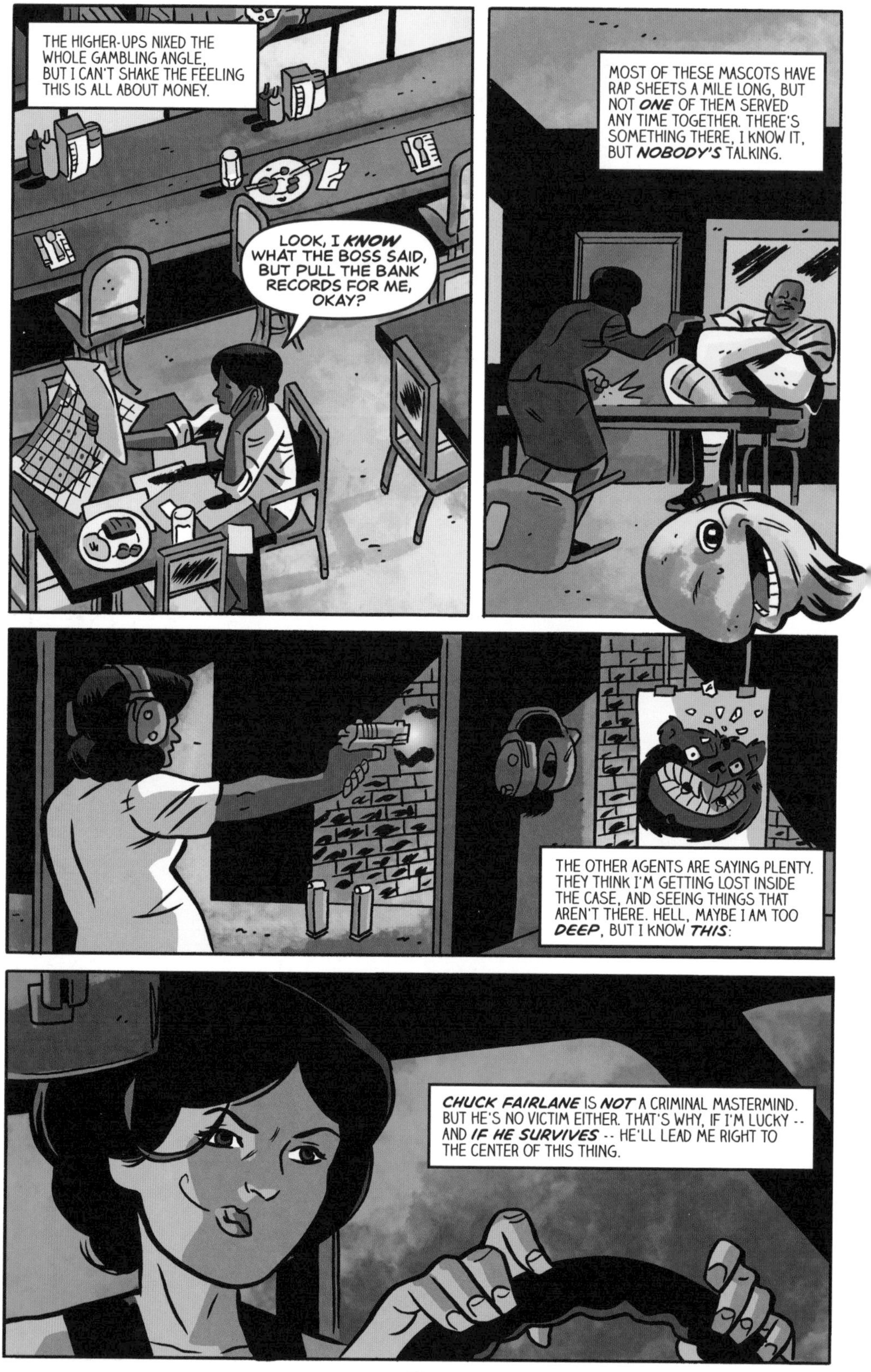
THE HIGHER-UPS NIXED THE WHOLE GAMBLING ANGLE, BUT I CAN'T SHAKE THE FEELING THIS IS ALL ABOUT MONEY.
LOOK, I KNOW WHAT THE BOSS SAID, BUT PULL THE BANK RECORDS FOR ME, OKAY?
MOST OF THESE MASCOTS HAVE RAP SHEETS A MILE LONG, BUT NOT ONE OF THEM SERVED ANY TIME TOGETHER. THERE'S SOMETHING THERE, I KNOW IT, BUT NOBODY'S TALKING.
THE OTHER AGENTS ARE SAYING PLENTY. THEY THINK I'M GETTING LOST INSIDE THE CASE, AND SEEING THINGS THAT AREN'T THERE. HELL, MAYBE I AM TOO DEEP, BUT I KNOW THIS:
CHUCK FAIRLANE IS NOT A CRIMINAL MASTERMIND. BUT HE'S NO VICTIM EITHER. THAT'S WHY, IF I'M LUCKY -- AND IF HE SURVIVES -- HE'LL LEAD ME RIGHT TO THE CENTER OF THIS THING.

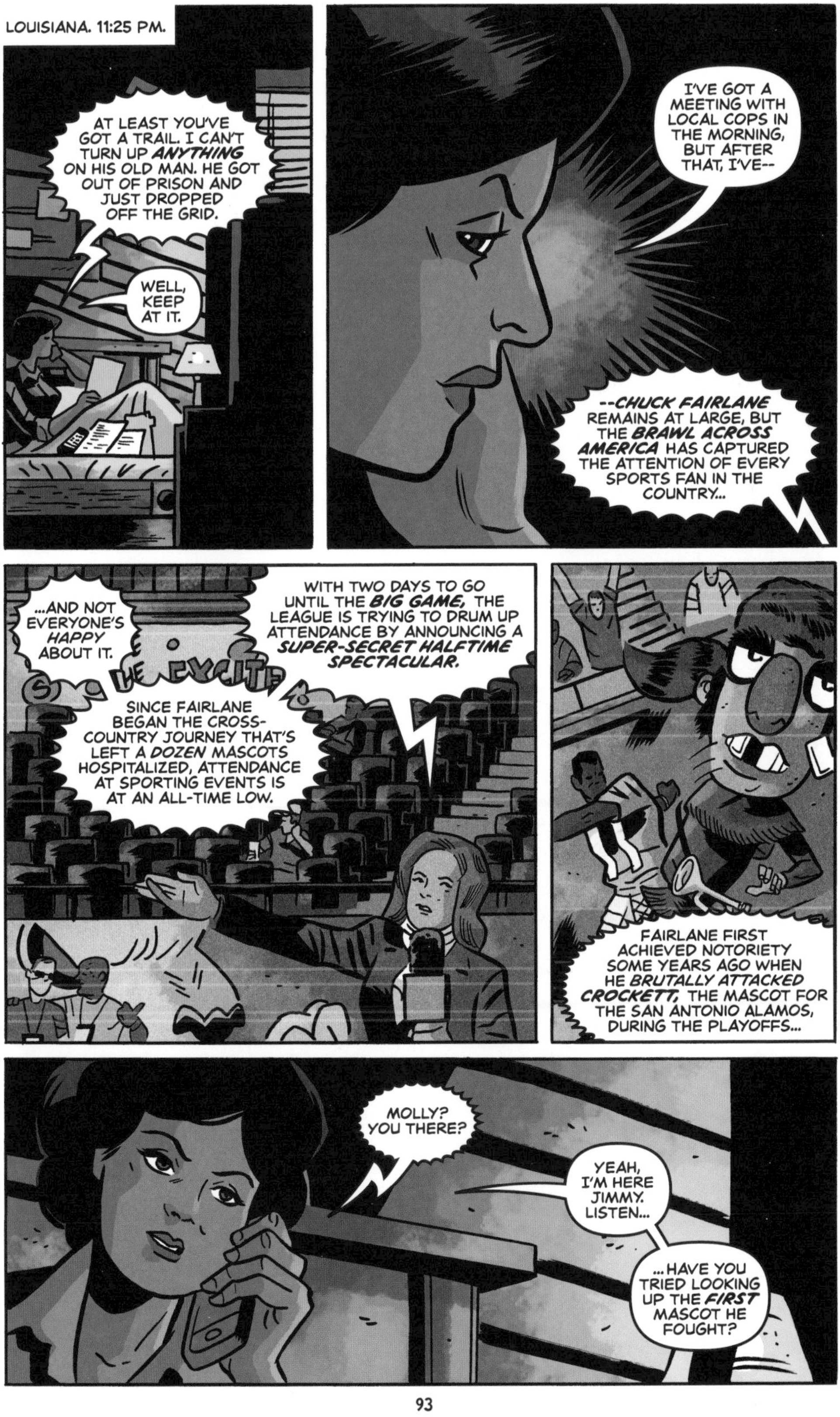
LOUISIANA. 11:25 PM.
AT LEAST YOU'VE GOT A TRAIL. I CAN'T TURN UP ANYTHING ON HIS OLD MAN. HE GOT OUT OF PRISON AND JUST DROPPED OFF THE GRID.
WELL, KEEP AT IT.
I'VE GOT A MEETING WITH LOCAL COPS IN THE MORNING, BUT AFTER THAT, I'VE--
--CHUCK FAIRLANE REMAINS AT LARGE, BUT THE BRAWL ACROSS AMERICA HAS CAPTURED THE ATTENTION OF EVERY SPORTS FAN IN THE COUNTRY...
...AND NOT EVERYONE'S HAPPY ABOUT IT.
WITH TWO DAYS TO GO UNTIL THE BIG GAME, THE LEAGUE IS TRYING TO DRUM UP ATTENDANCE BY ANNOUNCING A SUPER-SECRET HALFTIME SPECTACULAR.
SINCE FAIRLANE BEGAN THE CROSS-COUNTRY JOURNEY THAT'S LEFT A DOZEN MASCOTS HOSPITALIZED, ATTENDANCE AT SPORTING EVENTS IS AT AN ALL-TIME LOW.
FAIRLANE FIRST ACHIEVED NOTORIETY SOME YEARS AGO WHEN HE BRUTALLY ATTACKED CROCKETT, THE MASCOT FOR THE SAN ANTONIO ALAMOS, DURING THE PLAYOFFS...
MOLLY? YOU THERE?
YEAH, I'M HERE JIMMY. LISTEN...
...HAVE YOU TRIED LOOKING UP THE FIRST MASCOT HE FOUGHT?

IT'S A **CONSPIRACY**.

IT'S GOT TO BE.

CHUCK GOES AFTER THE MASCOTS, INSPIRING OTHERS TO START **"FAIRLANING."**

NOW THEY'RE OUT FOR **REVENGE**. SHOULD'VE SEEN IT BEFORE.

THE DAILY NEWS
BRAWL ACROSS AMERICA

EYES ALL OVER THE COUNTRY. ANYONE IN A **COSTUME** COULD BE PART OF THE CARTEL.

THAT'S HOW THEY'RE TRACKING HIM DOWN.

THAT'S HOW THEY'RE TRACKING **US**.

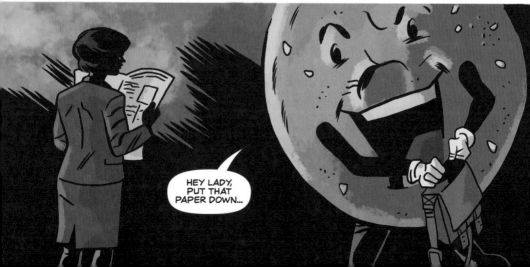

HEY LADY, PUT THAT PAPER DOWN...

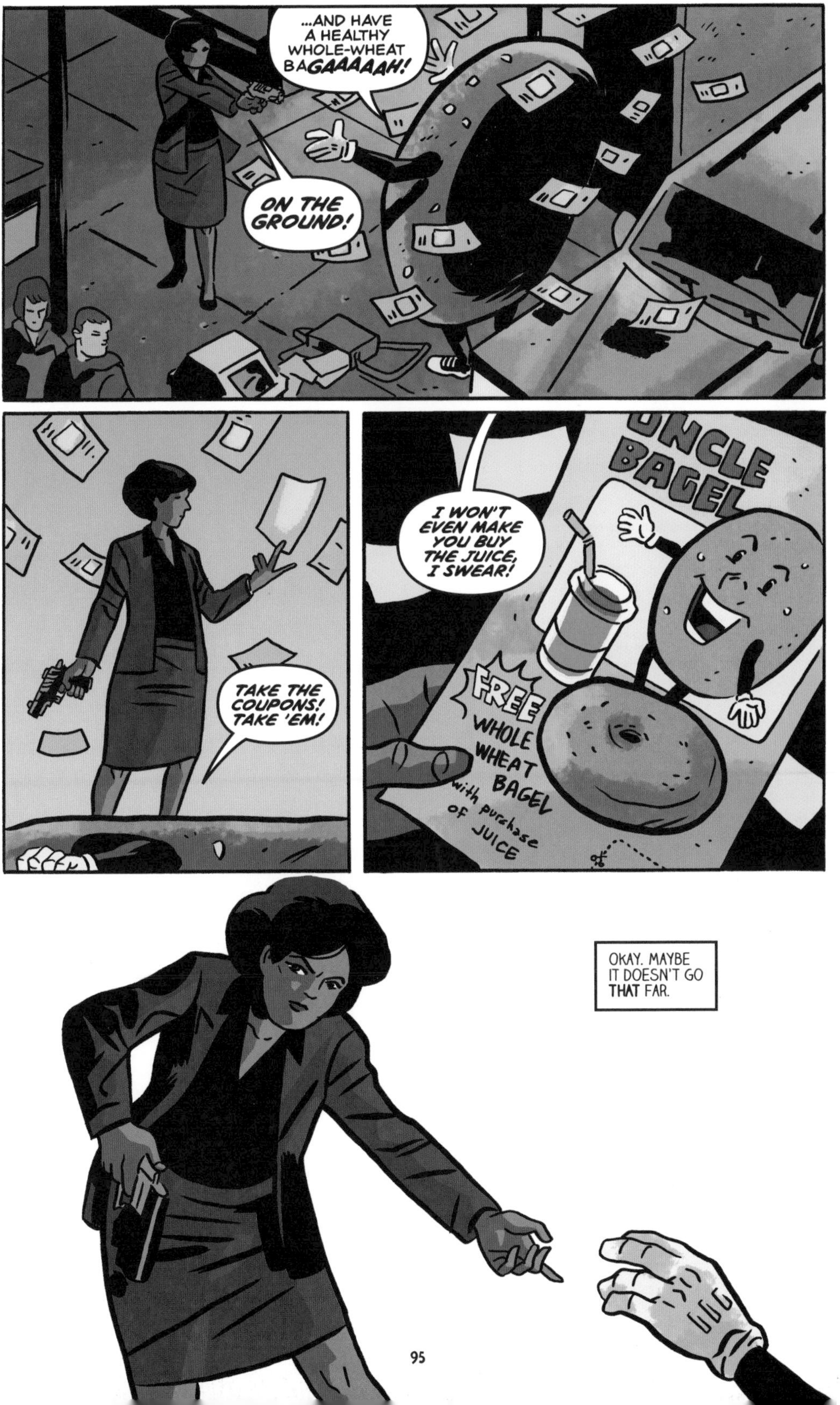
...AND HAVE A HEALTHY WHOLE-WHEAT BAGAAAAAH!
ON THE GROUND!
UNCLE BAGEL
I WON'T EVEN MAKE YOU BUY THE JUICE, I SWEAR!
TAKE THE COUPONS! TAKE 'EM!
FREE WHOLE WHEAT BAGEL with purchase of JUICE
OKAY. MAYBE IT DOESN'T GO THAT FAR.

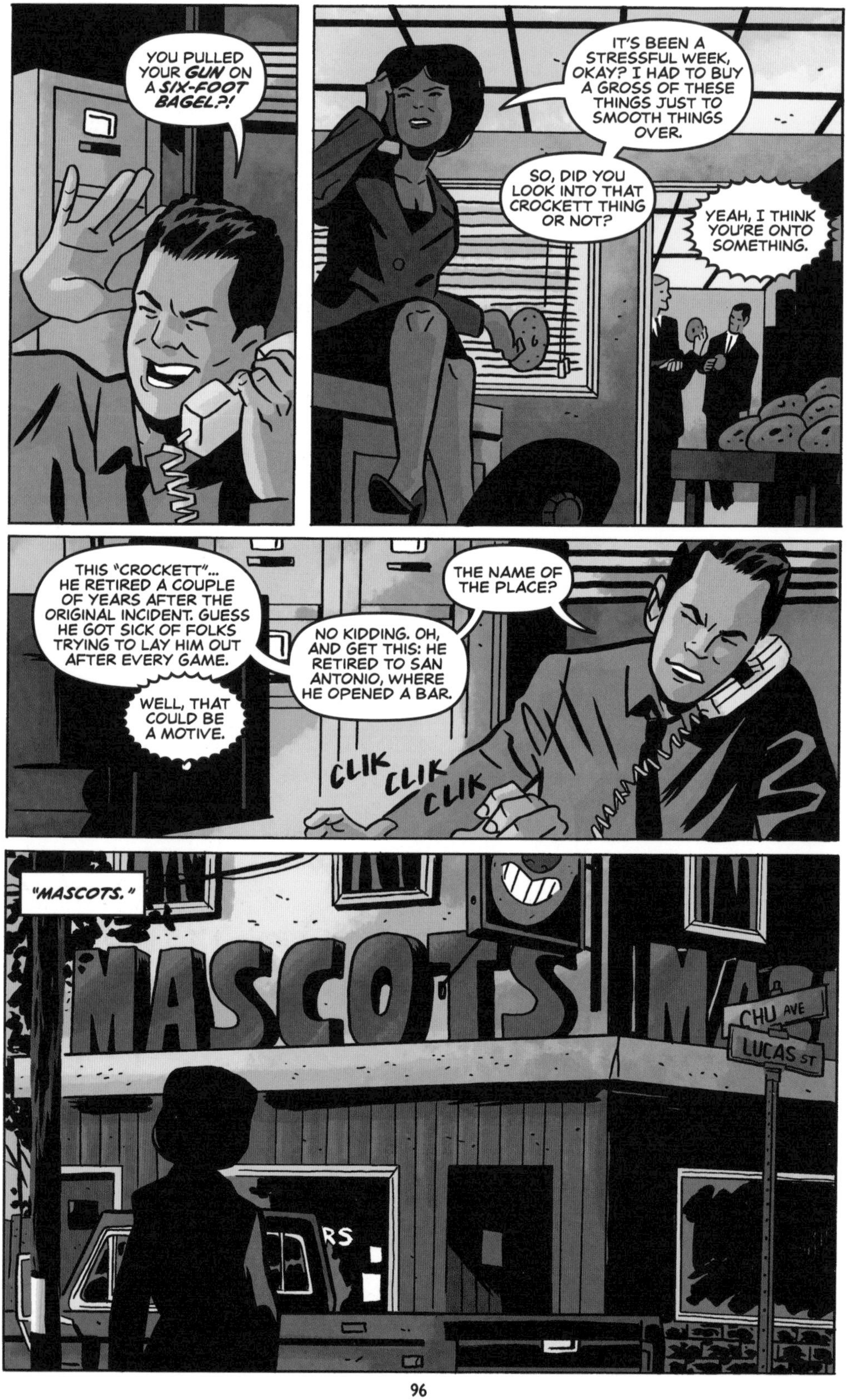

YOU PULLED YOUR GUN ON A SIX-FOOT BAGEL?!
IT'S BEEN A STRESSFUL WEEK, OKAY? I HAD TO BUY A GROSS OF THESE THINGS JUST TO SMOOTH THINGS OVER.
SO, DID YOU LOOK INTO THAT CROCKETT THING OR NOT?
YEAH, I THINK YOU'RE ONTO SOMETHING.
THIS "CROCKETT"... HE RETIRED A COUPLE OF YEARS AFTER THE ORIGINAL INCIDENT. GUESS HE GOT SICK OF FOLKS TRYING TO LAY HIM OUT AFTER EVERY GAME.
WELL, THAT COULD BE A MOTIVE.
NO KIDDING. OH, AND GET THIS: HE RETIRED TO SAN ANTONIO, WHERE HE OPENED A BAR.
THE NAME OF THE PLACE?
CLIK CLIK CLIK
"MASCOTS."
MASCOTS
CHU AVE
LUCAS ST

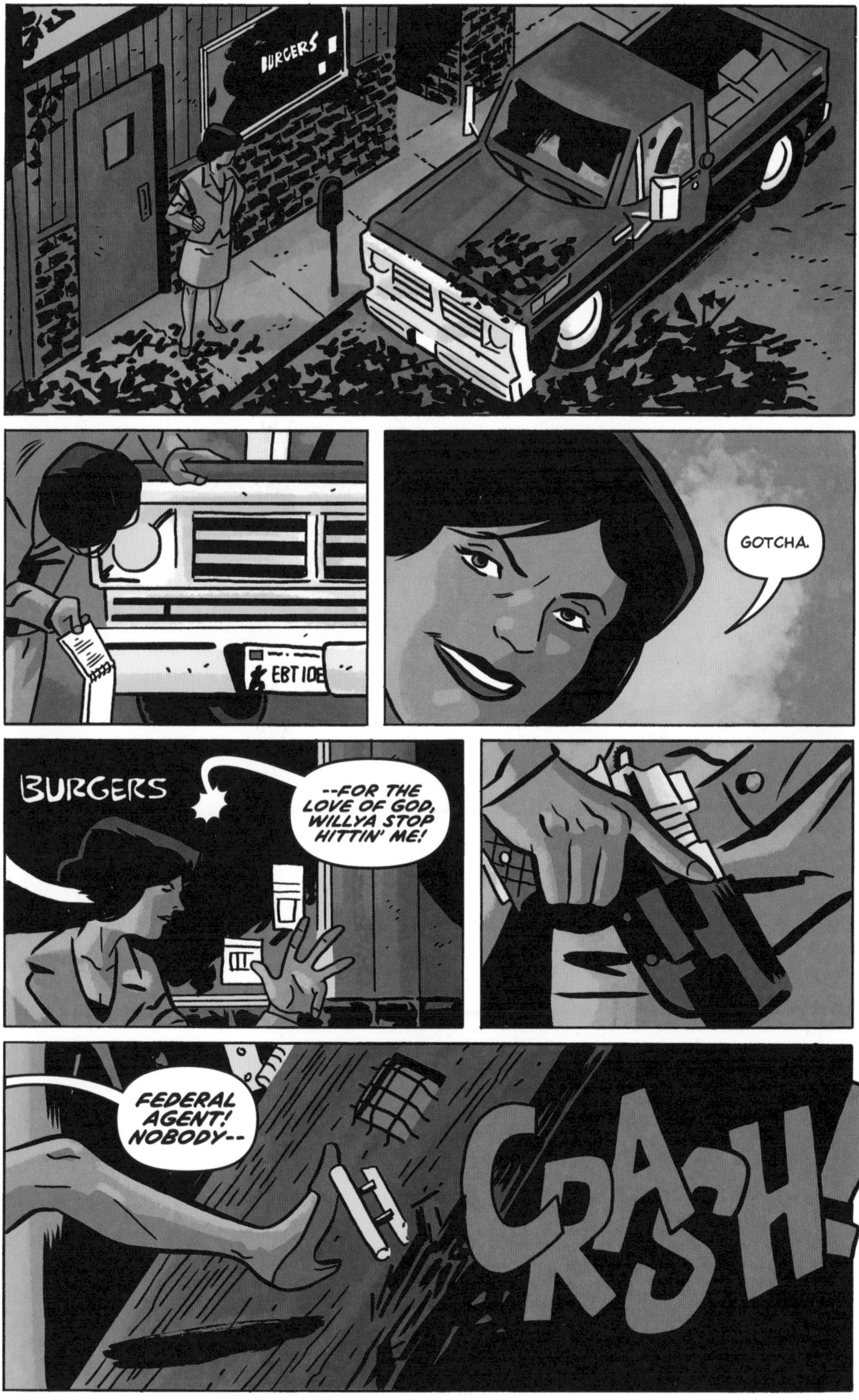
BURGERS
EBT IDE
GOTCHA.
BURGERS
--FOR THE LOVE OF GOD, WILLYA STOP HITTIN' ME!
FEDERAL AGENT! NOBODY--
CRASH!

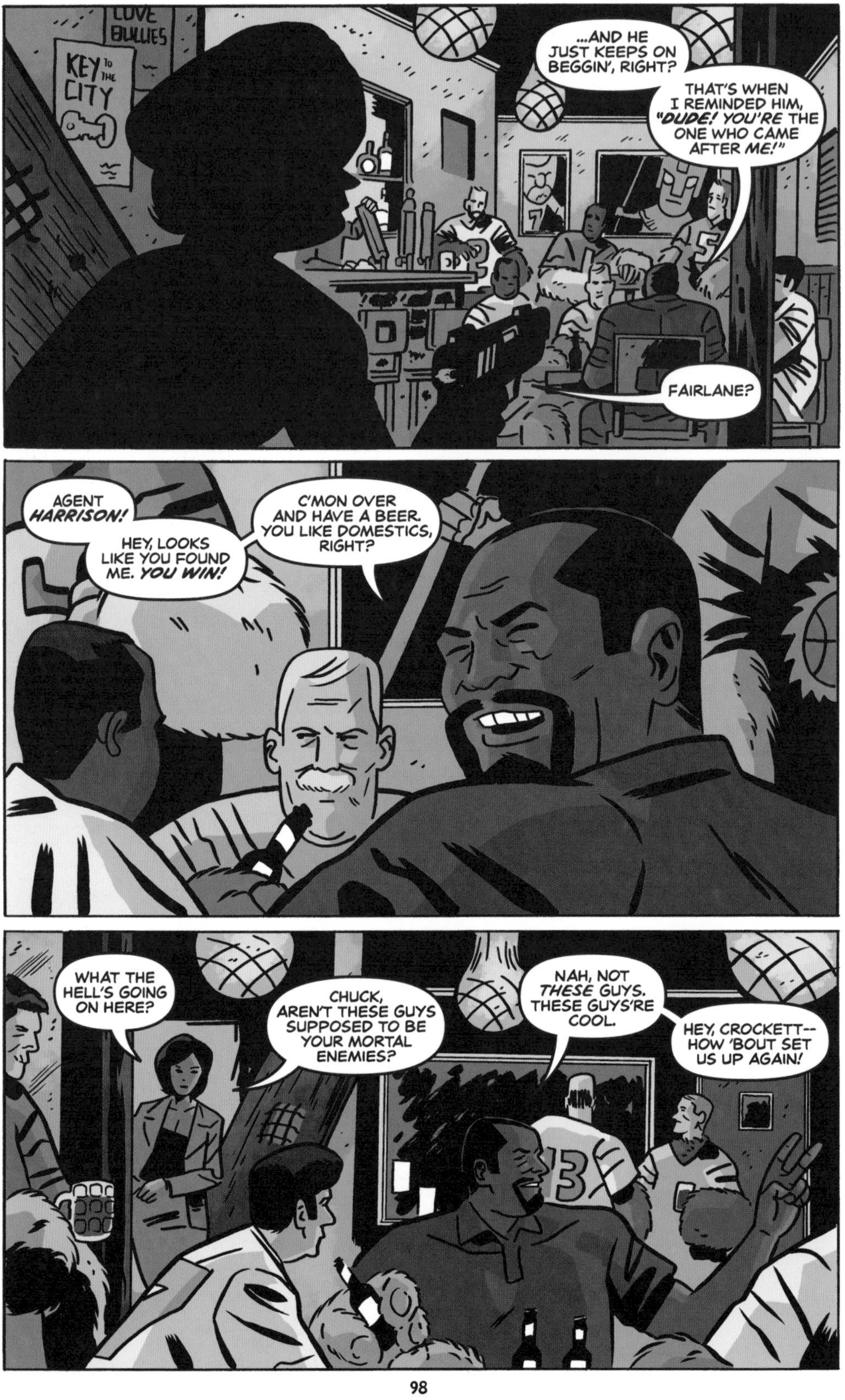
LOVE BULLIES
KEY TO THE CITY
...AND HE JUST KEEPS ON BEGGIN', RIGHT?
THAT'S WHEN I REMINDED HIM, "DUDE! YOU'RE THE ONE WHO CAME AFTER ME!"
FAIRLANE?
AGENT HARRISON!
HEY, LOOKS LIKE YOU FOUND ME. YOU WIN!
C'MON OVER AND HAVE A BEER. YOU LIKE DOMESTICS, RIGHT?
WHAT THE HELL'S GOING ON HERE?
CHUCK, AREN'T THESE GUYS SUPPOSED TO BE YOUR MORTAL ENEMIES?
NAH, NOT THESE GUYS. THESE GUYS'RE COOL.
HEY, CROCKETT-- HOW 'BOUT SET US UP AGAIN!

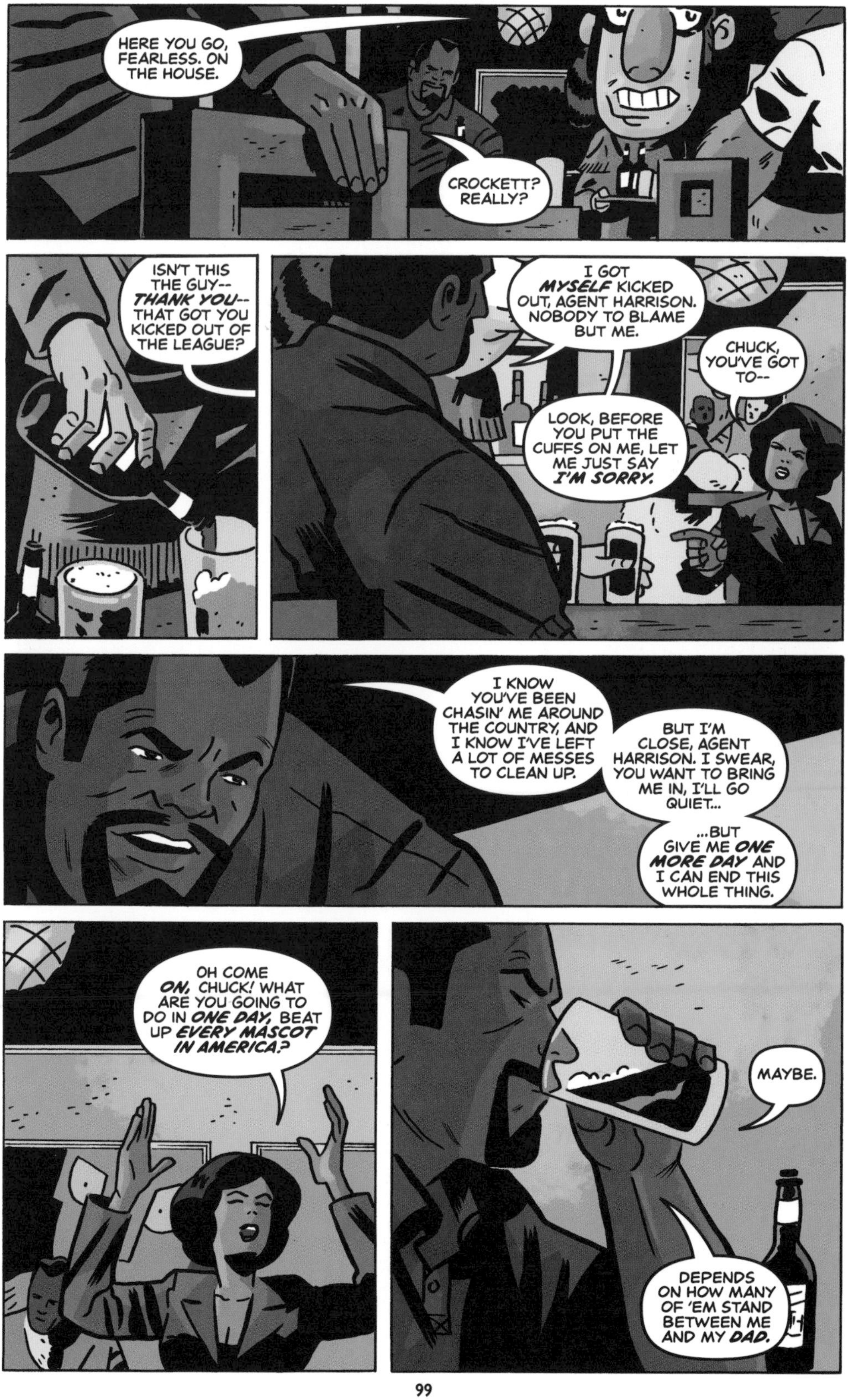
HERE YOU GO, FEARLESS. ON THE HOUSE.
CROCKETT? REALLY?
ISN'T THIS THE GUY-- THANK YOU-- THAT GOT YOU KICKED OUT OF THE LEAGUE?
I GOT MYSELF KICKED OUT, AGENT HARRISON. NOBODY TO BLAME BUT ME.
CHUCK, YOU'VE GOT TO--
LOOK, BEFORE YOU PUT THE CUFFS ON ME, LET ME JUST SAY I'M SORRY.
I KNOW YOU'VE BEEN CHASIN' ME AROUND THE COUNTRY, AND I KNOW I'VE LEFT A LOT OF MESSES TO CLEAN UP.
BUT I'M CLOSE, AGENT HARRISON. I SWEAR, YOU WANT TO BRING ME IN, I'LL GO QUIET...
...BUT GIVE ME ONE MORE DAY AND I CAN END THIS WHOLE THING.
OH COME ON, CHUCK! WHAT ARE YOU GOING TO DO IN ONE DAY, BEAT UP EVERY MASCOT IN AMERICA?
MAYBE.
DEPENDS ON HOW MANY OF 'EM STAND BETWEEN ME AND MY DAD.

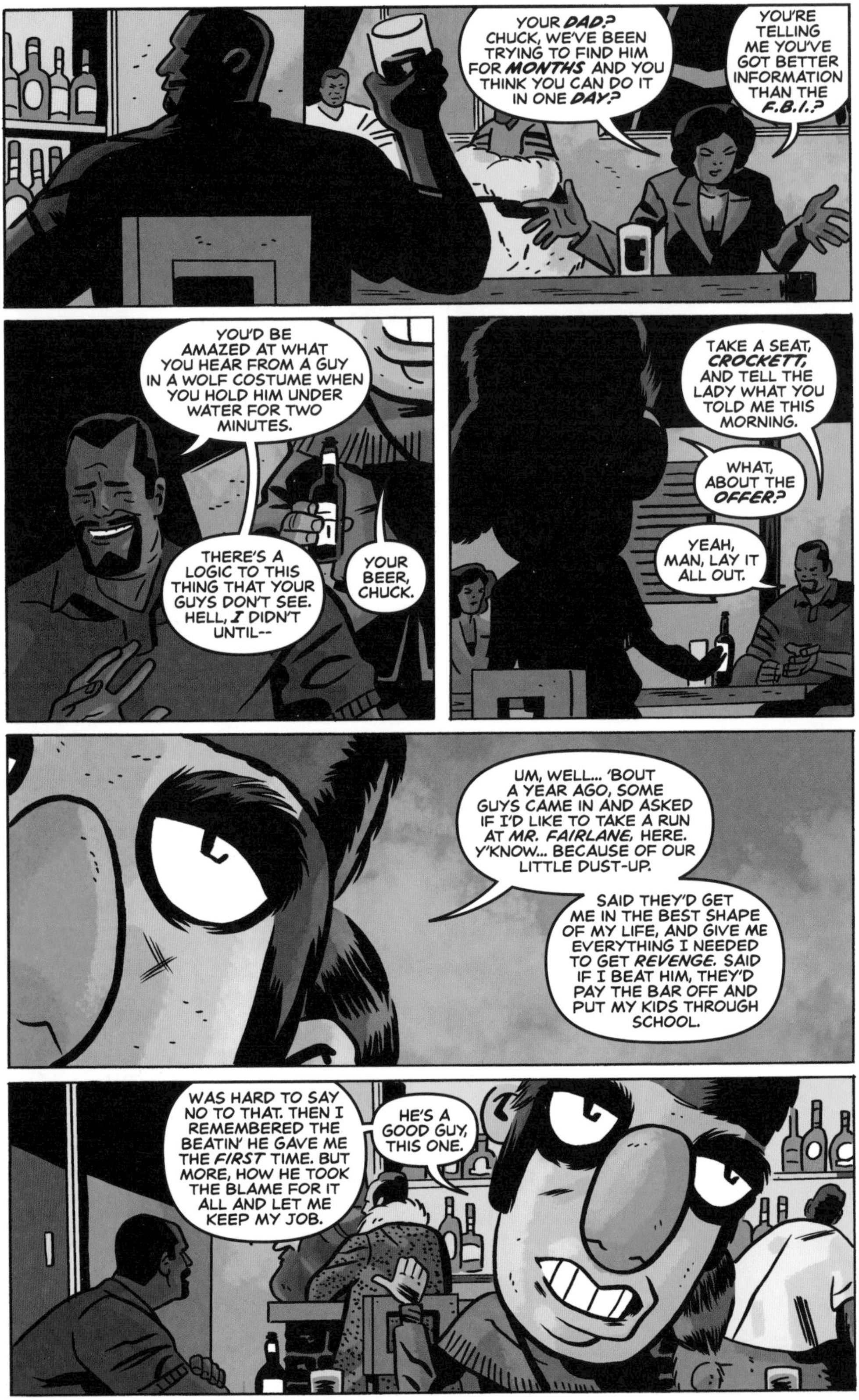
YOUR DAD? CHUCK, WE'VE BEEN TRYING TO FIND HIM FOR MONTHS AND YOU THINK YOU CAN DO IT IN ONE DAY?
YOU'RE TELLING ME YOU'VE GOT BETTER INFORMATION THAN THE F.B.I.?
YOU'D BE AMAZED AT WHAT YOU HEAR FROM A GUY IN A WOLF COSTUME WHEN YOU HOLD HIM UNDER WATER FOR TWO MINUTES.
THERE'S A LOGIC TO THIS THING THAT YOUR GUYS DON'T SEE. HELL, I DIDN'T UNTIL--
YOUR BEER, CHUCK.
TAKE A SEAT, CROCKETT, AND TELL THE LADY WHAT YOU TOLD ME THIS MORNING.
WHAT, ABOUT THE OFFER?
YEAH, MAN, LAY IT ALL OUT.
UM, WELL... 'BOUT A YEAR AGO, SOME GUYS CAME IN AND ASKED IF I'D LIKE TO TAKE A RUN AT MR. FAIRLANE, HERE. Y'KNOW... BECAUSE OF OUR LITTLE DUST-UP.
SAID THEY'D GET ME IN THE BEST SHAPE OF MY LIFE, AND GIVE ME EVERYTHING I NEEDED TO GET REVENGE. SAID IF I BEAT HIM, THEY'D PAY THE BAR OFF AND PUT MY KIDS THROUGH SCHOOL.
WAS HARD TO SAY NO TO THAT. THEN I REMEMBERED THE BEATIN' HE GAVE ME THE FIRST TIME. BUT MORE, HOW HE TOOK THE BLAME FOR IT ALL AND LET ME KEEP MY JOB.
HE'S A GOOD GUY, THIS ONE.

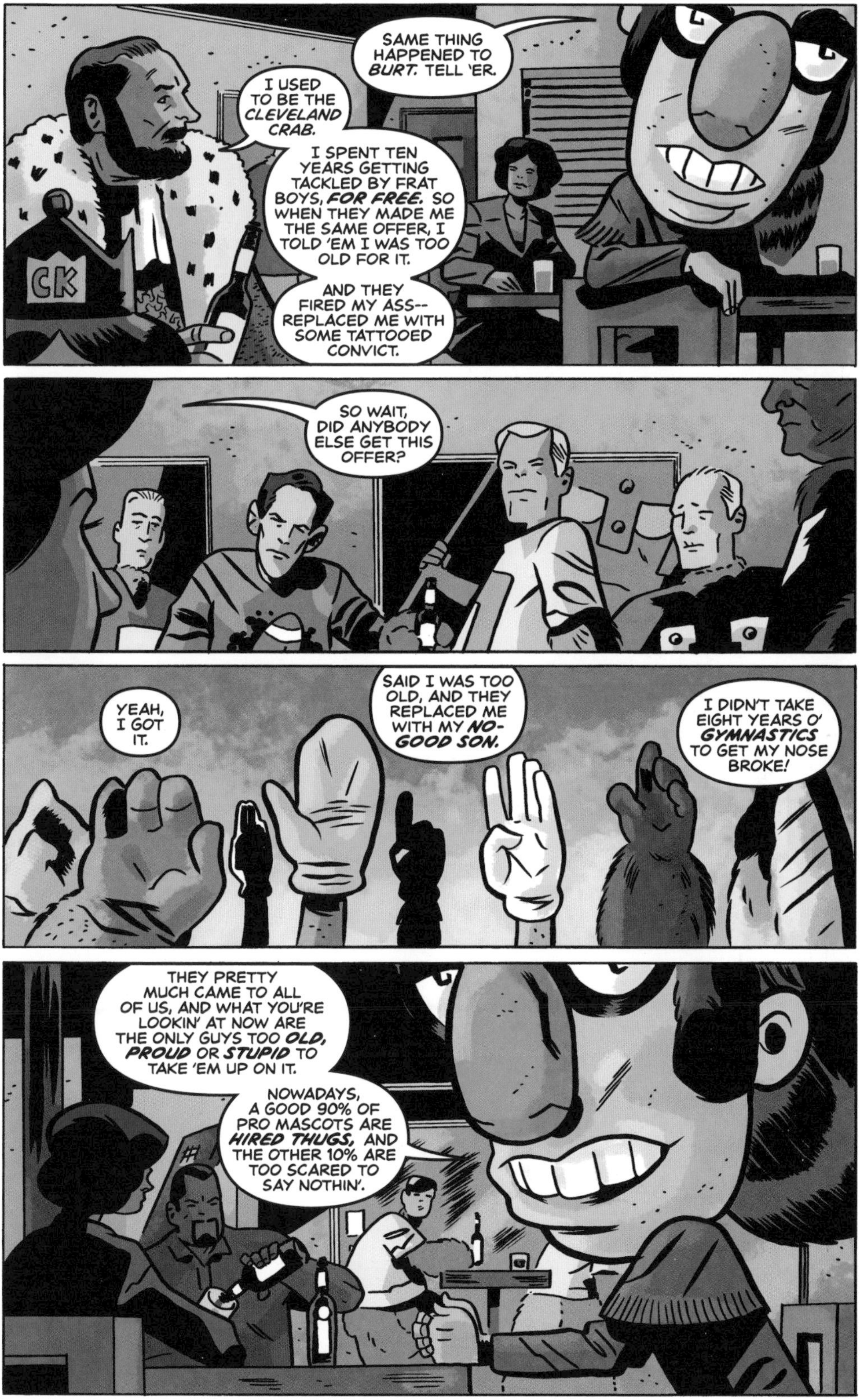
SAME THING HAPPENED TO BURT. TELL 'ER.
I USED TO BE THE CLEVELAND CRAB.
I SPENT TEN YEARS GETTING TACKLED BY FRAT BOYS, FOR FREE. SO WHEN THEY MADE ME THE SAME OFFER, I TOLD 'EM I WAS TOO OLD FOR IT.
AND THEY FIRED MY ASS-- REPLACED ME WITH SOME TATTOOED CONVICT.
CK
SO WAIT, DID ANYBODY ELSE GET THIS OFFER?
YEAH, I GOT IT.
SAID I WAS TOO OLD, AND THEY REPLACED ME WITH MY NO-GOOD SON.
I DIDN'T TAKE EIGHT YEARS O' GYMNASTICS TO GET MY NOSE BROKE!
THEY PRETTY MUCH CAME TO ALL OF US, AND WHAT YOU'RE LOOKIN' AT NOW ARE THE ONLY GUYS TOO OLD, PROUD OR STUPID TO TAKE 'EM UP ON IT.
NOWADAYS, A GOOD 90% OF PRO MASCOTS ARE HIRED THUGS, AND THE OTHER 10% ARE TOO SCARED TO SAY NOTHIN'.

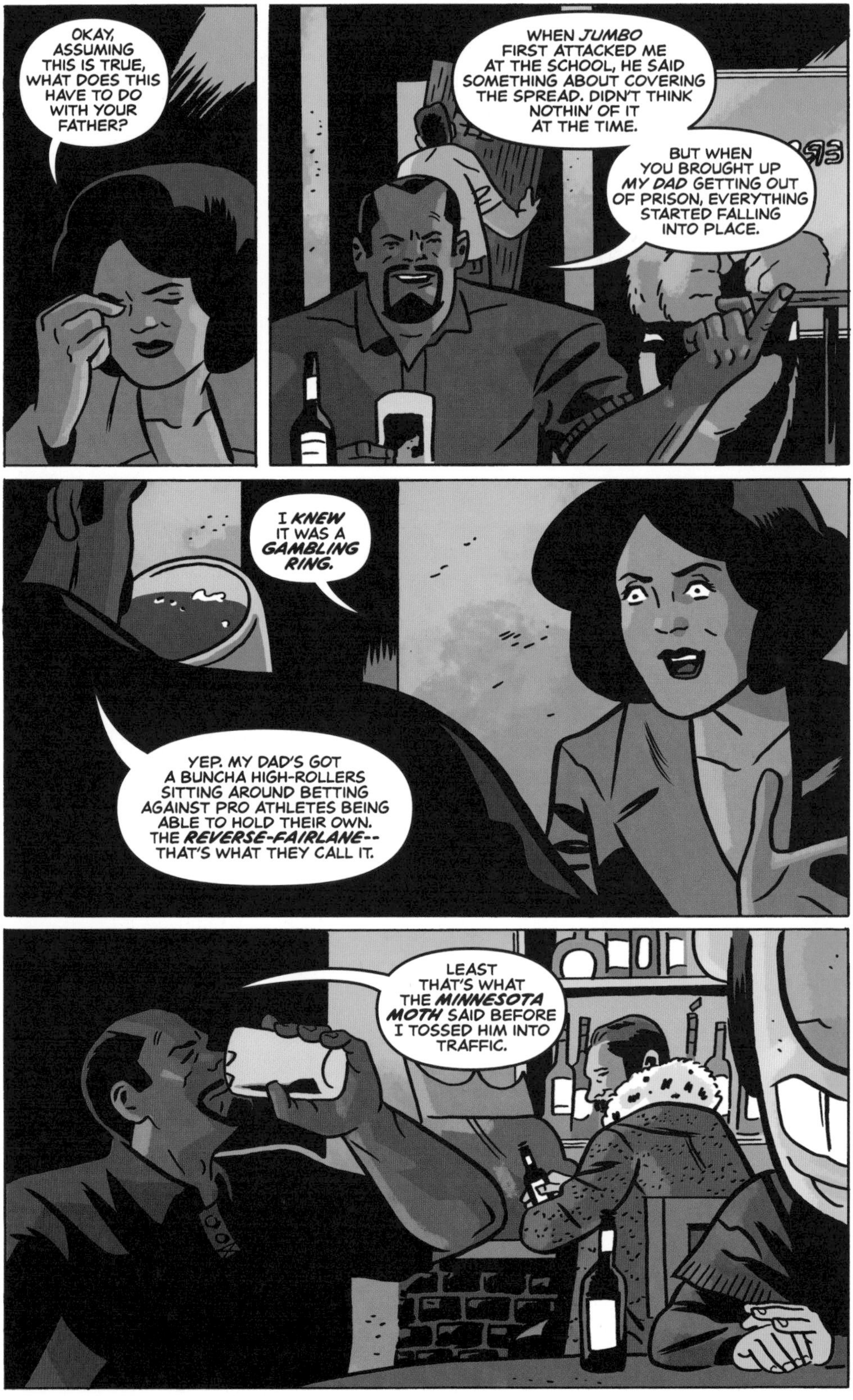
OKAY, ASSUMING THIS IS TRUE, WHAT DOES THIS HAVE TO DO WITH YOUR FATHER?
WHEN *JUMBO* FIRST ATTACKED ME AT THE SCHOOL, HE SAID SOMETHING ABOUT COVERING THE SPREAD. DIDN'T THINK NOTHIN' OF IT AT THE TIME.
BUT WHEN YOU BROUGHT UP *MY DAD* GETTING OUT OF PRISON, EVERYTHING STARTED FALLING INTO PLACE.
I ***KNEW*** IT WAS A ***GAMBLING RING.***
YEP. MY DAD'S GOT A BUNCHA HIGH-ROLLERS SITTING AROUND BETTING AGAINST PRO ATHLETES BEING ABLE TO HOLD THEIR OWN. THE ***REVERSE-FAIRLANE***-- THAT'S WHAT THEY CALL IT.
LEAST THAT'S WHAT THE ***MINNESOTA MOTH*** SAID BEFORE I TOSSED HIM INTO TRAFFIC.

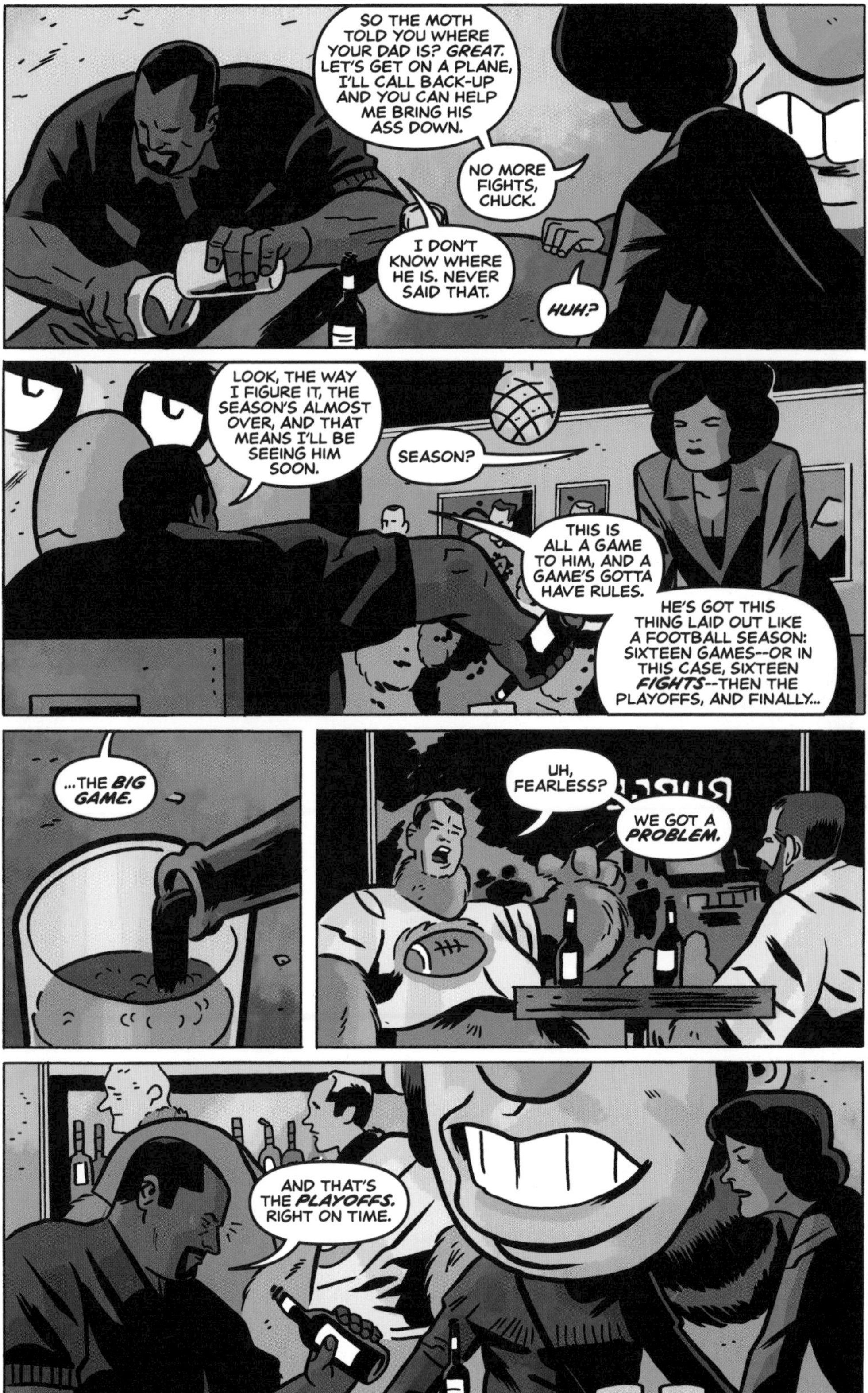
SO THE MOTH TOLD YOU WHERE YOUR DAD IS? GREAT. LET'S GET ON A PLANE, I'LL CALL BACK-UP AND YOU CAN HELP ME BRING HIS ASS DOWN.
NO MORE FIGHTS, CHUCK.
I DON'T KNOW WHERE HE IS. NEVER SAID THAT.
HUH?
LOOK, THE WAY I FIGURE IT, THE SEASON'S ALMOST OVER, AND THAT MEANS I'LL BE SEEING HIM SOON.
SEASON?
THIS IS ALL A GAME TO HIM, AND A GAME'S GOTTA HAVE RULES.
HE'S GOT THIS THING LAID OUT LIKE A FOOTBALL SEASON: SIXTEEN GAMES--OR IN THIS CASE, SIXTEEN FIGHTS--THEN THE PLAYOFFS, AND FINALLY...
...THE BIG GAME.
UH, FEARLESS?
WE GOT A PROBLEM.
AND THAT'S THE PLAYOFFS. RIGHT ON TIME.

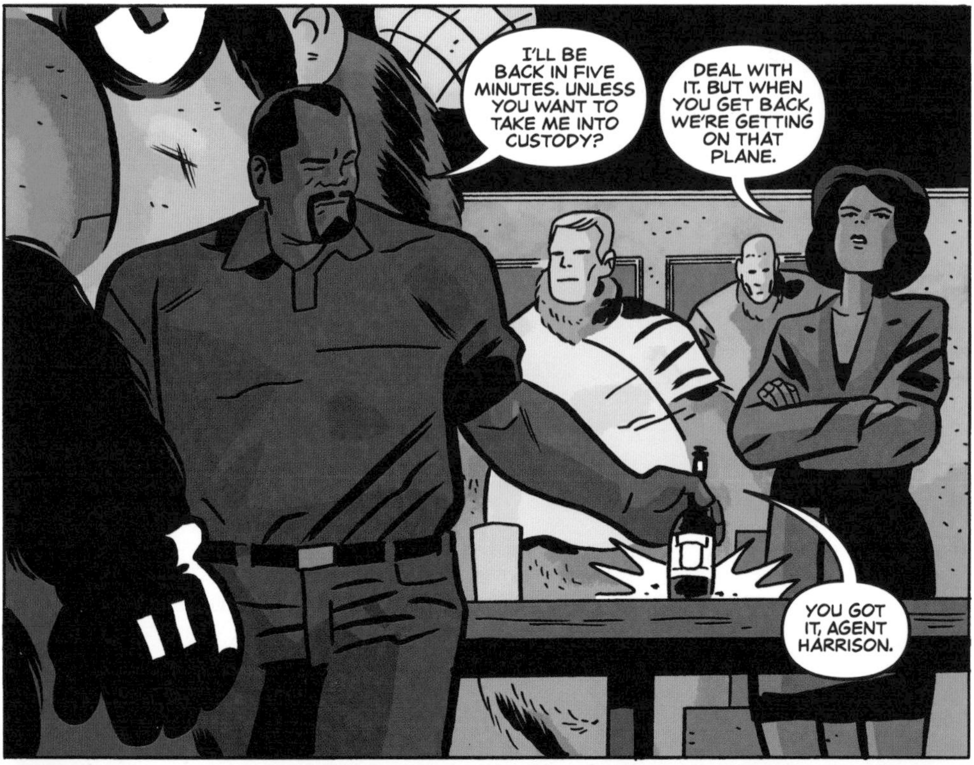
I'LL BE BACK IN FIVE MINUTES. UNLESS YOU WANT TO TAKE ME INTO CUSTODY?
DEAL WITH IT. BUT WHEN YOU GET BACK, WE'RE GETTING ON THAT PLANE.
YOU GOT IT, AGENT HARRISON.

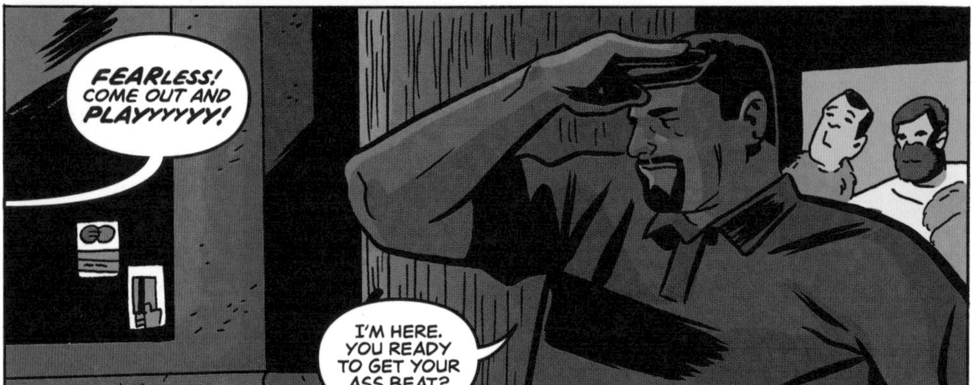
FEARLESS! COME OUT AND PLAYYYYYY!
I'M HERE. YOU READY TO GET YOUR ASS BEAT?

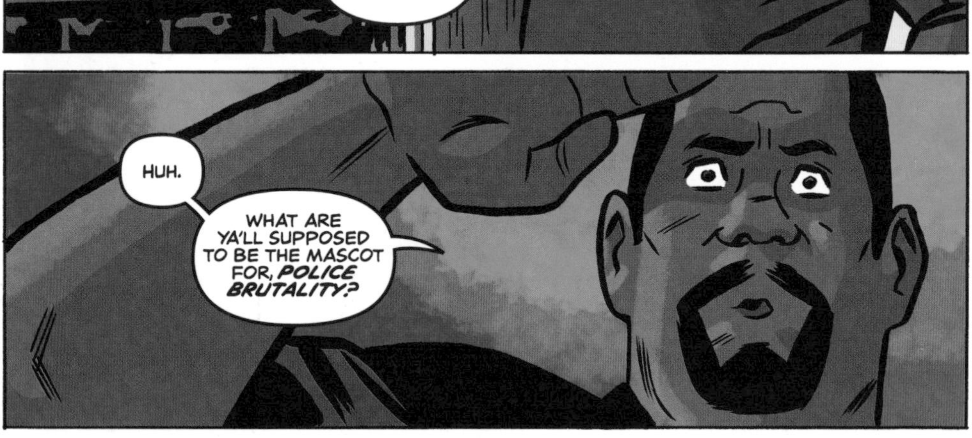
HUH.
WHAT ARE YA'LL SUPPOSED TO BE THE MASCOT FOR, POLICE BRUTALITY?

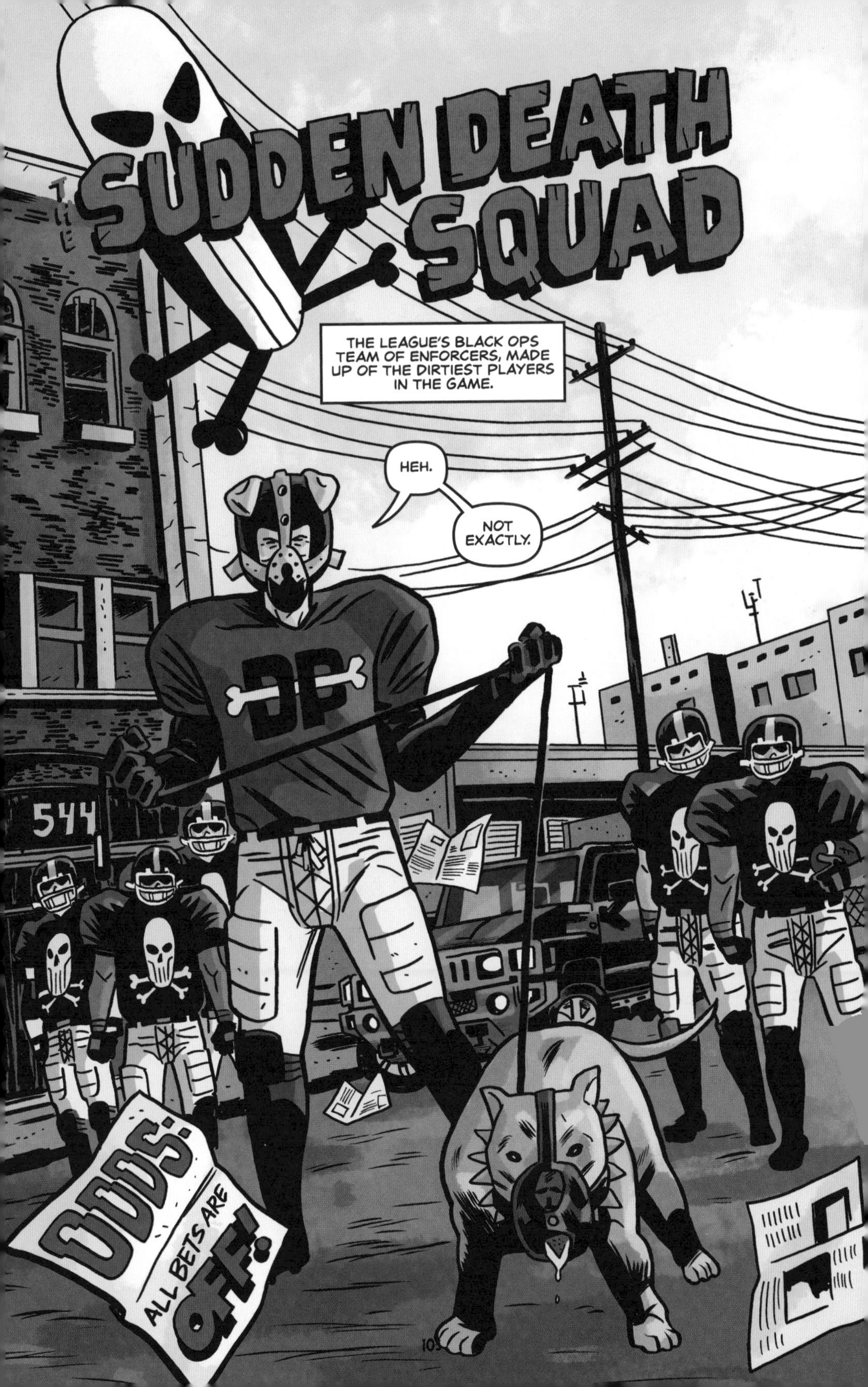
THE
SUDDEN DEATH
SQUAD
THE LEAGUE'S BLACK OPS TEAM OF ENFORCERS, MADE UP OF THE DIRTIEST PLAYERS IN THE GAME.
HEH.
NOT EXACTLY.
DP
544
ODDS:
ALL BETS ARE
OFF!

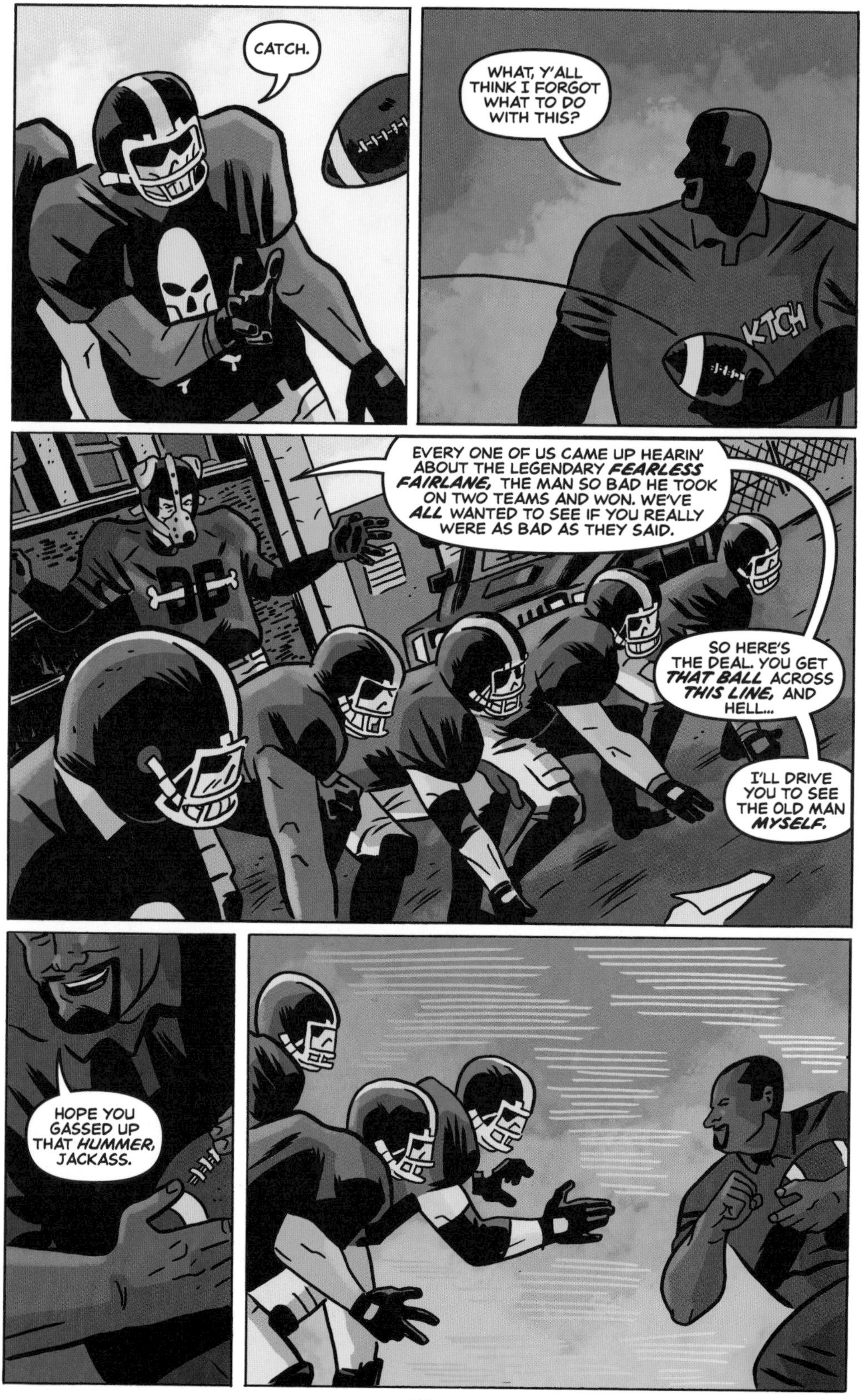
CATCH.
WHAT, Y'ALL THINK I FORGOT WHAT TO DO WITH THIS?
KTCH
EVERY ONE OF US CAME UP HEARIN' ABOUT THE LEGENDARY FEARLESS FAIRLANE, THE MAN SO BAD HE TOOK ON TWO TEAMS AND WON. WE'VE ALL WANTED TO SEE IF YOU REALLY WERE AS BAD AS THEY SAID.
SO HERE'S THE DEAL. YOU GET THAT BALL ACROSS THIS LINE, AND HELL...
I'LL DRIVE YOU TO SEE THE OLD MAN MYSELF.
HOPE YOU GASSED UP THAT HUMMER, JACKASS.

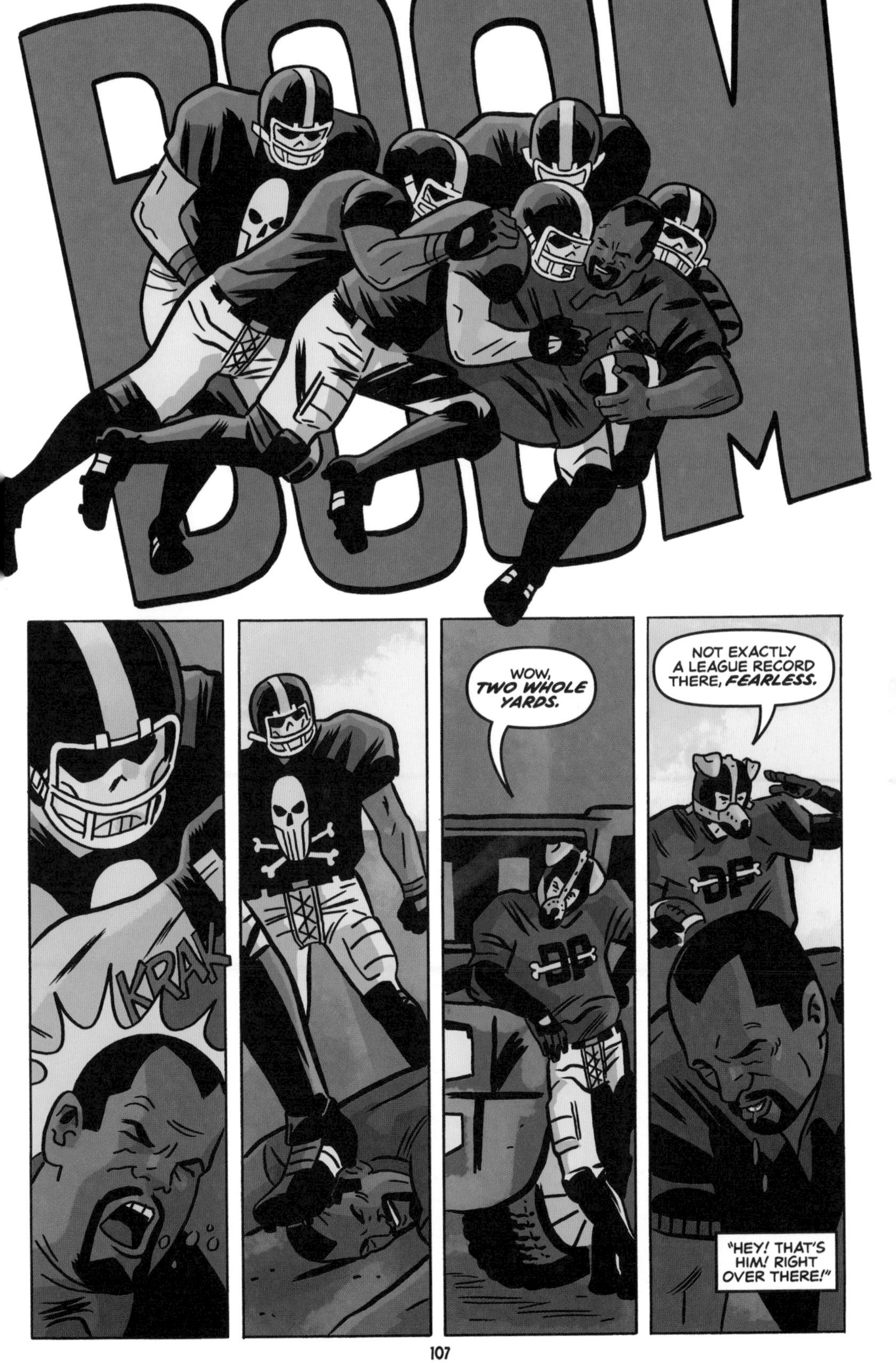
BOOM
KRAK
WOW, TWO WHOLE YARDS.
NOT EXACTLY A LEAGUE RECORD THERE, FEARLESS.
"HEY! THAT'S HIM! RIGHT OVER THERE!"

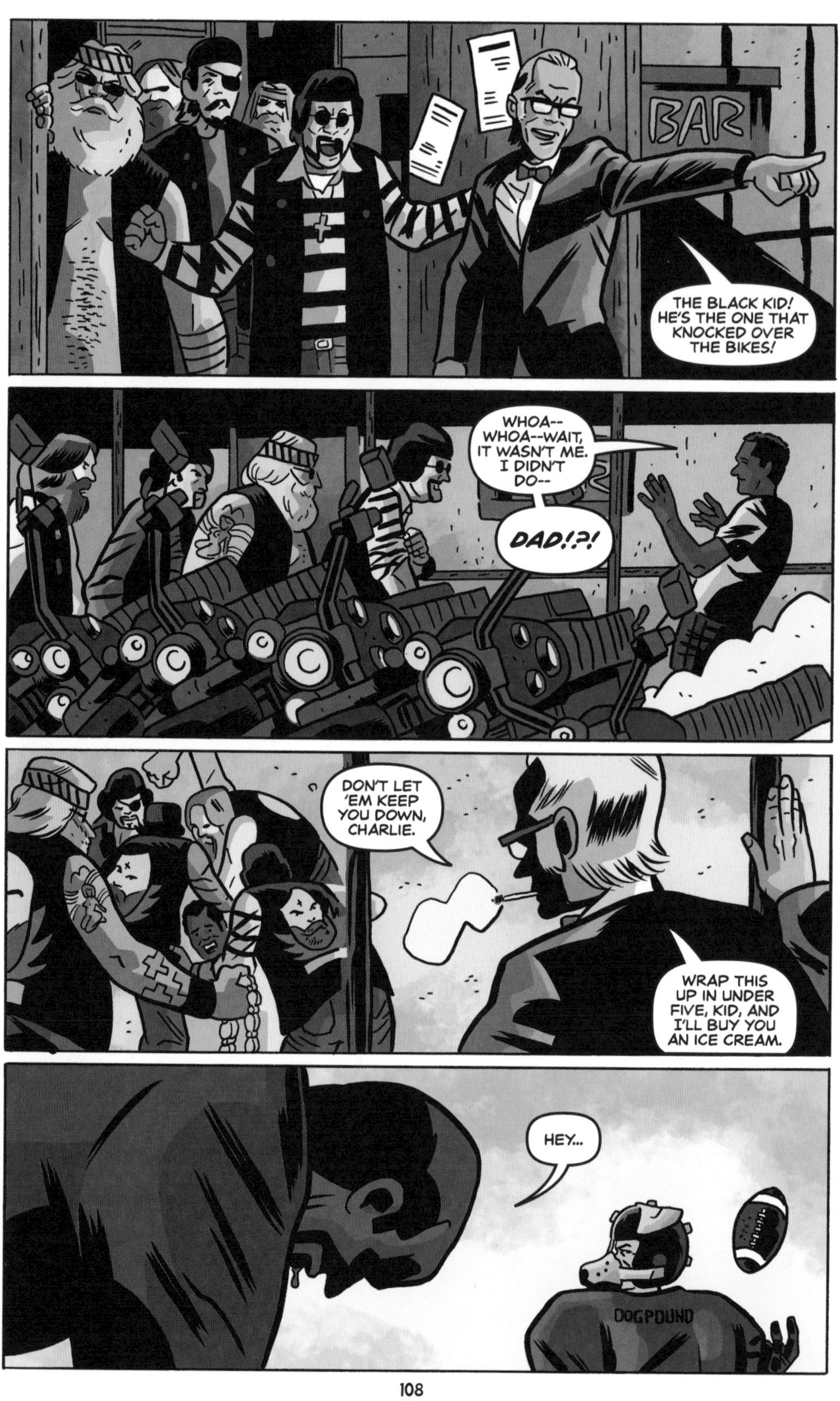
BAR
THE BLACK KID! HE'S THE ONE THAT KNOCKED OVER THE BIKES!
WHOA--WHOA--WAIT, IT WASN'T ME. I DIDN'T DO--
DAD!?!
DON'T LET 'EM KEEP YOU DOWN, CHARLIE.
WRAP THIS UP IN UNDER FIVE, KID, AND I'LL BUY YOU AN ICE CREAM.
HEY...
DOGPOUND

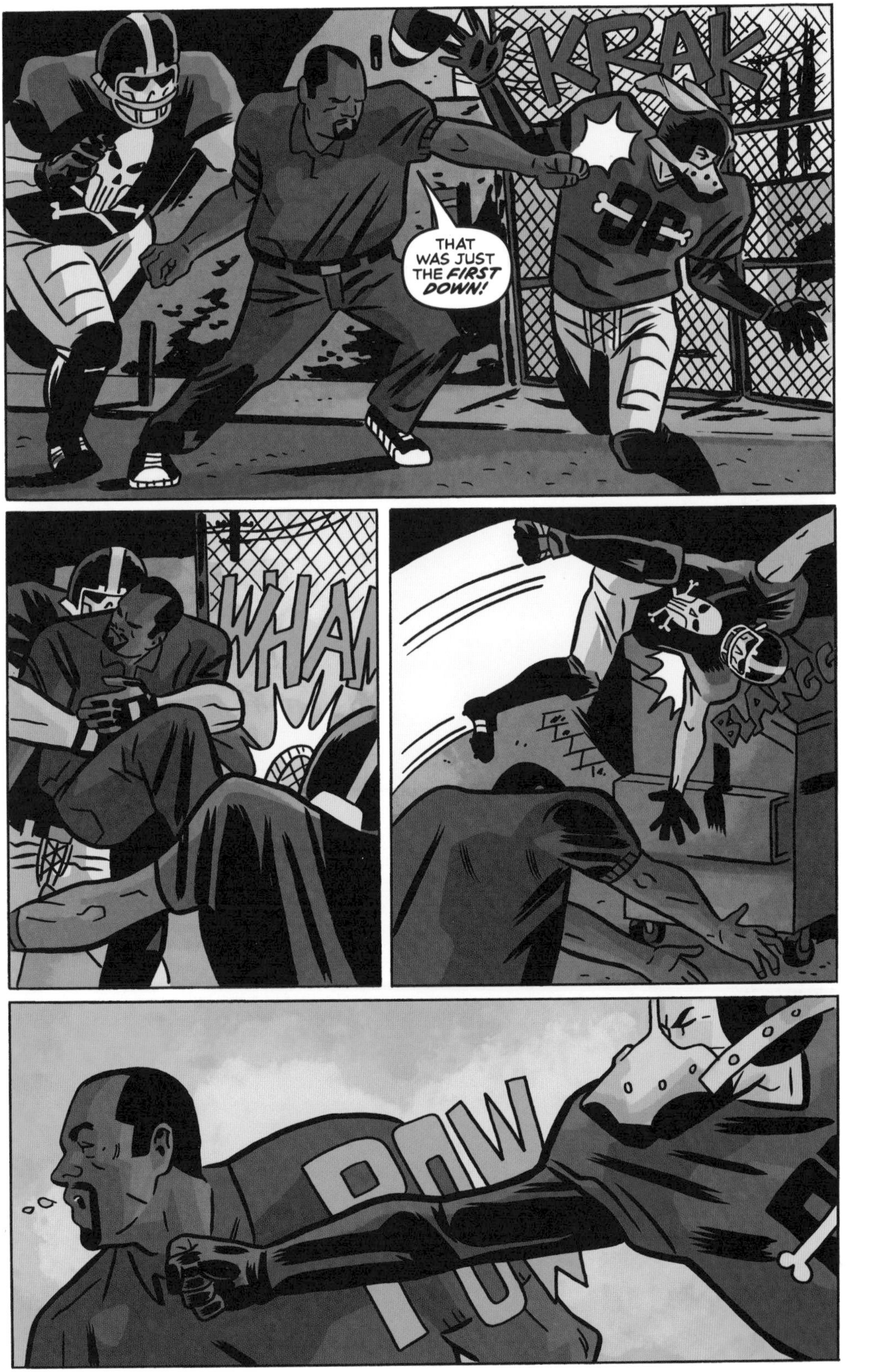
KRAK
THAT WAS JUST THE *FIRST DOWN!*
WHAM
POW

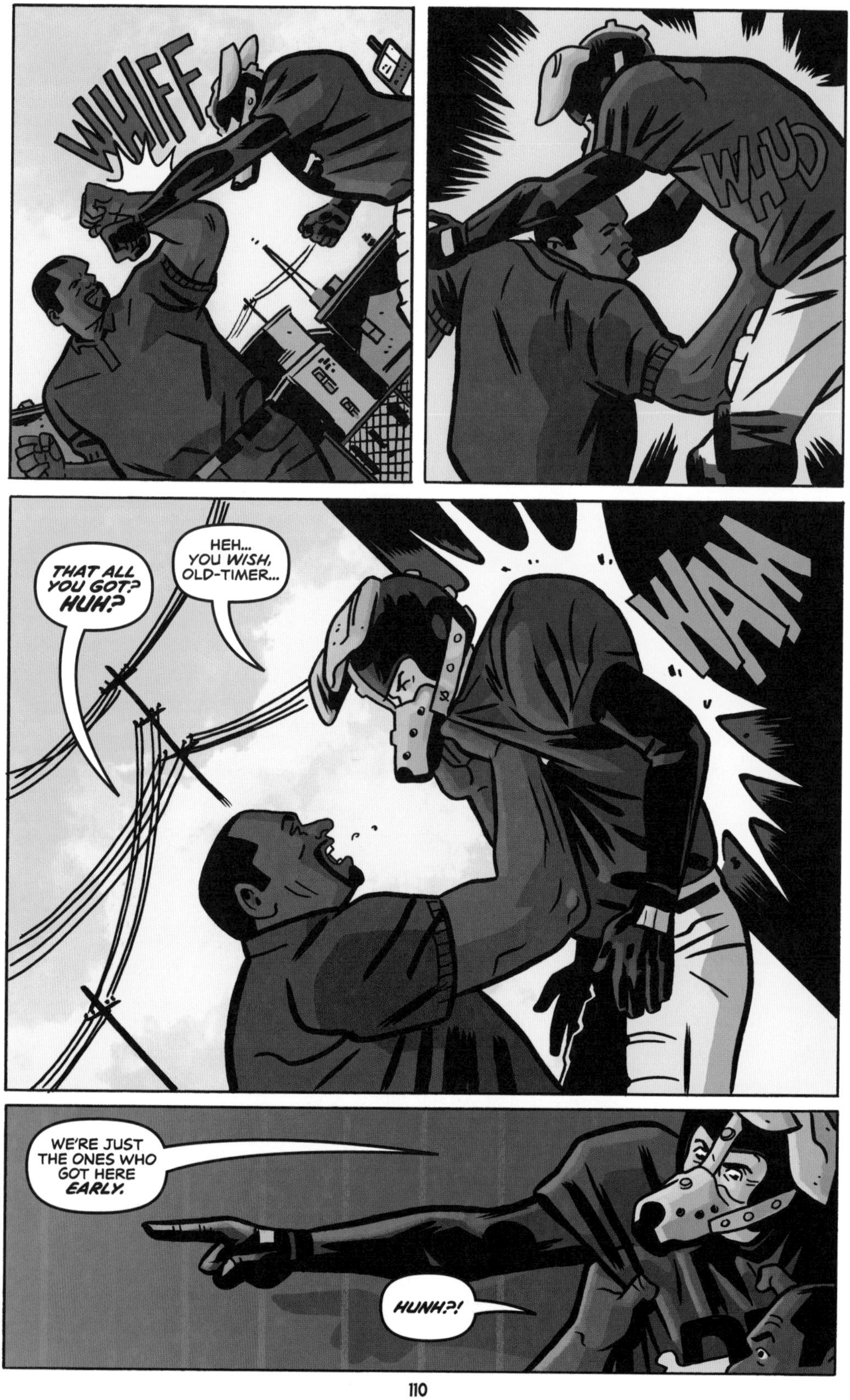
WHIFF
WHUD
HEH... YOU WISH, OLD-TIMER...
THAT ALL YOU GOT? HUH?
WHAM
WE'RE JUST THE ONES WHO GOT HERE EARLY.
HUNH?!

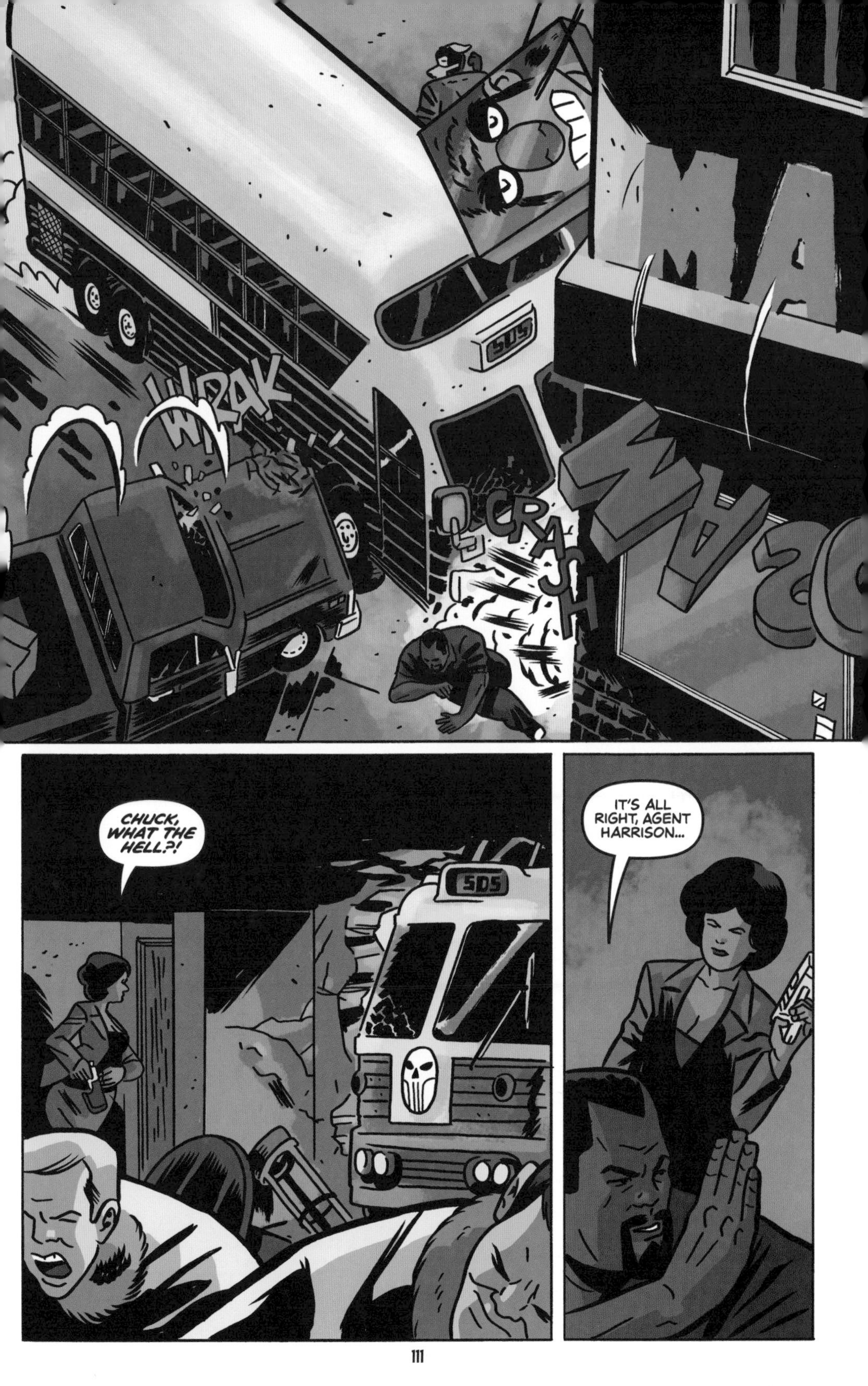
WRAK
CRASH
CHUCK, WHAT THE HELL?!
IT'S ALL RIGHT, AGENT HARRISON...

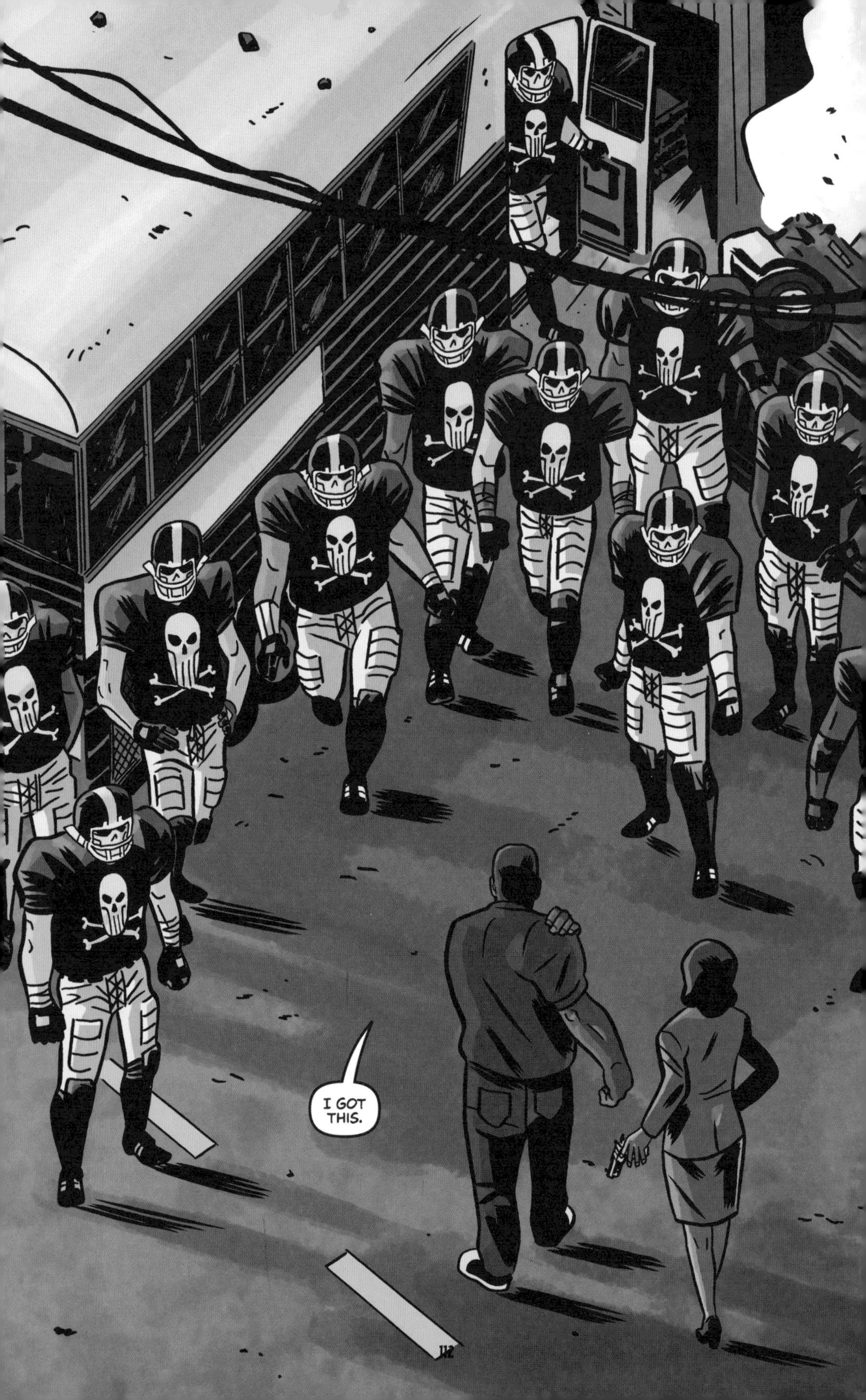
I GOT THIS.

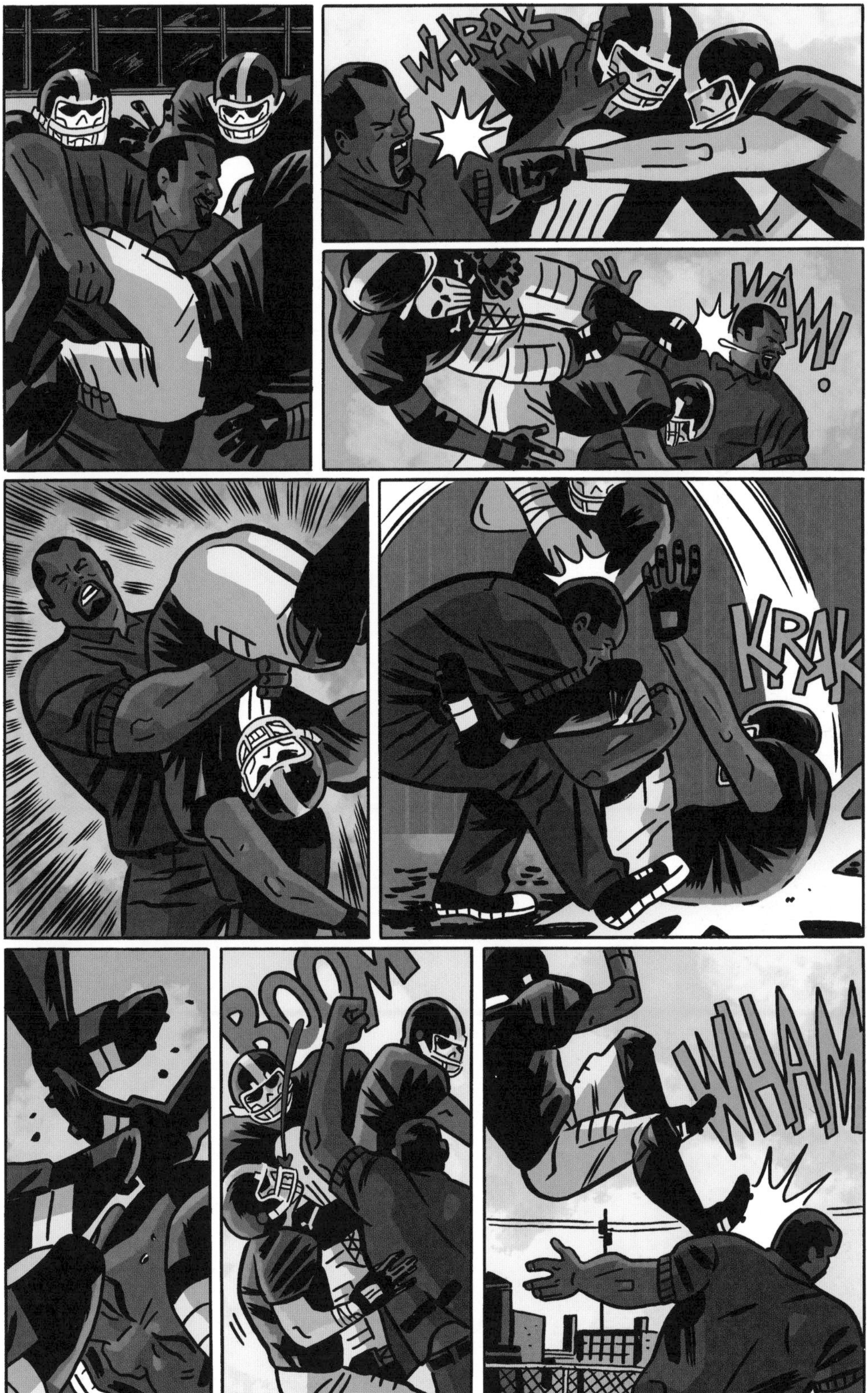
WHRAK
WAM!
KRAK
BOOM
WHAM

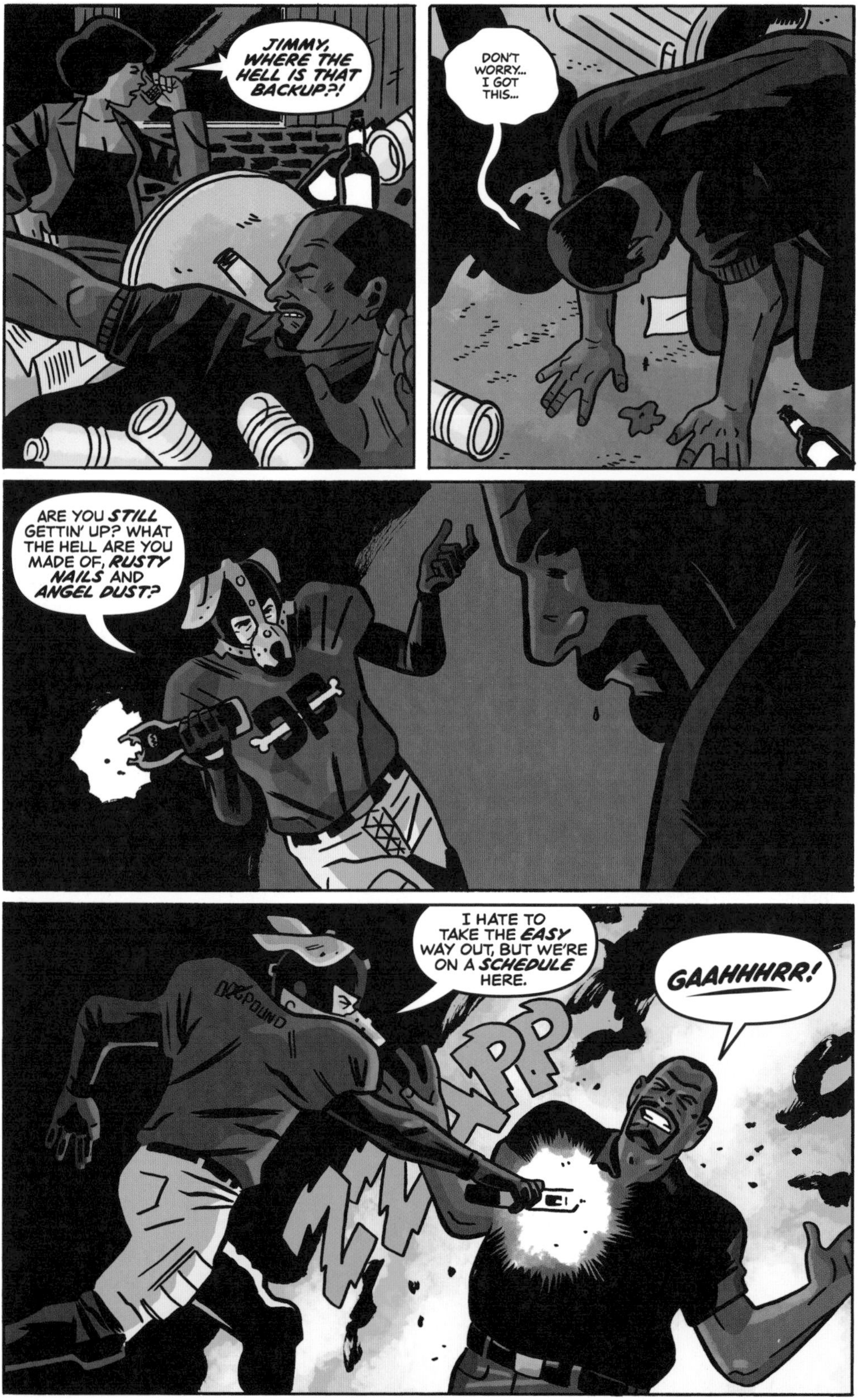
JIMMY, WHERE THE HELL IS THAT BACKUP?!
DON'T WORRY... I GOT THIS...
ARE YOU STILL GETTIN' UP? WHAT THE HELL ARE YOU MADE OF, RUSTY NAILS AND ANGEL DUST?
I HATE TO TAKE THE EASY WAY OUT, BUT WE'RE ON A SCHEDULE HERE.
GAAHHHRR!

HUH. BETTER GIVE HIM ANOTHER ONE JUST TO MAKE--

BANG!

FLAG ON THE PLAY, MORON.

FEDERAL AGENT. YOU'RE UNDER ARREST. NOW STEP AWAY OR THE NEXT ONE GOES THROUGH YOUR FACE.

FBI

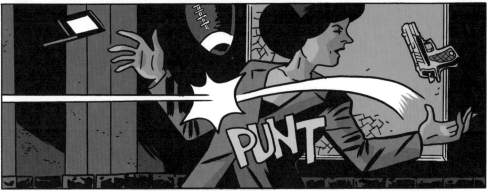

PUNT

GAME'S OVER, BABY. OUR TEAM DON'T NEED NO CHEERLEADERS.

NEVER WAS MUCH OF A CHEERLEADER...

...BUT I MADE ONE *HELLUVA* MAJORETTE.

POP

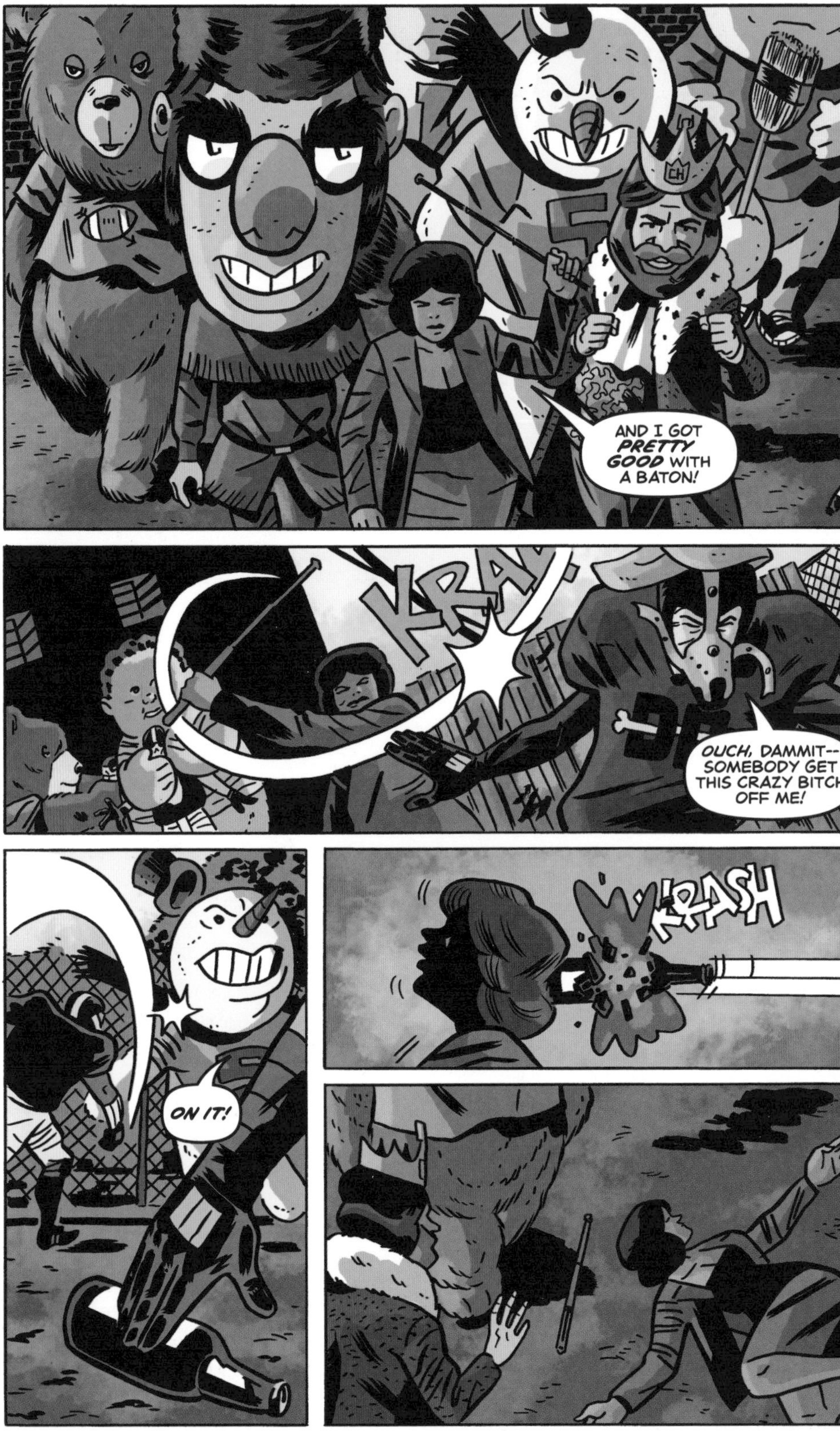
AND I GOT PRETTY GOOD WITH A BATON!
KRASH
OUCH, DAMMIT-- SOMEBODY GET THIS CRAZY BITCH OFF ME!
ON IT!
KRASH

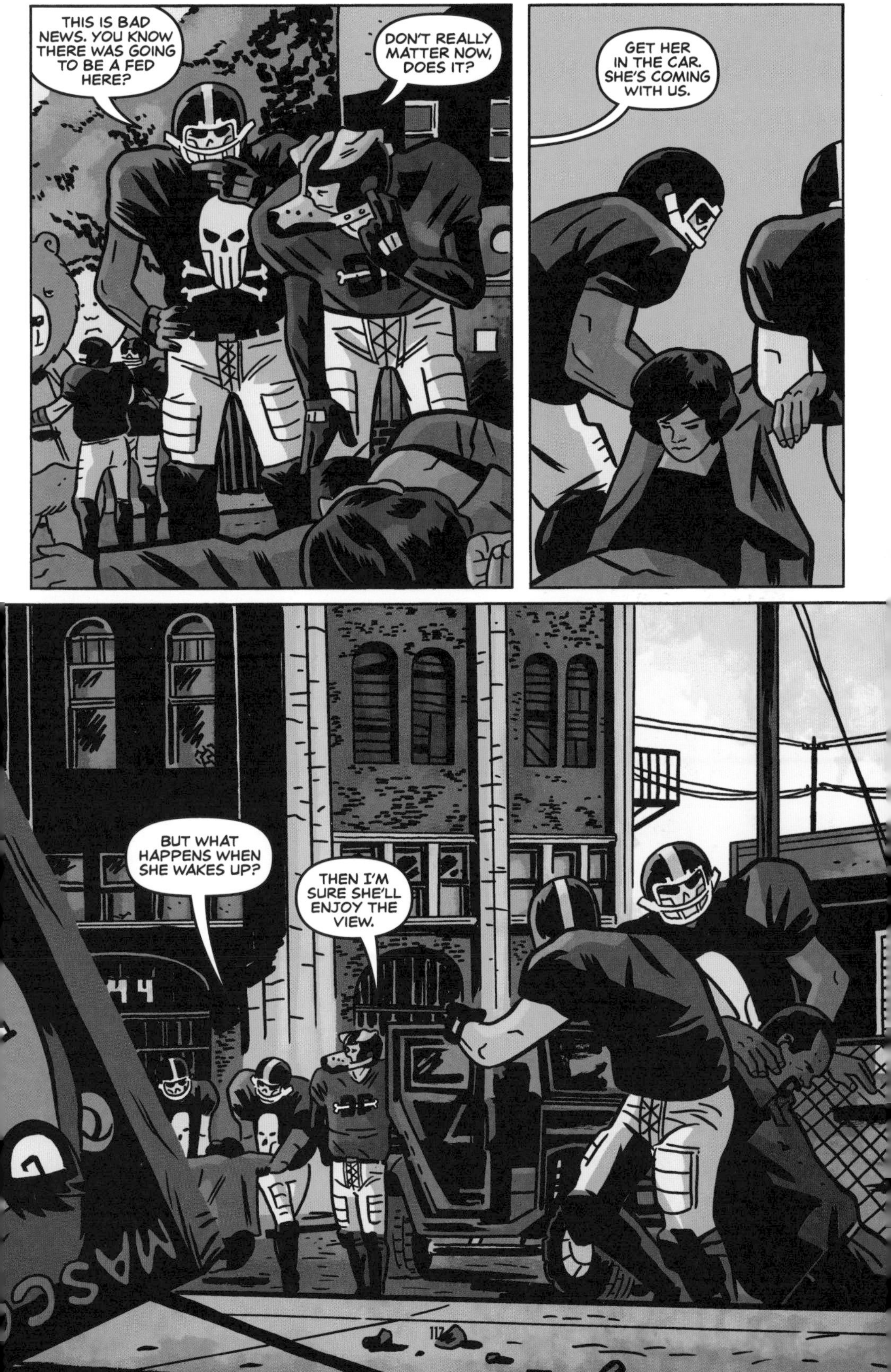
THIS IS BAD NEWS. YOU KNOW THERE WAS GOING TO BE A FED HERE?
DON'T REALLY MATTER NOW, DOES IT?
GET HER IN THE CAR. SHE'S COMING WITH US.
BUT WHAT HAPPENS WHEN SHE WAKES UP?
THEN I'M SURE SHE'LL ENJOY THE VIEW.

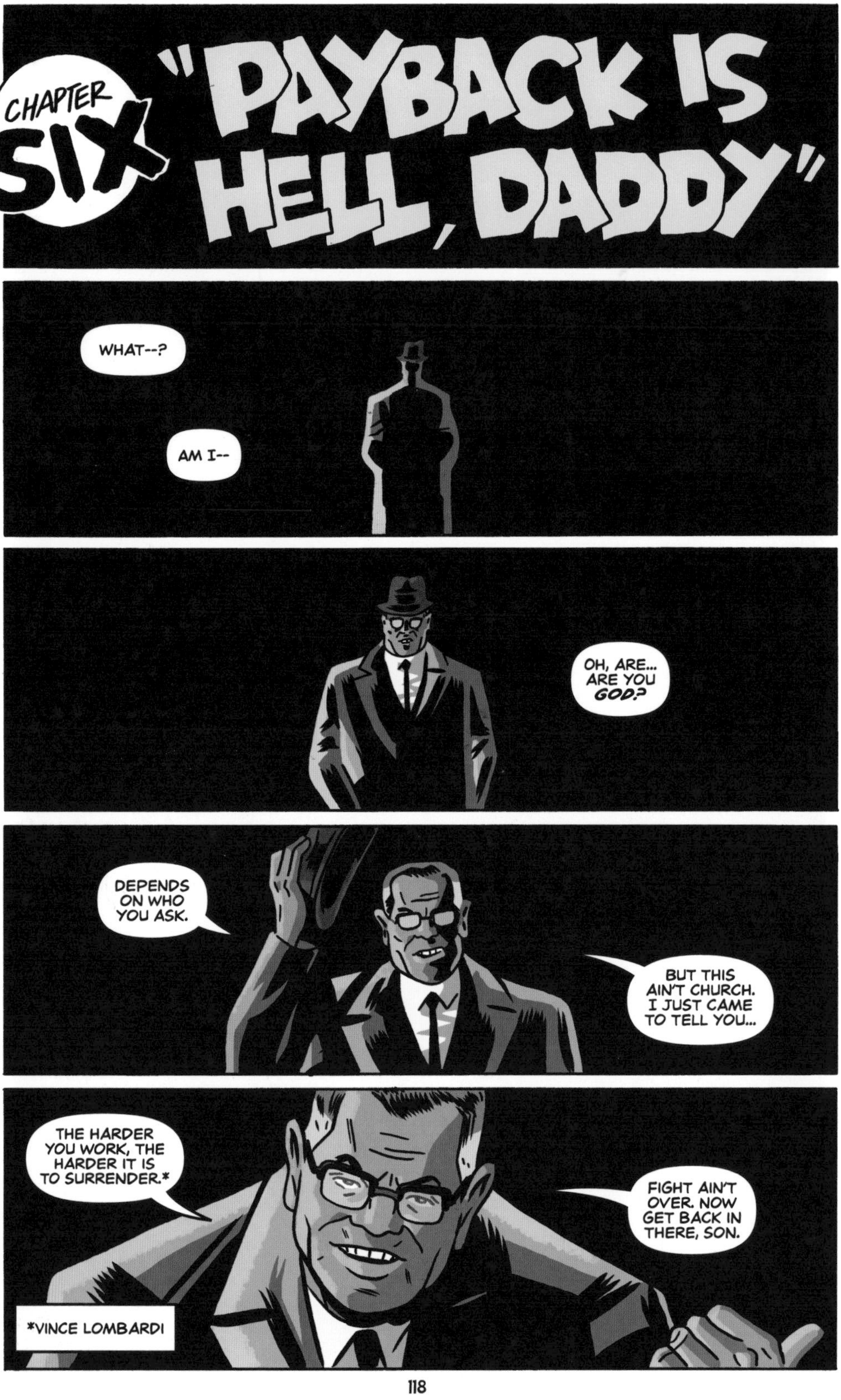
CHAPTER SIX
"PAYBACK IS HELL, DADDY"
WHAT--?
AM I--
OH, ARE... ARE YOU GOD?
DEPENDS ON WHO YOU ASK.
BUT THIS AIN'T CHURCH. I JUST CAME TO TELL YOU...
THE HARDER YOU WORK, THE HARDER IT IS TO SURRENDER.*
FIGHT AIN'T OVER. NOW GET BACK IN THERE, SON.
*VINCE LOMBARDI

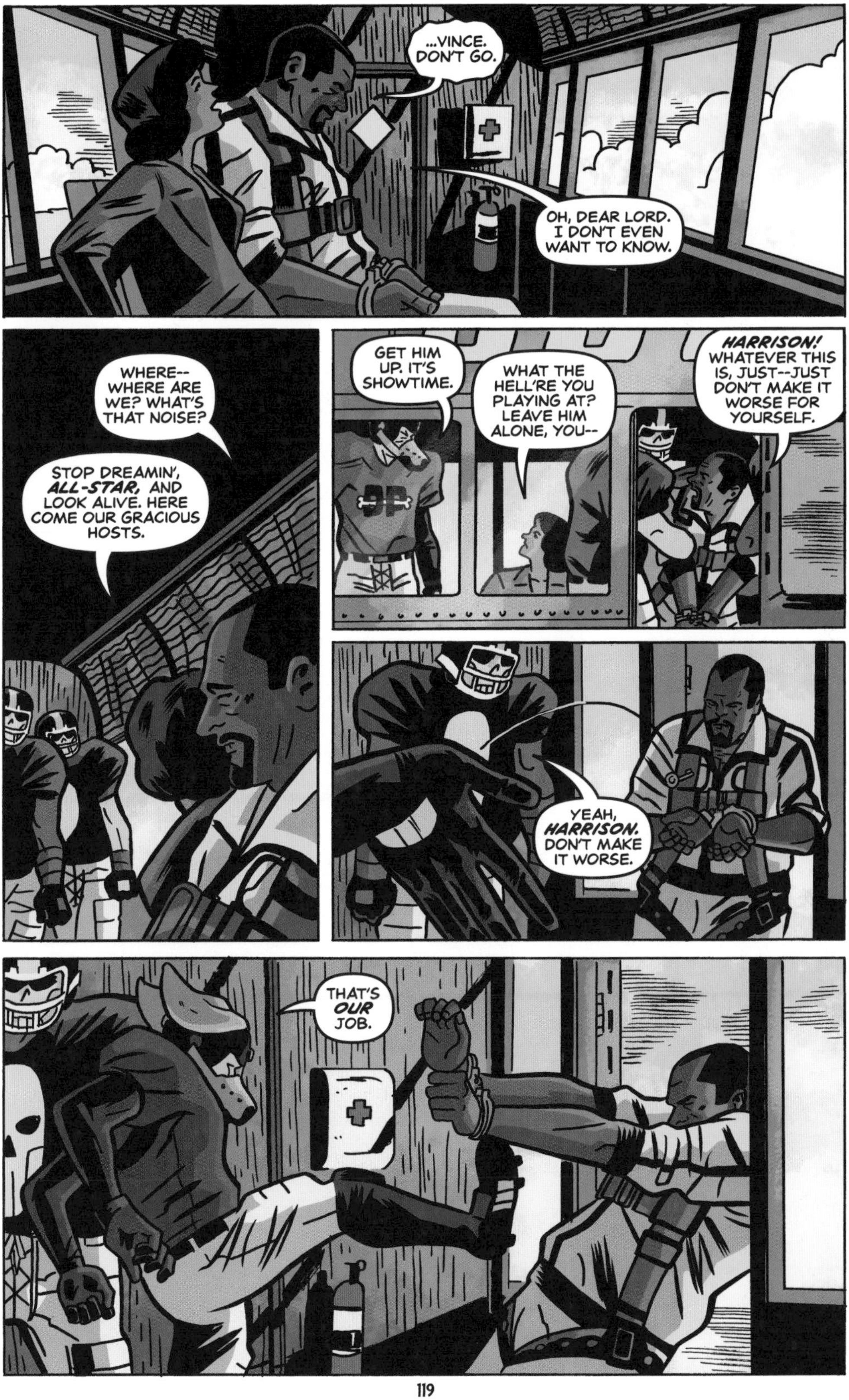
...VINCE. DON'T GO.
OH, DEAR LORD. I DON'T EVEN WANT TO KNOW.
WHERE-- WHERE ARE WE? WHAT'S THAT NOISE?
STOP DREAMIN', ALL-STAR, AND LOOK ALIVE. HERE COME OUR GRACIOUS HOSTS.
GET HIM UP. IT'S SHOWTIME.
WHAT THE HELL'RE YOU PLAYING AT? LEAVE HIM ALONE, YOU--
HARRISON! WHATEVER THIS IS, JUST--JUST DON'T MAKE IT WORSE FOR YOURSELF.
YEAH, HARRISON. DON'T MAKE IT WORSE.
THAT'S OUR JOB.

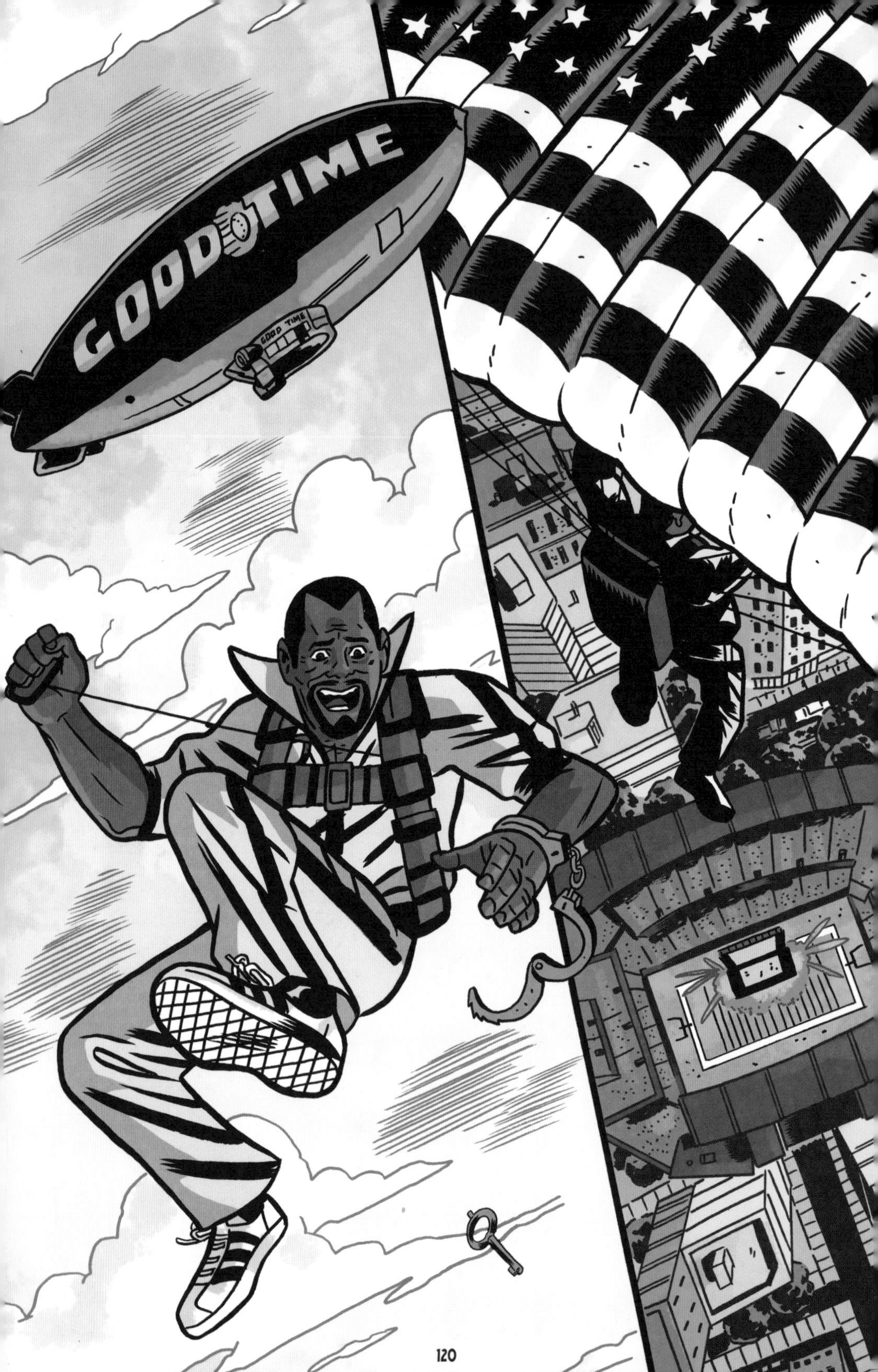
GOOD TIME
GOOD TIME

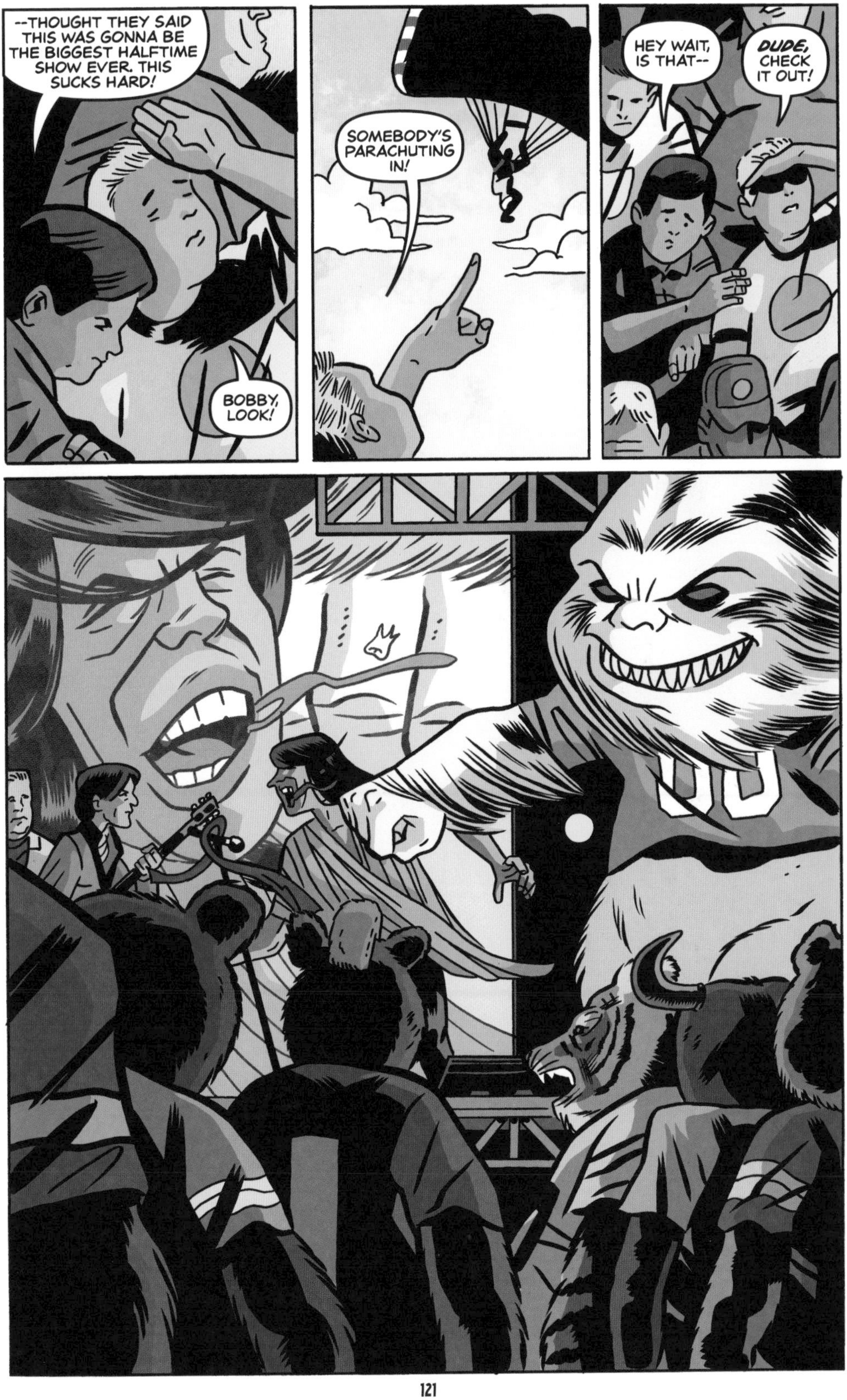
--THOUGHT THEY SAID THIS WAS GONNA BE THE BIGGEST HALFTIME SHOW EVER. THIS SUCKS HARD!
BOBBY, LOOK!
SOMEBODY'S PARACHUTING IN!
HEY WAIT, IS THAT--
DUDE, CHECK IT OUT!

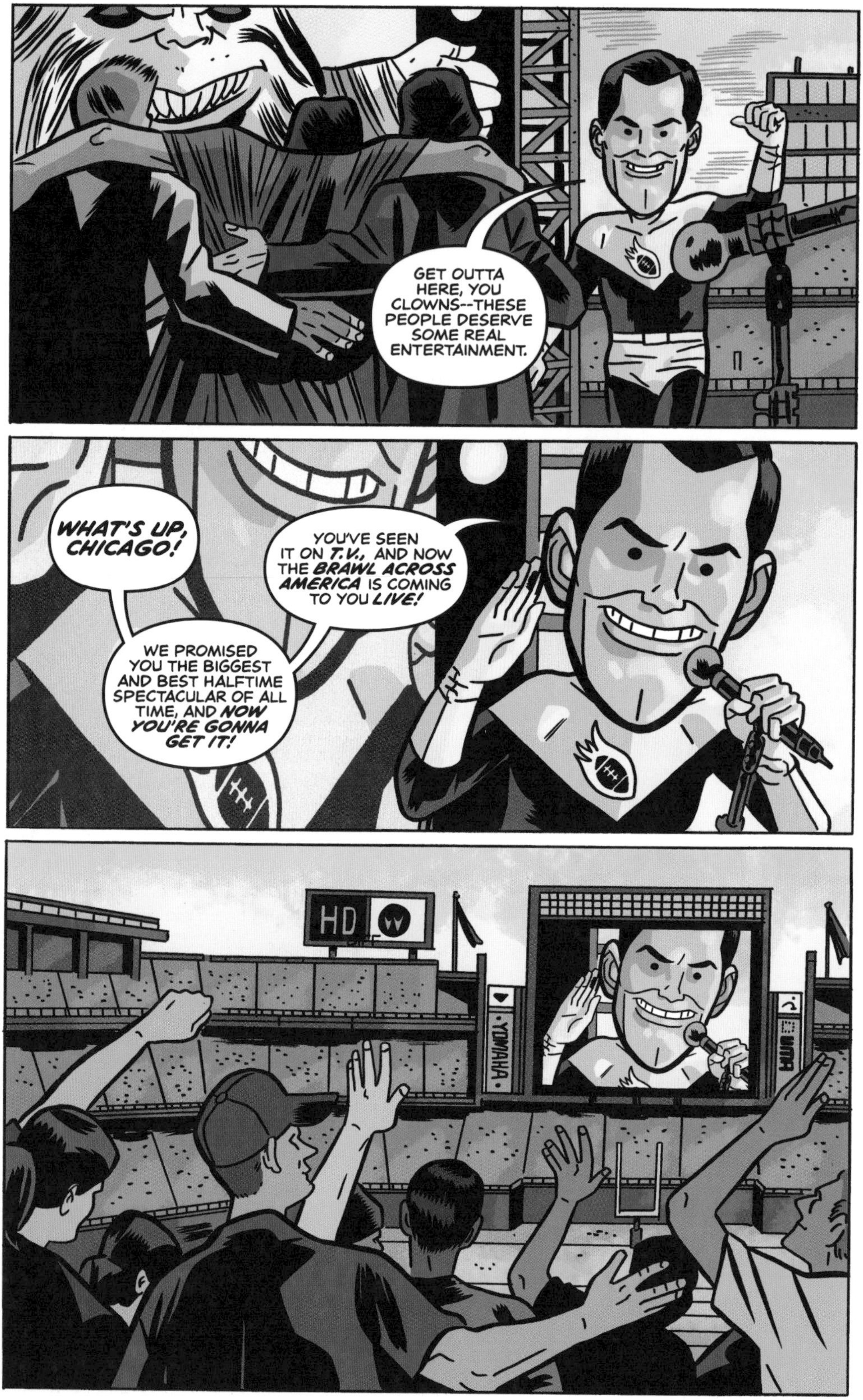
GET OUTTA HERE, YOU CLOWNS--THESE PEOPLE DESERVE SOME REAL ENTERTAINMENT.
WHAT'S UP, CHICAGO!
WE PROMISED YOU THE BIGGEST AND BEST HALFTIME SPECTACULAR OF ALL TIME, AND NOW YOU'RE GONNA GET IT!
YOU'VE SEEN IT ON T.V., AND NOW THE BRAWL ACROSS AMERICA IS COMING TO YOU LIVE!
HD
YAMAHA

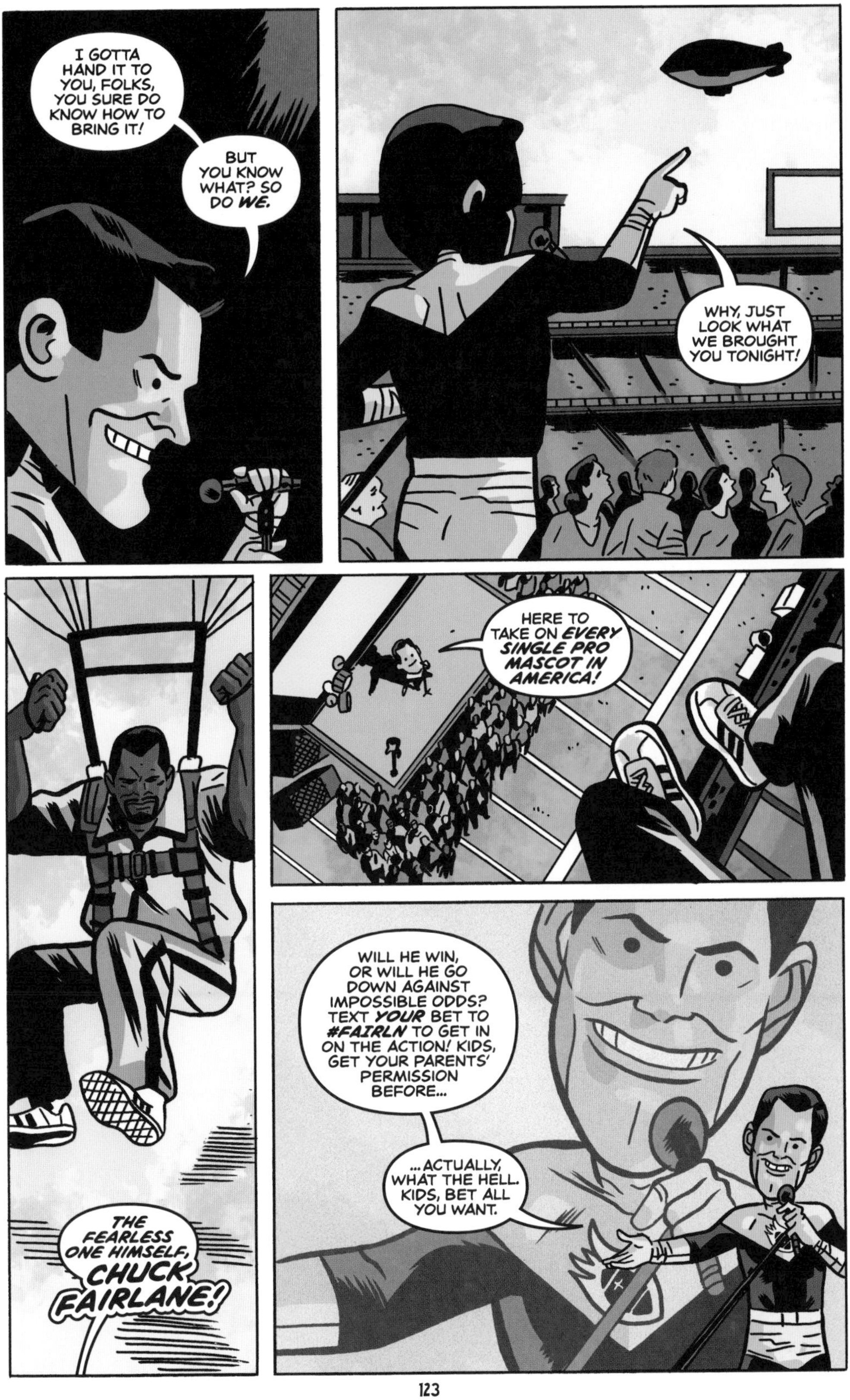
I GOTTA HAND IT TO YOU, FOLKS, YOU SURE DO KNOW HOW TO BRING IT!
BUT YOU KNOW WHAT? SO DO WE.
WHY, JUST LOOK WHAT WE BROUGHT YOU TONIGHT!
THE FEARLESS ONE HIMSELF, CHUCK FAIRLANE!
HERE TO TAKE ON EVERY SINGLE PRO MASCOT IN AMERICA!
WILL HE WIN, OR WILL HE GO DOWN AGAINST IMPOSSIBLE ODDS? TEXT YOUR BET TO #FAIRLN TO GET IN ON THE ACTION! KIDS, GET YOUR PARENTS' PERMISSION BEFORE...
...ACTUALLY, WHAT THE HELL. KIDS, BET ALL YOU WANT.

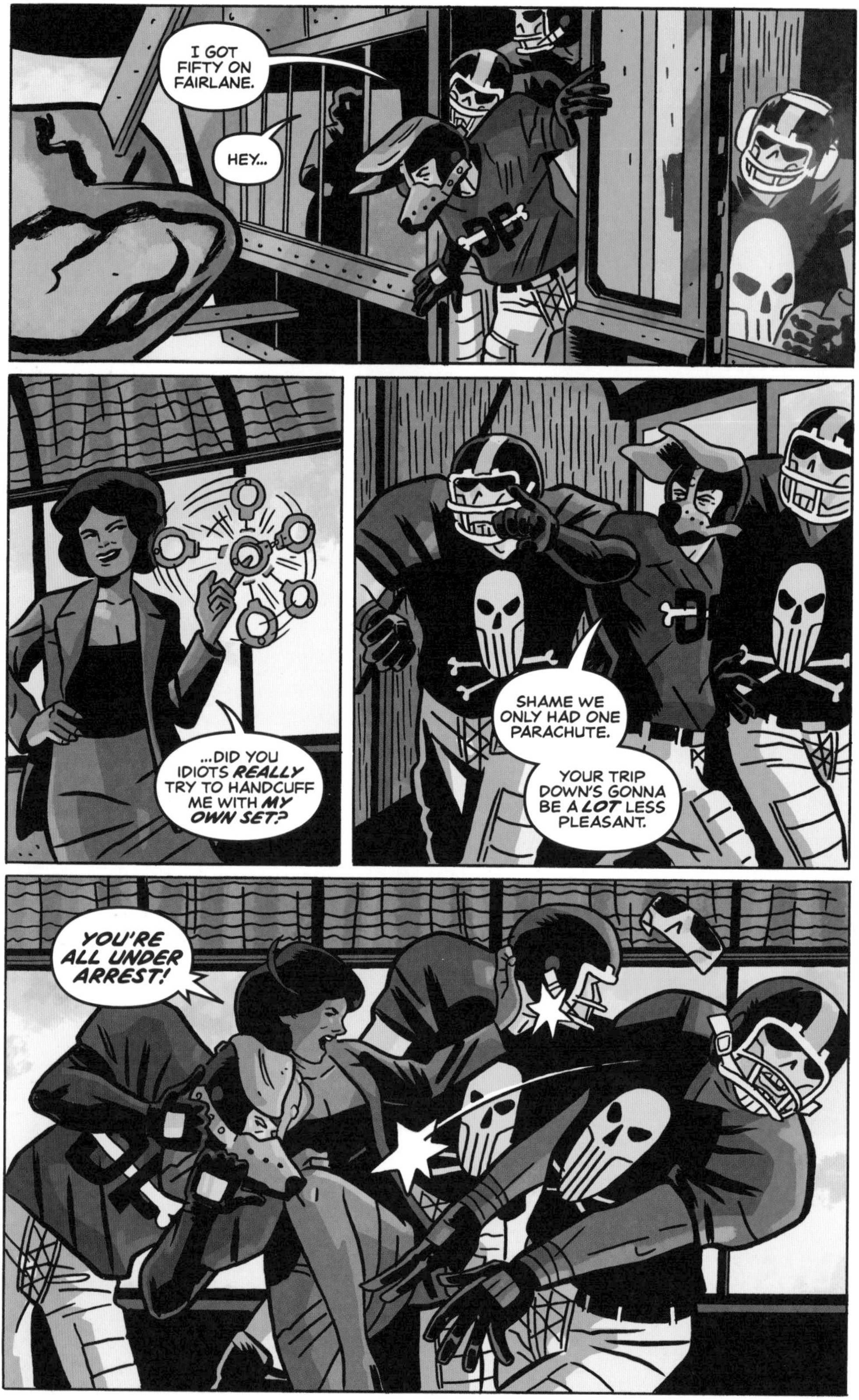
I GOT FIFTY ON FAIRLANE.
HEY...
...DID YOU IDIOTS *REALLY* TRY TO HANDCUFF ME WITH *MY OWN SET?*
SHAME WE ONLY HAD ONE PARACHUTE.
YOUR TRIP DOWN'S GONNA BE A *LOT* LESS PLEASANT.
YOU'RE ALL UNDER ARREST!

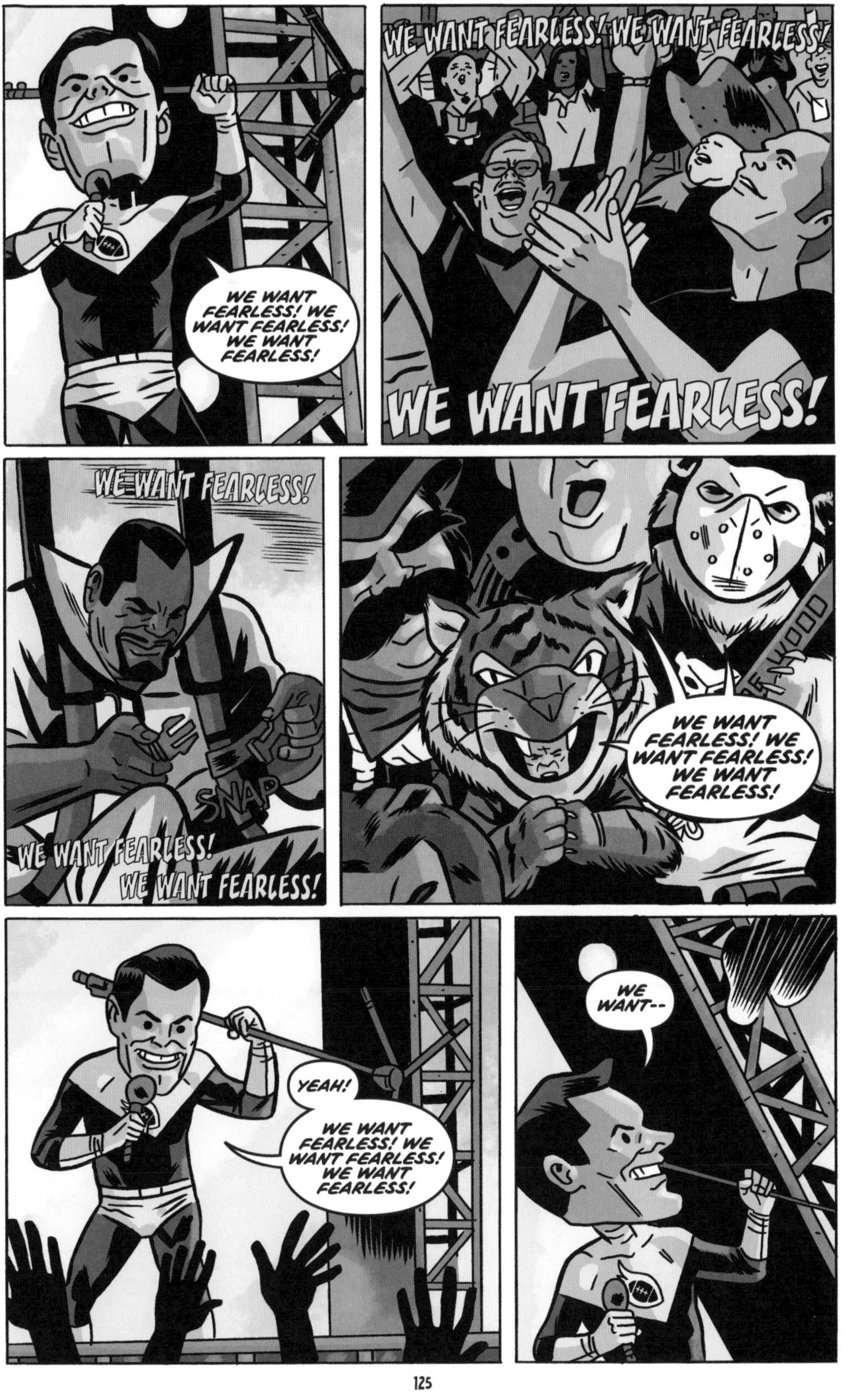
WE WANT FEARLESS! WE WANT FEARLESS! WE WANT FEARLESS!
WE WANT FEARLESS! WE WANT FEARLESS!
WE WANT FEARLESS!
WE WANT FEARLESS!
SNAP
WE WANT FEARLESS!
WE WANT FEARLESS!
WE WANT FEARLESS! WE WANT FEARLESS! WE WANT FEARLESS!
YEAH!
WE WANT FEARLESS! WE WANT FEARLESS! WE WANT FEARLESS!
WE WANT--

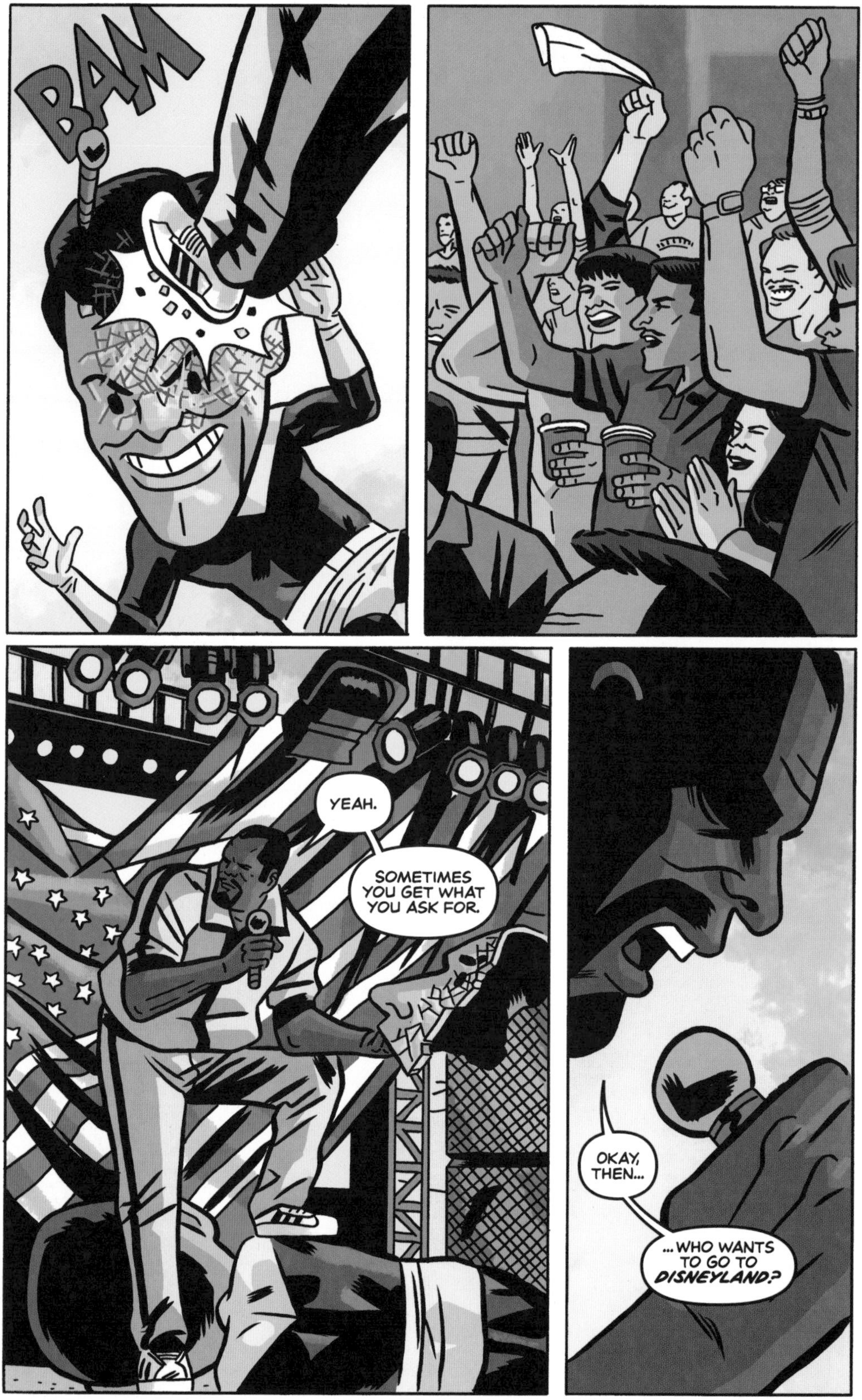
BAM
YEAH.
SOMETIMES YOU GET WHAT YOU ASK FOR.
OKAY, THEN...
...WHO WANTS TO GO TO *DISNEYLAND?*

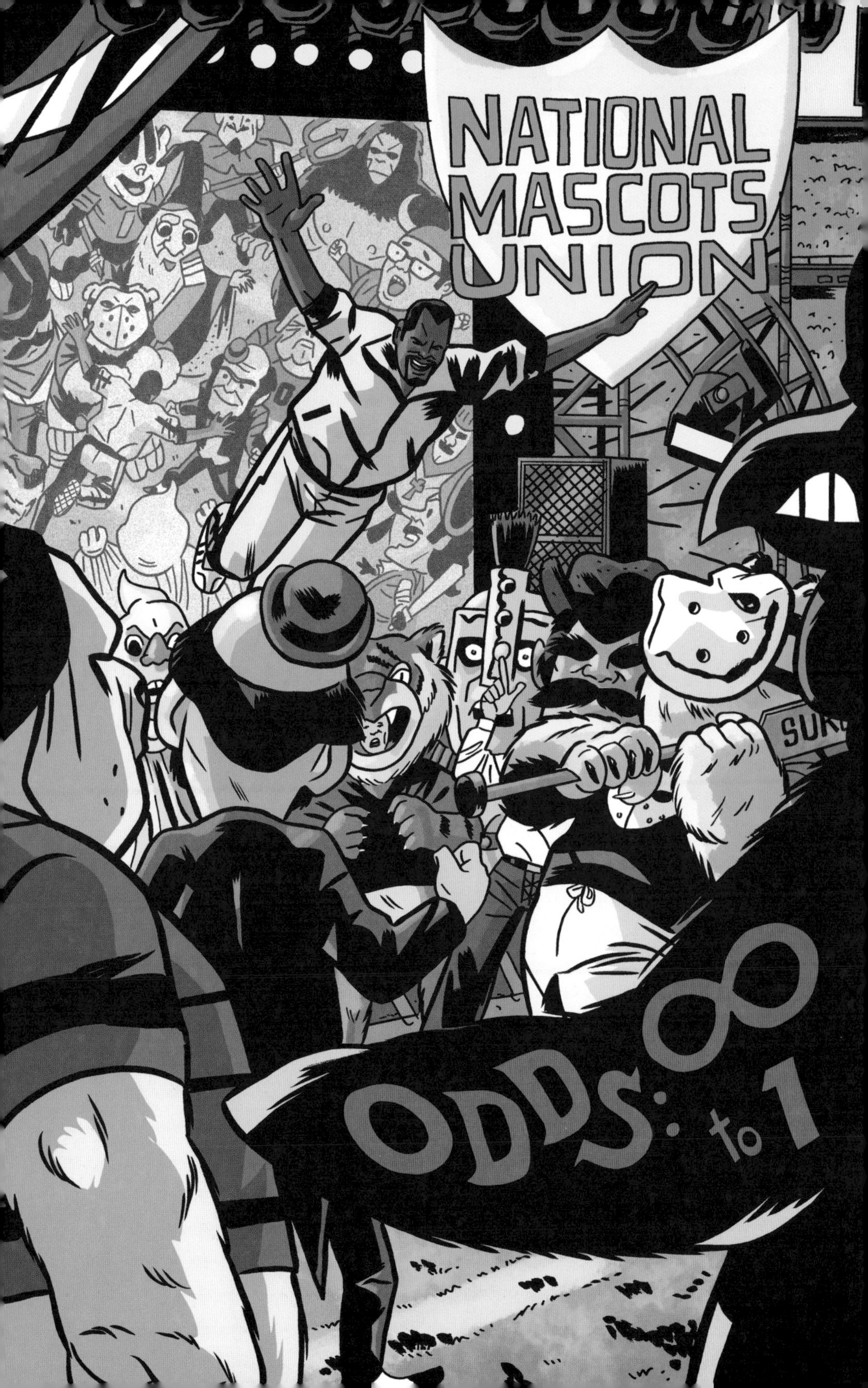
NATIONAL
MASCOTS
UNION
ODDS: ∞ to 1

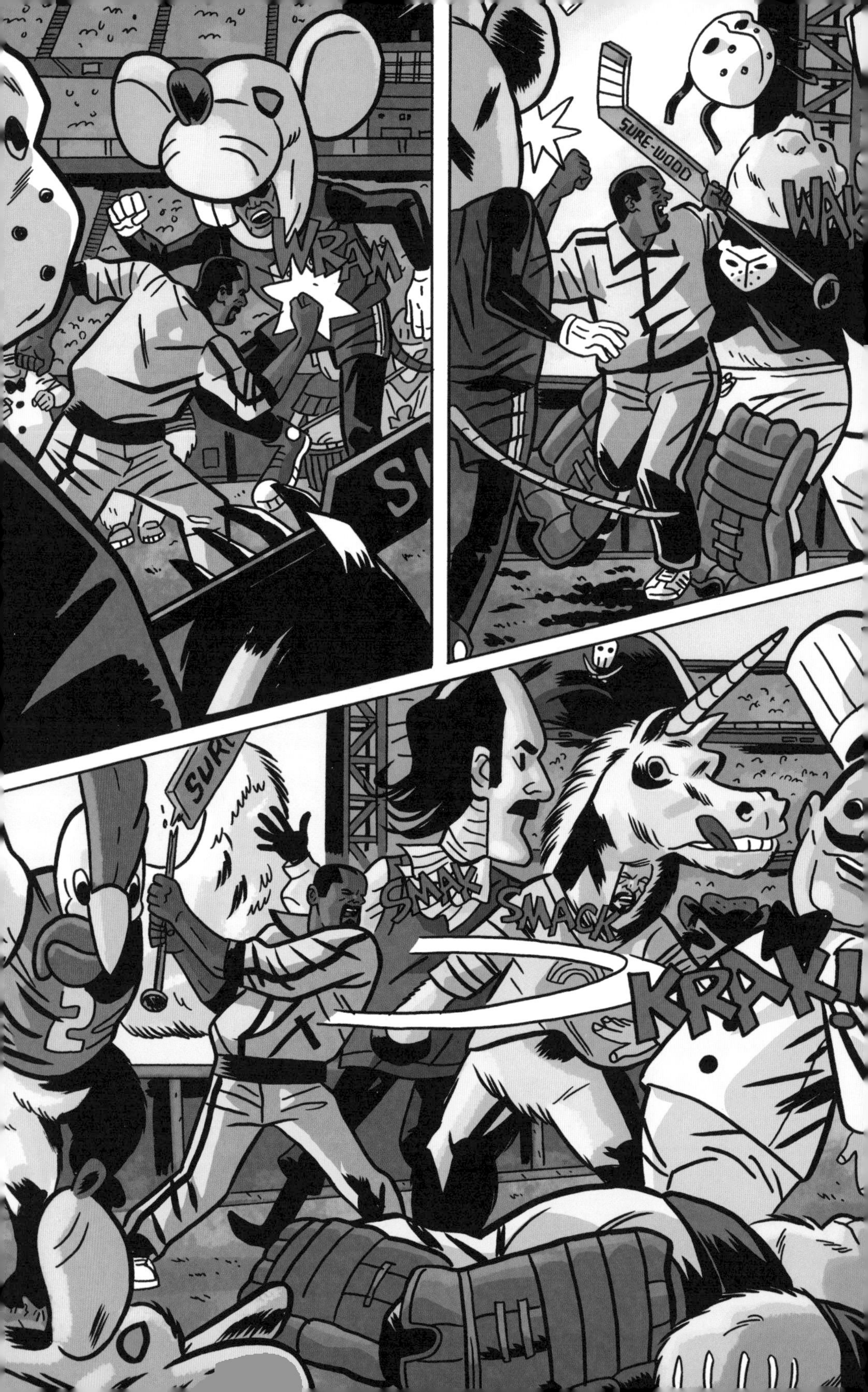
WRAM
SURE-WOOD
SMAK
SMACK
KRAK

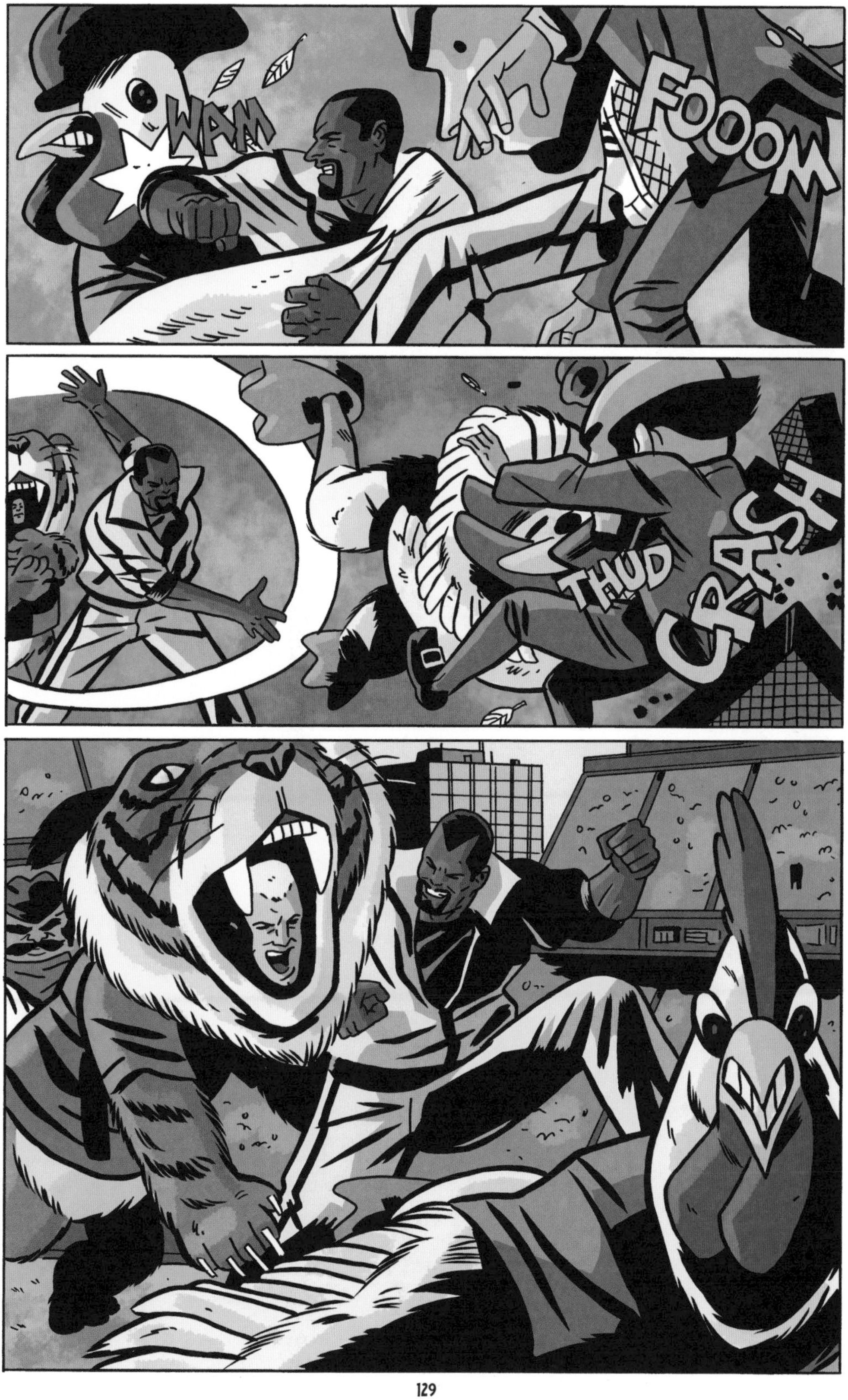
WAM
FOOOM
THUD
CRASH

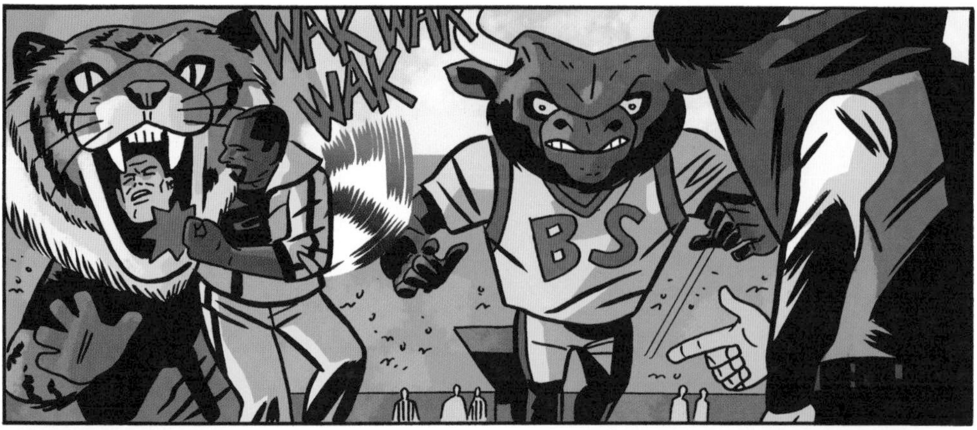
WAK WAK
WAK

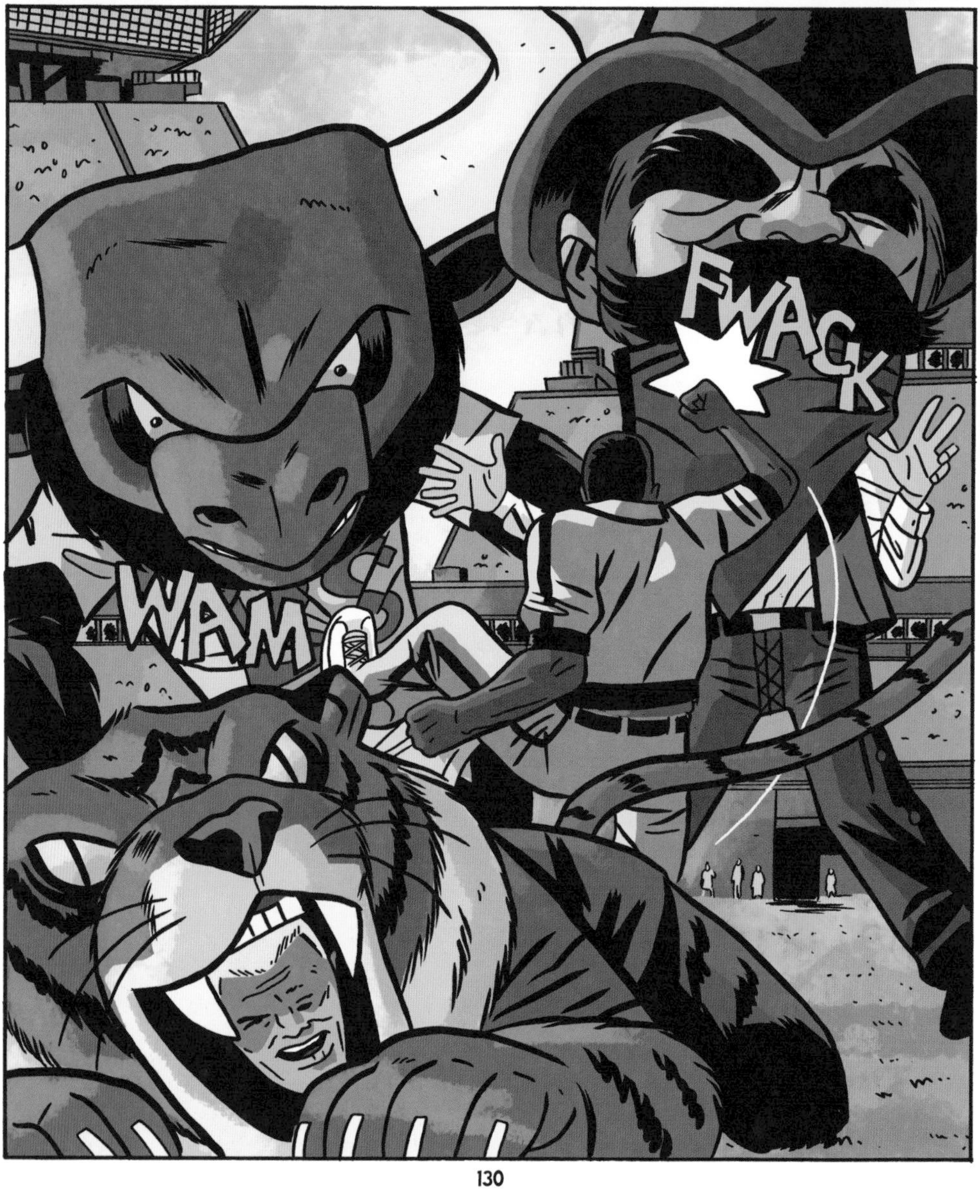
FWACK
WAM

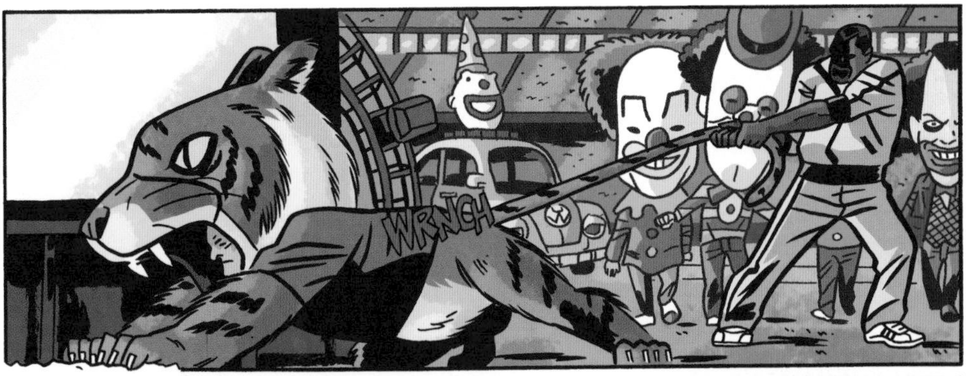
WRNCH

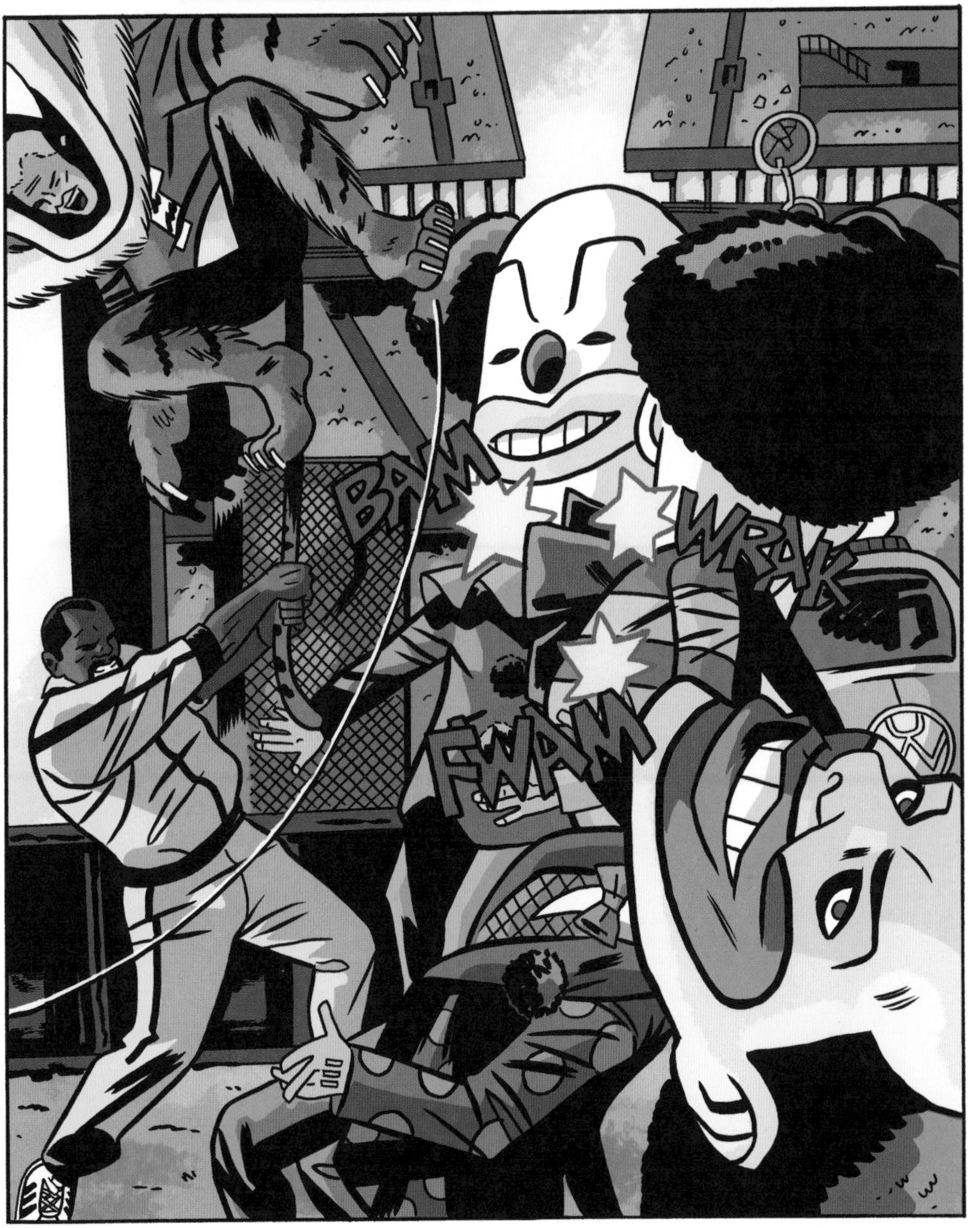
BAM
WRAK
FWAM

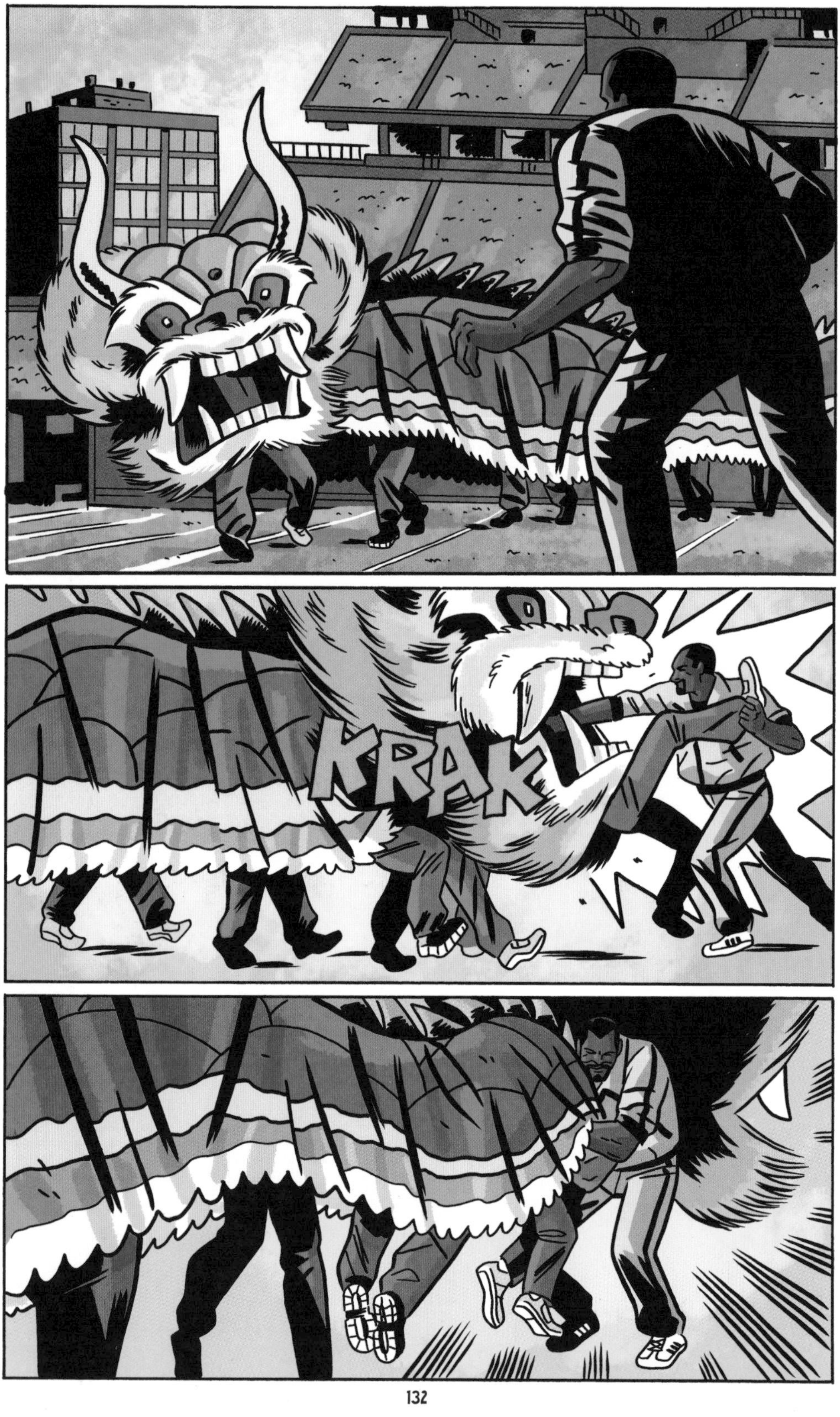
KRAK

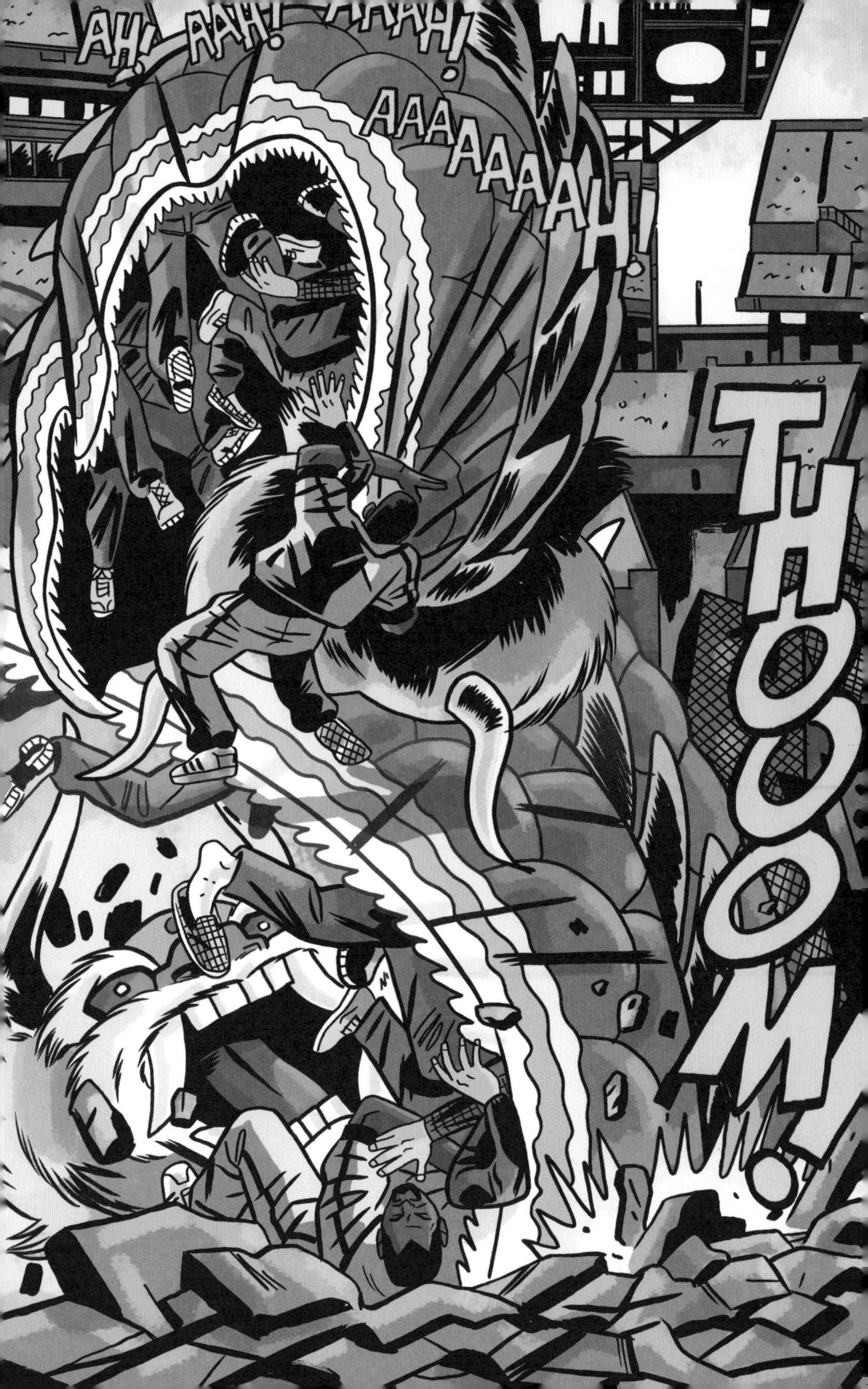
AH! AAH! AAAH!
AAAAAAAH!
THOOOM!

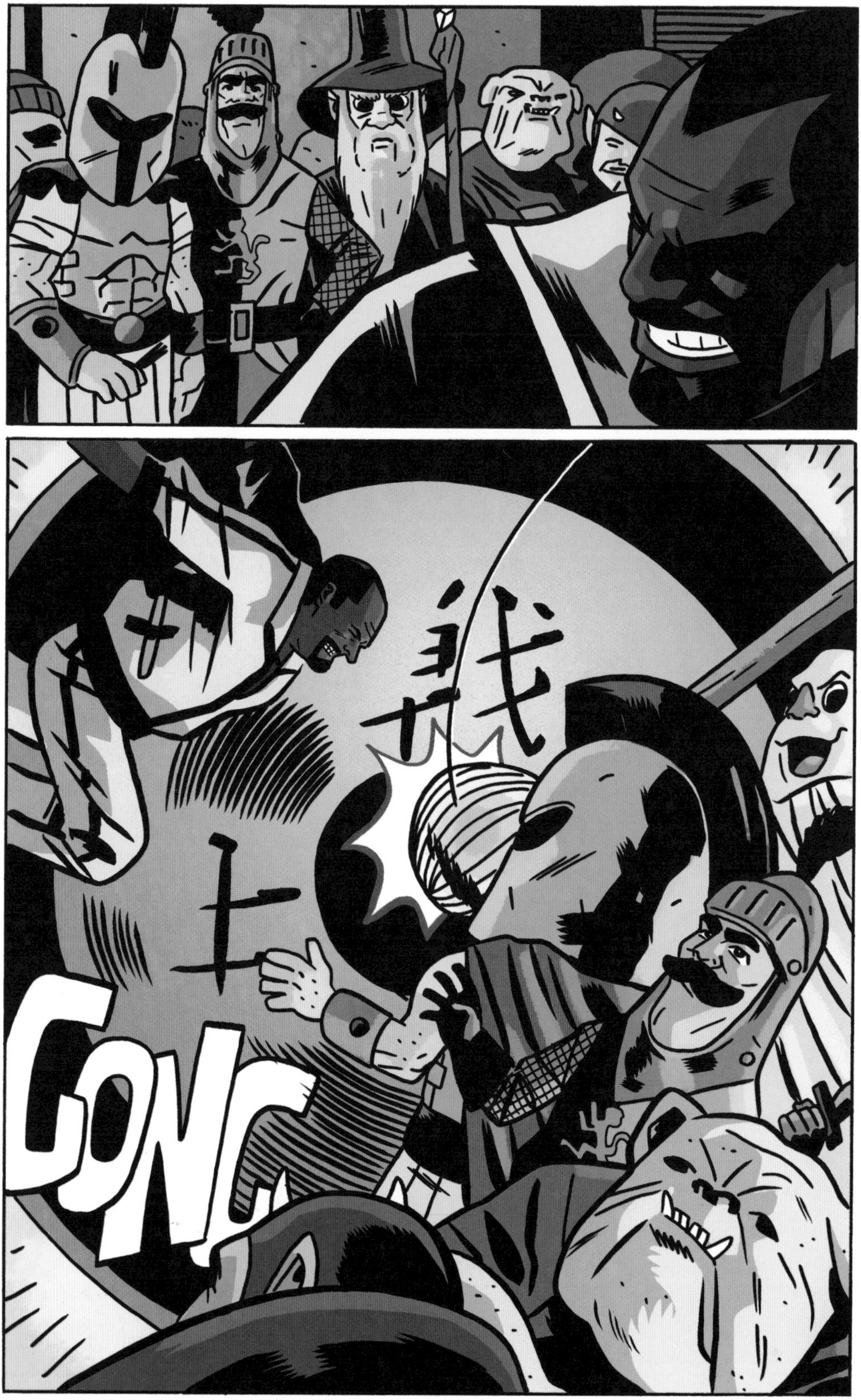
GON

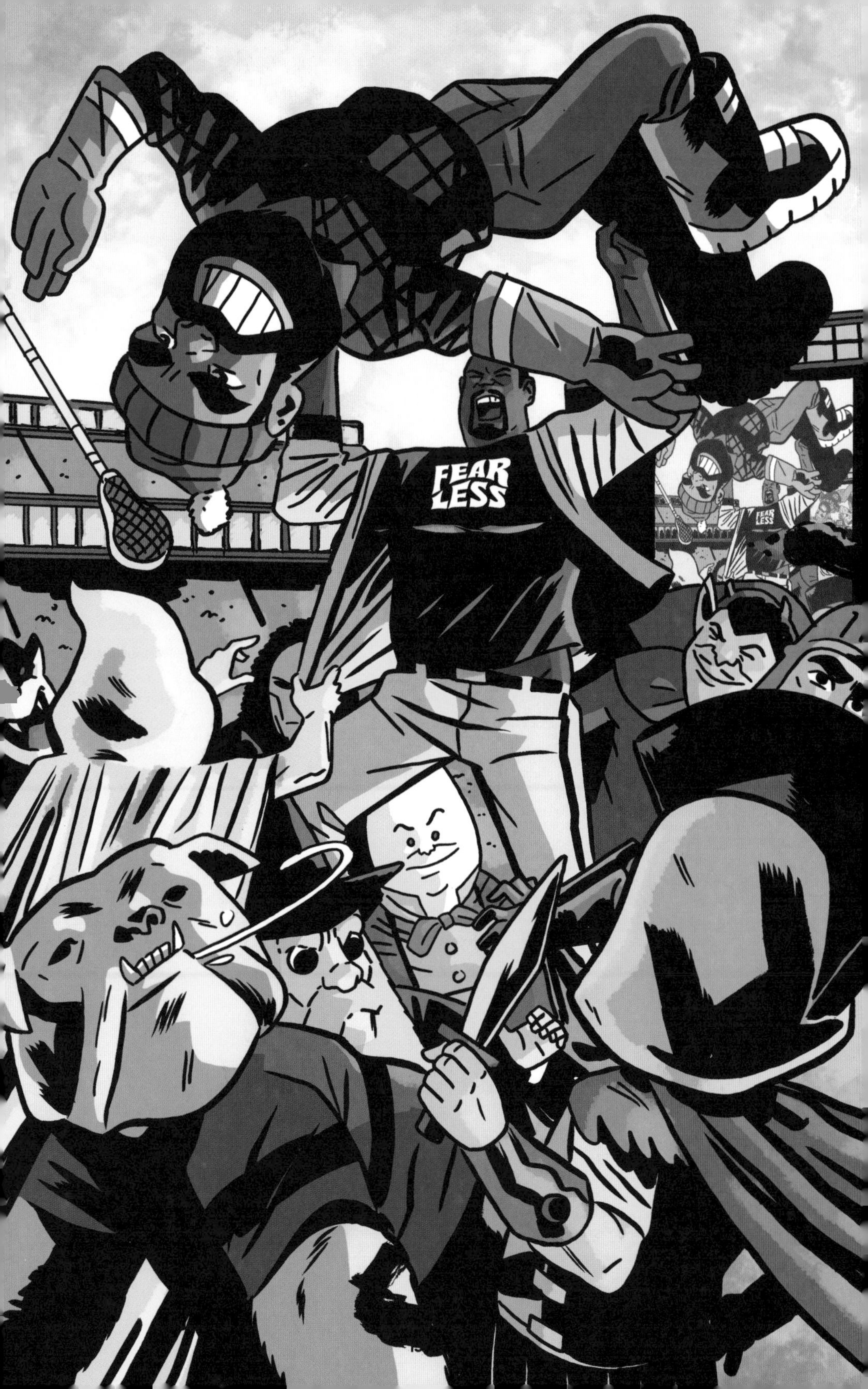
FEAR
LESS
FEAR
LESS

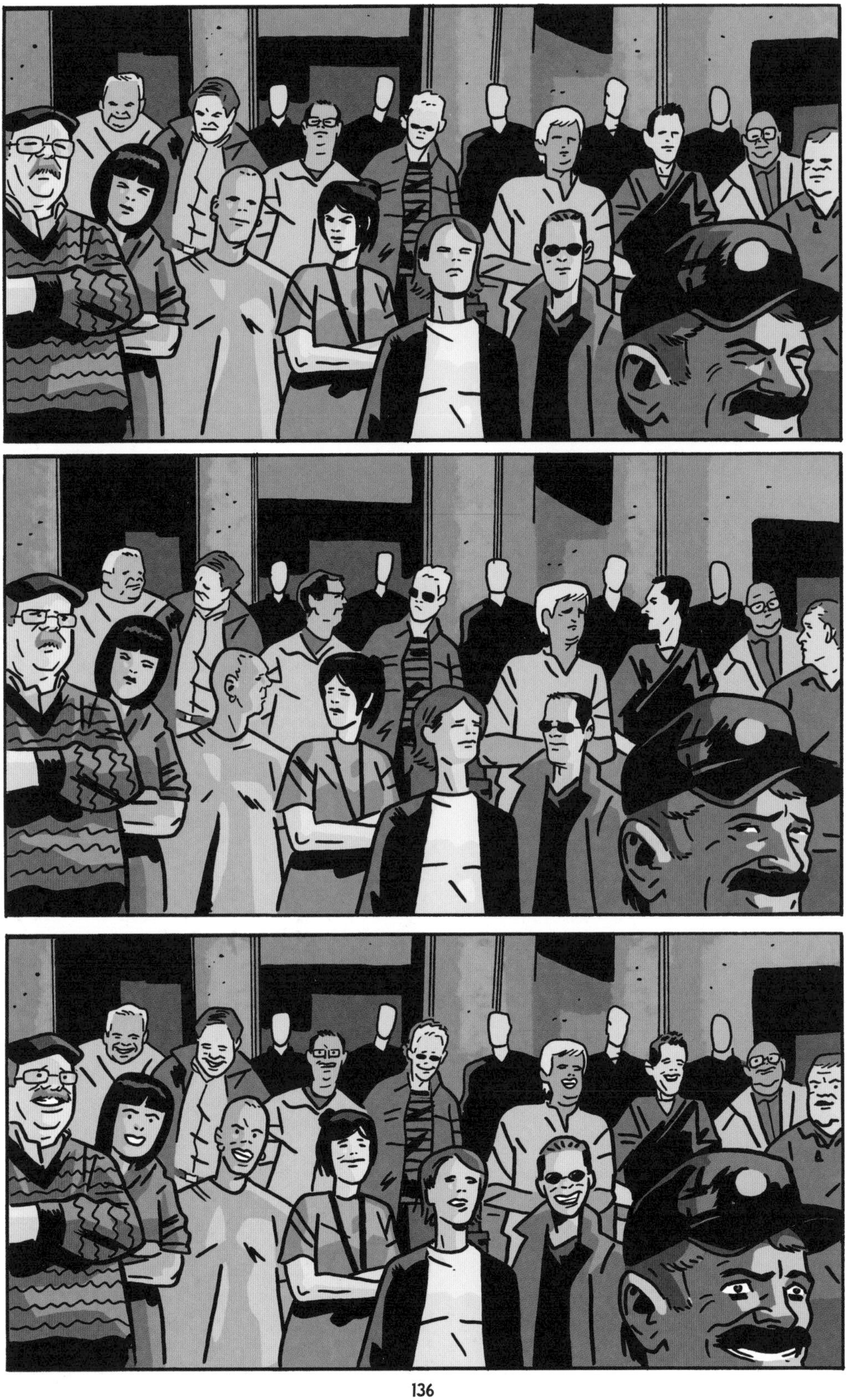

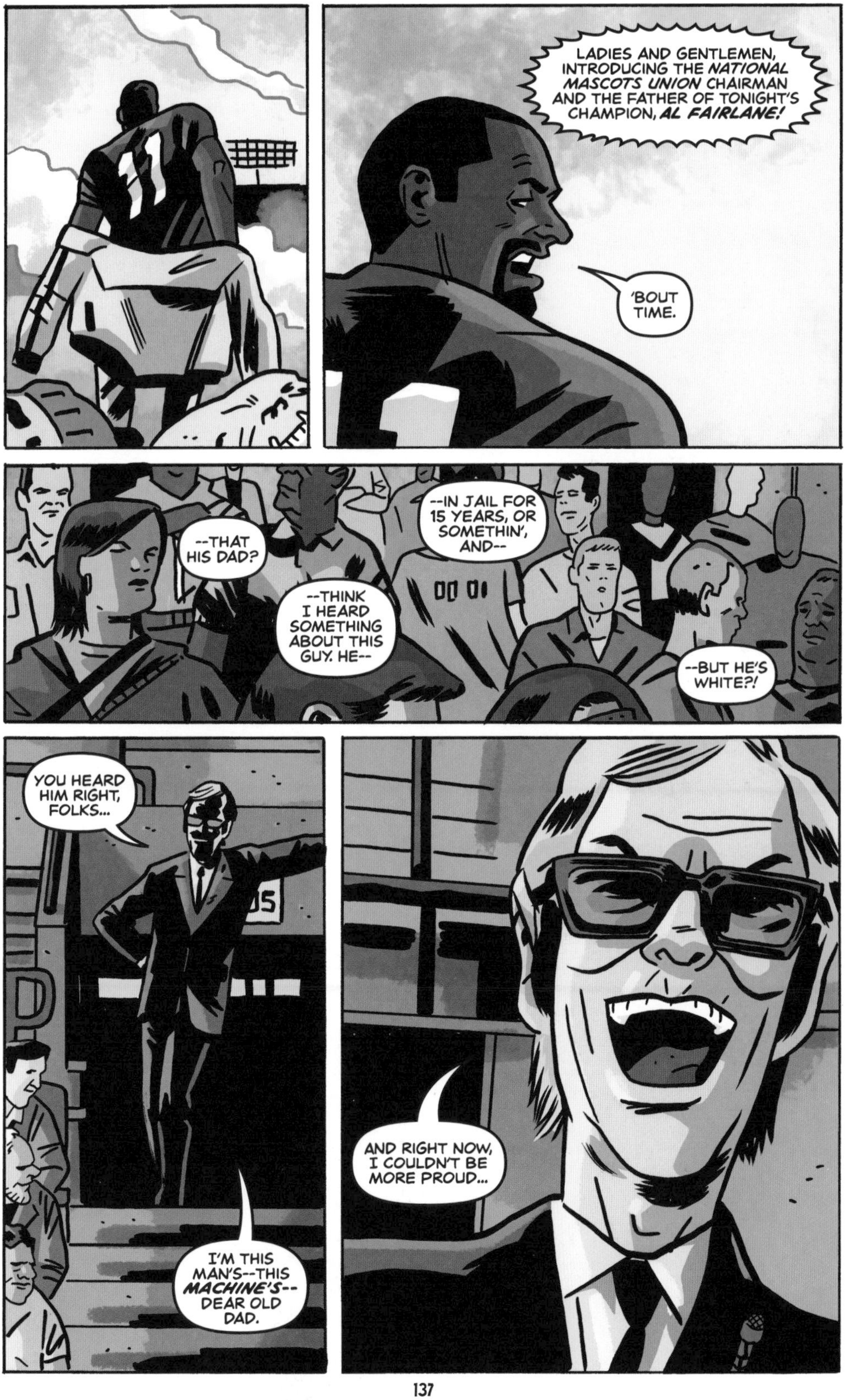
LADIES AND GENTLEMEN, INTRODUCING THE *NATIONAL MASCOTS UNION* CHAIRMAN AND THE FATHER OF TONIGHT'S CHAMPION, ***AL FAIRLANE!***
'BOUT TIME.
--THAT HIS DAD?
--THINK I HEARD SOMETHING ABOUT THIS GUY. HE--
--IN JAIL FOR 15 YEARS, OR SOMETHIN', AND--
--BUT HE'S WHITE?!
YOU HEARD HIM RIGHT, FOLKS...
I'M THIS MAN'S--THIS ***MACHINE'S***--DEAR OLD DAD.
AND RIGHT NOW, I COULDN'T BE MORE PROUD...

...OR ANY RICHER FROM THE LOOKS OF TONIGHT'S TOTALS. WHO KNEW THEY MADE THAT MANY ZEROES?

I'LL BE DAMNED, CHARLIE--YOU DID IT, BOY-- *YOU WON.* EVERYBODY HERE, EVERY OBSTACLE I PUT IN FRONT OF YOU, YOU BEAT 'EM.

THE *REBIRTH* OF *FEARLESS CHUCK FAIRLANE!*

'YEAHAHAHAH!

ALL RIGHT, SHUT UP, YOU JACKALS.

I'M TRYIN' TO TALK TO MY KID, HERE.

BOoOO

Y'KNOW, IF YOUR MOM HAD TAUGHT YOU ANY MANNERS, YOU'D THANK ME RIGHT NOW, KIDDO.

I SET THIS WHOLE THING UP. THE *BRAWL,* THE *MEDIA STORM,* IT WAS *ALL ME!*

AND YEAH, SURE I MADE SOMETHING OFF OF IT, BUT YOU'D *LOST* EVERYTHING BEFORE THIS... YOU WERE TEACHING AT A *PUBLIC SCHOOL* IN *SOUTH CAROLINA.* JESUS, CHARLIE. IT DON'T GET MUCH LOWER THAN THAT.

WHAT THE HELL HAPPENED TO YOU, HUH?

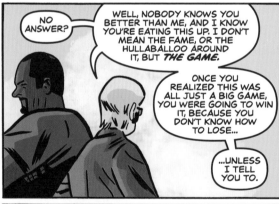

NO ANSWER?

WELL, NOBODY KNOWS YOU BETTER THAN ME, AND I KNOW YOU'RE EATING THIS UP. I DON'T MEAN THE FAME, OR THE HULLABALLOO AROUND IT, BUT *THE GAME.*

ONCE YOU REALIZED THIS WAS ALL JUST A BIG GAME, YOU WERE GOING TO WIN IT, BECAUSE YOU DON'T KNOW HOW TO LOSE...

...UNLESS I TELL YOU TO.

OH MY GOSH, WOULD YOU LISTEN TO 'EM? JUST LISTEN...

I MEAN, ISN'T THIS AMAZIN'?

YOU'VE BEEN GOING TO FOOTBALL GAMES SINCE BEFORE YOU COULD WALK, AND HAVE YOU EVER HEARD ANYTHING LIKE THAT BEFORE?

FEARLESS!

FEARLESS!

FEARLESS!

SON, I--I REALLY DID IT WITH THIS ONE, DIDN'T I?

TOOK IT ALL THE WAY TO THE TOP. THE LEAGUE CALLED ME-- *THEY CALLED ME*--AND ASKED ME TO SET THIS UP TONIGHT. THEY SAID THAT IN LESS THAN A YEAR "FAIRLANING" HAD GOTTEN MORE POPULAR THAN FOOTBALL. CAN YOU BELIEVE THAT?

AND THEN, WHEN I TOLD 'EM HOW MUCH MONEY WE MADE...

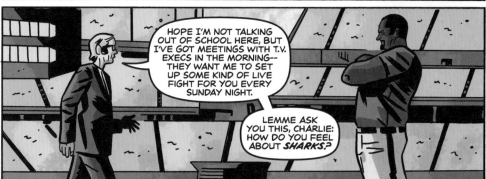

HOPE I'M NOT TALKING OUT OF SCHOOL HERE, BUT I'VE GOT MEETINGS WITH T.V. EXECS IN THE MORNING-- THEY WANT ME TO SET UP SOME KIND OF LIVE FIGHT FOR YOU EVERY SUNDAY NIGHT.

LEMME ASK YOU THIS, CHARLIE: HOW DO YOU FEEL ABOUT *SHARKS?*

ALL THAT WORK I PUT INTO MAKIN' YOU WHAT YOU ARE HAS *FINALLY* PAID OFF.

FOR *BOTH* OF US.

SO C'MON, CHARLIE. DO RIGHT BY YOUR OLD MAN FOR *ONE TIME* IN YOUR MISERABLE LIFE.

THIS IS *FAME!* THIS IS *MONEY!* THIS IS EVERYTHING YOU'RE GOOD AT AND EVERYTHING YOU'VE WANTED! HELL, CHARLIE, IF YOU DON'T WANNA DO IT FOR *ME...*

...DO IT FOR *YOURSELF.*

OKAY, DAD.

YOU WANT ME TO DO SOMETHIN' FOR MYSELF? FINE.

THIS ONE'S FOR *ME!*

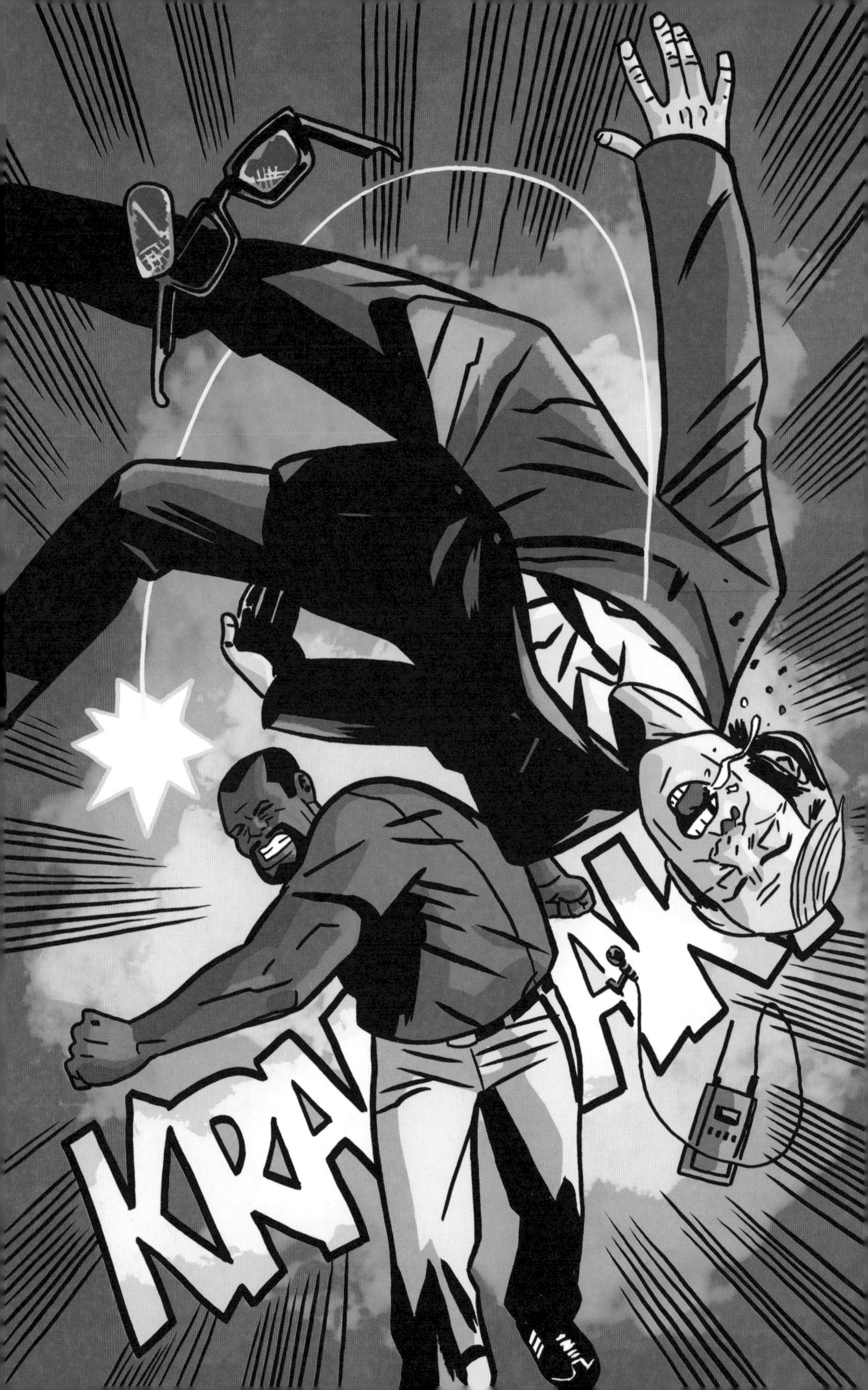

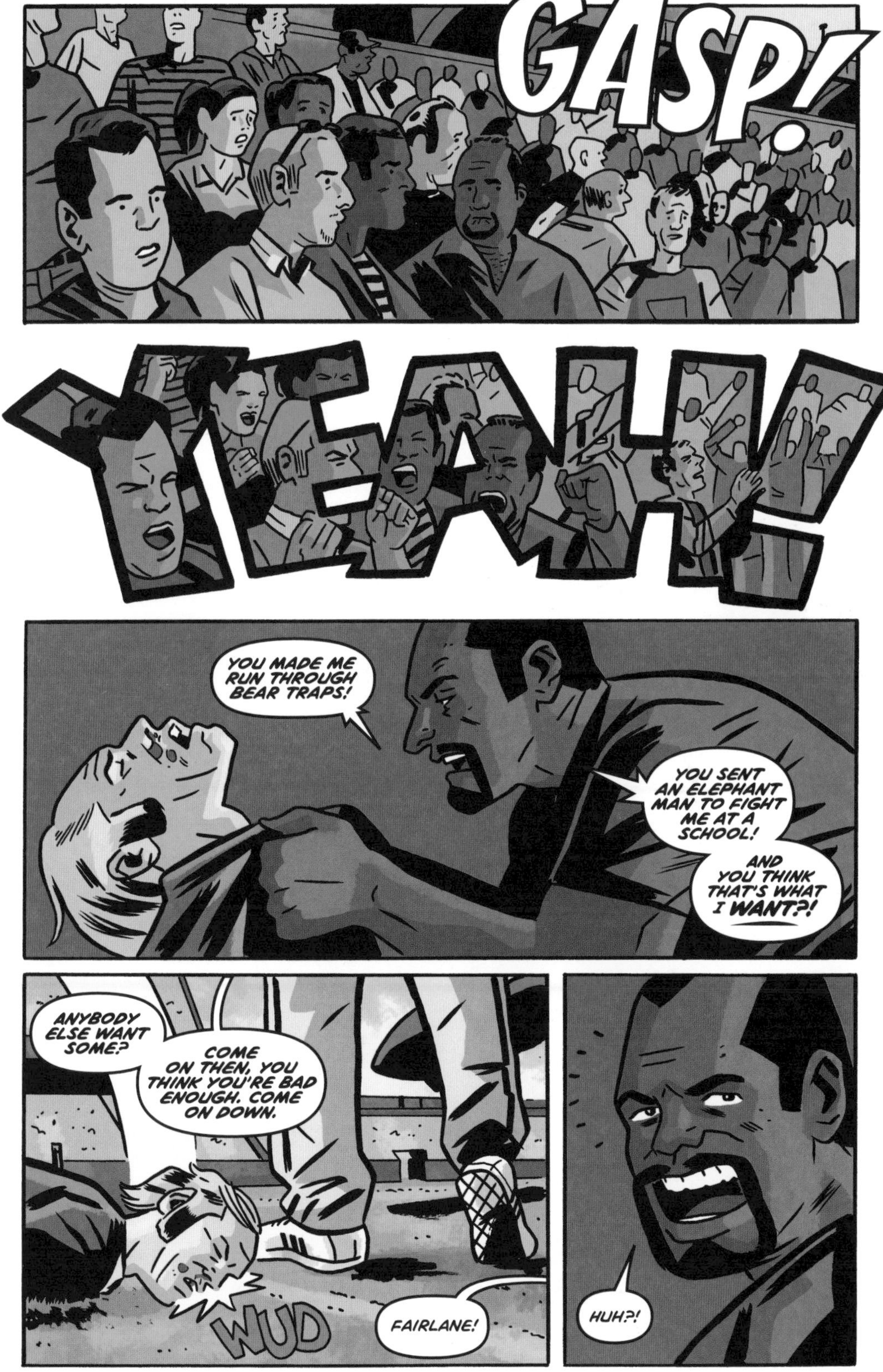

GASP!
YEAH!
YOU MADE ME RUN THROUGH BEAR TRAPS!
YOU SENT AN ELEPHANT MAN TO FIGHT ME AT A SCHOOL!
AND YOU THINK THAT'S WHAT I WANT?!
ANYBODY ELSE WANT SOME?
COME ON THEN, YOU THINK YOU'RE BAD ENOUGH. COME ON DOWN.
WUD
FAIRLANE!
HUH?!

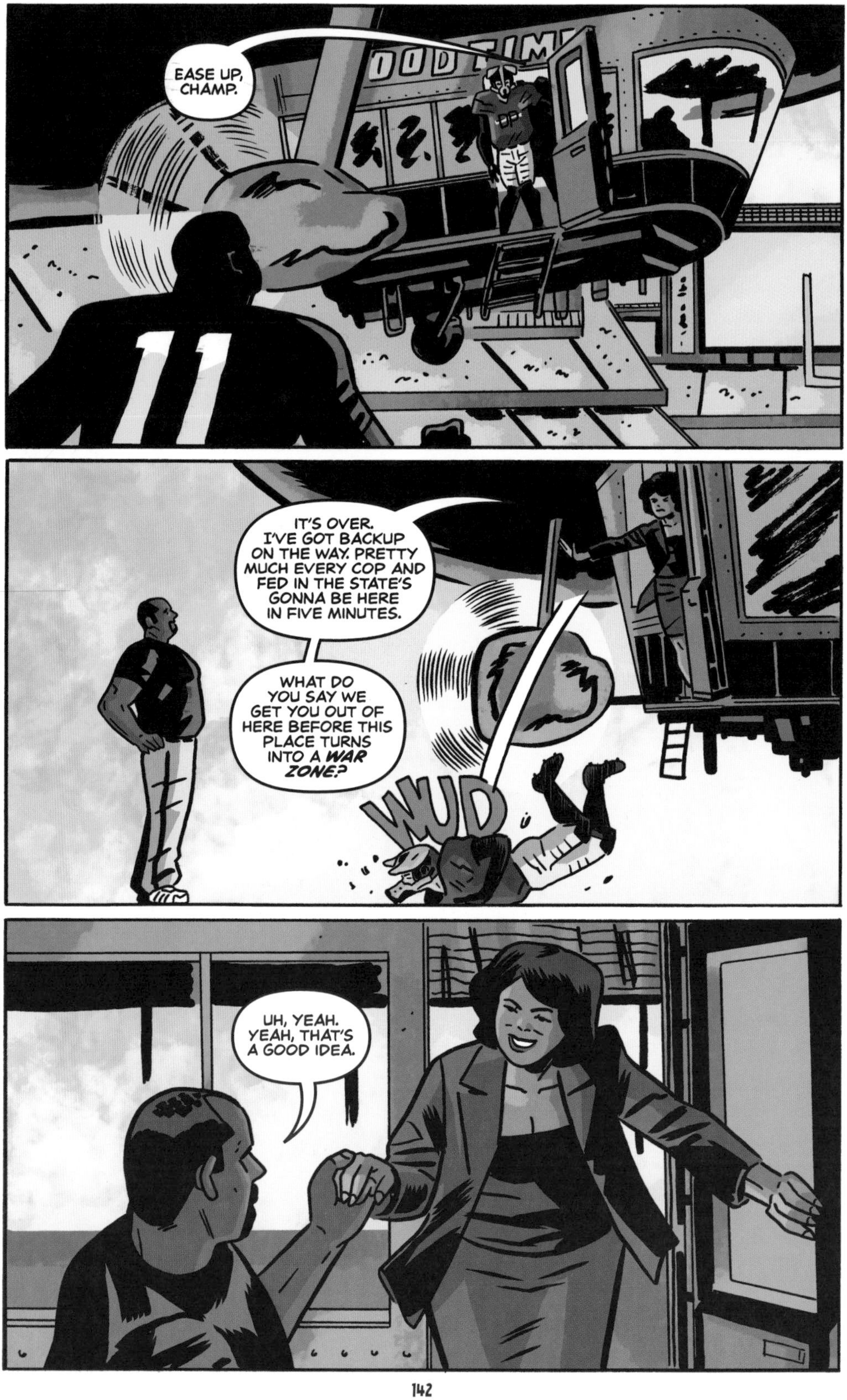
EASE UP, CHAMP.
IT'S OVER. I'VE GOT BACKUP ON THE WAY. PRETTY MUCH EVERY COP AND FED IN THE STATE'S GONNA BE HERE IN FIVE MINUTES.
WHAT DO YOU SAY WE GET YOU OUT OF HERE BEFORE THIS PLACE TURNS INTO A *WAR ZONE?*
WUD
UH, YEAH. YEAH, THAT'S A GOOD IDEA.

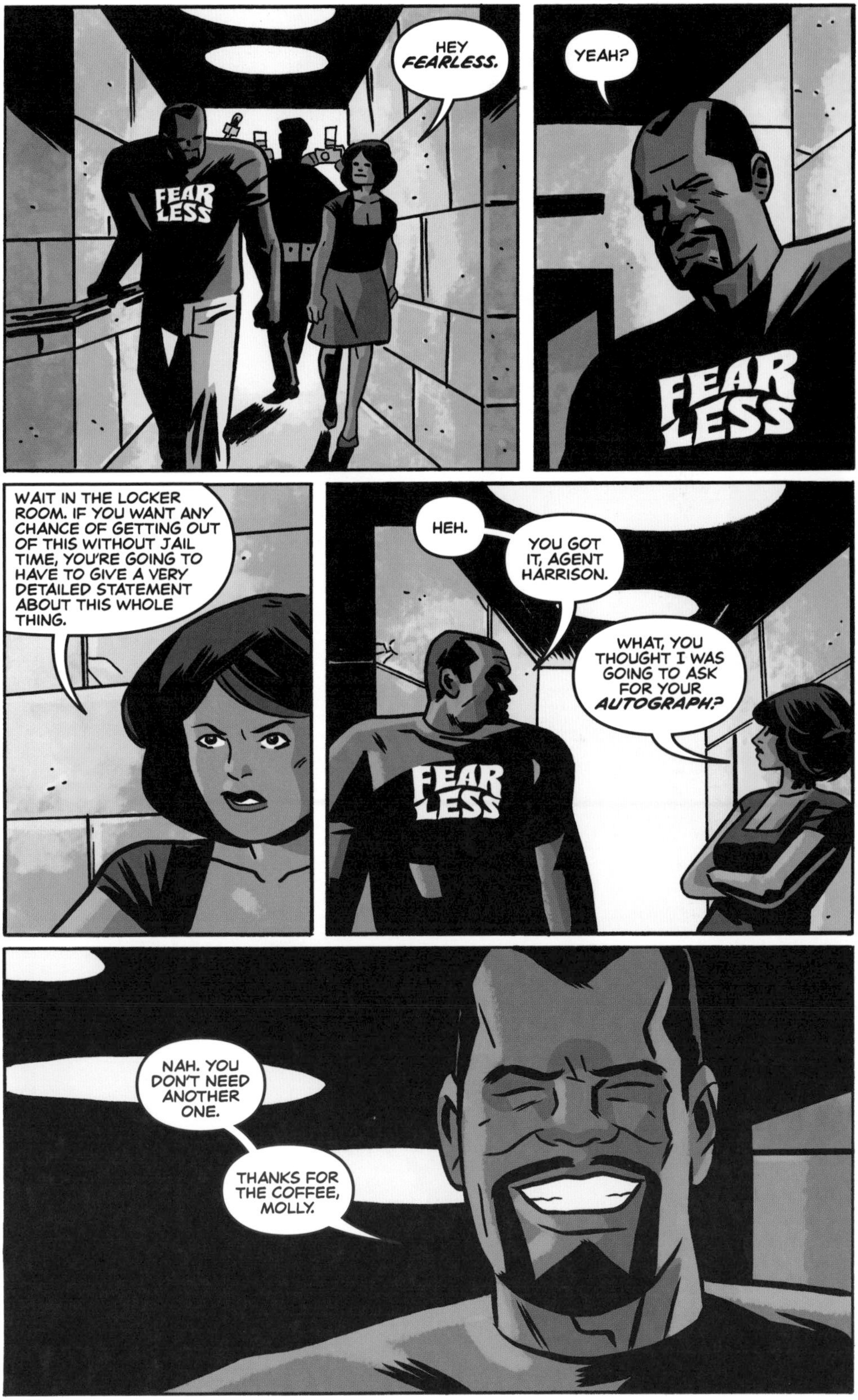
HEY *FEARLESS.*
FEAR LESS
YEAH?
FEAR LESS
WAIT IN THE LOCKER ROOM. IF YOU WANT ANY CHANCE OF GETTING OUT OF THIS WITHOUT JAIL TIME, YOU'RE GOING TO HAVE TO GIVE A VERY DETAILED STATEMENT ABOUT THIS WHOLE THING.
HEH.
YOU GOT IT, AGENT HARRISON.
WHAT, YOU THOUGHT I WAS GOING TO ASK FOR YOUR *AUTOGRAPH?*
FEAR LESS
NAH. YOU DON'T NEED ANOTHER ONE.
THANKS FOR THE COFFEE, MOLLY.

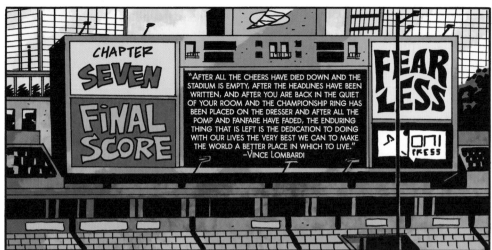

CHAPTER
SEVEN

FINAL SCORE

"AFTER ALL THE CHEERS HAVE DIED DOWN AND THE STADIUM IS EMPTY, AFTER THE HEADLINES HAVE BEEN WRITTEN, AND AFTER YOU ARE BACK IN THE QUIET OF YOUR ROOM AND THE CHAMPIONSHIP RING HAS BEEN PLACED ON THE DRESSER AND AFTER ALL THE POMP AND FANFARE HAVE FADED, THE ENDURING THING THAT IS LEFT IS THE DEDICATION TO DOING WITH OUR LIVES THE VERY BEST WE CAN TO MAKE THE WORLD A BETTER PLACE IN WHICH TO LIVE."
—VINCE LOMBARDI

FEAR LESS

ONI PRESS

SPECIAL AGENTS *MOLLY HARRISON* AND *JAMES PARK* RECEIVED A PRESIDENTIAL COMMENDATION FOR THEIR ROLE IN BRINGING DOWN THE BIGGEST *UNDERGROUND GAMBLING RING* IN DECADES.

SHE CELEBRATED WITH DINNER FOR TWO.

NO BEARS WERE SIGHTED DURING THE EVENING.

WHEN HE REGAINED CONSCIOUSNESS, *AL FAIRLANE* WAS ARRESTED ON CHARGES OF RACKETEERING AND ASSAULT AND SENTENCED TO *99 YEARS* IN FEDERAL PRISON, WHERE HE HAS SINCE FOUND JESUS.

STANLEY "CROCKETT" WENTZLER'S BAR BECAME A POPULAR TOURIST SPOT FOR *BRAWL ACROSS AMERICA* FANS.

HE PLANS TO FRANCHISE NEXT YEAR.

CHUCK FAIRLANE RETURNED TO SOUTH CAROLINA TO RESUME HIS JOB AS HEAD COACH AT DARIUS RUCKER HIGH SCHOOL.

HEY COACH...

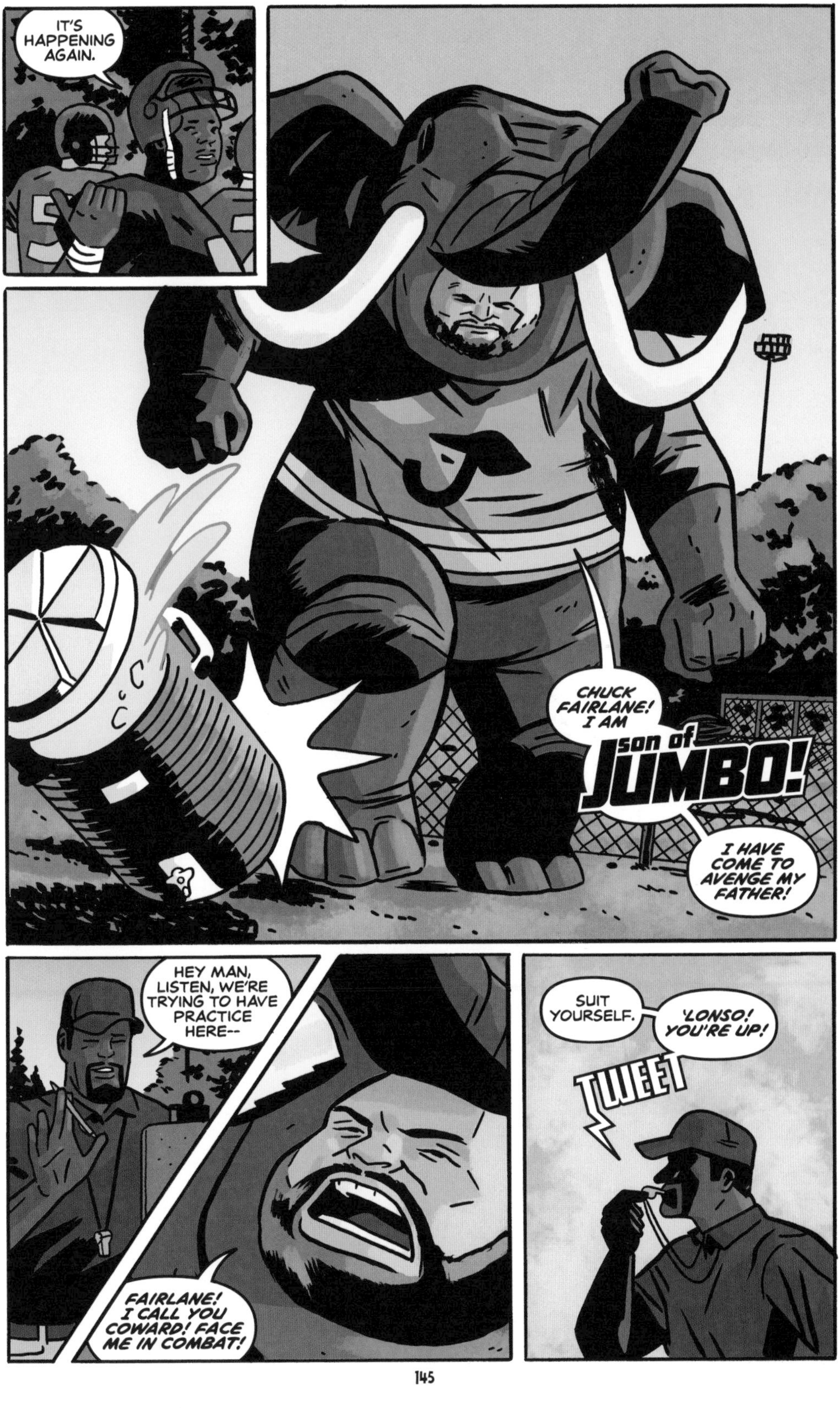
IT'S HAPPENING AGAIN.
CHUCK FAIRLANE! I AM
SON OF JUMBO!
I HAVE COME TO AVENGE MY FATHER!
HEY MAN, LISTEN, WE'RE TRYING TO HAVE PRACTICE HERE--
FAIRLANE! I CALL YOU COWARD! FACE ME IN COMBAT!
SUIT YOURSELF.
'LONSO! YOU'RE UP!
TWEET

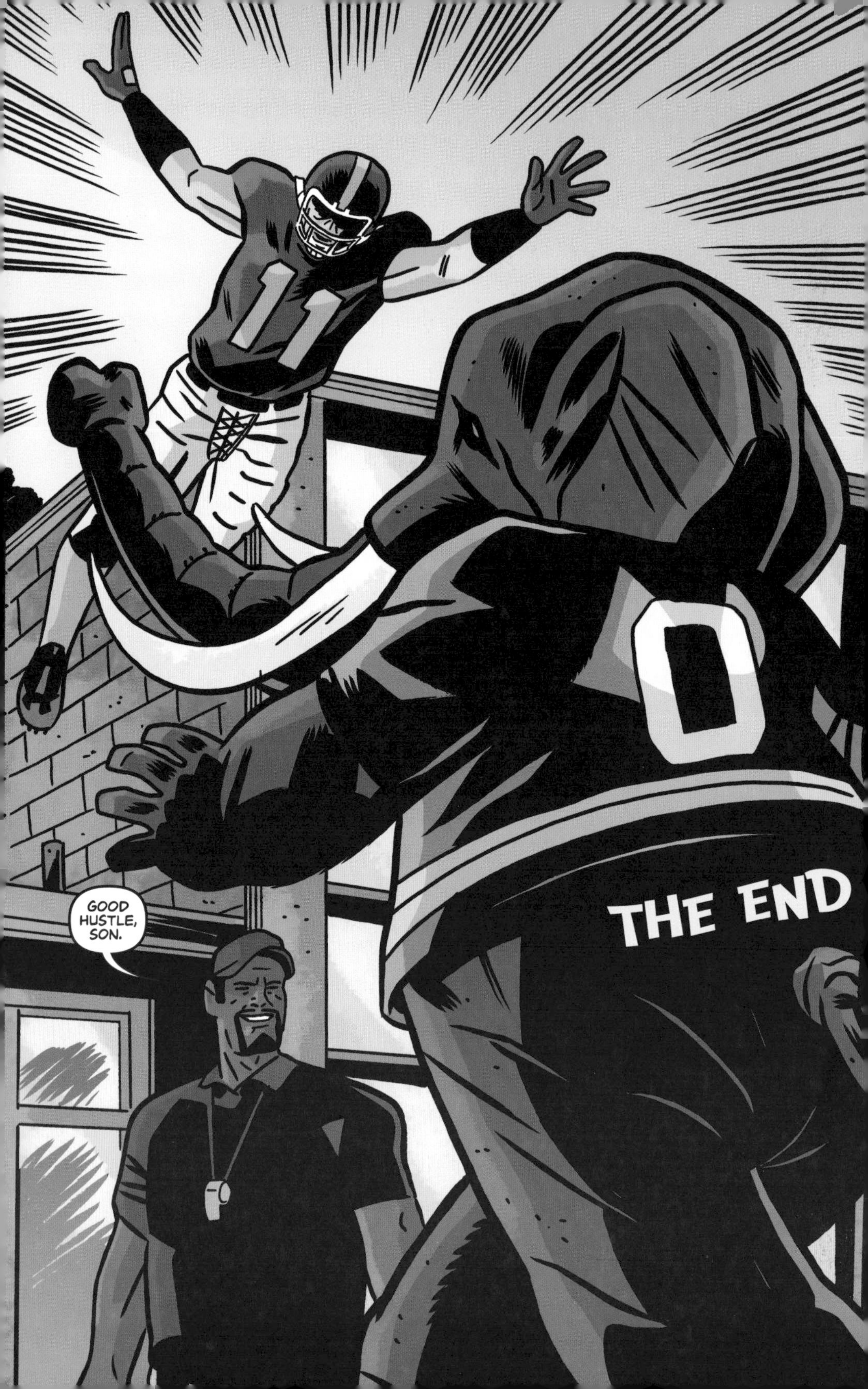
GOOD HUSTLE, SON.
THE END

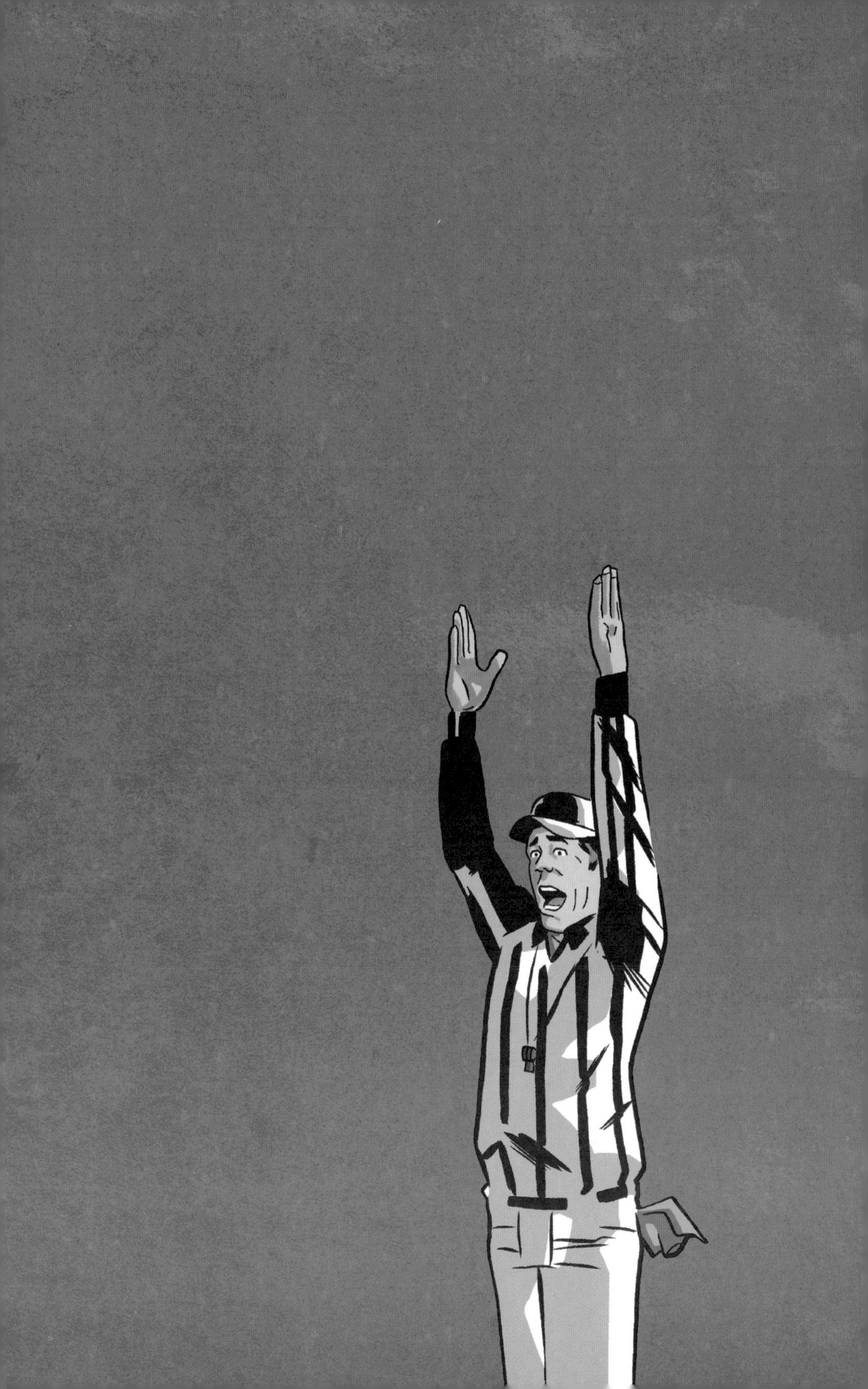

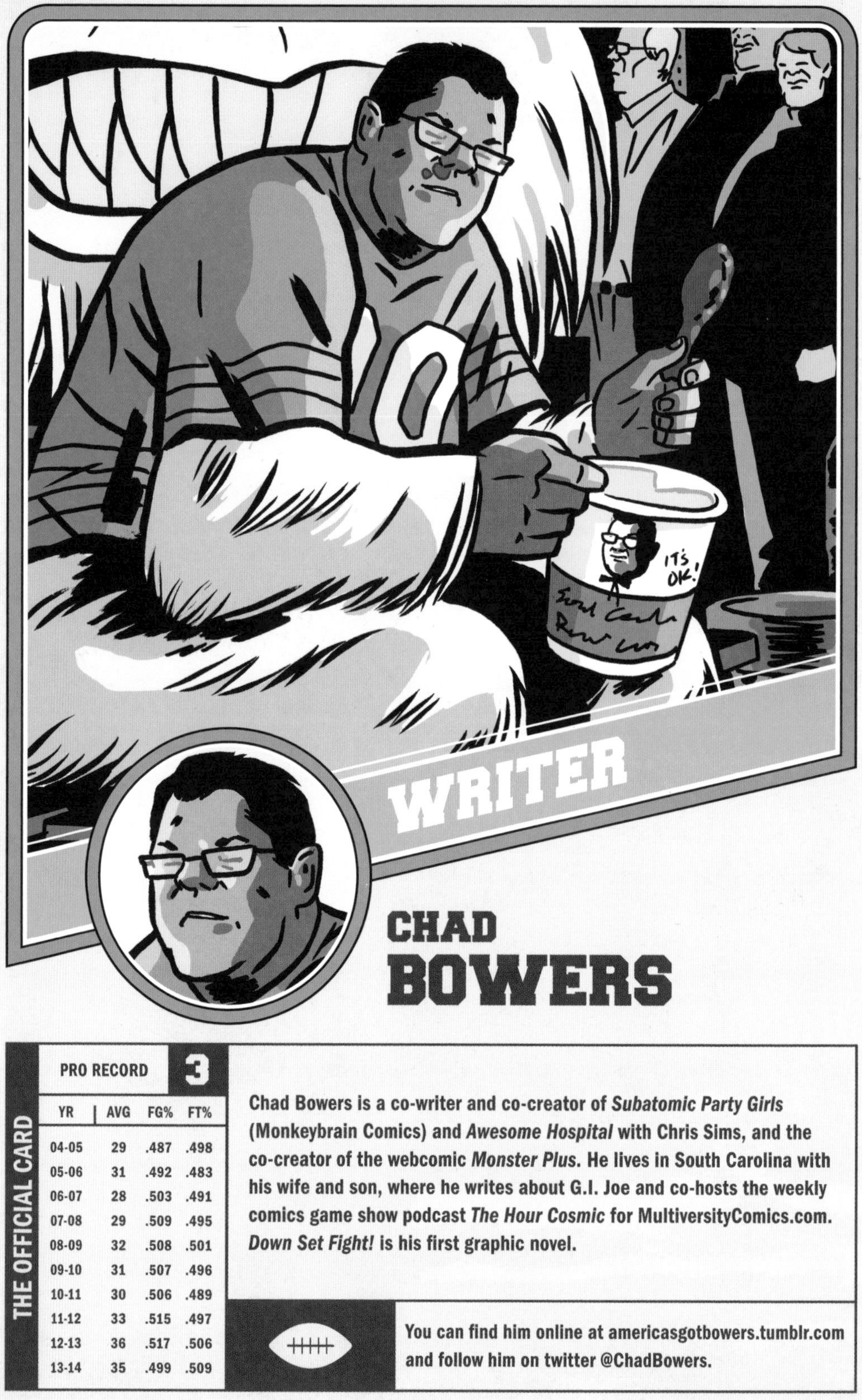
IT'S OK!

WRITER

CHAD BOWERS

THE OFFICIAL CARD

PRO RECORD **3**

YR	AVG	FG%	FT%
04-05	29	.487	.498
05-06	31	.492	.483
06-07	28	.503	.491
07-08	29	.509	.495
08-09	32	.508	.501
09-10	31	.507	.496
10-11	30	.506	.489
11-12	33	.515	.497
12-13	36	.517	.506
13-14	35	.499	.509

Chad Bowers is a co-writer and co-creator of *Subatomic Party Girls* (Monkeybrain Comics) and *Awesome Hospital* with Chris Sims, and the co-creator of the webcomic *Monster Plus*. He lives in South Carolina with his wife and son, where he writes about G.I. Joe and co-hosts the weekly comics game show podcast *The Hour Cosmic* for MultiversityComics.com. *Down Set Fight!* is his first graphic novel.

You can find him online at americasgotbowers.tumblr.com and follow him on twitter @ChadBowers.

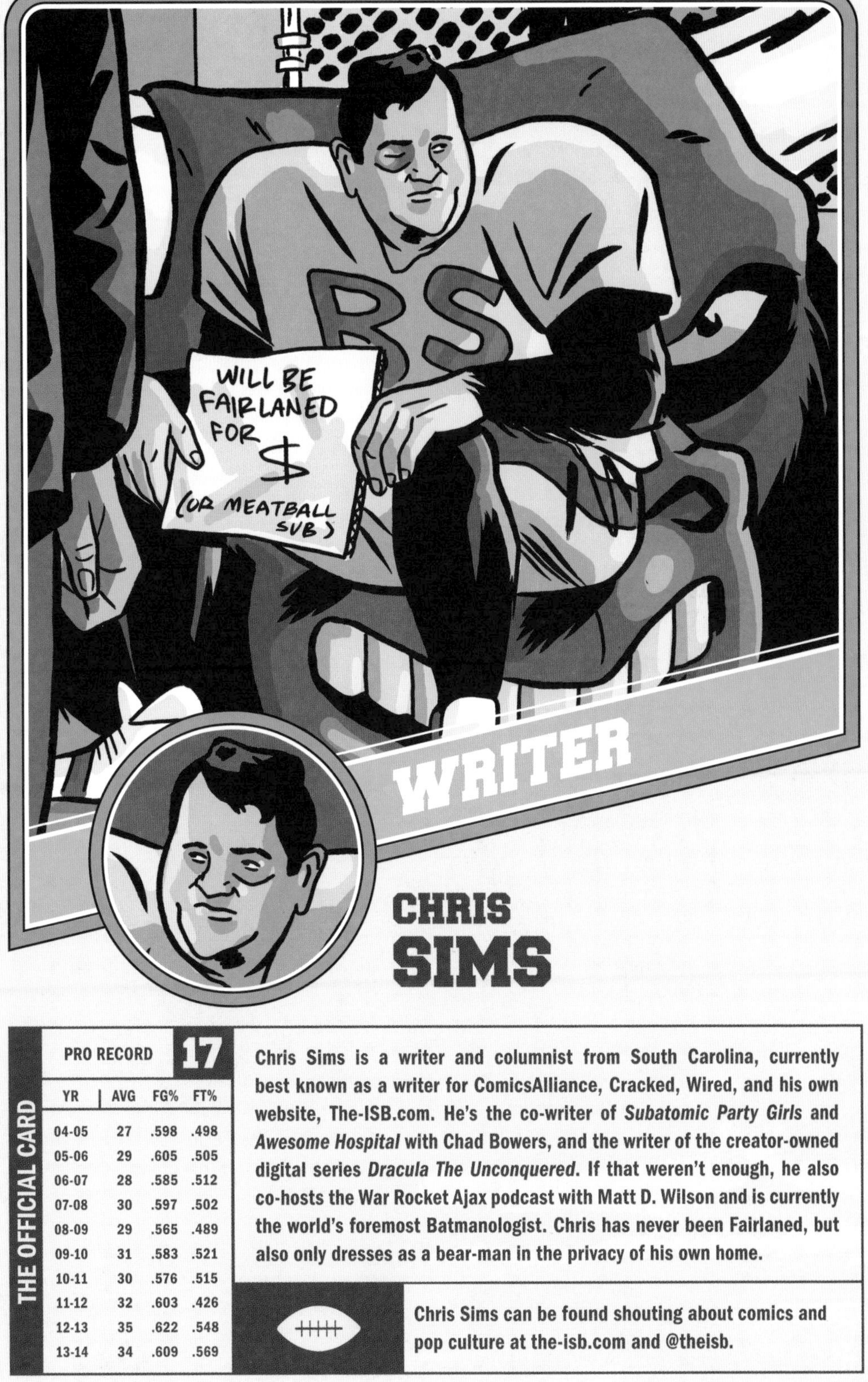
BS
WILL BE FAIRLANED FOR $ (OR MEATBALL SUB)

WRITER

CHRIS SIMS

THE OFFICIAL CARD

PRO RECORD **17**

YR	AVG	FG%	FT%
04-05	27	.598	.498
05-06	29	.605	.505
06-07	28	.585	.512
07-08	30	.597	.502
08-09	29	.565	.489
09-10	31	.583	.521
10-11	30	.576	.515
11-12	32	.603	.426
12-13	35	.622	.548
13-14	34	.609	.569

Chris Sims is a writer and columnist from South Carolina, currently best known as a writer for ComicsAlliance, Cracked, Wired, and his own website, The-ISB.com. He's the co-writer of *Subatomic Party Girls* and *Awesome Hospital* with Chad Bowers, and the writer of the creator-owned digital series *Dracula The Unconquered*. If that weren't enough, he also co-hosts the War Rocket Ajax podcast with Matt D. Wilson and is currently the world's foremost Batmanologist. Chris has never been Fairlaned, but also only dresses as a bear-man in the privacy of his own home.

Chris Sims can be found shouting about comics and pop culture at the-isb.com and @theisb.

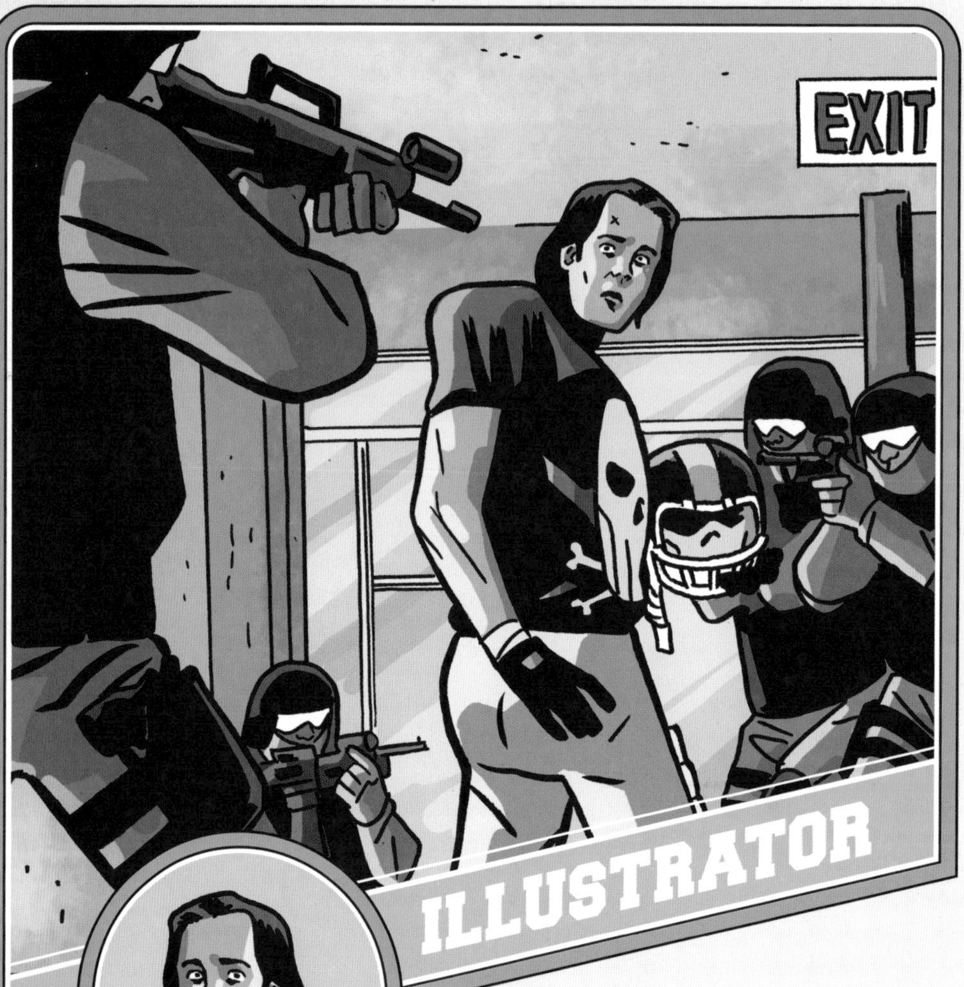
EXIT
ILLUSTRATOR

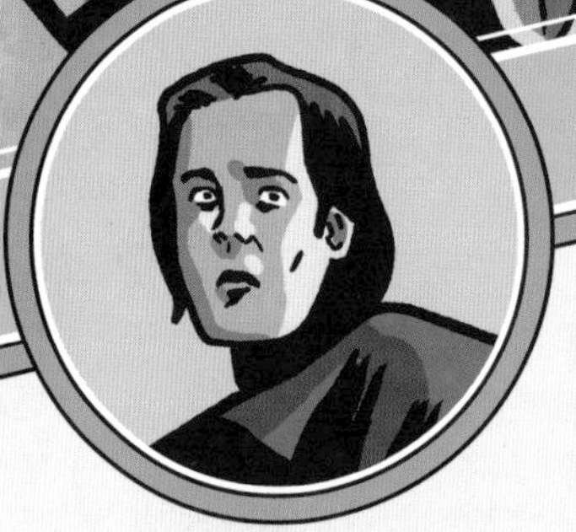

SCOTT KOWALCHUK

THE OFFICIAL CARD

PRO RECORD			9
YR	AVG	FG%	FT%
04-05	34	.519	.574
05-06	33	.527	.561
06-07	35	.545	.558
07-08	34	.521	.568
08-09	36	.537	.559
09-10	32	.541	.596
10-11	36	.535	.605
11-12	35	.541	.619
12-13	38	.552	.621
13-14	37	.549	.615

Scott Kowalchuk is a Canadian comic book artist who first made the scene in 2011 co-creating the sci-fi adventure series *The Intrepids* for Image Comics. His latest trippy adventure book *The Mysterious Strangers* is a 1960s-inspired supernatural spy-fi published by the fine folks at Oni Press. When not drawing comics, Scott enjoys 'Fairlaning' various locals, mostly those living at the old-folks home across the street from his house, and going on bike rides with his wife and daughter.

Find him online at scottkowalchuk.com and on twitter @ScottKowalchuk.